Cosmos and Community

COSMOS

AND

COMMUNITY

The Ethical Dimension

of Daoism

Livia Kohn

Three Pines Press
303 Cambridge Street, #410071
Cambridge, MA 02140
www.threepinespress.com

9   8 7 6 5 4 3 2 1

First Edition, 2004
Printed in the United States of America
⊗ This edition is printed on acid-free paper that meets
the American National Standard Institute Z39.48 Standard.
Distributed in the United States by Three Pines Press.

Library of Congress Cataloging-in-Publication Data
Kohn, Livia, 1956-
  Cosmos and community : the ethical dimension of Daoism / Livia Kohn.
        p. cm.
Includes bibliographical references and index.
  ISBN 1-931483-02-7 (alk. paper)
1. Taoist ethics. 2. Taoism. I. Title: Ethical dimension of Daoism. II. Title.
  BJ1290.8.K65 2004
    299.5'145--dc22   2004009397

CONTENTS

SUPPLEMENT TO *COSMOS AND COMMUNITY*

(ELECTRONIC PUBLICATION FROM WWW.THREEPINESPRESS.COM)

ACKNOWLEDGMENTS

This study began in 1992 during a research stay in Japan sponsored by the Japan Society for the Promotion of Science. It was inspired by the varied information on Daoist daily life and practice as well as the many texts on ethical behavior discussed in *Laughing at the Dao* (*Xiaodao lun*), the translation of which I had just completed (published in 1995). At the time, I pursued my understanding of the five precepts in both a Buddhist and Daoist context and prepared a first study in this area. It focused on the *Precepts of the Highest Lord Lao* (*Taishang Laojun jiejing*) and appeared under the title "The Five Precepts of the Venerable Lord" in *Monumenta Serica* 42 (1994). Also in this early phase of the study, I prepared translations of related texts, which came to form the backbone of the present project. The translations are now contained partly in this volume, partly in the "Supplement," published electronically.

For their support of the work in its early stages, I am particularly indebted to the Japan Society for the Promotion of Science for their generous financial support; to Boston University for granting me leave of absence; to Professor Yoshikawa Tadao and the Institute for Research in Humanities of Kyoto University for providing library resources and pertinent advice; to Dr. Roman Malek, editor of *Monumenta Serica*, for his support in conceiving and editing the first article on the subject; and to my many friends and colleagues in Kyoto who listened to ethical issues time and again.

After my return to Boston in 1993, I got involved with other projects. I only came back to working on Daoist ethics and communities after concluding a study on medieval monasticism, which appeared under the title *Monastic Life in Medieval Daoism* in 2003. For this second phase of work on *Cosmos and Community*, I am again indebted to Boston University for giving me leave of absence to pursue research as well as to the National Endowment of the Humanities whose support enabled me to bring the monasticism study to a timely conclusion. The study of monastic rules and institutions more than anything made me aware of the details of daily life and conduct and brought Daoist ethical visions and behaviors to life in previously unanticipated depth.

One sideline on monastic practice took me also into texts of the Complete Perfection school. In their study, I have benefited especially from the help of Dr. Martin Kraatz, curator of the Religionswissenschaftliche Sammlung at the University of Marburg, Germany. He granted me easy access to the legacy of Heinrich Hackmann, including several relevant texts on precepts, and greatly encouraged me to write an article on the subject. Entitled "Monastic Rules in Quanzhen Daoism: As Collected by Heinrich Hackmann," it is found in *Monumenta Serica* 51 (2003). The translations and discussion of all Complete Perfection materials in this volume follow directly from this work.

One chance to present on general issues of Daoist ethics arose at the conference on "Daoist Cultivation: Traditional Models and Contemporary Practices," held on Vashon Island near Seattle in May 2001. Here I presented a first theoretical discussion of Daoist ethics under the title "Morality and Daoist Cultivation." Especially Liu Ming, leader of Orthodox Daoism of America, was very inspiring in his discussion of the nature of the precepts and provided his contemporary version of the early rules. Louis Komjathy was of great help in formulating complex issues and rethinking theoretical dimensions.

Another inspiring opportunity to present arose in November 2002, at the international conference held in memory of Julia Ching at the University of Toronto, Canada. Here I presented a more comparative examination of ethical justification in Daoism. It will appear under the title "The Wisdom of Moral Conduct: Why Daoists Practice the Precepts" in *Wisdom in China and the West: Essays in Honor of Julia Ching*, edited by Vincent Shen. I benefited greatly from the suggestions of the conference participants whose comments helped me focus further on the comparative and theoretical aspects of the subject.

The last stages of preparation of this volume were greatly aided by the kind comments and suggestions of friends and colleagues. Most important among them are Daniel Overmyer, David Chappell, Vincent Goossaert, Lai Chi-tim, and Victor Mair. Also, the book owes much of its final shape to Shawn Arthur, who worked hard in proofreading and editing. Last but certainly not least, I am deeply grateful to my husband for his great patience with the tight work schedule that allowed the conclusion of this study.

Dynastic Chart

B.C.E.	Shang	1766-1122
	Western Zhou	1122-770
	Eestern Zhou	770-221
	Qin	221-206
	Former Han	206-6
C.E	Later Han	23-220
	Three Kingdoms	220-265
	Western Jin	265-317
	Eastern Jin	317-420
	Six Dynasties	420-589
	Sui	589-618
	Tang	618-907
	Five Dynasties	907-960
	Northern Song	960-1126
	Southern Song	1126-1260
	Mongol-Yuan	1260-1368
	Ming	1368-1644
	Manchu-Qing	1644-1911
	Republic (Taiwan)	1911-
	People's Republic	1949-

INTRODUCTION

The common view of Daoism is that it encourages people to live with detachment and calm, resting in nonaction and smiling at the vicissitudes of the world. Most people assume that Daoists are separate from the human community, not antisocial or asocial but rather supra-social and often simply different. Daoists neither criticize society nor support it by working for social change, but go along with the flow of the cosmos as it moves through them. They are not much concerned with rules and the proprieties of conduct, which they leave to the Confucians in the Chinese tradition.

Contrary to this common view, Daoists through the ages have developed various forms of community and proposed numerous sets of behavioral guidelines and texts on ethical considerations. Beyond the ancient philosophers, who are well-known for the moral dimension of their teachings,[1] religious Daoist rules cover both ethics, i.e., the personal values of the individual, and morality, i.e., the communal norms and social values of the organization (Trauzettel 2002, 137). They range from basic moral rules against killing, stealing, lying, and sexual misconduct through suggestions for altruistic thinking and models of social interaction to behavioral details on how to bow, eat, and wash, as well as to the unfolding of universal ethics that teach people to think like the Dao itself. About eighty texts in the Daoist canon and its supplements describe such guidelines and present the ethical and communal principles of the Daoist religion.[2] They document just to what degree Daoist realization is based on how one lives one's life in interaction with the community—family, religious group, monastery, state, and cosmos. Ethics and morality, as well as the creation of community, emerge as central in the Daoist religion.

In this regard Daoism does not stand alone. Rules and community structures play an important role in all religious traditions. They are often placed at the very foundation of religious aspiration and practice, formulating the proper way of conducting oneself in daily life and in relation to others, prohibiting destructive and disruptive behaviors, while encouraging practitioners to develop a positive and helpful outlook toward themselves and the world. Only on this basis of essentially moral conduct and a functioning human community can true inner cultivation grow and can higher levels of spirituality be attained.

Daoism shares with other religions the emphasis on ethical guidelines requisite to serious attainment and its support of three fundamentally different types of community: lay organizations, monastic institutions, and the closed communities of millenarian or utopian groups. It is unique in that its rules, which make use of both traditional Chinese values and Buddhist precepts, are highly varied and specific not only to these communities as they change over time but also to different levels of ordination and types of rituals. Furthermore, the rules are manifold, there are numerous different terms for them, and they appear in different grammatical formats.

---

[1] On ethics in early philosophical Daoist texts, see Graham 1983; Girardot 1985; Peerenboom 1991; Ames 1992; Kjellberg and Ivanhoe 1996; Kirkland 2001; and Vankeerberghen 2001

[2] Only two studies discuss religious Daoist ethics: Kleeman 1991; Liu 1990, 133-46. For a complete list of precepts texts in the Daoist canon and its supplements, see "The Texts" below.

On the basis of their terminology and grammar, four types can be distinguished: prohibitions formulated as "do not" (*bude* 不得); admonitions including the term "should" (*dang* 當) or "should always" (*changdang* 常當); injunctions that deal with concrete daily behavior; and resolutions that focus on a specific mindset, are phrased in the first person, and usually contain expressions like "pray" (*yuan* 願), "be mindful" (*nian* 念), or "bring forth [the good] intention" (*faxin* 發心).

The presentation in this volume, after a general description of the cosmic dimension of Daoist rules in chapter 1, follows the order of these four types, studying their appearance and role in the three different kinds of communities. Chapters 2 and 3 deal with prohibitions, first with the five great moral rules, then with specific guidelines regarding the use of food, wine, and sex. Chapters 4 and 5 focus on admonitions, beginning with a general survey of the ten precepts, then moving on to the use of positive encouragement in community building and organization. Chapter 6 explores monastic injunctions and the transformation of daily behavior, and chapter 7 concentrates on mental resolutions and other guidelines that create a cosmic mind.

In all cases, the communities are predominantly medieval (3rd through 9th centuries), mainly because that is where the sources emerged. But materials from Song ritual collections as well as from the monastic school of Complete Perfection are also included. Since the discussion is organized thematically, it does not follow a chronological order, and information on certain communities appears in different chapters, depending on the type of rules studied. For a chronological overview of the tradition, as well as a detailed outline of the textual resources, the reader is directed to the chapter on "The Texts" and the subsequent translation of sources.

KINDS OF PRECEPTS

The most general word for rule in China is *jie* 戒, commonly translated "precept." It follows the radical *ge* 戈, "spear" or "lance," to which it adds *gong* 共, the image of joined hands. The picture of the entire graph shows a phalanx of people with spears in hand who guard something or warn someone off. More psychologically, the word means to be prepared for unforeseen dangers, to guard against unwholesome influences, and to abstain from harmful actions. It occurs in the *Book of Rites* (*Liji* 禮記) to denote a sense of preparedness against the dangers lurking in the workings of the cosmos. In the *Analects* (*Lunyu* 論語), the recorded sayings of Confucius, it is seen more in a social context:

> The Master said: The gentleman has three things to be cautious about [*jie*; abstain from]: In his youth, when his blood and energy are not yet settled, he must be cautious about sex. In his middle years, when his blood and energy are just strong, he must be cautious about fighting. In his old age, when his blood and energy already weak, he must be cautious about greed [gain]. (16.7)

Jie can be described as occurring on three levels in Chinese culture. Most fundamentally, they match the basic moral rules against killing, stealing, lying, and sexual misconduct that are also found in other religions. Studied cross-culturally by moral philosophers and scholars of religion, they are considered great and universal, essentially rational, non-religious, geared to the individual, essential to civilization, and beyond the limitations of particular societies or cosmologies (Gert 1970, 60-69). In addition to being punished by the society and various cosmic forces or deities, their central agency for judgment is internal: the individual's conscience, sense of guilt, and awareness of what is right. These moral rules are so basic that, even if formulated in a specific social and historical context, they are not primarily social or cultural, but should be followed for their own sake, for the pure dictates of reason and humaneness (Green 1987, 94-96; Kant 1960). They appeal to the innate goodness in people and are monitored internally by their conscience, allowing the creation of an absolute morality that is valid for all and based on being essentially human (Bergson 1933, 22).

Beyond this, *jie* in China also include prohibitions (*jin* 禁) of certain socially disruptive behaviors and detailed taboos (*ji* 忌) of time and space. Unlike the universal rules, prohibitions focus on specific social actions and attitudes that are considered detrimental to the group and may lead to the disruption of social bonds and the destruction of integration and harmony. Represented by the ancient Confucian tradition, they are geared toward the upholding of propriety and social order, controlling sex, aggression, greed, and so on. Violations are punished by preventing people from attaining the established social goals of long life, prosperity, respect, and well-being.

Taboos, in contrast, are cosmically defined and center on space and time, prohibiting people from stepping on certain areas or committing specific acts at defined times, such as not eating crab on days associated with this animal (see Wagner 1987). Their violation creates a form of cosmic impurity and is punished by temporary exile from the tribe. If severe, their violation can lead to natural catastrophes and epidemics sent by the gods.

As described in the *Book of Rites,* taboos were wide-spread in ancient China. They hoped to create cosmic harmony through correct seasonal behavior (Emmrich 1992, 52-68). They prohibited not only the commission but even the watching of impure activities and prevented all close contact among unrelated members of the opposite sex (Emmrich 1992, 72-75). They also guarded against the taking of improper foods that would violate the harmony of yin and yang, the balance among the food groups, and the law of moderation (Emmrich 1992, 93-99; Chang 1977, 10).

Western scholars see distinct differences in kind, social context, and human consciousness among moral rules, prohibitions, and taboos. Paul Ricoeur, in his pioneering study of the symbolism of evil (1967) on the basis of Western religions, presents an evolution of ethical thinking from taboos through prohibitions to moral rules. Their violation causes different forms of the awareness of evil, which he calls defilement, sin, and guilt.

Defilement is characterized by the relation between the individual and the cosmos, and its practice consists of "a dread of the impure and rites of purification" (Ricoeur 1967, 25). Evil is externalized. Heaven and the gods cause natural catastrophes, fires, droughts, famines, and diseases. Purity, moral good, and good fortune are one and the same. To prevent evil, people create a detailed system of interdictions, "minute prescriptions in domains that for us are ethically neutral" (Ricoeur 1967, 27).

Sin, second, is the "violation of a personal bond" (1967, 52). It signifies the development of greater individual awareness yet still defines people as predominantly social beings. During the stage of sin sets of prohibitions emerge, which "elaborated ritual, penal, civil, and political codes to regulate conduct" (Ricoeur 1967, 53). People at this stage recognize their personal involvement in events but do not fully separate the independent self from nature and others and accordingly make no distinction between sickness and fault. What they experience within is linked with events without; sickness is the punishment for sin and misfortune is the result of evil intentions.

Only at the stage of guilt does the individual come fully into his own. Guilt means the emergence of a delicate and scrupulous conscience, the recognition of personal responsibility for one's own intentions and actions and the acceptance of an inner rather than a cosmic or a social control of evil impulses (Ricoeur 1967, 100). Punishment, too, is internalized as pure guilt—the unadulterated feeling that one deserves punishment and the powerful anxiety that comes with its anticipation. In its fully developed and conscious form, guilt is the eternal strife for altruistic perfection, the never-ending fight against egoistic impulses. It can be expiated through penance, confessions, and altruistic good deeds.

From cosmos to society to the individual, the punishment framework is narrowed successively as evil is increasingly internalized. While a similar development also took place in China and it is possible to apply Ricoeur's stages here (see Lai 1984; Kohn 1995a; 2002a), it is important to understand that Daoist rules intermingle all three and see violations in cosmic as well as social and personal terms. The universal moral rules, joined by specific social prohibitions and cosmic taboos, thus create a fundamental level of Daoist morality, which can be called ordinary morality or conventional morality. It reflects values also found in Chinese society in general and supported by Confucian doctrine. This kind of morality serves to define a clear sense of reciprocity within the community and provides limitations on specific modes of behavior. It is practiced in a tight hierarchical setting, where both individuals and groups interact in a given pattern, striving for the realization of socially defined moral goodness.

ADMONITIONS, INJUNCTIONS, AND RESOLUTIONS

Beyond *jie*, a second form of Daoist rules is found in positively formulated guidelines, encouraging followers to develop virtues of kindness and compassion and to become considerate toward others. Often called admonitions (*quan* 勸), they are the Daoist equivalent of what moral philosophers call supererogatory rules. Supererogation literally means "paying out more than required" and involves acts that are not obligatory but go beyond the call of duty and are thus of special value. They can be acts of heroism, beneficence, kindness, or forgiveness and always carry a special extra level of goodness (Heyd 1982, 115, 144-64). Supererogation creates merit and enhances virtue as a moral quality (Kant 1948, 57-58).

Rules of this type are formulated as "should," indicating a preferred course of action, "what one should do if one desires to achieve moral perfection" (Heyd 1982, 182). In Daoism, they include precepts such as: "Always create fields of blessedness," or "Always be careful where you take lodging," as well as detailed instructions on how to behave in certain situations. For example: "When walking with others, always let them go first," or "Every time you receive food from someone, cast a spell of good wishes to the effect that the donor may attain good fortune and be always full and satisfied."

Admonitions both limit certain physical actions and encourage others. They focus increasingly on the mind of the practitioner and serve to create a different level of moral awareness that could be called altruistic morality. Not unlike the bodhisattva ideal in Buddhism (see Kawamura 1981), it includes a non-ego-centered approach to the world, encompassing positive attitudes that are not reciprocal but one-sided in that they teach one to do good without expecting anything in return. Virtues include compassion, love, generosity, and an openness toward all beings that realizes an ideal within the person rather than in society. The practitioner of this level of morality is envisioned as standing outside society's hierarchical structures, yet his or her actions, undertaken in pure unselfish goodness, have a strong impact on the harmony and well-being of all. The basic pattern is impulse and response (*ganying* 感應): the practitioner giving pure love as an impulse, while society and the universe respond by becoming better and more harmonious.

A third type of Daoist rules appears as practical injunctions or rules (*ke* 科; *gui* 規 after the Song), dignified observances (*weiyi* 威儀), and statutes (*lü* 律). They prescribe in detail how and when to perform a certain action. Injunctions regulate every aspect of life and physical activity, causing the submission of the individual to the communal pattern and enabling the complete transformation of personal reality toward a celestial level.

Injunctions create a system of "ordered, authorized, tested actions," a *habitus* sanctioned by the group that shapes the reality and identity of its members (Mauss 1979, 102). Ranging from body movements (walking, squatting) through ways of caring for the body (washing, grooming) to consumption techniques (Mauss 1979, 98-100, 117-18), injunctions cover everything: attitudes to food, authority, sexual relations, nakedness, pleasure and pain, medicine and healing, and the use of 'body' metaphors (Coakley 1997, 8; see also Bourdieu 1977; 1990). Daoist examples include: "To bow, stand upright with palms joined at chest level;" "At meals, always first rinse your mouth and chant a blessing;" and "After use carefully fold your ritual vestments." They provide instructions on body techniques that constitute a sense of culturally and communally determined personhood realized in ordinary, daily life. Similarly, dignified observances prescribe proper ritual behavior, while statutes detail the administrative proprieties of the priestly hierarchy.

The ethics encapsulated in these rules serve the submission of ordinary bodily and social modes of behavior under the discipline of the institution (see Reinders 1997). Creating a new celestial way of being on the fundamental level of everyday activities, this transformative ethics is inward-focused and complements socially-centered prohibitions and admonitions. It takes Daoists further toward the goal of cosmic oneness in that it helps them to create a concrete basis of Dao-life in their bodily, personal, and ritual interactions.

Beyond all this is the fourth and highest level of Daoist rules representing the moral position of the perfected Daoist, fully at one with the cosmos and intimately perceptive of the cosmic flow. The dominant form of rules at this level is the resolution (*yuan* 願) or remembrance (*nian* 念). Unlike the other rules which are formulated as imperatives, these are phrased in the first person. They are declarations of positive intent and personal guidelines for developing a cosmic attitude and mindset. They go beyond even supererogatory rules in that they focus on the welfare of all beings and engage practitioners in universal ethics. Creating a culture of pure altruism, resolutions guide adepts to feel benevolence, sympathy, love, and compassion; to regard themselves as merely one person among others; and to find identity as part of the larger universe (see Nagel 1970; Munroe 1996).

Resolutions include specific prayers or good wishes, such as: "When I encounter clouds and rain, I pray that all may be soaked with kindness and be full to overflowing, so there is nothing that does not grow;" or "I will constantly practice a compassionate mind and pray and be mindful that all beings equally get to see the divine law." They may also create a mindset conducive to meditation and advanced Daoist practice. An example is: "May I wander to the Golden Towers in Highest Clarity, to pay my respects to the perfected and the Highest Lord."

Then again, resolutions can appear as strong declarations of determination, as in "I'd rather be harmed by wild tigers and poisonous snakes than ever harm the rules and prohibitions of the Heavenly Worthies." Developing a mind of such resolutions and remembrances, Daoists spontaneously avoid violating any rules and step in harmony with all. They no longer have an impact on the running of the universe, but flow along with the larger pattern, rejoicing in the inner harmony of the world and finding total freedom in it.

Taken together, these four kinds of rules present a comprehensive guide to the Daoist enterprise in this world. They are formulated and activated in different communities and change in expression and scope over the centuries of Daoist history. Their first appearance is among the millenarian community of the Celestial Masters.

EARLY MILLENARIAN COMMUNITIES

The earliest Daoist communities were the Celestial Masters (Tianshi 天師) and Great Peace (Taiping 太平) movements in the second century C.E., located in Sichuan and Shandong respectively. They focused on preparing their members for the coming end of the world and were essentially millenarian in nature (see Seidel 1969; 1984).

Millenarian organizations are a form of liminal communities or *communitas* as described by Victor Turner (1969); they resemble utopian communes as studied by Rosabeth Kanter (1972). Such groups tend to insist on a high degree of order and control, coordinating all activities and planning every aspect of life, however personal. Labor, property, personal items, kin, food, and sex—the core values and markers of rank in normative society—are shared and managed by the group. This leads to the practice of communal kitchens, dormitories, and childcare, as well as to the control of sexuality through either celibacy, communal sex, or arranged marriages (Kanter 1972, 44). Internally more open than conventional society in that they cut across ethnic, caste, and national divisions, such groups define themselves through being on the margins of ordinary social structure, whose existence they need as a counterpoint to their own place (Turner 1969, 127).

Like millenarian or utopian groups in general, early Daoist communities defined their organizational structures in religious terms and disregarded common social distinctions such as class, gender, and ethnicity. They also used ritual to determine their calendar and communal activities; they valued the community above individual needs and desires; they required strict humility and obedience as well as sexual control; and they demanded their members to accept pain, suffering, and humiliation as part of community life.

More specifically, among the Celestial Masters and to a lesser degree in the Great Peace movement,[3] followers were ranked hierarchically on the basis of ritual attainments, with the so-called

---

[3] On the history of both movements, see Hendrischke 2000; Robinet 1997. On the Celestial Masters, see Levy 1956; Stein 1963; Schipper 1984; Kleeman 1998;. Ōfuchi 1991; 1997. On Great Peace, see Kaltenmark 1979; Petersen 1989-90. For contemporary Daoist community as practiced among the Yao in northern Thailand, see Strickmann 1982; Lemoine 1982; Höllmann and Friedrich 1999.

libationers (*jijiu* 祭酒) at the top. They served as leaders of the twenty-four districts established by their founder Zhang Daoling 張道陵 and reported directly to the Celestial Master himself.

Beneath them were meritorious household leaders who represented smaller units in the organization and who guided the demon soldiers (*guizu* 鬼卒), the lowest level of initiates. Members came from all walks of life and included many non-Chinese—notably Ba and Banshun Man (Kleeman 1998, 74; 2002, 27)—and leadership positions could be filled by either men or women, Han Chinese, or ethnic minorities. Ranks were attained through ritual initiations, at which followers received lists of spirit generals for protection against demons. The earliest initiations were given to children at age seven, then continued at regular intervals, depending on the follower's devotion and community service. The list of spirit generals was called a register (*lu* 籙) and was carried, together with protective talismans, in a piece of silk around the waist.

Each household paid a rice tax or its equivalent in silk, paper, brushes, ceramics, or handicrafts. Its exact amount varied according to the number of productive members in each family. The tax was assigned and collected on the three major festival days of the year: the fifteenth day of the first, seventh, and tenth months. These days were called the Three Primes (*sanyuan* 三元). They were celebrated in honor of the celestial administration, the Three Bureaus (*sanguan* 三官) of Heaven, Earth, and Water, which kept records of life and death. Festivities involved large community assemblies and banquets known as kitchen-feasts (*chu* 廚), when the consumption of meat and wine was allowed. In addition, each smaller unit or village had a community or parish hall, where members would assemble weekly to perform rituals, confess sins, and discuss local affairs.[4]

Everybody had to participate in these events and perform community service on a regular basis, repairing roads and bridges and maintaining so-called lodges of righteousness where travelers could stay on their journeys (Stein 1963, 56). In addition, community life dominated the individual through sets of rules. Prohibitive in nature, they controlled various kinds of disruptive behavior while encouraging simplicity and obedience. The earliest code of twenty-seven precepts is found in a commentary to Laozi's 老子 *Daode jing* 道德經, followed later by a set of twenty-two statutes against demons and a code of 180 precepts revealed by Lord Lao. Punishments for transgressions were executed by demons who would invade members' bodies and cause sickness and disease (see Harper 1985).

While the precepts demanded humility and obedience and generally encourage submission of the senses, sexual control among the Celestial Masters was exerted in an initiatory practice known as the "harmonization of *qi*" (*heqi* 合氣), a form of choreographed intercourse between selected couples in an elaborate ritual. Practitioners underwent this rite when they were promoted from one level of ritual standing to the next, enacting the matching of yin and yang in their bodies and contributing to greater cosmic harmony (Stein 1963, 57-68).[5]

The acceptance of suffering and pain, moreover, appears in the Celestial Masters' understanding of sickness and sin. Sickness was seen strictly in supernatural terms as an attack by a demon,

---

[4] On the festivals of the Three Primes and other community events, see Ōfuchi 1991, 367-77, 396-400; Kleeman 1998, 72; Stein 1963, 70-71; Schipper 1984, 206.

[5] On the sexual practices, see also Kobayashi 1992, 27-31; Schipper 1994, 205; Ōfuchi 1991, 330-34; Kleeman 1998, 73; Yan 2001.

who could only gain entry into a person's body if the latter was weakened by moral failure. As a result, all healing of the early Celestial Masters was undertaken through ritual and magic; acupuncture, herbs, and other medical treatments were expressly prohibited. First the sick person was isolated in a so-called chamber of tranquility or oratory (*jingshi* 靜室; see Yoshikawa 1987), an adaptation of a Han institution for punishing wayward officials involving solitary confinement. There they had to think of their sins going all the way back to their birth to try and find an explanation for the illness.

Once certain sins had been identified, a senior master would come to write them down in triplicate, joined by a formal petition for their eradication from the person's divine record. Next, the three copies would be transmitted ceremonially to the Bureaus of Heaven (by burning), Earth (by burying), and Water (by casting into a river). The divine officials would then set the record straight, expel the demons, and restore the person's good health. Additional measures of purification involved the ingestion of "talisman water" (the ashes of a talisman dissolved in water), gymnastic exercises patterned on cosmic energy movements, and meditations.

The early organization of the Celestial Masters did not survive untroubled for very long. In 215, their leader Zhang Lu 張魯 got involved in the battles at the end of the Han dynasty and had to submit to the warlord Cao Cao 曹操, who in due course decided not to tolerate a separate organization in his territory (see Mather 1979; Kobayashi 1992). As a result, large numbers of Celestial Masters followers were forced to migrate to different parts of the empire, spreading their cult as they went and creating a different, more open form of their religion. Over time their community structures declined, giving rise to reform movements and new revelations which increasingly changed the nature of the religious Daoist organization.

One such reform was undertaken by Kou Qianzhi 寇謙之 (365-448), a son of a Celestial Masters family in north China. In 415 and 423, he received revelations from Lord Lao that appointed him the new Celestial Master and provided him with both longevity methods and community rules. The latter consisted of twenty *juan* 卷 (scrolls) and were known as the *New Code*, today partially extant in the Daoist canon. Taking his new vision and community organization to court, Kou found the support of the prime minister Cui Hao 崔浩 and became head of a state-sponsored Daoism, the so-called Daoist theocracy, which was geared to expand the Celestial Masters community to a national level and bring peace and harmony to the Toba-Wei empire. After establishing Daoist institutions widely, the emperor himself accepted Daoist initiation in 440, but the theocracy declined soon after Kou's death in 448 (see Mather 1979; Yang 1956; Tang and Tang 1961). Despite its early end, the theocracy laid the foundation for the earliest monastic community at Louguan 樓觀 and Kou's rules continued to be influential in later Daoist codes (see Kohn 1997b; 2000a).

While Kou Qianzhi took the millenarian organization of the Celestial Masters and expanded it to encompass the empire as a whole, creating a political as well as religious vision, other reforms of the group changed its character completely, so that from millenarian *communitas* it became one among several lay Daoist organizations in the fifth century.

LAY ORGANIZATIONS

Lay organizations differ from millenarian or utopian communities in that their followers join a specific school or group for devotional purposes while remaining the subjects of the worldly ruler and obeying the laws of the state. Their rank in civil society, their economic status, and their social connections are not predominantly defined through the religious organization. Their community is not total as in a cult or monastic situation (see Goffman 1961), they do not pay taxes to religiously appointed officials, and there are no civil sanctions for failure to attend assemblies or ceremonies. Rather, members join voluntarily as their schedule permits, they give donations as they can, and they come back only if services prove efficacious and worthwhile.

Rules in lay Daoist organizations of the middle ages were not normative for the whole social order but consisted of specific pledges which included both prohibitions and admonitions. Besides controlling disruptive behavior, they also encouraged a positive, supportive attitude toward the organization. People took these precepts in order to undergo minor ordinations; to join an elite group; and to participate in a ritual, retreat, or festival. They also used them to enhance their purity, religious dedication, and spiritual progress.

Tailoring rules to the individual member's capacity, situation, and ambitions, different lay organizations created various sets of precepts and ethical guidelines. One such group is the Celestial Masters as reformed in south China under the guidance of the Daoist master and ritualist Lu Xiujing 陸修靜 (406-477). As described in his *Abbreviated Rules for Daoist Followers*, he exhorted members to obey community rules, pay taxes, attend assemblies, and honor the libationers (Nickerson 1996). His work in turn inspired new guidelines, such as the sixth-century *Statutes of Mystery Metropolis*, which also continues Kou Qianzhi's *New Code*. By the late sixth century, the Celestial Masters had created a strong lay organization that has remained the foundation of Daoism to the present day.

The Celestial Masters were not the only Daoist group that created lay organizations in the middle ages. Other major schools of the fourth century, based on traditional methods and new revelations, similarly sponsored lay communities of dedicated seekers and lineages of self-cultivation. Among self-cultivation lineages, especially alchemical practitioners have left behind a set of rules, listed by Ge Hong 葛洪 (283–343) in his *Book of the Master Who Embraces Simplicity*. His outline of fifteen admonitions to prepare for the great work begins with: "Accumulate goodness and establish merit, be compassionate to other beings, maintain reciprocity between self and others, be benevolent even to the wriggling worms" (6.5a). It is followed by a set of seventy prohibitions that strongly discourage socially and cosmically harmful actions.

Another self-cultivation group was the school of Highest Clarity (Shangqing 上清). It began in 364-70 with the efforts of several southern aristocratic clans to contact their ancestors so they could find causes for unexplained illnesses and misfortunes and learn about the otherworld. The medium Yang Xi 楊羲 was particularly skilled and established contact with underworld rulers, spirit masters, divine officers of the dead, denizens of local grottoes, and past leaders of the Celestial Masters. They provided him with a detailed description of the organization and population of the otherworld, especially the heaven of Highest Clarity. They also revealed specific methods of soul travels or ecstatic excursions, visualizations, and alchemical concoctions; gave thorough instructions on how to transmit texts and methods; and provided prophecies about the golden age to come (see Strickmann 1978; 1981; Robinet 1984; 2000; Kamitsuka 1999). Moral and ethical rules play a secondary role in the revelations. They only appear in Highest Clarity materials of the sixth century when the school rose to central prominence in the integrated system of the Three Caverns.

The most popular lay organization in medieval Daoism was the Numinous Treasure (Lingbao 靈寶) school. It began in the 390s with the inspiration of Ge Chaofu 葛巢甫, a descendant of the alchemist Ge Hong and practicing member of the Highest Clarity group. His vision of the universe adopted the ideas of multiple layers of heaven, celestial administration, and an extensive host of divine beings from Highest Clarity, while also integrating Han-dynasty cosmology of the five phases and Celestial Masters ritual. In his seminal first work he emphasized spells, talismans, cosmic sounds, and mysterious signs as key sto creation and empowerment. He also stressed the importance of political stability and social harmony, and he established communal rituals that involved formal purifications and the sending of petitions to the otherworld. Over time, these rituals grew to be splendid, large-scale affairs with music, wine, and drama, led by professional masters and geared to move the cosmos in its roots. Known as purgations (*zhai* 齋), they aimed to create harmony and immortality not only for individuals but for entire clans and society as a whole, and they became highly attractive to large numbers of people (see Ōfuchi 1974; Bokenkamp 1983; Yamada 2000).

As it began to grow, the Numinous Treasure school integrated large segments of Buddhist worldview and practices. Buddhism had entered China already in the first century C.E., but it did not come fully into its own until around the year 400, when a group of aristocratic monks in the south asserted the independence of the Buddhist community, and the Toba-Wei dynasty in the north invited the Central Asian scholar Kumārajīva from Kucha to head a translation institute in their capital (see Zürcher 1959; Tsukamoto and Hurvitz 1985). As a result, Chinese Buddhists were able to rely on texts that represented accurate presentations of Buddhist doctrine, and the religion began to develop greater autonomy.

The increased translation of the *Vinaya*, or collection of Buddhist rules, inspired monks to standardize their practice and greatly contributed to the improved quality of both monastic and lay discipline. Daoists of the Numinous Treasure school looked to Buddhism as a model and integrated its doctrines and practices into their system, especially in the areas of rebirth, karma, and precepts (see Zürcher 1980). Texts arose that contained sets of ten precepts and ten items of goodness, bodhisattva-like vows, guidelines toward selflessness and compassion, rules for proper ritual preparation, as well as a new version of *The 180 Precepts of Lord Lao*, now called *Precepts of the Three Primes*. The first examples of universal ethics appear in this school. Followers joined by becoming members of dedicatory societies who organized regular worship of the Dao, special purgation ceremonies, and the sponsorship of sacred images (see Yamada 2000; Liu 2003, 59).

Similar activities were also undertaken by another lay Daoist organization, the school of the Three Sovereigns (Sanhuang 三皇). Followers believed that the talismans and teachings of these sage monarchs of antiquity guaranteed the perfect harmony of the universe and strove to make them accessible and applicable in the world. With a vision toward creating a state-wide community of Great Peace, their followers obeyed the five great moral rules and a set of eight precepts based on ancient Chinese rulership guidelines. Not well-known since their sources survive only in fragments, it appears that members of the Three Sovereigns school emphasized personal integrity and the correct ritual writing and activation of talismans (see Ōfuchi 1964, 277-343; Chen 1975, 71-78; Kobayashi 1990).

MONASTIC INSTITUTIONS

In the late sixth century the different Daoist schools began to integrate themselves into one organization under the system of the Three Caverns (*sandong* 三洞) which placed Highest Clarity first, Numinous Treasure second, the Three Sovereigns third, and included the Celestial Masters as the underlying foundation of all (see Ōfuchi 1979b). At this time a full-fledged monastic institution arose that served to train priests and religious specialists of the higher schools. Daoist monasteries followed Buddhist structural models, integrated the lay guidelines of the medieval schools, and continued the organization and buildings of Celestial Masters communities (see Kohn 2003a).

In general, monasteries can be described as institutions that allow religious seekers "to undertake an intense personal spiritual activity which separates them from ordinary society and binds them together in same-sex kindred fellowships that provide ideal alternatives to the ordinary world" (Juergensmeyer 1990, 556; Kohn 2003a, 3). Monasticism as a cross-cultural phenomenon represents a "purer, more lonely vision of the religious life" (1990, 558) and can be found in various expressions in different areas, cultures, and periods. Another form of *communitas*, it has four main characteristics.

First, it is the active expression of an inherently individual impulse that leads men or women to dedicate their lives to a quest of higher truth, an attainment of holiness, and a search for the perfect life. Second, it requires the separation from ordinary life: a need to die to the old and be reborn to a new, divinely-based identity. Consciously and actively choosing the divine over the mundane, the seeker moves away from society to a state of separateness and isolation, where traditional values count for nothing and emptiness and purity are the highest good.

Third, monasticism involves "the evolution of a same-sex kindred community," which Juergensmeyer describes as a kind of "spiritual factory" or "project," a "Los Alamos of spiritual technology" (1990, 550). As organized community, monasticism rejects and transforms the social patterns of the ordinary world, yet in certain ways also maintains and develops them. Monks and nuns are not sexless, homeless, or kinless beings, but people who have redirected their inherent needs toward a spiritual goal and the community of the divine. Fourth and finally, monasticism provides an alternative to ordinary society through its creation of specific religious rules, patterns, schedules, and hierarchies that hold up a mirror to society at large and show the way to an ideal, perfect form of the communal life (Kohn 2003, 4-5).

Following their monastic urge, Daoist monks and nuns in the middle ages joined communities to practice meditation and self-cultivation. Segregated from society and bound by detailed injunctions of propriety, these communities allowed them to worship and work together in a Daoist life on earth. Monastic rules are guidelines for daily conduct and dignified observances, as well as mental prescriptions for a universal mind. They appear in a group of texts from the seventh and eighth centuries (Kohn 2003a, 203-26). Concrete daily behavior and proper interaction with the community were essential to the Daoist enterprise in this setting, which dominated the religious scene in the Tang dynasty (618-907).

After the Tang, in the tenth century, a general collapse of political and organizational structures occurred, and court subsidies for religious institutions ceased. Temples declined, the ordination system broke down, and techniques and doctrines were suspended. Individual practitioners of Daoist training no longer had key places to go or officially recognized masters to follow. They were on their own, wandering to sacred mountains, occasionally connecting with isolated hermits or discovering efficacious techniques by trial and error. These practitioners had no financial cushion on which to fall back, and thus had to find ways of serving communities for a fee so they could continue their quest. Serving villages and towns whose citizens increasingly joined devotional groups in worship of local gods and saints, Daoists began to offer practical rites of veneration, healing, exorcism, and protection. They issued spells and talismans for concrete goals and undertook funerals and communication with ancestors to set people's minds at rest.

Daoists of this type became common in the Song (960-1260) and were known both as Daoists (*daoshi* 道士) and ritual masters (*fashi* 法師) (see Davis 2001; Kohn 2001a; Hymes 2002). They did not take a standardized set of precepts once at a formal ordination but instead made specifically tailored vows for specific rituals. Rules from this time accordingly focus on the proper moral attitude in preparation of rituals and self-cultivation practices, as well as on the salvation of the dead. They are most commonly found in ritual collections, often appearing in newly created sets of ten but also recapturing lists from the middle ages.

Monasticism did not survive as an active institution in the Song and only rose again in the late twelfth century with the school of Complete Perfection (Quanzhen 全真) (see Yao 1980; 2000; Tsui 1991). Founded by the ascetic Wang Chongyang 王重陽 (1112-1170), it encouraged followers to leave society, become celibate, and dedicate themselves fully to the Dao, thus living either in thatched huts on lonely mountain sides or in larger communities structured in imitation of Chan Buddhism.

As common in all monasticism, Complete Perfection communities had a systematic hierarchy and followed a tight schedule that kept everyone busy meditating, worshiping, and working from 3:00 a.m. until 9:00 p.m. (Yao 2000, 589). With such strict organization, the school developed many rules, laid out from its earliest texts. Its monastic ordination and precepts system is still in place today. It was created in the mid-seventeenth century under the guidance of Wang Kunyang 王崑陽 (d.1680), leader of the Longmen subsect and abbot of the White Cloud Monastery (Baiyun guan 白雲觀) (Esposito 2000, 629). Three texts are attributed to him, which match three levels of ordination and outline behavioral patterns for beginners, intermediate practitioners, and celestial immortals.

Still observed today, these texts are important also because they contain the culmination of all guidelines developed in the Daoist tradition, integrating many different strands and patterns into one systematic whole. In many ways, they close the circle to the earliest communities of the Celestial Masters. Thus, from its earliest organization to the present day, concrete behavior and community interaction have been at the heart of Daoist practice and have formed the basis for the successful attainment of personal cultivation and celestial realization.

CHAPTER ONE

Human Behavior and Cosmic Goodness

In the Daoist world, human beings are an integral part of nature and the greater universe, which functions in perfect harmony and is fundamentally good. Created in a series of transformations without a radical break from the pure, formless Dao (see Girardot 1983; Le Blanc 1987; Major 1993), the universe manifests itself in a wondrous combination of manifold forces that ideally work together to constitute a cosmos of perfect goodness.

The goodness of the cosmos is not necessarily a moral goodness that can be expressed in sets of rules and enforced by laws and other restraints. The goodness of the cosmos goes beyond human morality because it is cosmic and natural, and both cosmos and nature are cruel and unjust at times; they do not have a set of values that can be defined or to which they can be held. At the same time, the goodness of the cosmos is intuited by human beings as a sense of well-being and inner harmony which, if it is to be achieved with their limited sensory and intellectual faculties, can be expressed in moral rules. Morality is thus part of the cosmic harmony which Daoists embody, and their being in the world increases the ethical quality of life around them. Nevertheless, perfected Daoists are not *per se* moral, but rather transmoral or supramoral, going beyond the demands of human society in a spontaneous sense of cosmic oneness (Kohn 2002, 289).

Although expressed most strongly in resolutions and mindful intentions, all the rules and precepts of the Daoist religion serve to create an attitude that realizes the universal interconnectedness in everything one is and does. They acknowledge that while the cooperation of all things and beings in the universe constitutes its perfection and is its ultimate and most natural state, any particular individual or entity can realize its pure Dao-nature to a greater or lesser degree. Ideal Daoists have realized their Dao-nature to the utmost and are naturally who they were meant to be, thus able to spread the purity of underlying goodness.

People living in conflict and trouble, on the other hand, have not realized their true potential, but they have become removed from the inherent harmony of the Dao, developing patterns of disharmony and an inclination toward immoral and harmful actions. Still, because they too are part of the system as a whole, which is ultimately one, they are immediately affected by the condensed power of purity embodied in a realized Daoist if and when they come in contact with him or her. Through the latter's purity and Dao-ness, ordinary people transform over time, and without consciously wishing or even noticing it, to a higher degree of goodness and harmony. The moral rules on their different levels thus may reform specific individuals and communities, but they also affect the functioning of human society in general and impact the greater universe. They represent the goodness of the universe on a tangible, human plane.

HEAVEN AND EARTH

Daoists express this thought first and foremost in the claim that Heaven and Earth wish people to be good and to act morally so that they can fulfill their proper destiny. An early formulation of this thought, which is the background of all Daoist ethics, is found in *The Essential Precepts of Master Redpine* (*Chisongzi zhongjie jing* 赤松子中戒經, DZ 185).[1] Cited already in Ge Hong's *Book of the Master Who Embraces Simplicity* (*Baopuzi* 抱朴子, DZ 1185) of about 320 C.E., this text goes back to the fourth century and is extant in a Song-dynasty edition (see Yoshioka 1960; Kohn 1998c).

The text presents a dialogue between the Yellow Emperor and Master Redpine, both classical figures in the Daoist tradition who have early hagiographies in the *Immortals' Biographies* (*Liexian zhuan* 列仙傳, DZ 294) of the Former Han dynasty (see Kaltenmark 1953; Yamada 1989, 104). They discuss nine questions posed by the Yellow Emperor, including why people are different in their fortunes, what sins offend Heaven and Earth, and what one can do to improve one's lot. The fundamental concept is that as people consist of the *qi* of Heaven and Earth, their thoughts and actions have a direct impact on the functioning of the world. The text says:

> Human beings live between Heaven and Earth and are endowed with the two *qi* of yin and yang. Sovereign Heaven, although high, yet has its correspondence down below. Mother Earth, although low, yet has its correspondence far above. Heaven does not speak, yet the four seasons move in order. Earth does not speak, yet the myriad beings come to life.
>
> People reside right between the two. All their licentious intentions and passionate desires, whatever they do or do not do, Heaven and Earth know all about it. For this reason we say that Heaven has four-sided [all-round] knowledge. (2a)

This knowledge not only extends to people's overt and open actions but also involves their hidden thoughts and secret intentions. All these have an immediate effect, so that "when the people of the world commit violations, bad actions, or faults, or speak contrary words, Heaven's way is no longer even; instead, it is bent and loses its spontaneity" (5b). All bad deeds, all vicious thoughts, all cursing and scolding upset Heaven and create cosmic imbalance. So does the suffering that people undergo as a result of their bad deeds. Even worse, Heaven is strongly discomfited when people afterwards try to implore it and garner favor. The text says:

> Getting imprisoned and locked into the cangue [punishment board] upsets Heaven. Being hungry and poor, ill and sick upsets Heaven. Unseasonable cold and heat, frost and snow upset Heaven. Irregularities in the length of day and night upset Heaven.
>
> It upsets Heaven even more when people do evil then come to pray and besiege it [for help]. Or go against the four seasons, disobey the five phases, expose their naked body to the Three Luminants [sun, moon, planets], and then come to request a benefit at a shrine or temple of the Three Luminants or the various stars and constellations. (5b-6a)

People cause cosmic disharmony by not having respect for Heaven and Earth, the demons and spirits, by cursing the wind and the rain, by denigrating the sages and the scriptural teachings, and by desecrating shrines and temples (6a). Not only religious and cosmic violations, but all manner of social harm disturbs the cosmos: being unfilial toward their father and mother; dig-

---

[1] "DZ" stands for *Daozang* 道藏 or Daoist canon. Texts in this collection are referred to according to numbers in Schipper 1975; Komjathy 2002.

ging up tombs to steal the valuables of the dead; cheating the blind, the deaf, and the dumb; throwing impure substances into food and drink; killing other beings; accusing and slandering others or spying on their affairs; obstructing roads and letting drains be blocked; stealing and cheating, destroying nature's riches, and in other ways harming society and the life around them (6ab). All these acts cause Heaven and Earth to be upset and imbalanced. They in turn do not keep their displeasure a secret but give human beings ample warning that something is amiss. As *The Essential Precepts of Master Redpine* states:

> Heaven never cheats on living beings but shows them its inclinations, like a shadow following a shape. It has day and night, light and darkness, thunder and lightning, rain and snow, intertwining rainbows, eclipses of the sun and the moon, and floating characters of wisdom. All these are signs given by Heaven.

> Similarly Earth never cheats on living beings but shows them its inclinations, like an echo following a sound. It makes rivers and streams dry up and brings forth landslides and earthquakes, hurricanes and tornadoes, sandstorms and moving stones, floods and locust plagues, famines and droughts, epidemics and other disasters. All these are signs given by Earth. (2b)

In order to right the situation and to allow Heaven and Earth to come back to a balanced state, "all people need to do is honor and venerate Heaven and Earth and the Three Luminants, never violate the prohibitions and taboos, love and obey their fathers and mothers, maintain harmony with their siblings, be compassionate and empathic to the orphaned and lonely, save and support the poor and sick, and respect and honor their teachers and elders" (8a). People should retain a strong sense of interconnectedness in all they do, developing feelings of compassion and sympathy, well-wishing and support.

> Seeing people suffering loss should give them pain and a sense of urgency; seeing others win and gain should make them feel joyous. Supporting the emaciated and protecting the weak, they should be generous and kind, help and cherish the orphaned and poor, and honor and care for the lowly and humble. As they yield their emoluments to others, so Heaven records their merit, increases their age and longevity, and grants protection and good fortune to their sons and grandsons. (8b)

As people realize that they ultimately are at the root of Heaven and Earth and have the power to make the cosmos move in harmony or go out of balance, they act more and more in goodness—a moral goodness that abstains from harmful actions and supports the community of all life. They replace negative and destructive attitudes with supportive and helpful ones. For example, instead of "when burdened by debt, they wish that the moneylender may die and the debt expire," they now strive to pay back the money. "When they see someone who in the past was in debt to them run afoul of the officials, they develop an intention of helpfulness and support." Or again, when they see someone blessed with beautiful wives and concubines, instead of developing an intent toward adultery they now count their blessings and "realize that their own partner does not create quarrels or upheaval" (10b-11a). They begin by observing the precepts and prohibitions, then gradually develop a greater awareness of Heaven and Earth and come to create good fortune for themselves, the society around them, and the world at large.

Concepts of Heaven and Earth as central agents of morality are found throughout Daoist literature. Another text that spells them out in some detail is the *Precepts and Rules Taught by the Celestial Master* (*Tianshi jiao jieke jing* 天師教戒科經, DZ 789), a work of the early fifth century. It begins:

> The Dao takes harmony as its virtue and opposes what is not harmonious. For this reason, if Heaven and Earth are united in harmony, the myriad beings grow and prosper, plants blossom and lush growth develops. If the state is united in harmony, there is Great Peace in all-under-Heaven and the myriad families live in security and peace. If the family is united in harmony, the father is caring and the sons are filial, and Heaven spreads good fortune and blessings everywhere. (1a)

This passage expresses a direct link between the internal harmony of the Dao and the correct functioning of Heaven and Earth, which in turn creates prosperity among people and social peace. The virtues of humanity are the direct outcome of the harmony of the heavenly spheres, and at the same time people can create harmony on all other levels of life by being virtuous on the human plane. This, however, only works when there is deep sincerity and honesty. Both *The Essential Precepts of Master Redpine* and the *Precepts and Rules Taught by the Celestial Master* strongly object to people committing evil and then coming to beg the gods and the Dao for help. Unlike the former, though, the latter insists that this begging will be quite useless:

> Whenever people encounter disasters, emergencies, danger, sickness, pain, or other afflictions of their bodies, they look to the Dao for support and protection. But the Dao will not rescue them. Even if they are invaded and harmed by evil forces and demonic warriors, the Dao will not come to their help. On the contrary, it actively rejects people who are unsettled and ignorant, who never make any effort to control their minds, turn to repent their sins, or sincerely seek refuge in the Dao. (7a)

It is, therefore, not only an act of great wisdom but of elementary prudence to follow the Dao and obey the basic moral rules, for one's own protection and the greater good of all.

THE CELESTIAL ADMINISTRATION

When directly impacted by human activities, Heaven and Earth react by showing their signs immediately. Beyond this, they also have ways of mediating their effects on people's lives. The most important among these ways is through the celestial administration which supervises human behavior and adjusts people's life expectancy in accordance with their deeds. [2] Among the early Celestial Masters, this administration was described in terms of the Three Bureaus of Heaven, Earth, and Water, each with groups of officers who administered people's fates (see Kobayashi 1992). In the medieval schools, the system was expanded and the Daoist otherworld became an elaborate construction of manifold offices. As the *Illustrious Regulations of the Four Ultimates* (*Siji mingke* 四極明科, DZ 184), a fifth-century text of Highest Clarity, describes the central offices in heaven:

1. The office to the left presides over transgressions of a yang nature, such as killing, theft of celestial treasures, unwarranted spread of sacred texts, cursing and swearing.
2. The office to the right presides over transgressions of a yin nature, including harboring schemes in one's heart, disobedience, planning harm to others, and never remembering the Dao.

---

[2] The notion of a hierarchically organized otherworld with supervising functions over the living goes back far in Chinese history and can be traced back to the ancestor worship of the Shang dynasty. For a discussion of the early system, see Chang 1980; Keightley 1978a; 1978b. On its later development, see Poo 1997; Shahar and Weller 1996.

3. The office in the center presides over more essential shortcomings, such as doubts and duplicity, lack of reverence and faith in heavenly perfection, desecration of heavenly treasures, and thoughts of removing the scriptures of the Dao or of defiling perfected writings. (1.4b)[3]

To fulfill their function, these offices controlled a big staff of divine guards, bailiffs, and local agents, who resided in the nine provinces of the earth (1.5a). They ruled the souls of the sinful dead and kept them revolving in the cycle of transmigration for countless kalpas, letting them go only after unthinkable pain and torture (1.5b-6a). The only way to prevent falling into their hands was to act morally and with proper virtue (1.7b-8a) and to practice the meditations and recitations described in the text (chs. 2-5).

How exactly the celestial administration kept track of people's deeds and punished them was seen differently in the texts. *The Essential Precepts of Master Redpine* presents the idea of a personal star that people receive at birth and which shines or dims in accordance with their celestial standing. According to the text, everyone who comes to life is connected "to one particular star, which may be big or small, but in each case governs the person's longevity and shortness [of life], decline and prosperity, poverty and wealth, death and life" (1a). This star is used by the celestial administrators, notably by the Director of Fates (Si-ming 司命) and the Director of Emoluments (Silu 司綠), to gauge people's moral mettle by "placing a talisman of the Great One on people's heads to examine whether they are full of sins. In accordance with their finding, they then make a subtraction from the life expectancy" (2a). Although most people begin life with a standard longevity "of 43,800 days, i.e., 120 years of life"(1b), this may change rapidly as their behavior does not measure up.

The starry essence of the talisman changes in accordance with the subtractions made by the gods. As the text has it:

If they subtract one year, the star on the person's head becomes lackluster and he or she runs into lots of difficulties. If they take off ten years, the star begins to fade and the person encounters disasters and disease. If they subtract twenty years, the star is extinguished and the person runs into legal trouble and is imprisoned. If they make a reduction of thirty years, the star dissolves and the person dies. (2ab)

Here the lessening of human life expectancy, as a result of evil deeds and their punishment by the gods, is envisioned as the gradual dimming and extinction of a bright star. At the same time, the energetic fading has physical and social consequences in the person's life, making it clear that punishment is not only a shorter life but also a much less happy, healthy, and successful one. Both sickness and legal troubles are part of the overall fortune of the person, brought about through immoral acts. Also, the ensuing troubles often are in direct resonance with the sins committed. The text says:

Someone who killed, for example, will himself be caught up between two armies and suffer death on the battlefield. If he has killed only once, he will be harmed in his own body and that will even the score of his fate. If he has killed twice, he will be caught between five armies and the Great One will come to slay him. Plus, the evil deed will continue to follow him and create continued misfortunes for his descendants. (7b)

---

[3] Numinous Treasure Daoism has a similar threefold division under the name of the Three Primes in its *Precepts of the Three Primes*. See Text 6 below.

The bottom line is that no bad deed ever goes unpunished and that cosmic justice will prevail through the management of the celestial administration.

DIVINE RETRIBUTION AND MEASUREMENTS

Further questions about the celestial administration arise. What happens when a person has committed more evil than can be punished by subtractions from his or her life? How exactly do the celestial officials know what people do in the privacy of their homes and thoughts? And how can we know where we stand in relation to our heavenly reckoning?

To answer the first, early texts present the concept of "inherited evil" (*chengfu* 承負). Already *The Essential Precepts of Master Redpine* notes that innocent babies die in the womb or in infancy "because the sins of the ancestors and forebears bequeath calamities upon their descendants" (1b). The *Book of the Master Who Embraces Simplicity* lists both fifteen good deeds to cultivate and seventy bad behaviors to avoid, stating that "every one of these activities constitutes one sin, and according to its being either serious or light, the Director of Fates subtracts a unit of reckoning or a period [from the life expectancy]. When no more units remain, the person dies" (6.7a; Yoshioka 1970a, 190). Even bad thoughts count: "If there is evil intention without evil action, one unit is subtracted; if there is evil action that causes a loss to another, a whole period is taken off" (6.7a). It then notes that the bad fortune so created is transmitted to family and descendants:

> Whenever you interfere with or steal another's goods, the gods may take into account [the life expectancy] of your wife, children, and other household members in order to compensate for it, causing them to die, if not immediately. Even if your evil behavior is not quite bad enough to bring death upon the members of your household, for a long time you will be plagued by floods, fires, burglaries, and other losses. (6.7b)

The same notion, including also the importance of thoughts and attitudes, is further formulated in the *Scripture of Great Peace* (*Taiping jing* 太平經, DH 86; DZ 1101; ed. Wang 1979), a sixth-century collection that contains reconstituted materials of the Great Peace movement of the second century.[4] It says that "when someone strives to be good but evil results, this is because he receives and transmits the mistakes men have formerly made" (Hendrischke 1991, 10; Kamitsuka 1988). The concept also extended to other social units beyond the family, such as the village or the groups of five families that had joint responsibility according to the legal codes. In the case of an emperor, it might even involve the fortune of the entire country (Hendrischke 1991, 16-17). Belief in inherited evil explained why innocent children or good people had to suffer. The concept took some pressure off the present generation in that reasons for failure could be found among earlier family members and often were addressed through the performance of rituals (Kaltenmark 1979, 24). However, it also heightened the responsibility of the individual for his current family and future descendants (Hendrischke 1991, 11).

The second question about the celestial administration addresses the issue of how the supernatural officials received their information. The answer given in the *Book of the Master Who Embraces Simplicity* and later expanded in other Daoist texts, states that there are Three Corpses or Deathbringers (*sanshi* 三尸) in the body (6.4b; Ware 1966, 177). A mixture of demons and parasites, they reside in the head, torso and lower body of the individual and are assisted by a group

---

[4] On the history of the text, see Michaud 1958; Kandel 1979; Mansvelt-Beck 1980; Petersen 1989-90.

known as the Nine Worms (*jiuchong* 九蟲), physical entities that cause illnesses and look like ordinary worms or insects— some long and slithering, others round with little leg-like extensions, yet others spongy or crab-like.[5]

The Three Deathbringers are deputies of the celestial administration who deliver regular reports to the Director of Fates above, as does the Stove God from his residence in the family kitchen (see Chard 1988; 1990; 1995). Instructed by the celestials to punish people, the Deathbringers cause them to be sick, suffer misfortunes, and eventually die. After the death of the host, when the various souls have been sent off to the otherworld, they remain with the corpse and gorge themselves on its blood, bones, and muscles. Having partaken of the human body, they are able to assume its former intact shape and appear as ghosts, feasting further on the offerings laid out for the dead. They have thus a vested interest in bringing a person to death quickly and without mercy, and accordingly incite them toward evil.

Measures against them begin with virtuous behavior in accordance with moral rules and social harmony, as well as continued meditation on the pure gods of the Dao. For those who lack saintly virtue, there are more physical countermeasures, such as a vigil on the *gengshen* 庚申 night once every two months, when the Three Deathbringers ascend to heaven to report. The idea is that the parasites are like souls who can only leave the body when the person is asleep. Without proper directives for destruction, they will be helpless and disoriented and eventually die. For those who cannot stay awake long enough or lack the moral purity required for the vigil, various drugs and medicines as well as talismans, incantations, and the observation of taboos may keep the Three Deathbringers from doing too much harm (Yamada 1989, 107-12). While these remedies will not eradicate them and people may still die from their activities, they at least hamper them in their ways, and one can breathe a little easier (Kohn 1995b, 44).

To keep track of the activities of the celestial administration and to learn about their current status, Daoists further answered the third question on how people can keep track of their current standing by attributing specific numerical values to particular deeds. The currency selected consisted of single days of life called a "reckoning" (*suan* 算) and a longer time span known as a "period" (*ji* 紀) which could be 60, 100, or 300 days, or even twelve years (Yoshioka 1970a, 190). For example, the *Demon Statutes of Nüqing* (*Nüqing guilü* 女青鬼律, DZ 790) of the fourth century, an outline of protective measures against demons that may well be the "most ancient doctrinal work of the Celestial Masters" still extant (Schipper 1994b, 69; Lai 2002a, 268), says:

> Do not claim to hold on to perfection while entering falsehood, or to quarrel with and disturb the sages and enlightened ones. Do not drink wine, eat meat, or revile and curse the Dao. For this Heaven will subtract 1,300 days [from your life]. (1b)

`Another Celestial Masters text, the sixth-century *Statutes of Mystery Metropolis* (*Xuandu lüwen* 玄都律文, DZ 188), similarly states that lying costs fifty reckonings, deceiving one's teacher costs 400 reckonings, and lack of compassion and filial piety costs seven periods. The *Rules and Precepts for Worshiping the Dao* (*Fengdao kejie* 奉道科戒, DZ 1125; trl. Kohn 2004), a monastic manual of the early Tang, insists that Daoists who pass others without proper greeting suffer a loss of 120 reckonings, those who place their shoes directly on the ground instead of on a proper rack

---

[5] An illustrated description is found in the ninth-century *Scripture on Preserving Life by Removing the Three Deathbringers* (*Chu sanshi baosheng jing* 出三尸保生經, DZ 871). See Kohn 1995b.

lose 280, and those who do not line up in proper accordance with their ritual rank will live 1,200 days less than originally destined (Kohn 1998c, 856-58).

A different approach to the problem lists numbers of good and bad deeds with various celestial rewards and punishments. A first example is found in *The Essential Precepts of Master Redpine*. It states that one good deed causes spirit and intention to be calm and at peace, ten give the person strong physical energy, twenty keep the body free from affliction, thirty ensure that all one's goals are achieved as planned, and so on, until hundreds of good deeds will make certain that one's family brings forth noble, prosperous, and honored people. In reverse, one bad deeds makes one restless and nervous, ten cause one's *qi* to decline, twenty cause physical afflictions, thirty prevent one's plans from being realized, forty will put one in constant difficulties, and so on, until hundreds of bad deeds cause one's family to decline and one's descendants to become lowly, destitute, and criminal.

The effects of increasing numbers are roughly parallel among good and bad deeds and expand in concentric circles. Beginning with influencing the person's mind and attitude toward life, they cause changes in physical well-being and a greater tendency to succeed or fail in one's ventures. This leads to gain or loss in social standing, which influences the prosperity of one's descendants for several generations. The list of how many deeds create what kind of fortune has survived through the ages and is still actively present today in the most basic ordination text of the monastic school of Complete Perfection.[6]

Among lay followers, the concept of numerical values has been popularized since the Song dynasty in the so-called ledgers of merit and demerit (*gongguo ge* 功過格), a kind of religious diary that allows people to keep track of their actions and supernatural standing (see Yoshioka 1959; Brokaw 1990). Around the same time, the methods of the celestial administration were modernized also, so that today it features a celestial treasury whose divine officers issue a set amount of credit to everyone at birth—primordial *qi* seen as a sum of money—which has to be repaid over one's lifetime in good deeds and through the burning of spirit money. Anyone who commits bad deeds or otherwise wastes their credit will suffer in the prisons of hell (see Hou 1975). All in all, the celestial administration is actively present in people's lives and ensures the proper rewards and punishments for all thoughts and actions.

BODILY EFFECTS

Besides sending sickness and misfortune through the celestial administration, Heaven and Earth also make people pay for their sins directly through their bodies. According to this understanding, failure to behave properly causes internal stress; invites demonic influences. It harms the spirit, the souls, the essence, and the *qi* in the body and thereby creates first psychological ten-

---

[6] The text is the *Precepts of Initial Perfection* (*Chuzhen jie* 初真戒), translated below (see Text 11). In between, the list appears in the *Statutes of Mystery Metropolis* 2a-3a; the *Comprehensive Perfect Words* (*Zhiyan zong* 至言總, DZ 1033), 5.5b-6a, 9ab; in Du Guangting's 杜光庭 *Record of the Assembled Immortals in the Heavenly Walled City* (*Yongcheng jixian lu* 墉城集仙綠, DZ 783) 1.4a-5a (Kohn 1989a, 88-89); and in the supplement to the *Treatise on Impulse and Response* (*Ganying pian* 感應篇, DZ 1167), 11.2b-3b. For a comprehensive survey of all lists and their variants, see Yoshioka 1967, 294-99.

sion, then physical ailments, and eventually death. This notion is at the root of the understanding of sickness and healing among the early Celestial Masters, for whom disease was caused by demons who could only gain entry into a body if the person was weakened by sin. It also appears in the medieval schools, especially in the *Immortals' Taboos According to the Purple Texts Inscribed by the Spirits* (*Lingshu ziwen xianji* 靈書紫文仙忌, DZ 179), a fifth-century document of the Highest Clarity school. It begins by emphasizing the need to keep one's sexual essence to oneself and not to squander it in immoral acts. It says:

> Do not delight in licentiousness. As and when you engage in licentiousness, your spirit souls and bodily fluids leak to the outside and your essence and radiance wither and dry up. Your spirit gets scorched, your material souls scatter, your bones turn brittle, and your marrow rots.

> Then your spirit souls will cry out to the numinous offices and report to the three celestial pavilions. The Three Palaces [cinnabar fields] will squabble over their jurisdiction, and your embryonic florescence will be sad and wronged. (1b; see Bokenkamp 1997a, 363)

This understanding relies on the notion of Chinese medicine that sexual activity, especially when undertaken to excess, leads to a loss of the vital fluid known as essence (*jing* 精). Essence is a form of *qi* in the body that is responsible for procreation but also maintains the person's vitality and is at the root of one's brain, bones, and marrow. Its continued loss results in physical weakness and leads to death. The text further connects this notion with the idea of various divine entities residing in the human body who are impacted by debauched thoughts and activities. No longer with a clear sense of rank and duty, they will create great confusion which in turn causes to physical decline.

A similar case is made for stealing. The text says:

> Do not steal or bring about misfortune and evil. As and when you bring about misfortune and evil, your Yellow Court [spleen] is thrown into confusion, and the Three Deathbringers delight in the kill.

> Your spirit souls and body gods start quarreling with each other; your material souls and inner demons fight for residence. The radiance of your eyes is besieged and scattered, and your mouth emits a noxious vapor. (1b; see Bokenkamp 1997a, 363)

Again the link between moral failure and illness is made through the action of inner forces, envisioned as deities and demons, such as the Three Deathbringers, who fight with each other for dominance in a person's body. Any disturbance of their equilibrium creates disorder and encourages the bad elements to rise to the fore, making the person sick. More so than in the rule against sexual misconduct and intoxication where the connection is directly physical, in the precept against stealing the supernatural intercession is essential. It reflects the Daoist view of the body as a microcosm of the universe that is inhabited by countless deities and body gods whose continued presence and harmonious interaction are essential to health, longevity, and spiritual attainment.[7]

Another connection between moral behavior and the body is made in the *Precepts of the Highest Lord Lao* (*Taishang Laojun jiejing* 太上老君戒經, DZ 784; Kohn 1994; Jan 1986), a late fifth-century

---

[7] On the Daoist understanding of the body, see Schipper 1978; 1994a; Kohn 1991b; Kroll 1996; Saso 1997; Bumbacher 2001.

text associated with the northern Celestial Masters. Here the five precepts are linked with traditional cosmology and thus with the five inner organs. The text says:

> The precept to abstain from killing belongs to the east. It embodies the energy of Germinating Life and honors natural growth. People who harm and kill living beings will receive corresponding harm in their livers.

> The precept to abstain from stealing belongs to the north. It embodies the essence of Great Yin and presides over the resting and storing of nature. People who steal will receive corresponding calamities in their kidneys.

> The precept to abstain from licentiousness belongs to the west. It embodies the material power of Lesser Yin and preserves the purity and strength of men and women. People who delight in licentiousness will receive corresponding foulness in their lungs.

> The precept to abstain from intoxication belongs to the south and the phase fire. It embodies the energy of Great Yang and supports all beings in their full growth. People who indulge in drink will receive corresponding poison in their hearts.

> The precept to abstain from lying belongs to the center and the phase earth; its virtue is faithfulness. People who lie will receive corresponding shame in their spleens. (14a-15b; Kohn 1994, 204-5)

In each case, sickness and physical decline appear in the organ that matches the phase and direction of the precept violated, placing physical well-being in an immediate relationship to the morality of thoughts and actions.[8] Just as the human body is part of the greater universe and matches Heaven and Earth in its constitution and functioning, so all activities undertaken in and through it have a direct impact on the cosmic pattern and reverberate back to take their toll or give their benefits. The body becomes the central agency in the understanding of the close connection between morality and well-being, connected to Heaven and Earth either directly or mediated through the activities of the body gods. It is an essential indicator of moral standing and the key vehicle for transformation to immortality, purified not only through proper insights and dedicated self-cultivation but in the moral purity of everyday activities and thoughts.

RITUAL PURITY

Another way in which Heaven and Earth demanded moral action is that they would not accept ritual offerings or petitions without proper purification, both physical and moral. Even in ancient China purity was an essential prerequisite for the performance of rituals, typically undertaken as a set of purifications known as *zhai* 齋 that included baths, fasting, sexual abstention, and the avoidance of death, blood, and other forms of defilement.

The Daoist alchemical tradition, too, placed strong emphasis on purifications. Before even the first ingredient could be placed in the alchemical cauldron, the stage had to be set in an uninhabited area far removed from the impurities of ordinary folk, in a grove planted with the right combination of trees for proper *qi*, near an eastward flowing stream, and generally in a pure en-

---

[8] A comparative modern understanding similarly states that physical symptoms can be manifestations of guilt or forms of self-punishment for actions interpreted as wrong or evil. See Belgum 1963; 1967; Siivals 1962. The concept has also been linked with cases of cancer (Simonton 1956).

vironment. Then several ritual purifications had to be undergone. As the *Book of the Master Who Embraces Simplicity* describes them:

> Begin by purifying yourself and fasting for one hundred days. Wash your body and hair in water en- riched with the five fragrances, and make yourself utterly clean. Never approach any defiling or dirty object or let ordinary people come anywhere near you! Let no disbelievers know of your plans. If they denounce the divine medicine, successful preparation will be impossible. (4.5b)

In addition, the seeker had to set up protective talismans, offer a sacrifice to the gods, swear an oath of secrecy, and make a formal pledge (often involving substantial gifts) to the master al- chemist. All these measures served to create the proper atmosphere and mindset for the great work, which could not be completed without the ethical protection of virtues and merits.

Formal purifications were also demanded for all sacred practices of Daoism, both meditations and rituals. Before one could practice in the oratory, for example, one had to undergo prepara- tory periods of fasting, bathing, and abstentions, then don proper garb, burn incense, and per- form a series of bows, prostrations, and incantations (see Yoshikawa 1987, 140-44). Similarly, the practice of purgations, the formal ceremonies of Numinous Treasure, also called *zhai* (Yamada 2000, 248-49; Benn 2000, 310), involved ten preparatory measures of physical purification, as well as the taking of ten precepts for moral and spiritual purity.

An early document on these rites is the *Observances for Lamps, Spells, and Vows* (*Dengzhu yuan yi* 燈祝願儀, DZ 524), a fifth-century text ascribed to Lu Xiujing. It begins with ten measures of pu- rification:

1. taking baths in fragrant waters;
2. separating from worldly duties and ordinary relationships;
3. fasting to cut off desires for fancy foods and cleanse the organs and digestive tract;
4. donning proper garb to symbolize the majesty and power of the gods while encouraging humility in the practitioner;
5. maintaining silence to avoid speaking wrong or harsh words and only issuing sounds to intone scrip- tures;
6. cleansing all intentions from the heart by avoiding false imaginings and harmonizing the six senses;
7. burning incense and sending up a memorial to invite the gods;
8. repenting one's sins and begging for forgiveness
9. developing compassion and empathy for all beings;
10. bowing down in faith, opening one's self to the Dao, and pledging to follow the divine law. (1b-2a; see Kleeman 1991, 179-80; Yoshioka 1961a)

Beyond this preparatory purification which involves cleansing intention, developing compas- sion, and surrendering to faith, practitioners also had to take ten precepts based on the Buddhist model. They discourage feelings of "evil and envy in the heart" and prohibit killing, licentious- ness, passions, impure speech, intoxication, competitiveness, scriptural criticism, and quarrel- ing. They end with the general admonition that one should always be "of even and unified mind" in all activities (2ab). Not only in the fifth-century *Observances for Lamps, Spells, and Vows*, these rules were widely applied in various ritual settings and are listed as necessary prerequi- sites for the performance of the Nocturnal Annunciation, the Golden Register Purgation, and the Rite of Mud and Ashes.

The tendency to require the taking of precepts as a necessary purification before the performance of any ritual continued in later Daoism and also played a role in the establishment of the ordination system, according to which only masters who had taken the highest and most extensive precepts were empowered to perform the great rites. The notion that rituals were only effective if undertaken by someone of proper moral and ritual purity was thus another way in which Heaven and Earth inspired ethical thinking among Daoists.

KARMA AND RETRIBUTION

Under the influence of Buddhism, fifth-century Daoists began to adopt the doctrine of karma and retribution to explain how Heaven and Earth provided rewards and punishments for human behavior. The karma doctrine, as is commonly known, has been part of Indian religion since the *Upanishads*. It states that all actions have inevitable consequences and, after a period of maturation, revert to their perpetrator. As the individual's soul or *ātman* is the carrier of this load, it must continue to be embodied in a physical form to receive the rewards and punishments necessitated by its former actions. Thus the notion of rebirth, including that in nonhuman and hellish states, became a close correlate to the idea of personally created and suffered karma (Mahony 1987, 262). In Buddhism, which denied the existence of an eternal soul, karma was understood more as a function of the intention, transmitted in "consecutive moments of a psychic continuum," unstable and impermanent like the light of a candle (Mizuno 1987, 267). It was, at least according to ancient Buddhist doctrine, entirely centered within the individual and could be neither worsened nor improved by the actions of others.

This notion was later challenged by the Mahāyāna, whose followers claimed that good karma in the form of merit accumulated over long periods of time not only served as a positive inspiration to others but could also be transferred to improve their lot (Mitomo 1991, 19). This gave rise to devotional cults toward savior figures or bodhisattvas, to rituals that would transfer merits for the sake of one's ancestors, and to the swearing of so-called bodhisattva vows. The latter placed the practitioner immediately on a high level of karmic attainment and gave him a "karmically protective coding" (Mizuno 1987, 267), with the help of which he or she could fulfill the spiritual goal of universal salvation and compassion for all that lives.

Placing a strong emphasis on the community of all beings, Mahāyāna practitioners believed that the karmic activities of each being had an influence on all and that the country and even the world would benefit from the religious activities of the people. The king, therefore, participated in the merit or demerit created by all his subjects, and society as a whole became a forum for karmic and religious unfolding (Mizuno 1987, 268).

The Chinese, confronted with the karma doctrine in the first century C.E., found the intensely personal responsibility it implied not only surprising but abhorrent (Tsukamoto and Hurvitz 1985, 42). However, they could accept the more socially centered vision of its Mahāyāna developments, and Daoists tended to follow Mahāyāna lines. For them, the key concept was the contrast between "sin" and "good fortune" (*zuifu* 罪福). The term *zui* here indicates three different aspects of wrongdoing: the bad deed itself, the guilt that accompanied it (see Eberhard 1967), and the resulting suffering through disasters and diseases, bad rebirths and the tortures of hell. Bad deeds could be acts of evil (*wu* 惡), transgressions (*guo* 過) or faults (*yan* 衍). They led to *zui* as bad karma because one had violated or gone against the precepts; this eventually would bring great suffering (*ku* 苦), defined as physical pain, psychological frustration, and an overall sense of hopelessness (see Bemporad 1987).

Fu, "good fortune," on the other hand, meant the positive conditions attained through the practice of the precepts, both in this world and the next, from good health through wealth and intact family relations, and to fortunate rebirths and residence in heaven. *Fu* led to the creation of "fields of blessedness" (*futian* 福田). Understood like physical fields plowed and cultivated by farmers (see Cole 1998), they were essentially areas of goodness that eventually created the conditions necessary for liberation and immortality.

In the Buddhist context, these "fields" referred to the acquisition of virtues, such as charity, kindness, and goodness toward all beings; they did not protect against the vagaries of karma but endowed the person with the power to remain mentally calm and inwardly happy (Nakamura 1975, 1187; Mochizuki 1936, 4396b-97c). In Daoism, as described in the *Scripture of Karmic Retribution* (*Yinyuan jing* 因緣經, DZ 336; see Nakajima 1984; Kohn 1998b), they were more concrete, denoting the activities and wishes to create good living conditions for all beings, from the emperor and the aristocracy to the poor and orphaned (1.1a-9b). Also, beyond providing the mental stamina to deal with adversities, they guaranteed that one would encounter mainly positive and fortunate situations.

Daoists also identified the punishments for evil deeds in concrete terms, adapting Buddhist notions such as the "three bad rebirths" (*santu.*三途), "five realms of suffering" (*wuku* 五苦), "eight difficult conditions" (*ba'nan* 八難), and "ten situations of intense suffering" (*shiku* 十苦). As described in the fifth-century *Scripture of Controlling Karma and Original Conduct* (*Jieye benxing jing* 戒業本行經, DZ 345), the three bad rebirths are in the hells, as hungry ghosts, or among animals (15b), while the five realms of suffering include all areas of rebirth. The eight difficult conditions are life on the borders or among the barbarians; as a slave or servant; in poverty, as an orphan, or as a lowly person; as a sick or person; as a mentally retarded, mad, or disabled person; in situations of trouble and distress; with no filial piety or compassion for life and death; and in a country that lacks the Dao (14a). The ten situations of intense suffering are specific punishments in the hells, also adapted from Buddhism.[9] As the text lists them:

1. to have to step on the mountain of knives;
2. to have to climb the tree of swords;
3. to be thrown into the boiling cauldron;
4. to be tied to the hot iron pillar;
5. to have to lie on the bed of spikes;
6. to be tied to a fiery chariot and plunged into icy water;
7. to have one's head grasped and one's tongue twisted;
8. to have to swallow fire and to eat burning charcoal;
9. to be tied and locked up by the three officers, hit with metal cudgels, and beaten with iron staffs;

---

[9] Further Daoist descriptions of hell are found in the *Scripture of the Three Bad Rebirths and Five Sufferings* (*Santu wuku jing* 三途五苦經, DZ 455) and the *Scripture on Removing Sins from the Nine Realms of Darkness* (*Jiuyou bazui jing* 九幽拔罪經, DH 84). A modern description of the punishments of hell as still taught in tantric Nyingma practice is found in Hopkins 1982, 64-72. For traditional Buddhist sources, see Mochizuki 1936, 1132a.

10. to come to life only to be tied in fetters, to be deeply in trouble and distress, and to be eventually killed. (12b)[10]

The process by which one is affected by bad karma is gradual. As the *Scripture of Prohibitions and Precepts* (*Jinjie jing* 禁戒經, DH 35)[11], an early Tang text found at Dunhuang, points out, people who violate the precepts will first encounter various forms of misfortune, such as "the calamities of water and fire, swords and weapons, capture and prison, many thousands of strokes, evil winds and nasty demons" (l. 71). This will put great stress on their minds and cause increasing madness, while their bodies "will overflow with rot, they will be covered with boils, their hands will be crippled, and their feet deformed" (l. 72). Too sick to live yet not sick enough to die, they are caught in a living hell on earth. Even after death, there is no respite. On the contrary, the real suffering starts in the various depths of hell for kalpas eternal.

Then, "when they finally attain rebirth, they will come back in the body of a domestic animal; pauper or lowly person; or as a dumb, deaf, mute or crippled man;with warped hands and deformed feet and an overall ugly and repulsive appearance, suffering from hunger, cold, and chronic diseases, a myriad pains stabbing the entire body" (l.74). This situation, of course, gives rise to more inner tension and greed for food, wealth, and well-being, making it doubly difficult to create the good karmic conditions necessary for a better life. The precepts are the last straw to be grasped by the sinking sufferer, the first foothold in a new way of life away from evil and its bad consequences. Even the most elementary prohibitions against killing, stealing, and lying help to create a setting that allows relief and eventual growth in the Dao. The karmic power of the precepts is enormous on all levels; yet each level of the rules can only be attained with a background of goodness already accumulated, bringing the practitioner closer to Heaven in the process.

The connection to Heaven and Earth as expressed through their immediate signs, the workings of the celestial administration, the development of sickness and health, the efficaciousness of rituals, as well as through karma and retribution is at the core of Daoist ethics. It establishes a close connection of the individual's thoughts and actions to the workings of the cosmos. Because of this, ethical guidelines not only modify a person's behavior and intentions, creating more harmony in people's lives and a more stable community, but their observance also creates positive and spiritually beneficial situations.

A person in good karmic standing will always step into lucky circumstances, while one who fails to follow the precepts will be haunted by back luck—the direct result of bad karmic connections, medical violations, ritual impurity, and punishments imposed by the celestial authorities. Obeying the precepts is thus a safeguard against the vagaries of fate. It serves as the ultimate

---

[10] A more complete list of Daoist hells is found in the sixth-century *Twenty-four Precepts for Followers* (*Ershisi menjie jing* 二十四門戒經, DZ 183). Each precept here is associated with punishment in a specific hell—of the boilding caudron, the mountain of knives, the tree of swords, the stove full of coal, the iron plow that cuts the tongue, the steel pestles that grind down the body, the poisonous snakes that eat away the heart, the molten copper, the hot copper pillar, the iron wheel, the heavy boulders, the bed with iron spikes, the forest of swords, the lake of ice, and so on. For a full translation of this text, see the "Supplement."

[11] "DH" stands for Dunhuang and refers to Daoist texts found among Dunhuang manuscripts. The numbering follows Komjathy 2002. Citations are given by lines (l.) in the edition in Ōfuchi 1979a.

control over things commonly associated with luck or external factors: infections and diseases, accidents and mishaps, natural disasters, political upheavals, and even cosmic catastrophes.

The metaphors and images used for the precepts bear this out. For example, the *Scripture of Prohibitions and Precepts* describes the precepts as "the medicine of the divine law" with the power to "eradicate life and death and all serious illness," "the raft of the divine law which can take us beyond life and death and the ocean of suffering," "the sharp sword of the divine law that can cut down all entanglements and attachments of life and death" (l. 53-54). The *Rules for a Thousand Perfected* (*Qianzhen ke* 千真科, DZ 1410), a monastic code of the early Tang, notes that the rules are the guarantee of liberation, helping people to accumulate merit with every thought just as "polishing a mirror makes it gradually brighter," inevitably taking them beyond the ocean of life and death, just as "a boat will cross the great sea" (10a).[12] Daoist ethics is thus an essential vehicle that can take people from this life to celestial transcendence, from human self-interest to cosmic goodness.

---

[12] These and other images for the precepts echo the metaphors used for *sīla* in Buddhism, including those of a solid basis upon which to stand, such as roots, the Earth, or the foundations of a city; of protection, e.g., a guide in the wilderness, a safeguard, and a destroyer of poisons; of motion, such as the raft crossing the ocean or the feet; of purification, including water, fire, and wind; and of precious objects, including perfume, jewels, ornaments, treasures, and fabric. See Keown 1992, 48-54.

CHAPTER TWO

Moral Rules and Sensory Transformation

The most fundamental ethical guideline in Daoism is the observation of the basic moral rules. The five precepts against killing, stealing, lying, debauchery, and intoxication occur in all major collections of Daoist rules, sometimes as a block, sometimes scattered in the larger context. Clearly present in Daoist texts from the fifth century onward, they closely imitate the five abstentions (*pañca sīla*) of Buddhism, which in turn go back to the five basic prohibitions for Brahmanic priests already used in Vedic times. These prohibitions were integrated into the various Indian ascetic movements that sprang up in the sixth century B.C.E., of which mainly Jainism and Buddhism survive today.

In due course the five Buddhist precepts made their way into China, where as in India they served to create an awareness of community organization, but where they were also seen as a way to ensure good fortune and earthly well-being. Also, the five precepts were connected with traditional Chinese cosmology and the understanding of the human body as an energetic system and a major vehicle for cosmic retribution. The five senses in particular came to be understood both as the root cause of possible violations of the precepts and as the main means toward ethical and immortal transformation.

THE BUDDHIST BACKGROUND

The most ancient list of Buddhist rules we know is the *Pratimokṣa* (see Prebish 1974; 1975). It consisted of 250 rules for monks and was recited twice every month at the new and full moon as a formal declaration of intent and communal commitment, offering the opportunity for self-awareness and the confession of transgressions. Arranged according to the severity of the offense, it begins with four of the five abstentions: prohibiting killing, stealing, lying, and sexual misconduct. They are called the four *pārājika* rules, those to be punished with excommunication and expulsion from the order.[1]

Following this, the five precepts occur in the *Āgamas* or *Nikayas*, the sūtra-collections containing the sermons of the Buddha. Here they appear in four different ways, subtly corresponding to the development of Buddhism from a loose confederation of like-minded ascetics to an organized monastic religion (Ōno 1954, 379-80). First, they are implied in mentions of the formal refuge in the Three Jewels, the confession of trust in buddha (enlightenment), dharma (teaching), and saṇgha (community). This refuge was to be recited three times by all followers, an act which made them, in the most perfunctory way, members of the Buddhist community. It was consid-

---

[1] A translation of the *Pratimokṣa* is found in Beal 1871, 204-39. For more on ancient Buddhist rules and monastic life, see Dutt 1924; Dutt 1960; Lamotte 1987; Prebish 1975; Groner 1990a; Holt 1981; Keown 1992. For the precepts in Jainism, see Jaini 1979.

ered essential for Buddhist practice on any level, and the five precepts went with it, whether stated explicitly or not (Yifa 2002, 3).

Next, the five precepts are mentioned explicitly as the foundation for lay practice. Any lay devotee had to observe them since they were the beginning of Buddhist cultivation and the outward sign that one strove to care for others, to support the community of monks, and to walk on the eightfold path. More than just prohibitions of bad conduct, the five precepts were guidelines for good behavior, means to raise the conscience and consciousness of practitioners to honor and cherish all that lives. Only a householder who based his behavior on them could ever hope to be a good Buddhist. The constitution of community, from an oral declaration of faith had shifted to the performance of morally impeccable behavior (Mochizuki 1936, 2:1118-20).

Third, the *Āgamas* mention the five precepts expressedly in connection with the refuge in the Three Jewels. The formal vow that combined a declaration of faith with a taking of the precepts indicated a yet more devout level of Buddhist practice. This formalization also shows the beginning of the integration of the precepts into a more standardized legal system of Buddhist rules.

Fourth and finally, the *Āgamas* contain passages where the five precepts and the refuge are described as absolutely imperative for Buddhist practice. This reveals a stage in the development of Buddhist organization where even lay followers are formally recognized as official members of the religious group (Ōno 1954, 380). Laymen, moreover, were promised a set of benefits that would accrue because of their moral virtue, such as wealth, good repute, self-confidence in public, an untroubled death, and rebirth in heaven (Keown 1992, 44-45). The different ways in which the *Āgamas* mention the precepts, therefore, show how important their practice and standardization was for the evolution of the religious organization of ancient Buddhism.

In China, the five precepts are mentioned first as being transmitted to a lay follower in 65 C.E. It appears that in the early stages of the adaptation of Buddhism, they were given orally and practiced in accordance with local customs and individual preference (Yoshioka 1961a, 51; Yifa 2002, 2-3). Both monks and lay followers took them, but laymen soon eagerly began to reinterpret them in light of Chinese cosmology and point out their practical benefits. Thus Mouzi's 牟子 essay *To Dispel Doubts* (*Lihuo lun* 理惑論, T. 2102, 52.1a-7a) [2] and Xi Chao's 郗超 *Essentials of Venerating the Dharma* (*Fengfa yao* 奉法要, T. 2102, 52a.86-89b), both influential guides for lay practice of the fourth century, list the five precepts and link them with good fortune and a long life. Xi Chao says:

1. Do not kill or make others kill; always firmly persist in this to the end of your life.
2. Do not steal or make others steal; always firmly persist in this to the end of your life.
3. Do not be licentious or make others be licentious; always firmly persist in this to the end of your life.
4. Do not lie or make others lie; always firmly persist in this to the end of your life.
5. Do not drink wine or use it as a gift; always firmly persist in this to the end of your life. If wine is used as a medicine, the dosage must be weighed, the main point being that it should not cause intoxication. Intoxication is followed by the thirty-six evils, and the teachings of the *sūtras* prohibit it most strongly.

---

[2] The abbreviation "T." stands for *Taishō daizōkyō* 大正大藏經, the Japanese edition of the Buddhist canon. It is followed by the numbers of text, volume, and page.

If you do not kill, you will have a long life. If you do not steal, you will have lasting prosperity. If you are not licentious, you will be pure. If you do not lie, you will always be respected and trusted by others. If you do not drink wine, your spirit will be clear and orderly. (52.86ab)[3]

However similar in basic formulation and essential usage to their Indian original, the five precepts in Chinese Buddhism have shifted in emphasis. No longer merely the condition for membership in the Buddhist community and a way to earthly well-being, they have become the means to long life, prosperity, purity, intelligence, and social position. Thisworldly concerns and values intimate to Chinese society have superseded the spiritual and community outlook of original Buddhism. This tendency is continued in the fifth century in the *Sūtra of Trapusa and Bhallika* (*Tiwei boli jing* 提謂波利經),[4] a Chinese apocryphon dated to 450 and compiled by Tanjing 曇靜, a disciple of Tanyao 曇曜, the creator of the saṇgha-households under the Toba-Wei.[5] It consists of a dialogue between the Buddha and the two gentry devotees Trapusa and Bhallika, who allegedly came to him with five hundred followers shortly after his enlightenment and received instruction in the five precepts and other essentials for lay practice. The text describes the five precepts in terms of traditional Chinese cosmology in relation to the five phases, five planets, five inner organs, and five Confucian virtues, making them accessible to a Chinese lay audience. The first systematic Daoist presentation of the five precepts in the *Precepts of the Highest Lord Lao* appears contemporaneous with the *Sūtra of Trapusa and Bhallika* and closely echoes its understanding. Both works formed the center of dedicatory societies of lay followers (Liu 2003, 60; Qing 1996, 42). The texts show the ethical efforts of lay followers and the degree to which Buddhism and Daoism intermingled in medieval China.

COSMOLOGY AND MEDICINE

The *Precepts of the Highest Lord Lao* (DZ 784; trl. Kohn 1994; see Jan 1986) lists and explains the five precepts, claiming that they were revealed as part of the transmission of the *Daode jing* to the border guard Yin Xi 尹喜 when Laozi crossed the pass to emigrate to the west (see Kohn 1998a, 255). After a three-stanza poem in which Lord Lao encourages Yin Xi to follow the Dao with his whole heart, the text gives a short list of the basic precepts, followed by an introductory explanation. For example:

The precept to abstain from killing means that you must not kill any living being or anything that contains vital *qi*, be it flying or merely wriggling.

The precept against stealing means that you must not take anything that does not belong to you, be it owned by someone or without obvious owner, even a single copper coin. (6b-7a)

---

[3] The translation is my own. See also Kohn 1994, 175-76. For complete renditions of the text, see Zürcher 1959, 164-76; Ch'en 1963; Tsukamoto and Hurvitz 1985, 1110-28. For a discussion of the text and its rules in relation to Daoism, see Yoshioka 1961a, 51-54; Jan 1986, 287.

[4] The text survives in a Dunhuang manuscript (S. 2051) and is edited in Makita 1968; 1971. A discussion is found in Lai 1987. On early textual references, see Hurvitz 1956, 33-36. On Chinese Buddhist apocrypha in general, see Buswell 1990.

[5] Saṇgha -households consisted of families who paid taxes in the form of grain to the Buddhist community but were exempt from all other state duties. The saṇgha would store the grain for redistribution during famine or sell it to satisfy their own needs. The variant form of Buddha-households included freed criminals or slaves who did manual labor in the monasteries, putting state offenders to religious use. See Ch'en 1964, 153; Sargent 1957.

Next, Lord Lao explains why there are five precepts by relating them to the cosmology of Heaven and Earth: Heaven has the five planets that keep it on its course; Earth has the five sacred mountains which provide its stability; the seasons function according to the five phases which stabilize their rhythm; the state has the five emperors who set up proper culture; and human beings have the five inner organs which keep them supplied with *qi* (12b-13a). The implication is that the precepts in human behavior are as essential and as stabilizing as the different cosmological agents in the greater universe and form part of the cosmos as it functions in perfect harmony.

This point is expanded by setting the five precepts into a relationship with the five phases, five directions, and five inner organs. For example, the text links licentiousness with the west and the phase metal, and notes that it will have a negative impact on the lungs (14a). The *Sūtra of Trapusa and Bhallika* matches this and explains it in more detail:

> The precept to abstain from adultery is assigned to the west, to metal, for metal is righteousness, and the righteous one would not be licentious. . . . In the seventh and eighth months, Lesser Yin dominates. Avoid jealousy and envy, for they endanger your body. Retain and preserve life within and avoid excesses without that might deplete your essence. Refrain from selfish desires and licentiousness. (Lai 1987, 22)

In both texts, the inner organs and directions are matched with the precepts, but the Buddhist text also connects them to the five virtues— benevolence, wisdom, righteousness, propriety, and faithfulness—originally part of the Confucian system (Trauzettel 2002, 147-51). While all actions have a direct impact on the health of the inner organs, the five virtues supersede all impulses to break the precepts and are a higher form of their observance. The Daoist system, therefore, combines the medical understanding of the relation between body and cosmos with Buddhist precepts and Confucian virtues.

Aside from the close cosmological connection of the five precepts, they are also essential for developing good karma, so that only people who observe them properly can prosper and progress over lifetimes. Those who are honest in their dealings will be honored in the community, but those who lie and cheat during this life will not be believed either now or later (19ab). Taking the five precepts requires a formal presentation by a master and comes with the commitment to perform regular rites to the Dao, including the daily recitation of scriptures, monthly observance of retreats, and three major annual festivals (22b). They are the foundation of Daoist practice and establish both the healthy body and the compassionate mind set that will take adepts to immortality, making them benevolent givers and models of the world:

> With soft countenance and benevolent energy, these [Daoists] admonish all men and women to harmonize their minds. Getting far away from the five evils and firmly upholding the five precepts, they continuously worship the Three Treasures [Dao, scriptures, masters].[6] Accepting the commands [of the Dao] and working to fulfill them, they are not choosy about what may be sweet or bitter. Upholding the great precepts, they go through hardship with firmness and zeal. They give freely with indulgence and sacrifice themselves to save all beings. (24ab)

An expansion and more detailed psychological explanation of the five precepts is found in the short work *The Five Precepts of Orthodox Unity* (*Zhengyi wujie* 正一五戒), cited in the sixth-century

---

[6] On this Daoist adaptation of the Three Jewels, see Lagerwey 1981, 31; Benn 1991, 66; Zürcher 1959, 115.

encyclopedia *Secret Essentials of the Most High* (*Wushang biyao* 無上秘要, DZ 1138, 46.16b-18a; hereafter abbreviated WSBY). Setting the precepts in the context of visualizing the One and guarding the gods of the five inner organs, the text explains that bad behavior comes from a lack of control over the senses. As the five senses are exercised, the five psychological agents are labored. For example, "the eyes desire to see the five colors; overwhelmed by color, the spirit souls are labored" (16b). When the five psychological agents are labored, the five organs do not function properly and induce the person to engage in further sensory excesses which lead to violations of the precepts and prevent virtue. Thus, the text says:

> When the will is dissipated, the spleen is harmed, and one indulges in sensual pleasures. When the spirit is muddled, the heart is confused, and the mouth becomes talkative. When the essence is dispersed, the kidneys become empty, and there are wrong views and crazy ideas. When the material souls suffer, the lungs are depleted, and the ears go deaf. When the spirit souls are labored, the liver is exhausted, and the eyes go blind. With these five desires, there is confusion and darkness, and the body loses its life. (17a)

The correspondences of the system are as follows:

sense	psych. agent	organ	precept	virtue
eyes	spirit souls	liver	killing	benevolence
ears	material souls	lungs	stealing	righteousness
mouth	spirit	heart	licentiousness	propriety
nose	essence	kidneys	intoxication	wisdom
body	will	spleen	lying	faithfulness

This means that people only create problems for themselves and society when they are under stress through their sensory desire which causes their inner organs to stop functioning properly. Morality becomes an aspect of psycho-physical health and the proper *qi*-flow in the individual so that physical and mental health are only possible as and when the precepts are observed.

The understanding of disharmony as caused by the senses goes back to the *Daode jing*, which already points out the dangers of engaging in sensory pleasures. It warns:

> The five colors make the eyes go blind.
> The five sounds make the ears go deaf.
> The five flavors make the palate be spoiled.
> Racing and hunting make the mind go mad. (ch. 12)

The *Five Precepts of Orthodox Unity* also makes use of the standard system of Chinese medicine which associates specific psychological agents and senses with the five main organs that store *qi* and are essential for human health. The difference is that in common medical usage the ears are associated with the kidneys and the nose with the lungs, and not vice versa as presented here. Also, in medical literature, the will is associated with the kidneys and the intention is the psychological agent of the spleen (see Porkert 1974; Liu 1988).

Still, the system applies the principles of Chinese medicine to Daoist morality, in each case proposing that indulgence in the senses causes a disturbance to the resident interior gods and creates "confusion and darkness, so that the body loses its life" (16b-17a). To prevent this from happening, practitioners should follow the five virtues and will eventually be free from all troubles and disturbances. *The Five Precepts of Orthodox Unity* concludes:

> [Practicing this] you will never again be plagued by sadness or worry. The five desires are eliminated, the five evils are dissolved, the five disasters are forever gone, the five sufferings are over once and for all. With the five gods well-settled, the five good deeds come of themselves, the three states of good fortune increase daily, and the five pleasures are constantly renewed. (17b-18a)

SENSORY TRANSFORMATION

Another presentation of the five precepts in Daoism places an even greater emphasis on the senses and psychological attitudes. Found first in the *Precepts and Rules Taught by the Celestial Master*, they are:

1. Do not engage in licentiousness or let your will and thoughts dwell upon wrong ideas. This will labor your spirit and deplete your essence, and your spirit souls and material souls will no longer be kept. Then pain and sickness will come to harm you.
2. Do not develop violence and anger through passions and bad temper or let your heart boil over and explode in fury. Do not let your mouth spout loud sounds—cursing, reviling, scolding, abusing. This will agitate Heaven and shake Earth, startle the spirits and terrify the demons. . . .
3. Do not harbor intense imaginings and poisonous thoughts, develop envy and jealousy toward others, or contain any evil in your heart. The god of the heart is the ruler of the five inner organs, and if you only think of evil things, this central god will not be at peace. All the inner gods will duly be restless, and as they are restless, they will cut into your longevity. . . .
4. Do not defile yourself by becoming reckless and muddled-headed by drinking wine or otherwise disturb the natural transformations. If your inner nature is always disturbed and twisted, you will have no inhibitions. . . .
5. Do not develop greed for profit and material goods. Profit and material goods are just so much excrement and dirt; as time proceeds they return to just that. (3b-4a)

This list prohibits essentially the same actions as the standard set, i.e., debauchery, killing, lying, intoxication, and stealing, yet it does so in a more sophisticated and subtler way. It encourages people to modify the way they think and feel rather than imposing behavioral constraints upon them. The close connection of human beings to the greater universe through their inner organs, psychological agents, and body gods allows a formulation of the universal rules located deep within the person rather than at the surface of behavior. Although presented as prohibitions and focused on establishing a foundation of practice, these precepts already contain the seed for advancement to selfless perfection.

The same set of rules also appears in the *Scripture of Ascension to the Mystery* (*Shengxuan jing* 昇玄 經),[7] which presents a Mahāyāna-style exposition of the Daoist teaching, revealed by various deities to the first Celestial Master Zhang Daoling. The text, which dates from the sixth century, shows a high degree of integration among schools while still maintaining close allegiance to the Numinous Treasure school.

The precepts appear in chapter 7 (DZ 1122), where Lord Lao asks the Heavenly Worthy for instructions on the Dao. He wishes to be taught its origins and application, hoping to help Zhang

---

[7] First cited in WSBY 46, this consists of ten *juan*, which survive in fragments: DH 41 and DZ 1122, collected in Yamada 1992. See also Sunayama 1990, 227-29.

Daoling in his quest. The Heavenly Worthy explains that there are three ranks of attainments: higher, medium, and lower. Those of the higher level are spirit immortals who ascend to heaven in broad daylight, join jade maidens and pure lads, and transform physically into diamond bodies and radiant beings. Those of the medium level are the finders of nirvāna who serve as celestial officers of lower rank while attaining residence in the heavenly halls. Those of the lower level are longevity practitioners who undertake diets and gymnastics and extend their years; they will eventually become earth officials and sit in judgment over the souls of the dead. To attain any of these three ranks, however, one must thoroughly cultivate oneself, harmonize *qi* and inner nature, move away from the ordinary, cut off pleasures and sensuality, and join one's actions to the Dao (3b; Yamada 1992, 15).

In other words, all adepts must follow the precepts to establish themselves in the Dao and avoid harm to their bodies and psychological agents (4a-5b; Yamada 1992, 15). Adding to this, the text emphasizes that especially "sensuality and passions are destructive forces" and formulates a supplementary set of five rules to control the senses:

1. If you see sensuous colors woven in enticing patterns and variegated images—use my precept and cover your eyes.
2. If you hear words of good and evil or any of the five sounds—use my precept and block your ears.
3. If you are tempted by the delicacies of the eight marvels, or by the delights of the five fragrances—use my precept and stop your mouth.
4. If you find yourself imagining wealth and riches, the wondrous jewels of the seven treasures, and are drawn into emotions and at the extreme of desires—use my precept and dampen your heart.
5. If you hanker after lasciviousness and lust, coveting the pursuit of evil affairs—use my precept and cut off your intention. (36b; Yamada 1992, 21-22)

Expanding further on this set, a more extensive presentation of the same ideas is also found in chapter 9, which lists a set of nine precepts that will control body, mind, mouth, hands, eyes, ears, nose, feet, and intention, helping adepts to overcome their this-worldly attachments. Every precept in this list has the same refrain, emphasizing that "there can never be any satisfaction" and that people tend to be "utterly unaware of the sins of their very own body and soon let them become so great that they cannot be counted or controlled." To counteract this tendency everyone should "make sure that they do not violate [the precepts] or encourage any one else to do so," instead maintaining a firm determination toward the Dao (Yamada 1992, 42-47).

Beyond merely preventing harm, however, the sense-based precepts are also used to transform the practitioner to a higher level. To this end, the early Numinous Treasure text *Great Precepts of the Highest Ranks* (*Shangpin dajie* 上品大誡, DZ 177) presents a set of "Six Precepts of Wisdom" as essential blocks against the six passions and the basis for future transformation. For example,

1. Let not your eyes gaze widely or be confused by flowery colors lest you lose their clarity and diminish your pupils, their radiance no longer bright and penetrating.
2. Let not your ears be confused in their hearing or obscured by the five sounds lest you harm spirit and destroy uprightness, hearing bad sounds everywhere. (6a)

These precepts contain warnings against overindulgence in the senses, which cause turbidity among the body gods and loss of *qi* (6ab; WSBY 46.10a-12b), merging the *Daode jing* warning against overloading the senses with the medical understanding of moral action, while also adjusting the number to match the Buddhist system and adding the mind as a sixth sense.

Beyond curbing harmful tendencies, these precepts open the wisdom of awakening or immortality in the practitioner. The text defines wisdom as a state of sensory purity in complete openness to all, a state expressed as the mastery of the "six pervasions."[8] As the *Great Precepts of the Highest Ranks* says, they are:

> pervasive sight, pervasive hearing, pervasion of the void [air, smells], pervasion of emptiness [sound], pervasion of clarity [objects], and pervasion of the subtle [thoughts]. These six pervasions mean that nothing is left unpervaded. Through them the six passions are laid to rest and the inner spirits naturally return. The Great One naturally arises, and your essence is naturally strong. You reach long life and eventually go beyond death. (7a)

As each sensory organ is transformed and reorganized in the move from passion to compassion and from separation to oneness, ordinary sense faculties are reversed and developed into something new and unusual. This places the practitioner into the center of the universe and on equal footing with the gods. For example, supernatural sight, according to the text, involves the creation of universal vision:

> This means that with the eyes of Heaven one's understanding is lofty and wisdom pervades all without limits. Above and below, in the four corners and eight directions, nothing is not illumined, nothing is not radiantly bright. (10b)

The ordinary eyes of the practitioner, by avoiding the intricacies of worldly vision and being shaded against the enticing patterns of outside life, are made susceptible to the subtler and more brilliant vibrations of the light of Heaven. The inner eye joins with cosmic radiance, and their merged vibrations obliterate blockages to expose all to a pervading, penetrating light. "As long as people pattern themselves on Heaven, the bright pupils in the eyes can freely follow the radiance of the five colors" (10b). Similarly all the other senses are transformed from a mundane to a cosmic level, so that the Daoist becomes able to see, hear, and feel with the *qi* of the Dao rather than through the limited agents of the body. The vision reflects the earlier encouragement in the *Zhuangzi* 莊子 to practice "the fasting of the mind" (*xinzhai* 心齋):

> Make your mind one. Don't listen with your ears, listen with your mind. No, don't listen with your mind, but listen with your spirit. Listening stops with the ears, the mind stops with recognition, but spirit is empty and waits on all things. (ch. 4; Watson 1968, 57-58).

The five precepts in their Daoist formulation, therefore, go far beyond the creation of social harmony and personal benefits. They ready practitioners for advancement toward the Dao, allowing them to attain a level of being and perception that is universal in all respects.

COMMUNITY APPLICATION

How, then, are the five precepts used in Daoist communities? What role do they play? And how are they activated?

To begin, they are present in all the major collections of precepts, the *180 Precepts of Lord Lao* of the Celestial Masters (nos. 2, 3, 4, 3, 24, 102), the *Precepts of the Three Primes* of Numinous Treas-

---

[8] Known as *liutong* 六通, this concept is adopted from Buddhism, where it indicates the six supernatural powers of a buddha: universal vision and hearing, knowledge of other minds, seeing former lives, multilocation, and superconsciousness (Mochizuki 1933-36, 5060a).

ure (nos. 26, 27, 34, 62, 80), the *Great Precepts of Self-Observation* of Highest Clarity (nos. 1, 3, 5, 7, 9) and the *Precepts of Medium Ultimate* of Complete Perfection (nos. 1, 3, 5, 8, 9). Translated below, these texts are central for ordination in these schools and form the backbone of advanced practice; they each contain 180 prohibitions, to which the latter two add 120 resolutions for ecstatic excursions and celestial interaction. The five precepts appear scattered among the rules in the first two texts, but are placed first in the latter two, showing the impact of the standard list as it was imported from Buddhism (Kohn 1994, 173-74).

In the *180 Precepts of Lord Lao,* the five precepts are dispersed and repeated with varying degree of detail, so that, for example the rule not to kill (no. 2) also appears as:

39. Do not engage in killing.
40. Do not encourage others to kill.
42. Do not kill another in hatred.
79. Do not fish or hunt and thereby harm and kill the host of living beings.

This not only repeats the basic prohibition several times, but also specifies particular situations in which killing might be indicated but should not be pursued. The text further notes that the group's followers should not eat any "birds or beasts, fish or other living beings" that were specially killed for them (nos. 172-173).

Similarly, the precept against stealing is specified to include a number of different ways of handling wealth and material goods. Here we have first a group of rules that prohibit the pursuit or wrongful use of other people's possessions. The text says:

5. Do not wantonly take other people's goods, even if worth only one cash.
6. Do not wantonly burn or destroy other people's goods, even if worth only one cash.
22. Do not covet or begrudge material goods.
25. Do not accumulate material goods and despise the orphaned and poor.
73. Do not obliquely pursue other people's goods.
94. Do not forcefully take other people's things and distribute them in charity.

Beyond this, the *180 Precepts of Lord Lao* also prohibits the acquisition of luxury goods and the pursuit of comfort and personal wealth. Rules include:

86. Do not select the best accommodation or room and most comfortable bed for sleep.
105. Do not accumulate and hoard material goods and treasures, thereby inviting bad luck and misfortune.
106. Do not covet or hanker after a nice residence.
107. Do not hide and bury vessels or other objects.
163. Do not own more than three sets of clothes.

The precept against stealing is, therefore, explained in great detail and made part of harmonious community interaction. It involves not merely abstention from taking what is not freely given but implies the reduction of greed and control over personal impulses towards grandeur and enrichment.

The same also holds true for the precept against lying. Here the text has various rules that prohibit using fancy language (no. 23), discussing other people's status and faults (nos. 31, 33, 54, 91), gossiping about their secrets (no. 32), claiming oneself to be skilled or noble (nos. 44, 45, 87), or in other ways abusing words, such as by yelling, cursing, scolding, or deceiving people (nos. 48, 50, 65, 88). In general, followers should not "talk too much and exert their mouth and tongue" (no. 111) or "make loud, harsh sounds" (no. 126), so that the precept covers many different kinds of verbal abuse.

While intoxication is mentioned only in one rule (no. 24) and linked with restraints on certain foods, sexual misconduct in the *180 Precepts of Lord Lao* is again specified in various rules that prohibit meeting, eating, speaking, traveling, and entering the mountains "with a woman alone" (nos. 117, 139, 161-64). Altogether, therefore, the five precepts as they are specified in the early codes provide the foundation of social interaction in a wide spectrum of behavioral guidelines. They apply to many situations and create a network of acceptable and unacceptable behavior that allows the community to function harmoniously.

In the lay communities of the medieval schools, as described in the *Precepts of the Highest Lord Lao* discussed earlier, the five precepts and the refuge in the Three Treasures established membership and prepared for ritual purity. Like in ancient Buddhism they were the sign that a person had accepted the basic rules of a religious lifestyle and was ready to pursue the path, which included the active participation in purgations, held in different formats throughout the year.

A purgation could be a simple fast day used by lay followers to behave with increased purity while in temporary renunciation. Inspired by the Indian Buddhist practice of bimonthly confession and the chanting of precepts, both Chinese Buddhists and Daoists instituted a number of one-day purgations in groups of six, eight, or ten per month, usually centered around the new and full moon (see Soymié 1977). Practitioners would take additional precepts and offer prayers to the deities, especially to the Great One, the Northern Dipper, and other central cosmic administrators who inspected their earthly charges on those days. It was hoped that the pious activities caused the celestial officers to be lenient in their adjustment of the person's life expectancy.

Larger purgations were festivals that could take from three to nine days. They were essentially audience rites during which the officiating priest became a celestial official and transmitted prayers and confessions to the celestial administration (Yamada 2000, 249; Benn 2000, 332-35). They, too, matched the days when the deities inspected humanity to update the records of life and death. By behaving with particular circumspection, confessing sins, and presenting offerings and memorials, they hoped that the gods would be merciful in their retributions. The actual ceremonies, then, undertaken after a period of purification and preparation, involved the taking or reinforcing of precepts, rites of confession and repentance, and prayers for blessings and good fortune.

TALISMANS AND EMPOWERMENT

In a different strand of medieval Daoism, the five precepts were applied in the proper writing and handling of talismans. Talismans (*fu* 符) were oblong pieces of wood, metal, or colored paper inscribed with figurative signs and formal symbols, written in black or red ink. Believed to contain the essence of a heavenly force or deity, they could be manifestations of cosmic energies, representations of a god, edicts from the spirit world, orders from the divine, or a spiritually perfect body. Their holder received complete control over spirits and demons and could travel to the heavens with great ease (Despeux 2000b, 498)

Talismans could only be handled and activated if the practitioner was in a high state of purity and mentally prepared to take on the powers they represented. All medieval Daoist schools made use of them for purification, exorcism, healing, and various rituals. They were particularly dominant in the school of the Three Sovereigns, which strove to continue the activation of talismans used by these sage rulers at the beginning of civilization to govern the world in perfect harmony. Revealed to the hermit Bo He 帛和 in the third century as writings in a cave,[9] the talismans were later found by Bao Jing 飽靚, Ge Hong's father-in-law, in a grotto on Mount Song. From him they passed down to Ge Hong, who links them with other cosmic charts such as the *Chart of the True Shape of the Five Sacred Mountains* (*Wuyue zhenxing tu* 五嶽真形圖, DZ 1223; see Schipper 1967). Through Ge Hong, the talismans became part of the Ge-family tradition and were duly expanded and interpreted in various texts, the most important of which are the *Inner Texts of the Three Sovereigns* (*Sanhuang neiwen* 三皇內文, DZ 855) and the *Scripture of the Eight Emperors* (*Badi jing* 八帝經, DZ 640).[10]

The school of the Three Sovereigns was influential in the middle ages but did not survive as an independent entity beyond the beginning of the Tang. Its end came in 646 when the noted Daoist thinker and *Daode jing* commentator Cheng Xuanying 成玄英 was asked to inquire into the authenticity of a newly discovered manuscript of the *Inner Texts of the Three Sovereigns*. Cheng refused to accept its third-century origins and advised the emperor to have it burned. The latter did so, and in the following years the *Daode jing* officially became the highest Daoist scripture, replacing the more talisman-centered approach of the earlier schools with more philosophical tendencies (Sunayama 1980, 126).

Followers of the Three Sovereigns school believed that the talismans and teachings of the ancient sage rulers guaranteed the perfect harmony of the universe. Safely stored in the higher reaches of heaven and accessible only to the gods, they were transmitted to earth by the Highest Lord (Taishang 太上) or the Yellow Emperor. Through them practitioners learned about the proper behavior, personal integrity, and correct procedures for the effective handling of the talismans. According to the *Scripture of the Eight Emperors*, personal integrity consisted of following a set eight precepts patterned on Buddhism which included the five precepts plus abstention from various luxury activities (1b). The text also emphasizes that Daoists are well advised to avoid any exhibition of vulgarity, as well as excesses in eating, drinking, heat, cold, gazing, listening, crying, shouting, thinking, and anger (13b). All these activities harm the *qi* and body gods and disturb the purity of life, thus preventing the activation of talismans.

To write a talisman, Daoists needed a special brush and ink. They began by purifying themselves with incense and by fasting in a secluded spot. They should act only at night and in a clean place, in perfect accordance with the phases of the moon. First they donned immortals' garb, then summoned the gods by writing the proper talisman. For the gods of Heaven, the

---

[9] This information comes from Ge Hong's *Biographies of Spirit Immortals* (*Shenxian zhuan* 神仙傳), ch. 7. See Güntsch 1988, 214-16; Petersen 1990, 177-82; Campany 2002, 135.

[10] Other fragments of the texts remain in WSBY 43.1a, *Pivotal Meaning of the Daoist Teaching* (*Daojiao yishu* 道教義樞, DZ 1129; 2.3a; see Wang 2001), and *Seven Tablets in a Cloudy Satchel* (*Yunji qiqian* 雲笈七籤, DZ 1032; hereafter abbreviated YJQQ) 6.5b. See also Ōfuchi 1964, 277-343; Chen 1975, 71-78; Kobayashi 1990. For a study of related Song-dynasty texts, see Andersen 1991.

characters should be written pointing upward; for those of Earth, downward. The deities would announce their presence after a few moments (29a).[11]

Precepts observed by practitioners are further detailed in a text entitled *Precepts of Spirit Cavern* (*Dongshen jiepin* 洞神戒品, WSBY 46.14a-16b). It notes:

> Developed by immediate transformation from the original mysterious source, they gradually became multiple. Thus there gradually came to be three, five, eight, nine, ten, a hundred, a thousand, even ten thousand precepts. They follow the laws of causation, and yet you must in no way add to or subtract from them. (15b)

Matching the Dao, the precepts form an original part of the world's creation and represent life in its primordial state. They participate in the ceaseless transformations of the world, changing according to the rhythms of the universe and appearing differently as the ages require. The inherent contradiction between unborn eternity and continuous transformation is a source of power, for the Dao as much as the precepts, which serves as a guide to gaining and exercising this might. The most basic rules, then, were the following three cautions:

1. Carefully understand the law of karma and causation; never forget the origin and pursue the far end.
2. Carefully keep yourself back; never harm others to gain profit for yourself.
3. Carefully practice with diligence; never get confused and lose your perfection. (14b)

These cautions aid the adept's focus on the divine law. They are "honored by the highest sovereigns, venerated by the Emperor-on-High, and cultivated by the highest divine gentlemen" (14b). Rules obeyed in heaven itself, they guarantee the completeness of life, integrity of body and spirit, and grant protection by the proper deities. Observing them, "you will attain the Dao, live forever, and be called Highest Lord yourself" (14b).

Next, adepts took five precepts as revealed by the Yellow Emperor, which are reminiscent of the precepts controlling the five senses but come with admonitions to dedicate oneself to the Dao. They are:

1. Let not your eyes covet the five colors; instead make a pledge to the right teaching and the study of long life.
2. Let not your ears covet the five sounds; instead vow to hear the good and follow it without error.
3. Let not your nose covet the five smells; instead burn incense for the divine law and drive out all stink and stench.
4. Let not your mouth covet the five tastes; instead practice embryo breathing and refrain from all bad language.
5. Let not your body covet the five silks; instead tread the path of diligence and duty and always follow the Dao. (15a)

Observing these five rules guarantees that a troop of spirit soldiers remains within the body and guards one's being, "protecting life and driving out death, warding off sickness and future calamity. It also helps to attain an extended life and find rebirth again on the human plane, while dissolving all disasters and saving adepts from all troubles" (46.15a).

Beyond the five precepts, the school of the Three Sovereigns had a set of advanced rules, formulated in a set of eight. Neither based on Buddhism nor on Confucian virtues, they follow the cosmology of the "Great Plan" (*Hongfan* 洪範) in the *Book of History* (*Shujing* 書經; trl. Legge

---

[11] More detailed instructions of a similar nature also survive from the Song dynasty. See Drexler 1994.

1969) and guide Daoists to act on the basis of a cosmic connection in imitation of the rulers of antiquity. They are:

1. Be studious in understanding the five phases [wood, fire, earth, metal, water] and always perform the five virtues [benevolence, righteousness, propriety, wisdom, faithfulness].
2. Be diligent in conducting the five activities [demeanor, speech, sight, hearing, and thought] and never be unsteady about them.
3. Be steadfast in controlling the eight policies [food, commerce, sacrifices, public works, instruction, justice, retainers, military] and perform them only in accordance with the proper times.
4. Be clear in comprehending the five mainstays [year star, moon, sun, planets, calendar] and always match your energy to their movements.
5. Be careful in examining the Sovereign Ultimate [central ruler of the universe] and always make sure above and below are in perfect harmony.
6. Be eager in cultivating the three virtues [uprightness, strength, gentleness] and always adapt all your actions to the Three Clarities.
7. Be resolute in examining doubts and errors [through consultation and divination] and always transform falsehood into pure perfection.
8. Be meticulous in verifying your experiences, so you can dissolve bad luck and approach only good fortune. Purify all that is common and ascend to sageliness, never burdening the Three Venerables with your sins. (15b)

This list is a close adaptation of the "Great Plan" (Nylan 1992, 14-19). Both guide the protagonist, the leading Daoist or the ruler, through various levels of decision-making. The Daoist/ruler is to take his own counsel first, then consult with officials, question the tendencies among the people, and finally use divination by tortoise shell and milfoil. Perfect agreement is the condition for perfect harmony, but if there is discord among the various levels of advice, operations will only meet with limited good fortune.

 The eighth rule is a guideline to verify experiences. Again the Daoist vision follows the "Great Plan," which sees certain government qualities in the seasonality or excess of natural phenomena. Thus seasonal rain, sunshine, heat, cold, and wind reveal the ruler's gravity, orderliness, wisdom, deliberation, or sageliness; their excess, on the other hand, show that he tends to be wild, presumptuous, lax, rash, or stupid (Nylan 1992, 19-20). Thus, if the seasonal patterns are in good order, the sovereign has done a superb job. If there are some errors over several months, his officials need to examine themselves more carefully. But if there is complete failure of seasonable weather, the entire government should be reorganized, and the moral qualities of the ruler strengthened. Daoists in the same way are to dissolve bad fortune and pursue celestial bliss by seeing whether their experiences are causing harmony or disturbance, whether the world around them is in line with the rhythm of the year, and whether the talismans are doing their work.

The result in the Daoist case, as much as in the ancient cosmology, is perfect happiness, defined in the ninth and last item of the "Great Plan" as the five attainments: long life., wealth, ease, virtue, and a natural end (Nylan 1992, 22). If the sovereignty of the ruler is properly established and he is the perfect channel for the goodness of the universe, these five crown the ruler and the entire country. On the contrary, if he fails in his efforts, there will be the six extremities-- premature death, sickness, sorrow, poverty, illness, and weakness (Nylan 1992, 22)—a list that closely resembles the effects of bad deeds in other Daoist texts.

Adapting the instructions and guidelines given to the ancient rulers, Daoists of the Three Sovereigns school individualized them to fit the format of eight precepts for their followers. Every single Daoist, with the help of the talismans and by virtue of being part of the power of the Dao, can become the very center of the universe. As in the other lay organizations, the precepts do not merely regulate moral conduct and maintain harmony in the community, but become guidelines for immortality and the transformation to perfection.

The various ways in which Daoists used the universal moral rules all begin with a clear adaptation of Buddhist models, revealing the same language and great similarities in organizational function. However, once fully integrated into the Chinese vision of cosmic goodness, Daoists interpreted the five precepts quite differently and connected them to traditional cosmology, the bodily organs, the senses, karmic benefits, and ritual purity. The basic moral rules thus reveal a uniquely Daoist ethical vision that relies on a detailed understanding of the cosmos and a subtle psychology of the individual. Everyone can attain the purity of Heaven and its immense powers through the dedicated observation of the fundamental five precepts. Everyone can transform their senses toward the Dao.

CHAPTER THREE

Impulse Control: Food, Wine, and Sex

The great moral rules laid a strong foundation for individual attainment and communal harmony. However, Daoists were also well aware that certain basic impulses needed more than general rules to be controlled. Especially the precepts against sexual misconduct and intoxication were not considered sufficient in and of themselves, but were bolstered by supplementary regulations, warnings, and prohibitions. The various communities, moreover, dealt with the issues differently, none simply pronouncing prohibitions but instead offering ways of sublimation or temporary release.

Early millenarian groups like the Celestial Masters had their followers obey strict rules of simplicity and abstention when it came to food and wine, and insisted on sexual satisfaction within the boundaries of married life. They opened the community to kitchen-feasts on the days of the great festivals, offering wine and meat and other foods not usually seen on their tables. As for sexual practices, they controlled members' urges not only by venerating the institution of marriage but also in the rituals of the harmonization of *qi*, in which men and women engaged in ritual intercourse to advance personal, communal, and cosmic harmony.

The lay communities of the middle ages in many ways reversed this pattern. They emphasized moderation in their precepts, allowed some personal freedom in daily life, and insisted on strict rules of purity with regard to food, wine, and sex at all purgations, whether one-day retreats or extended festivals. Any ritual activity had to be preceded by purifications and involved the abstention from unclean foods and acts, including even married sex.

In monastic life, the rules against intoxication and sexual misconduct were enforced most strongly and most consistently. Monastics followed tight restrictions on food and were encouraged to observe periods of fasting, not only by abstaining from eating after noon but also by training themselves to replace the intake of ordinary nourishment with breathing exercises and the iinternal circulation of *qi*. Still, even here sexuality was not denied or suppressed as in other religions that favor strict celibacy, but rather sublimated into an internal transformation of *qi*.

In all cases, the Daoist take on impulse control with regard to food, wine, and sex was not merely about creating social harmony and improving karma—although these factors certainly played a role. Rather, the central issue in the rules was the integrity and enhancement of the practitioner's *qi* (Strickmann 1978b, 473; Eskildsen 1998, 67). By eating right, abstaining from alcohol, and regulating sexual activity, adepts ensured that their *qi* continued to flow in harmony. They prevented the loss of vital essence and learned to increase the quality and smooth flow of their cosmic energy. Once again, the precepts created cosmic unity in addition to personal integrity and communal harmony.

UNDERSTANDING BODY ENERGIES

The body in Daoism is made up of *qi* 氣 or cosmic energy, which appears in three distinct forms. The first and highest is *shen* 神, spirit, the divine aspect of human vitality and the moving force behind all mental and bodily activities. It represents consciousness and constitutes the individual's awareness and mental direction. Impossible to be perceived directly and physically, spirit is a vitalizing force that exerts transformative influence on all aspects of the human being. Closely associated with personality, it resides in the heart and relates to the mind and the emotions (Porkert 1974, 181; see also Kaptchuk 1983; Liu 1988). In its more spiritual dimension, *shen* is present as the body gods and provides an intimate link to the celestial spheres.

Next is personalized, individual *qi*, a flowing force that constitutes health and sickness and determines how we move, eat, sleep, and work. Moving through meridians, it is the source of all movement. It can be lost or replenished through exchange with the outside world, where it appears in breath, food, drink, physical contact, sexuality, and emotions. *Qi* is limited in amount but can be *zheng* 正, i.e., proper, well-aligned, harmonious, and right in activity, thus bringing health and well-being; or *xie* 邪, i.e., wayward, heteropathic, off-track, and harmful, thus causing sickness and disease.

The third and most perceptible body force is *jing* 精, essence, described as the indeterminate aspect of *qi* or as *qi* in transition from one determinate form to another (Porkert 1974, 176-77). A classic example is man's semen that carries life from the parents to the offspring. Governed in the body by the kidneys and the phase water, *jing* is closely related to the psychological power of the will and provides the source of a person's charisma, sexual attraction, and sense of wholeness. It also controls the brain, the bones, and the marrow. In its most dominant and perceptible form, *jing* is sexual energy: semen in men and menstrual blood in women. Both develop from personal *qi* that sinks down from its center—the abdomen in men and the breasts in women—and becomes tangible in sexual fluids.

In ordinary life, *jing* is emitted from the body at regular intervals, causing loss of *qi* which over time leads to bodily weakness, disease, and death. This loss can be moderate, so that one's essence diminishes over a lifetime and leads to disease and death only gradually, as outlined in the life-cycle descriptions of the medical classics.[1] The loss can also be excessive, resulting in crippling illness and untimely demise. Or it can be prevented and controlled, leading to enhanced vitality and a longer life. The latter forms the basis for the subtler levels of Daoist cultivation that lead to immortality.

It is an important part of the Daoist enterprise not only to regulate and slow down the process of *jing*-loss, but even to stop and reverse it. The control of *jing* is a corner stone of Daoist practice and the goal of all rules on food, wine, and sex. *Jing* can be modified with medical methods, such as acupuncture and herbs, but in Daoism it is controlled primarily through physical discipline and meditation. Unlike other religions which insist on strict celibacy, Daoists even in the monastic setting never ignore or deny their sexual energy. Instead, they allow the *qi* to sink down and transform into *jing*, thereby rendering it tangible as sexual arousal, then prevent it from being emitted and instead revert it back to become refined *qi*.

---

[1] See, for example, *The Yellow Emperor's Inner Classic* (*Huangdi neijing*), ch. 1; trl. Veith 1972; Ni 1995.

Moved consciously around the body in various cycles, this refined *qi* is further rarified into *shen*, creating an increase in the higher vitality of life and spiritual dimension of being. Ultimately spirit is the goal of Daoist attainment: the transformation of a baser *qi*-being into an entity of pure spirit. But in all cases the holy work begins with *jing*, with the sexual nature and most essential human vitality. All rules and guidelines with regard to food, wine, and sex, therefore, serve the regulation, enhancement, and ultimate transformation of body energetics.

FOOD AND WINE IN THE EARLY COMMUNITIES

The early Celestial Masters instituted basic abstentions from wine and meat and set up close limits on sexual activity. The *Demon Statutes of Nüqing* states that followers should "not drink wine and eat meat" (no. 3, 3.1b; see Lai 2002a, 267-68). This is echoed in the *180 Precepts of Lord Lao*, which notes that "to be able to cut out all meat of living beings and the six domestic animals is best; without doing this, you will violate the precepts" (no. 176) and finds that eating "only vegetables is most excellent" (no. 177). The text further notes that followers should not eat anything that has been killed specifically for consumption (no. 173) or anything that is foul and smells rank (no. 174).

Besides meat, early Daoists also prohibited the consumption of the five strong vegetables (*wuxin* 五辛), i.e., leeks, scallions, onions, garlic, and ginger. Yang-enhancing and warm-ing foods, they serve as important herbal remedies in the Chinese pharmacopoeia (see Stuart 1976) and were originally part of the diet of Daoist hermits and immortals, who used them to replace grains and ordinary nourishment (Kohn 1993, 151). The five were prohibited in Daoist communities because their consumption was seen as leading to diminished purity of the inner organs and could result in socially obnoxious phenomena, such as bad breath and flatulence, which in turn might have a negative impact on discipline and community cohesion (Kohn 2003a, 127). [2]

Other food rules among the early Daoist communities as found in the *180 Precepts of Lord Lao* prohibit egoistic tendencies, such as greed for fine food (no. 149) or rich donated meals (no. 160), criticism of bad or ill-tasting food (nos. 133, 151), the tendency to eat all by oneself (no. 26), and the urge to make the meal special by using fine dishes and implements (no. 15). Practitioners should not consume to excess (no. 155), but "eat sparingly, like a deer" (no. 142). They should honor the value of food and not waste it by "throwing it into fire or water" (no. 7), but instead develop gratitude for it and always "cast a spell of good wishes to the effect that the donor may attain good fortune and be always full and satisfied" (no. 154). [3]

These precautions and restraints remained in effect throughout the year and governed the daily life of Celestial Masters practitioners. They were lifted for short periods at the festivals of the Three Primes and other major community occasions. At these times, kitchen-feasts were held that involved great banquets, imitating rites for the sun god in antiquity, during which followers

---

[2] The precept against the five strong vegetables appears in all major codes: *Precepts of the Three Primes*, no. 77; *Great Precepts of Self-Observation*, no. 45; *Precepts of Medium Ultimate*, no. 4.

[3] The rules against greed for food, against eating all by oneself, and against throwing foodstuffs into fire or water are also found in the other major codes: *Three Primes*, nos. 45, 90 and 71; *Self-Observation* and *Medium Ultimate*, nos. 44, 69 and 41.

enjoyed rich meals and took wine, offering matching morsels to the gods (Stein 1971, 489; Mollier 2000, 46).

The *New Code* of Kou Qianzhi divides feasts according to major, medium, and lesser, lasting seven, five, or three days respectively (Ware 1933, 233). Also called "fortunate feedings" (*fushi* 福食) or "rice for the wise" (*fanxian* 飯賢), a typical banquet consisted of three courses—a vegetarian meal, wine, and rice—but those who could not afford all three could also resort to having only wine, up to a maximum of five pints (no. 12; 8ab). The ritual activity during feasts, daily services, and ancestral worship also involved a series of bows and prostrations, as well as the burning of incense and the offering of a prayer or petition, which had to follow a specific formula (no. 19). Festivities were lavish, and all leftovers were to be distributed among the faithful (Mollier 2000, 46; Maspero 1981, 289).[4]

There were no blood sacrifices under Kou Qianzhi (no. 4; 2a) as in medieval Daoism in general, but occasionally the texts mention offerings of dried meat and wine (Stein 1971, 490; Ware 1966, 285). The *History of the Sui Dynasty* (*Suishu* 隋書) similarly describes such sacrifices in the context of a Daoist offering (*jiao* 醮):

> At night, under the stars and zodiac signs, Daoists offer wine and meat, cakes and cookies, sacrificing them one after the other to the Heavenly Emperor of the Great One, to the five planets, and to the twenty-eight lunar mansions. They also prepare a written document like a formally presented petition to address the gods. This is known as performing an offering. (35.12b; Ware 1933, 246)

Daoist millenarian communities, therefore, were very circumspect in the way they dealt with food, prohibiting the consumption of yang-enhancing foods, such as the five strong vegetables and all kinds of meat, as well as the taking of wine which might lead to intoxication and the disruption of *qi*-flow and communal harmony. On the other hand, they used these substances during their kitchen-feasts and in offerings to the gods, allowing for a release of impulses and acknowledging their divine potential in a controlled setting.

SEXUAL PRACTICES

A similar pattern of daily restraint and release at special occasions also holds true for the early communities' handling of sexual impulses. Following ancient cosmologies and medical teachings, Daoists saw sexual intercourse as a primary manifestation of the interaction of yin and yang, leading to a state of unitary *qi* and thus to harmony with the Dao (Reid 1989, 165-66). Regular sexual activity among married couples was encouraged, and the *Demon Statutes of Nüqing* prohibits members from "living in a separate dwelling from your father or son or otherwise being separated from your family," punishing this with a subtraction of twenty-two days from the life expectancy (no. 13; 3.2b). It also warns against failure to produce offspring and rejects homosexuality and the seduction of young girls. This is punishable by a subtraction of 300 days (no. 10). The *180 Precepts of Lord Lao* similarly focuses on the maintenance of social boundaries among the sexes and prohibits meeting, eating, speaking, traveling, and entering the moun-

---

[4] A mythological form of the great feast is described by Ge Hong as the "traveling kitchen," for which immortals conjure up celestial delicacies (Stein 1971, 490). The ceremonies were later replaced by the great purgations of Numinous Treasure and also continued in an internalized form as meditations of inner nourishment. See Mollier 2000.

tains "with a woman alone" (nos. 117, 139, 161-64). It also discourages spying on women (no. 99) and love relationships with female disciples (no. 81).[5]

While sex in daily life and social interaction was restrained, the Celestial Masters also encouraged the spiritual transformation of sexuality in their rites of the harmonization of *qi* (Ozaki 1986, 95; Schipper 1994b, 69). Adepts learned to detach themselves from desire and to dissociate orgasm from pleasure. The act itself was less important than its effect of setting the *qi* in harmonious motion along the bodily circuits, where it provided sustenance and nourishment instead of being wasted as outflow (Despeux 1990, 36; Despeux and Kohn 2003, 11).

The ritual consisted of highly complex ceremonies during which male sexual energies (known as yellow *qi*) and female sexual energies (red *qi*) joined together in accord with cosmic forces (Schipper 1984, 203; Yan 2001). They were practiced in the oratory in the presence of a master and an instructor. Adepts began with slow, formal movements accompanied by meditations to create a sacred space, then established the harmony between their *qi* and that of the cosmos through visualizations. For example, the *Observances for Salvation through the [Practice of the] Yellow Book* (*Huangshu guodu yi* 黃書過度儀, DZ 1294), a fourth-century manual of Highest Clarity that contains remnants of earlier materials (Schipper 1994, 252), says:

> May each person visualize the *qi* of his or her cinnabar field [below the navel] as large as a six-inch mirror, leaving the body through open space. Its light progressively increases to illuminate the head and bathe the entire body in radiance, so that the adept can clearly discern the five inner organs, the six viscera, the nine palaces, the twelve lodgings, the four limbs, as well as all the joints, vessels, pores, and defensive and nutritive *qi* within the body and without. (2a; Despeux and Kohn 2003, 12)

Next, adepts informed their master and various divinities that they were going to undertake the harmonization of *qi*. This involved ritualistic movements in precise directions and according to astronomically defined positions, as well as the concentration and firm maintenance of bodily essence and vital spirits through the retention of sexual fluids. Reverting them away from orgasmic expulsion, adepts moved these forces up along the spinal column and into the head to nourish the brain and enhance personal and communal harmony. The risen *qi* would also communicate with the celestial officers who erased the names of all participating members from the registers of death and inscribed them in the ledgers of long life (see Stein 1963; Yan 2001).

In this practice, control of sexual urges and desires was essential. As the *Esoteric Rites of the Perfected* (*Zhenren neili* 真人內禮), cited in a later Buddhist polemic, says:

> Do not fail to observe the proper order of attendance in the inner chamber. Do not harbor desire for the ordinary way [of intercourse] or fail to observe the teachings of [sexual] control. Do not lust for relations with outsiders or fail to observe the rituals of the proper nourishing of the inner chamber. Do not lust to be first or fail to observe the rules of cultivation of the inner chamber. (T. 2110; 52.545c; Kohn 1995c, 148)

---

[5] The rules against speaking, eating, or walking about with a woman alone as well as that against closeness with a disciple are also found in the other major codes: *Three Primes*, nos. 98, 100, 108; *Self-Observation*, nos. 79, 82, 93; *Medium Ultimate*, nos. 80, 82, 24.

This closely reflects the rules of the *Demon Statutes of Nüqing*. It warns followers not to "transmit the red energy [sexual practices] to ordinary people and not to interact with them with mouth, hands, chest, or heart" (no. 21; 3.3b; Schipper 1994b, 69). Their mental state during the rites, moreover, had to remain pure. The text says:

19. Do not on the days of rites for the Dao be lustful for sex or give in to your passions. Do not have preferences in activating the *qi* [during ritual intercourse] or keep on pleasuring yourself without stopping. . . . For this Heaven will subtract 300 days [from your life].

20. Do not make meditation on the spirits subject to personal reward. Do not give rise to [excited] *qi* while practicing the rites or let the primordial *qi* rise and fall, becoming greedy for love and sex. Never let your hands and feet stray, and whether day or night, never be without the Dao. For this Heaven will subtract 342 days [from your life]. (2.3ab)

Physical control over sexual impulses, therefore, is set into a ritual, communal, and cosmic context. The rules do not prohibit sexual activities but limit them to socially acceptable venues. They make sure intercourse is undertaken in a way that is pleasing to Heaven and Earth and aids the maintenance of cosmic harmony. Practitioners use their bodies to transform into holier and purer beings, transcending the urges for fine food, strong seasonings, and pleasurable sex in favor of a greater harmony with the universe in the Dao.

LAY RESTRICTIONS

Among the lay organizations of the middle ages, in Highest Clarity and Numinous Treasure, this pattern of restriction in daily life and activation during festivals and rituals is reversed. Throughout the year, practitioners observe the five precepts and are encouraged to be moderate in their consumption of wine, meat, and sex. As the *Great Precepts of the Highest Rank* of early fifth-century Numinous Treasure says:

Take care not to be too greedy for the five tastes or to delight in rich food that will overburden the five inner organs. Always maintain purity and cleanliness within, and wisdom will arise in you. (12b)

Reduce the wine you drink, always using it in moderation and harmonizing your *qi* and inner nature. Make sure your spirit is not diminished or harmed, and never commit the multitude of evils. (2a)

Do not engage in passions or desires, never giving free rein to your mind. Be chaste and pure, and maintain prudence in all actions without flaws and disgrace. (1b)[6]

Like medical manuals, the rules do not prohibit wine, meat, or sex, but encourage practitioners to be careful and moderate their intake, while remaining aware of the purity of their body and mind. This attitude is also echoed in the *Immortals' Taboos According to the Purple Texts Inscribed by the Spirits*. In addition to prohibiting the consumption of the five strong vegetables, it lists several kinds of that meat practitioners should avoid:

Do not eat the flesh of animals associated with the day of your parent's birth.
Do not eat the flesh of animals associated with the day of your birth.
Do not eat the flesh of the six domestic animals.

---

[6] Similar rules are also found in the *Scripture of Great Offerings* (*Daxian jing* 大獻經, ed. DH 23; DZ 370), a sixth-century work on ritual matters.

> Do not eat the meat of armored [shelled] animals like turtles or dragons on the days of Six Armored Gods [*liujia* 六甲].
> Do not eat pheasant on *bingwu* 丙午 days.
> Do not eat the meat of black animals on *bingzi* 丙子 days.
> Do not eat fish on the ninth day of the second month. (2ab; Bokenkamp 1997, 365)

Here meat is allowed but in controlled limits and in correlation with the cosmic constellation of the adept's birth date and that of his parents, as well as with various astrological constellations in the course of the year. The text also says that followers should "not get drunk on *yimao* 乙茂 days" (2b), implying that it was acceptable to partake of wine on other days of the sixty-day cycle.

This more open attitude toward meat and wine reflects the fact that lay leaders had much less control over what their followers did in their own homes than the libationers among the Celestial Masters who were immediately present in the community. Lay leaders then compensated for this by making a strong case for why indulgence should be avoided. Thus, the *Precepts of the Highest Lord Lao* establishes a chain of negative impact that leads from intoxication to loss of control and the breaking of precepts. It says:

> Dead drunk, people get into disputes and quarrels, bringing misfortune to their lives and shame on themselves. Lying and cheating, they lose all guidelines they could follow. Stealing even from their six relations, they grab from all, not just from strangers. Killing off a host of living beings, they are only interested in giving satisfaction to their mouths and stomachs. (17b-18a; Kohn 1994, 206)

Not only in this life, they will also experience negative consequences in their future rebirths. Being born among non-Chinese peoples and barbarians, they will have a husband or wife who is ugly and cruel. "Poor and destitute, cold and exposed, they will find no peace anywhere they live; whatever wealth and lifestock they may acquire will be stolen by others; whatever they say, nobody will believe them" (18b). In general, their minds will be dull and blocked, and they will be objects of contempt.

A similar list of consequences is also presented in the *Twelve Highest Precepts of Admonition* (*Shier shangpin quanjie* 十二上品權戒, DZ 182), a Numinous Treasure collection of the sixth century. It says:

> People who drink wine may expect three kinds of retribution for their sins:
> 1. In this world they hinder or lose all goodness and connection to the divine law. In future lives, they will be born with a dark and obtuse spirit.
> 2. They are crazy and confused in their minds, lacking clarity and radiance. Later they will fall among the bats, lizards, and similar creatures.
> 3. Even if they attain human birth again, their conscious minds and inner natures will be mad and deluded, full of evil and folly. (9b-10a)

On whichever level of the rebirth process, people who indulge in wine are likely to be deluded and subject to bouts of madness. This connection between madness and drinking is also pronounced in the Buddhist *Retribution Sūtra* (*Baoying jing* 報應經, T. 747, 17.562b-63b), translated in the mid-fifth century, and the Daoist *Scripture of Karmic Retribution* (Kohn 1998b, 19). The latter text links it to a lack of respect for the scriptures, which causes one to be reborn as a fish. Fish, as everyone knows, drink, so in one's next life one comes back into the world as an alcoholic. This alcoholism leads to madness and a rebirth in mud and filth, as a result of which one may again show disrespect for the scriptures and come back once more as a fish (Kohn 1998b, 30). The only way to avoid this vicious circle is to be careful in one's consumption of wine—and also of meat, which medieval texts commonly link with becoming the victim of violence and being reborn as a wild animal (Kohn 1998b, 31).

Sexual indulgence, too, is punished through karma. The *Twelve Highest Precepts of Admonition* says:

> People who engage in licentiousness may expect seven kinds of retribution for their sins:
> 1. They are born with withered roots [penises].
> 2. They are the source of foulness and afflictions.
> 3. They try to do good in vain.
> 4. They suffer a short life and lose their spirit souls.
> 5. They have troubled sleep and are confused and deluded in their minds.
> 6. After death they fall into the hells to suffer the tortures of the iron bed and the copper pillar. Their bodies burnt and their bones rotting, they are dumped in and out of the icy pool, speared by ice and knifed by frost. They die and are born time and again without respite, undergoing terrible suffering and afflictions.
> 7. In separation from human life, they are born as pigs, dogs, or other unclean animals, wild or domestic. (6ab)

This establishes a close connection between foulness and sexual indulgence, carried through this life and into the next, both in the form of physical defilements and mental unrest. Similar consequences are also spelled out in the sixth-century *Twenty-four Precepts for Followers* (*Ershisi menjie jing* 二十四門戒經, DZ 183, 4b) and the *Scripture of Karmic Retribution* (Kohn 1998b), both of Numinous Treasure provenance. In contrast, the *Immortals' Taboos* of Highest Clarity sees the harm of sexual indulgence more in physical terms and as affecting the body gods. It insists that licentiousness causes the spirit souls and bodily fluids to leak out, so that essence diminishes, the spirit suffers, the material souls scatter, the bones decay, and the bone marrow rots (1b).

In all cases, the texts warn practitioners in drastic and vivid terms of the consequences their uncontrolled behavior might have, raising the stakes for observing the precepts and the price to be paid for their violation in terms of health, good fortune, and future life experiences. During all retreats and festivals, they carry this tendency even further and insist on a high degree of purity. At those holy times, all sexual relations were prohibited, and participants not only avoided meat, wine, and the five strong vegetables but even fasted in order to cleanse themselves. The strictness of the rules made lay followers into temporary monks and nuns, allowing them to partake for a bit of the benefits of the monastic life.

MONASTIC PRACTICE

Monastic practitioners abstained from all inappropriate foods and sexual activity, as these substances and activities disturbed their celestial progress. Especially intoxication was seen as a great danger and source of uncontrolled behavior. As outlined in the early Tang code *Rules and Observances for Students of the Dao* (*Daoxue keyi* 道學科儀, DZ 1126), such behavior included sloth and torpor, violence and killing, eating meat, consuming the five strong vegetables, and disregarding taboos or the ritual schedule. Any of these offended the celestial officers, sickened the spirit and material souls, brought nightmares and bad fortune, and caused bad karma and rebirth (2.5a).

Wine was blamed for ten kinds of evils, including unfilial, offensive, and belligerent behavior, sexual hankerings and rule violations, as well as riding accidents and getting lost on the road. As in the lay texts, its consumption was associated with bad karma and the tendency to kill living beings. Over time, it would lead to the loss of the goodwill of one's masters, family, friends, and companions (1.3b-4a). The source of violence and aggression, wine was harmful to all forms of social interaction. The text also emphasizes that production of wine was a perfect waste of thousands of pounds of good grain that could feed the people. It was, therefore, best to stay away from wine completely and instead create one's own inner liquor from refined saliva and *qi* (Kohn 2003a, 122).

In addition to refraining from wine, Daoist monastics also avoided the five strong vegetables, seen as harmful in both practical and karmic terms. As the *Rules and Observances for Students of the Dao* explains, eating them will cause bad breath, which is harmful when one attends ritual ceremonies, sends a petition to the gods, or lectures to a group of commoners (1.4b-5a).

The *Scripture of Karmic Retribution* of the Sui dynasty, in a set of karmic consequences, links the five strong vegetables with the tendency to drink wine and eat meat (no. 44) and states that they frequently cause either a stuffy nose that prevents the person from "smelling either fragrance or stink" (no. 34) or a lascivious and uncontrolled nature, which will cause harm to one's karma (no. 58). Such karmic harm may lead to death by drowning (no. 44) or to rebirth in an unclean and foul-smelling body, be it human or animal (no. 26). At the worst, approaching the Three Treasures after having partaken of the noxious greens will cause one to be reborn as a flea or wood-louse (no. 78) (2.5b-9b; Kohn 1998b, 35-36; 2004, sect.1).

Monks and nuns of the Complete Perfection school, too, abstained from the five strong vegetables. They were seen as enhancing yang and thus heating the blood and raising internal fires, which may lead to an increase in passions, desires, and aggression. Although strengthening, taking these vegetables might thus increase the tendency to violate the precepts and cause communal disorder (Hackmann 1931, 8).

In all these arguments, the Daoist position closely matches that of Chinese Buddhism, which also places a strong emphasis on the prohibition of the five strong vegetables. Here it appears among the ten leading Mahāyāna precepts, formulated first in the apocryphal *Brahma Net Sūtra* (*Brahmajala sūtra, Fanwang jing* 梵網經, T. 1484, 24.997b-1010a; trl. DeGroot 1969, 42)[7] of the mid-fifth century, as well as in the *Surangama sūtra* (*Shoulengyan jing* 首楞嚴經, T. 945, 19.105b-55c), compiled around the year 700. The main reason for the prohibition is less their smelly nature than their aphrodisiac and anger-inducing qualities which lead to the creation of bad karma

[7] The text, which also has forty-eight lesser rules in addition to the ten precepts, is not mentioned in bibliographies before the year 730 but has had a major impact on East Asian Buddhist practice. Its role in Japanese Buddhism of the Heian period is discussed in Groner 1984, 215-20; 1990b; Stevens 1988, 22-26. On its use in Fujian monasteries of the late nineteenth century, see DeGroot 1969. For a general discussion of the text and its history, see Pruden 1967; Demiéville 1929, 146-47. On its importance for Daoism, see Yoshioka 1961a; Kusuyama 1982; 1983.

(19.141c; Ch'en 1973, 98; Kieschnick 1997, 24). This evaluation has persisted over the years, and the five are still forbidden in Buddhism today (see Welch 1967).

Unlike medieval Buddhists whose codes, at least in the early stages, still spoke about meat as part of the monastic fare,[8] Daoists ate a meat-less diet. Their meals consisted largely of rice, wheat, and barley, combined with various vegetables and tofu. In Daoist religious literature, meat is not even mentioned among the five main food groups. Echoing the *Book of the Master Who Embraces Simplicity* (ch. 11; Stein 1971, 492), the *Prohibitions and Precepts Regarding Ceremonial Food* (*Fashi jinjie jing* 法食禁戒經, DH 80) of the early Tang defines them five food groups as *qi*, medicines, grain, fruit, and vegetables. Prepared so that they are neither too hot or too cold, too spicy or too bland, and do not contain harmful substances, food serves "to harmonize the blood and body fluids, preserve and nourish the body and spirit, calm the spirit soul and settle the will, and in general expel all wind and dampness, thus greatly enhancing life and extending old age" (l. 17-18). Among these five, moreover,

> eating vegetables is not as good as eating grains; eating grains is not as good as eating fungi and excrescences; eating fungi is not as good as eating gold and jade;. eating gold and jade is not as good as eating primordial *qi*; and eating primordial *qi* is not as good as not eating at all. By not eating at all, even though Heaven and Earth may collapse, the body will remain eternally. (l. 9-11)

The ability to live on pure *qi* is a major characteristic of the gods and immortals, whom Daoist monastics are trying to emulate. At the same time, they also strive to return to the state of high antiquity, when people "only ate primordial *qi* and managed to live for millions of years, focused on guarding the Dao and never pursued the multiple states of mind" (l. 6-7). They hope to create a celestial life in this world, reversing the decline humanity went through after the invention of cooking and agriculture (see Lévi 1983).

To control their intake of food, monastics had meals only in the morning and before noon, fasting for the longer part of the day. They also engaged in breathing exercises to help them replace food with *qi* and thus sublimate the body to a more refined level. The technique they used was called "ingesting *qi*" (*shiqi* 食氣) or "swallowing *qi*" (*yinqi* 泅氣). As described in the *Record on Nurturing Inner Nature and Extending Life* (*Yangxing yanming lu* 養性延命綠, DZ 838), a medieval classic on longevity techniques (see Switkin 1987; Mugitani 1987), this breathing technique was undertaken while sitting down in a meditative posture, either kneeling or cross-legged, with the back and neck straight, the eyes closed, and the mind concentrated.

Inhaling *qi* through the nose, adepts held it in the mouth to form a mixture of breath and saliva—called "jade spring" or "sweet wine." They rinsed the mouth with it to gain a feeling of fullness, allowing the *qi* to envelope the tongue and teeth. Then they consciously swallowed it, visualizing the mixture as it moved through the torso into the inner organs. Once the *qi* was safely stored in its intended receptacle, they exhaled. As the text says, "If you can do one thousand swallowings like this in one day and night, this is most excellent" (2.1a).

---

[8] This is documented in the *Three Thousand Dignified Observances* (*Sanqian weiyi* 三千威儀, T. 1470, 24.912c-26a), which has a section on the proper way to purchase meat: make sure the meat is whole and not in pieces, is not left over by someone else, is weighed correctly, and is only bought in necessary quantities (T. 24.922c). The text is ascribed to An Shigao 安世高 of the second century, but more likely dates from the fifth (Hirakawa 1960, 193-96). It had a great impact on the Daoist *Rules for a Thousand Perfected*, however, not with regard to meat.

In the long run the practice eliminated the need for food and drink and thus served as a preparatory method of complete fasting or the "abstention from grains" (*bigu* 辟穀). To achieve this, as outlined in the *Great Clarity Oral Instructions on the Absorption of Qi* (*Taiqing fuqi koujue* 太清服氣口訣, DZ 822), Daoists gradually modified their diet in accordance with the five food groups. First they took simpler foods to harmonize spleen-*qi* and activate the saliva, such as rice porridge, boiled wheat dumplings, cooked barley, and dried meat, which they supplemented with raw pepper corns to make the *qi* flow harmoniously and to ward off cold, heat, and dampness.

After a few weeks of regular breathing practice and this simple diet, they could skip one or two meals. They then replaced the grains with steamed vegetables, seasoned with soy sauce or vinegar and enhanced with medicinal herbs. This was to cleanse the colon and wean the body from its need for grains. After about a week, adepts were able to do away with the vegetables and only take their juice. Three days later, food intake could be given up completely, but liquids—such as boiled water, wine, ginger soup, or vegetable juice—should still be taken until such time when reliance on primordial *qi* was complete (Huang and Wurmbrand 1987, 60).

While they were sill eating worldly food, however, as the *Prohibitions and Precepts Regarding Ceremonial Food* spells out, monks and nuns not only abstained from wine, meat, and strong vegetables, but also from all foodstuffs from far-away places, from families with a recent birth or death, and from robbers or lascivious people. They avoided anything that was left behind from offerings given to birds, beasts, worms, and fish; any food offered to spirits and demons at altars, shrines, or temples; anything unclean, rotten, moldy, broken, burnt, or defiled by birds; as well as any food that children had touched and returned to their mothers (l. 45-55). If any donor came to the monastery offering food of this type, it was considered "nonritual" (*feifa* 非法) and not accepted. Violations of the rules about food, especially if repeated, could result in expulsion from the institution—as did any commercial activities that involved them, such as dealing in wine, selling meat, or engaging in other forms of trade (*Rules for a Thousand Perfected* 9a).

Sensual attachments and sexual activity, too, were strictly controlled in medieval Daoist institutions. Men and women were segregated and had to avoid all contact or discussions. If they did not see an attractive person of the opposite sex, the *Rules for a Thousand Perfected* says, their minds would not be agitated (7a). Daoists had to remain distant whenever they found themselves in the presence of a person of the opposite sex.

However, even for this rule there were exceptions. For example, Daoists could lecture lay women on the scriptures, but they must never be alone with them nor develop lascivious intentions. Also, at the time of ordination it was permitted for men and women to enter each other's quarters after receiving permission from the masters. They were admonished, however, to behave with dignity and could not go off individually or in groups of two or enter private quarters (*Rules for a Thousand Perfected* 16a) (Kohn 2003a, 121-22).

If, furthermore, a monk came across a woman in danger of drowning or burning, he must not "hesitate to reach out a hand to help," because this contact was not in violation of the rules (11b). Similarly, when his own mother, sister, or aunt was "sick or in some kind of distress at home, he could go and serve to support her" (11b), or in some special cases bring her to the monastery and set up a hut for her nearby (Bumbacher 2000a, 246). This shows, as does the emphasis the texts place on filial piety as a key virtue of human life, that "leaving the family" in medieval Daoism did not mean the complete severance of all worldly ties but rather was a sign of serious dedication to the goals of the Dao (Tuzuki 2002, 64). These goals were best met in a life of self-control and abstinence, a life conducted closer to the rules of Heaven and Earth than to those of humanity, which demanded the complete control of impulses toward intoxication, gluttony, and sexual activities.

MODERN APPLICATIONS

The modern school of Daoist monasticism, Complete Perfection, has continued the medieval tradition in many ways. The *Precepts of Initial Perfection* (*Chuzhen jie* 初真戒, JY 278, 292; ZW 404; [9] trl. Hackmann 1920) begins by requiring ordinands to take refuge in the Dao, the scriptures, and the masters, then swear to obey a set of five and ten precepts. The latter specify, among others, that they should not "be lascivious or lose perfection, defile or insult the numinous *qi*." They should also avoid "ruining others to create gain for themselves and instead stay with their own flesh and blood," as well as abstain from "drinking wine beyond measure or eating meat in violation of the prohibitions" (22a). A complementary work, the *Pure Rules, Mysterious and Marvelous* (*Qinggui xuanmiao* 清規玄妙, ZW 361), similarly prohibits the consumption of wine and fancy foods, such as luscious mushrooms and meat, and punishes violations of this rule by caning and expulsion (see Yoshioka 1979; Kohn 2003b).

Food was precious and important. Monastics partook of it in formal meal-time ceremonies called *zhai* 齋 and to a certain degree begged for it. Using the begging bowl and eating from it was a highly ritualized activity, performed with great care. As the *Precepts of Initial Perfection* says:

> The begging bowl should have the shape of the eight trigrams. Only the opening for the lid should be round. It should be kept in a special bowl bag and taken out only when it is time to eat. After concluding the incantation [at meals], collect your *qi* and visualize the spirit, then eat without opening your mouth widely or making any sucking noises. Use the spoon when appropriate. After food has been taken, wash the bowl and return it to its bag. Every time you go against this, it will count as one transgression. (30a)

These rules applied both to men and women, however, the latter also received a set of twelve special precepts, listed in the nineteenth-century manual *Women's Golden Elixir* (*Nü jindan* 女金丹, ZW 871, 878; Tao 1989, 57-122). The rules emphasize the mental state women needed to cultivate, encouraging them to "restrain the recurrence of inappropriate thoughts;" to "cut off lust and sexual indulgence;" to avoid "flying into rages" or giving in to anger, fear, or anxiety; as well as to curb tendencies toward curiosity, gossip, stinginess, and scorn. Women were not supposed to "kill or harm any living being" and had to "avoid excess in eating meat" (1.4a-5a; Despeux and Kohn 2003, 165).

Most Complete Perfection followers underwent initial ordination simultaneously with that into the second level, which involved taking the *Precepts of Medium Ultimate* (*Zhongji jie* 中極戒, JY 293, ZW 405; trl. Hackmann 1931). Closely patterned on the medieval *Great Precepts of Self-Observation*, this contains three groups of rules: a set of 180 socially oriented prohibitions that

---

[9] The abbreviation "JY" stands for *Daozang jiyao* 道藏輯要 or "Collected Essentials of the Daoist Canon," a collection of Daoist texts dating from the early nineteenth century. "ZW" indicates *Zangwai daoshu* 藏外道書, "Daoist Texts Outside the Canon," a recent compilation. Both are numbered according to Komjathy 2002.

frequently follow the *180 Precepts of Lord Lao*, thirty-six admonitions that specify forms of monastic behavior, and eighty-four altruistic resolutions. With regard to food, the text prohibits killing for nourishment (no. 1), taking the five strong vegetables (no. 4), wasting food (no. 70), throwing it into water or fire (no. 41), and touching it with bare hands (no. 154). It emphasizes that one should live on a vegetarian diet (no. 217), be content with taking coarse and tasteless bits (no. 188), and "wish that the donor may attain good fortune and be always full and satisfied" when given a morsel during begging rounds (no. 195).

In terms of sexual activity, the *Precepts of Medium Ultimate* echoes its medieval forerunners in that it wishes to forestall all thoughts of licentiousness and prohibits close contact with members of the opposite sex, either by eating together or exchanging clothes (no. 82), by becoming an instructor (no. 83), by spying (no. 8), or in other ways intermingling (no. 81). The rules are similar to earlier precepts in that they circumscribe interaction with women to prevent practitioners from falling into the ways of the world. Adepts of Complete Perfection observed complete celibacy, seen as a fundamental condition for the concentration on the inner energies and the in-depth meditation practices necessary for successful transformation.

Even here, however, sexuality is neither denied nor suppressed. Rather, the transformation of sexual essence is at the root of the spiritual practice of Complete Perfection, the technique of inner alchemy.[10] To begin, adepts pursue longevity techniques to make the body healthy and strong, then they engage in mental concentration to make the mind tranquil and stable. The actual practice begins with focusing on one's essence, allowing it to sink from the centers of *qi* in the chest or abdomen and to become tangible. Instead of letting it leave the body, however, adepts refine and revert it, restoring their sexual essence back to its original form as *qi* and preventing its future disintegration.

To accomplish this, men should get aroused almost to the point of ejaculation, then mentally concentrate on making the semen flow upward and along spine into the head. Once a man has reached proficiency in the practice and will no longer ejaculate, texts say that he has "subdued the white tiger." Men then proceed to circulate the reverted energy—parallel to the reverted cinnabar in operative alchemy—along a cycle inside the torso known as the "microcosmic orbit" (*xiao zhoutian* 小周天) that follows the course of made up of the Governor and Conception Vessels, central *qi* meridians that run along the spine and in front of the torso. With prolonged practice, the practitioner's *qi* is refined and begins to form a divine "pearl of dew" in the lower cinnabar field. A first coagulation of stronger and purer *qi*, this lays the foundation for the next level.

In women the first stage of reverting *jing* back to *qi* begins with daily breast massages, a change in diet to lighter foods, and a series of meditations in which menstrual blood is visualized rising upward and transforming into clear-colored *qi*. After several months of this menstruation ceases, an effect called "decapitating the red dragon." It serves to stabilize the *qi*, which will then come to nurture the pearl of dew. Unlike in men, in women the pearl is naturally present but if left untended will dissipate with every menstrual cycle. The beginning of inner alchemical practice is the reversal of this natural tendency (Despeux and Kohn 2003, 223).

---

[10] On inner alchemy, see Needham et al. 1983; Robinet 1989; 1995; Lu 1970; Cleary 1987; 1992; Wilhelm 1984; Baldrian-Hussein 1994; Baryosher-Chemouny 1996; Skar and Pregadio 2000.

The second stage is the same for men and women. It focuses on the transformation of *qi* into *shen* or spirit. The pearl of dew is developed into the "golden flower" with the help of transmuted *qi*. For this, yin and yang are identified as different energies in the body and described with various metaphors including lead and mercury, dragon and tiger. Adepts learn to revolve these energies through an inner-body cycle that includes not only the spine and chest but leads all the way to the feet and is known as the "macrocosmic orbit" (*da zhoutian* 大周天). Gradually the bodily substances are refined to a point where they become as pure as the celestials and form the golden flower, the first trace of the immortal embryo in the lower cinnabar field. The process is complex and must be timed in exact correspondence with the cosmic patterns of yin and yang.

Once the embryo is started, adepts switch their practice to employ a method called "embryo respiration" (*taixi* 胎息) to nourish it for ten months. This is an inner form of breathing, combined with the meditative circulation of *qi*, which allows the embryo to grow and makes the adept increasingly independent of outer nourishment and air. Unlike the first phase, which was easier for men, the process at this stage is easier for women because they are naturally endowed with the faculty to grow an embryo. After ten months, the embryo is complete (Despeux and Kohn 2003, 234).

Adepts then proceed to the third stage. The as yet semi-material body of the embryo is transformed into the pure spirit body of the immortals, a body of primordial *qi*. To attain its full realization, the embryo has to pass through several phases. First it undergoes a spiritual birth by moving up along the spine and exiting through the acupuncture point Hundred Meeting (Baihui 百會) at the top of the head, now called the Heavenly Gate (Tianguan 天關). The first exit of the spirit embryo is known as "deliverance from the womb." It signifies the adept's celestial rebirth and is accompanied by the perception of a deep inner rumbling, like a clap of thunder. When the Heavenly Pass bursts wide, a white smoky essence can be seen hovering above the adept. The spirit passes through the top of the head and begins to communicate with the celestials, transcending the limitations of the body (Despeux and Kohn, 2003, 238).

Once the embryo has been born, it is nursed for three years. It gradually gets used to its new powers, moves faster and travels further afield until it can go far and wide without any limitation. As the spirit enters into its cosmic ventures, the adept exhibits supernatural powers, including the abilities to be in two places at once, move quickly from one place to another, know the past and the future, divine people's thoughts, procure wondrous substances, overcome hazards of fire and water, and have powers over life and death. Known as "spirit pervasion" in analogy of the six pervasions of the medieval texts, this indicates the freedom achieved by the spirit and evident in the practitioner. Going beyond this level, adepts eventually transform into pure light and melt into cosmic emptiness.

Daoist rules and precepts that control basic impulses of nourishment and sexual contact, therefore, are at the root of a transformative process that leads far away from ordinary human life and into the celestial spheres. Even early communities and lay groups were aware of this and emphasized the purity of body and mind necessary for community cohesion and the practice of rituals. They were conscious of the need to maintain a smooth flow of *qi* through both body and community and to revert and maintain internal essence rather than losing it in emotions, defilements, and sexual activity. But the full impact of the rules only becomes clear in the strict monastic setting, where adepts transform their need for food into the ability to nourish on primordial *qi* and their inherent sexual nature into a replica of the divine.

CHAPTER FOUR

Admonitions toward Goodness

Both the reorientation of the senses through the five precepts and the redirection of inner energies through the control of food, wine, and sex can lead to advanced states of oneness with the Dao and prevent upheaval in communal organizations. However, the establishment of boundaries for harmful and disruptive behavior alone does not create an ideal living situation on earth. Above and beyond the personal realization of the Dao, the ideal of Daoist practice has always been the state of Great Peace, a situation where humanity lives in perfect alignment with the forces of nature and the cosmos and where human society functions smoothly and to the greatest benefit of all. As Daoist communities strove to set an example for the state of Great Peace, they provided further guidelines on how practitioners should think and behave. Going beyond the great moral rules and specific prohibitions, these guidelines tended to be socially oriented and admonished practitioners to direct their thoughts and actions in specifically Daoist ways.

Admonitions in the Daoist tradition include both concrete instructions on how to behave and personal prescriptions for mental attitudes to cultivate. They are often presented in close connection with sets of prohibitions and preventative precepts, so that some lists begin with the five precepts then move on to five admonitions, while others have a list of prohibitions that are each supplemented with admonitions. The ultimate goal in either case is to instill in Daoist followers a sense of goodness toward others and an awareness of cosmic responsibility. Like the Dao itself, practitioners ultimately should come to be above moral issues yet incorporate an elementary goodness in all they do.

The *Twelve Highest Precepts of Admonition* has a vivid parable about the ultimate kindness of Daoists, formulated in the words of the Heavenly Worthy. Echoing the famous metaphor of Mencius (II.A.6), he begins by comparing the situation of humanity with that of a small child who has fallen into a well. He continues:

> The well is dark and full of dangers, pitch black, and inhabited by poisonous snakes. The parents hear the child scream and immediately feel great distress and sympathy. First they chant an incantation to the gods to stop the poisonous snakes from attacking. Thus they ensure that the child remains physically safe and will not be bitten or devoured. Then they take hold of a strong rope and long pole to use as a hook and ladder. They also find a valiant man who will enter the pit and rescue the child. Thus they plan to bring him out to safety.

> As things are going along smoothly, however, the child, ignorant and foolish and utterly unaware of the dangerous depths below, suddenly loosens his grip and falls down a second time. Hope for his life is almost lost. The parents once more call upon the gods and again set out to make rescue plans. They teach the child divine incantations to subdue the poisonous snakes. Then they again lower the pole and eventually get him out of the dangerous pit. (DZ 182, 2b-3a)

The Heavenly Worthy then notes that he uses the exact same methods to save human beings who have fallen into the three bad rebirths, dark and dangerous like the deep pit, and are constantly troubled by sufferings and vexations, symbolized by the poisonous snakes. The first thing he teaches people is to observe the precepts, which has the same effect as the chanting of divine incantations in the story in that it provides a prime line of defense. Then, caring for every single being as if he or she were his own child, the Heavenly Worthy strives to bring them all out of the darkness of the rebirth cycle (3a). In a similar way, Daoists are ultimately responsible for the well-being of all beings and come to care about the world at large. Admonitions are a first step to awaken the social responsibility and altruistic dimension of the teaching.

Positive rules for socially caring behavior are present from the earliest Daoist groups. The Celestial Masters had a set of nine attitudes for followers. Including nonaction, desirelessness, and purity, they were based directly on the *Daode jing* and appeared in the *Xiang'er Commentary* to the text. They guided practitioners toward realizing the qualities of the Dao within themselves and thereby support social harmony.

In the medieval schools, admonitions came for the most part in lists of ten. Both the numbering in tens and the first examples of ten precepts and ten items of goodness can be traced to Buddhism and especially its Mahāyāna development—including a greater focus on mental attitudes and a broader application to lay followers. Daoists adopted the Buddhist model, and some lists of rules closely echo Buddhist rules. However, the most prevalent Daoist sets, the classic Ten Precepts and the Ten Wisdom Precepts of Numinous Treasure, are quite different from their Buddhist counterparts. Also, they both come with supplementary lists of encouraging self-admonitions that focus on developing an altruistic mind-set. Several lists of ten, moreover, were also used in Daoist communities of later dynasties, mostly associated with ritual performances and in some cases presenting a shorthand for community regulations and major virtues.

THE *XIANG'ER* PRECEPTS

Among the early Celestial Masters, admonitions appear first in the precepts of the *Xiang'er Commentary* to the *Daode jing* (*Laozi Xiang'er zhu* 老子想爾注) as cited in the *Scriptural Statutes of Lord Lao* (*Laojun jinglü* 老君經律, DZ 786), a sixth-century collection. This collection only presents the precepts from the *Commentary*, of which larger fragments remain in a manuscript found at Dunhuang.[1]

The precepts are of two kinds: a group of nine that provide positive attitudes based on philosophical concepts of the *Daode jing* and a set of twenty-seven that present a mixture of general rules, behavioral regulations, and temporal taboos. They closely echo a set of admonitions contained in *The 180 Precepts of Lord Lao* (nos. 141-60) and a group of thirteen desirable attitudes listed in the *Statutes of Mystery Metropolis*. Also, they are important not only because they formulate what the Celestial Masters expected of their ideal followers, but also because they have been adopted by in various surviving branches of the school, including also the American lineage of Orthodox Daoism of America (O.D.A.).

The nine admonitions take technical terms from the *Daode jing* and make them into guidelines for Daoist behavior, such as nonaction, desirelessness, nonaggression, weakness, and softness

---

[1] DH 56. Reprinted with notes in Rao 1992. A complete translation is found in Bokenkamp 1997. Index in Mugitani 1985a. For discussions, see Akizuki 1965; Boltz 1982; Boken-kamp 1993; Mugitani 1985b.

(see Ames 1992, 126; Liu 1990, 137). The practice of these, as that of other sets of precepts, was closely related to physiological cultivation. Thus, "being pure and tranquil is a practice of *qi*-ingestion that serves to return human energy to its root and thus create a more stable sense of being in the world" (Bokenkamp 1997, 51). Along similar lines, nonaction was an admonition for concrete behavior, intending that people should act without artifice and in a way that was not contrived or willful. It involved a quiet mind, a laying-to-rest of the passions, and a sense of moving along with the Dao (Bokenkamp 1997, 52).[2]

In the text, the nine admonitions are formulated in descending order and divided into three groups. In contemporary American Daoism, they are called the "Nine Mandates." Unlike their classical forerunners, they are numbered consecutively and have been translated into modern values (O.D.A. 1998, Part 1). They are:

Xiang'er Commentary	O. D. A.
Highest	
nonaction	honesty
being soft and weak	weakness
guarding the female	modesty
Medium	
being nameless	humility
being pure and tranquil	serenity
doing only good	kindness
Lowest	
having no desires	desirelessness
knowing when to stop	restraint
yielding and withdrawing	nonaggression

While the original source leaves it at that, expecting the masters to clarify the meaning of the rules in oral instructions, contemporary Daoists provide a detailed guideline in each case. For example, "guarding the female" has the following:

3. The Mandate of Modesty. Be like a polite guest.

We are guests in the house of the Dao. Honor all the customs of the host family (Daoism) and wait to be invited into action. In this case, the Daoist is the guest and the host family is the Dao. The image here refers to a bride in ancient times. Act as a bride in the house of a new husband's family. (O.D.A. 1998, Part 1)

This not only changes the formulation into something modern practitioners can understand but also enhances the vision of the Daoist in contemporary society as someone who is modest and withdrawing, careful and solicitous.

In a similar fashion, O.D.A. provides consecutive numbering for the twenty-seven precepts of the *Xiang'er Commentary* and reformulates them in a modern style, in the process changing them

---

[2] In this sense, the *Xiang'er Comentary* precepts continue the practice of inner cultivation already associated with the *Daode jing* and related texts in pre-Han China. For details, see Roth 1999.

to admonitions. The original twenty-seven, with the exception of two rules, are presented as prohibitions and listed according to lower, medium, and higher.

The lower precepts guide people to behave with obedience toward the religious leaders and with reticence toward fellow members. They warn followers not to strive for positions beyond their status and to abstain from sacrifices for the dead and popular deities, i.e., the ghosts of dead humans rather than the pure, unborn deities of the Dao (Strickmann 1985, 188). The rules also prohibit the commitment of evil deeds, engagement in warfare, the accumulation of riches, and self-praise as a great sage. They closely reflect similar guidelines in the *180 Precepts of Lord Lao*.

The medium rules prevent followers from studying outside scriptures, pursuing fame and gain, giving rein to sensory pleasures, engaging in frivolous activities, and lacking in devotion and respect for the leaders and the Dao. Members should yield to the needs of others and always stay within the organization. The highest set of nine precepts, finally, represents a guide toward active service for the Dao—adherents on this level are ordered never to forget the divine law and keep strictly within its boundaries. They must not push things forward or reveal esoteric teachings to outsiders.

As advanced practitioners and leading members of the community, they must abstain from killing and eating the flesh of animals, strictly avoiding any harm or diminution of *qi*— their own or that of others. In addition, they are guided to be aware of the cosmic constellations, to pay attention to the currently dominant or "kingly" *qi* and never to harm it. This temporal taboo in conjunction with the other rules aims to raise the practitioner's awareness to the role of the Daoist group within the larger society and the natural universe. The rewards are accordingly: those who obey the highest rules become immortals, all others will extend their years and live happily (1b-2a).

In the modern reinterpretation, all of these rules are presented as admonitions, so that, for example, "Not to waste *jing* or *qi*" becomes: "Conserve your *jing* and *qi*." "Do not study false texts" evolves into: "Diligently study and practice the view and method of *Zhengyi dao*" (O.D.A. 1998, Part 2). Again, more so than in the ancient text, detailed explanations are given that provide guidelines beyond the mere skeleton of the rules. For instance, where the text has: "Do not engage in frivolous undertakings," *The Blue Book* says:

> 15. Embrace the real. Avoid the drama of anger.
>
> Emotions are a constant, gentle and natural flow of responses to the changing face of the Dao. Accepting the naturalness of emotion is not an attachment to emotional drama or passion. Embrace the real. The histrionic display of emotions is the result of inattention to the real. (ODA 1998, Part 2)

The fact that the ancient rules are still followed and used as the foundation of modern Daoist conduct speaks strongly for the continuity of the tradition and its valuing of the past. It shows the vitality and active strength of Daoism and its ability to use ancient models without allowing them to fossilize or become an obstacle to contemporary relevance. The translation of the rules into a more contemporary setting, their reinterpretation and expansion to include modern concerns with emotions, correct views, and reality, makes them accessible in a new way to practitioners who might otherwise not gain their benefits. Continuing the tradition of medieval China, the admonitions of the Celestial Masters today speak to the inner transformation of the individual's awareness as well as to the creation of a harmonious community in the Dao. Then as now the rules involve the creation of a new body-awareness and higher sense of cosmic alignment. Though changed in their interpretation and context, they still hark back to ancient patterns and carry important traditional values.

MAHĀYĀNA ADMONITIONS

Among lay organizations in the middle ages, sets of admonitions came mostly in tens. They tended to go back to Buddhist models, particularly the Mahāyāna precepts. In the Mahāyāna, the distinction between lay and monastic practitioners blurred, and the emphasis of Buddhist ethics shifted away from behavioral prohibitions toward a greater concern with inner awareness and a positive encouragement of bodhisattva virtues. As Tsuchihashi points out, there are several major differences between ancient and Mahāyāna precepts.

First, in content, the new precepts were concerned with benefiting others, while their precursors focused on self-enhancement. Second, they were understood as a visible part of the practitioner's inner nature and not, as in earlier Buddhism, cultivated as external rules. In other words, they were more mind-oriented and inward-looking than previously, when they focused on outward action. Next, in the Mahāyāna model, the precepts once taken became an integral part of the person and could never be lost, while in the old days failure to observe them would cause their loss. Also, in terms of social context, the precepts in ancient Buddhism used to be taken before three masters and seven witnesses, showing that the practitioner had become a member of the Buddhist community. The new precepts could be taken by oneself to enhance one's dedication to serve all beings. Finally, the punishment of any violation, originally meted out in the monks' community, was now located inside the practitioner, who experienced a sense of shame and guilt and underwent rituals of confession and repentance (Tsuchihashi 1980, 115-22).

With these differences in mind, the ten precepts of the Mahāyāna were founded on the ancient five precepts, supplemented with five more inward-looking prohibitions regarding speech and emotions:

6. Do not speak of the faults of the four orders.
7. Do not praise yourself while putting down others.
8. Do not be stingy and miserly and add to others' ruin.
9. Do not harbor anger and aggression in your heart without ever regretting it.
10. Do not slander the Three Jewels. (DeGroot 1969, 36-39)

In China, these rules were first formulated in the fifth-century *Brahma Net Sūtra* (T. 24.997c). They replaced earlier restrictions of concrete behavioral acts with rules furthering self-awareness and proper emotional attitudes. Correct speech was encouraged together with an emphasis on proper concern for others and a clear social conscience—plus a final injunction to maintain respect for the main pillars of the religion.

The same tendency toward greater mental awareness is also evident in another set of ten rules promoted by Mahāyāna followers under the title "ten items of goodness" or "ten good deeds" (*daśākuśala*; *shishan* 十善), a list of ten prohibitions conducive to wholesome behavior. They include the classic five precepts, then add rules against malicious speech, double-tongued speech, fancy language, anger and ill-will, and wrong views.[3] Understood to prevent bad actions as based on the karmic factors of body (1-3), speech (4-7), and mind (8-10), they serve to counteract commitment of the ten evils.[4] The latter led to appropriate karmic retribution in making people subject to ill health, poverty, adultery, fraud, violence, and other negative life events (Demiéville 1929, 1:20-21). While, therefore, the various actions of body, speech, and mind would lead to bad karma if unchecked, it was the firm conviction of Mahāyāna Buddhists that good actions were possible and that passion could be transformed into compassion.

The ten precepts and ten items of goodness in the Mahāyāna system were part of an overall cosmology arranged according to sets of ten, beginning with the ten buddhas of the ten directions and moving on to ten bodhisattva virtues, ten stages of enlightenment, ten powers, ten hindrances, ten activities, and many more. Its first clear formulation appears in the *Flower Garland Sūtra* (*Avatamsaka sūtra; Huayan jing* 華嚴經, T. 278, 9.395-674), translated under the guidance of Buddhabhadra in 418-420.[5] It contains sections on the "ten abodes" (sect. 15), "ten practices" (sect. 21), "ten dedications" (sect. 25), "ten stages" (sect. 26), "ten concentrations" (sect. 27), "ten superknowledges" (sect. 28), and "ten acceptances" (sect. 29; see Cleary 1984). This ten-based cosmology was continued in the *Brahma Net Sūtra* and elaborated further in the integrated system of Zhiyi 智顗 (538-598), founder of the Tiantai 天台 school.[6]

The most important sets of ten that pervaded Mahāyāna teachings and also had a major impact on Daoism were the ten virtues (*pāramitā*) and the ten bodhisattva stages (*bhūmi*) as presented in the *Flower Garland Sūtra* (ch. 26; 9.542c-43a).[7] While the ten virtues outlined qualities that the aspiring bodhisattva had to attain in his quest for enlightenment and universal salvation, the ten stages described the developmental phases he underwent, from the joyful contemplation of nirvāna through the unfolding of compassion and radiant wisdom to the stage when "everything is enveloped with the dharma-cloud of transcendental truth" (Suzuki 1968, 328). Both lists, as well as some of the other ten-based classifications of Buddhism, had a strong impact on Daoist cosmology and were closely linked with the observance of the ten precepts (see Bokenkamp 1990).

It is not clear how exactly Daoists picked up the Buddhist system of precepts, which specific sources they used, and what connections they established with the Buddhist community. There

---

[3] For a list in English, see Groner 1984, 216; Keown 1992, 30. The precepts are found in many Chinese Buddhist texts, beginning with the fifth century, but earlier versions, based on the *Āgamas*, appear even in third-century texts. For a discussion, see Ōno 1954, 370-86; Tsuchihashi 1957; 1980, 131-52. A general overview of the development of Buddhist precepts in China is found in Tsuchihashi 1956; 1980, 214-35.

[4] The ten evils are those of body: killing, stealing, licentiousness; those of speech: lying, malicious speech, double-tongued speech, fancy language; and those of mind: greed or covetousness, violence or anger, and wrong views. For a list and discussion, see Demiéville 1929, 1:20-21; Ōno 1954, 378.

[5] For an English rendition, see Cleary 1984. See also Cook 1977. On its history, see Gomez 1993. For its precepts, see Tsuchihashi 1980, 179-92. For a list of related Chinese texts, see Ōno 1954, 136-39.

[6] The *Brahma Net Sūtra* lists ten stages, ten diamond qualities, ten nurturing tendencies, and ten initial attitudes. See DeGroot 1969, 17-19; Ōno 1954, 183-94. Zhiyi has ten stages, ten powers, ten hindrances, ten aspects of suchness, ten characteristics of the diamond heart, ten universals, ten degrees of teaching, ten grades of faith, and many more. See Hurvitz 1962, 361-69. Tantric practice to the present day relies heavily on sets of ten. See Evans-Wentz 1983, 67-99.

[7] See Nakamura 1975, 1228. For English renditions and discussions, see Hurvitz 1962, 366-67; Suzuki 1968, 313-29; Cleary 1984, 695-811; Keown 1992, 130-32.

is strong evidence for the pervasiveness of the five precepts in the oral and lay Buddhist traditions throughout China, and a few rules in the *180 Precepts of Lord Lao* can be traced back to the *Pratimokṣa*, the oldest set of 250 rules for the Buddhist community (see Penny 1996). There is also some indication that Zhi Qian 支謙, translator of numerous texts in the third century (Tsukamoto and Hurvitz 1985, 145-51, 1139-42), had certain connections with the Ge family, home of both the alchemist Ge Hong and of Ge Chaofu, the founder of Numinous Treasure (Bokenkamp 1983, 466). Zhi Qian's *Sūtra on Original Karma* (*Benye jing* 本業經, T. 281) on the bodhisattva path seems to have had a certain impact on the *Scripture of Universal Salvation* (*Duren jing* 度人經, DZ 1), a central text of Numinous Treasure, as had his translation of the *Pure Land Sūtra* (*Sukhāvatīvyūha sūtra*, *Wuliang shou jing* 無量壽經, T. 360). His writings also contain a set of five precepts (T. 362, 12.311a), possibly creating some inspiration for Daoists (Bokenkamp 1983, 469-70; 1990, 126-27).

Beyond these specific connections, Buddhist and Daoists in general followed the same basic doctrines and observed highly similar practices, often mixing them together. Several images and stone steles show Lord Lao and the Buddha seated side by side with prayers to both Daoist and Buddhist deities attached. While Buddhist monastics and Daoist practitioners certainly recognized the differences between the doctrines and iconography of their teachings, for the majority of ordinary people such differences were not highly significant, and they tended to ignore or even intentionally obscure them (Liu 2003, 60). It is, therefore, not entirely surprising that Buddhist rules exerted a strong influence on Daoist practice, especially in the Numinous Treasure school of the early fifth century after translators rendered the major collections of the *Vinaya* and other major Mahāyāna texts into Chinese.[8]

THE TEN PRECEPTS IN DAOISM

Beginning with Numinous Treasure, there are numerous sets of ten precepts and items of goodness in Daoism (see Yoshioka 1961a; Kusuyama 1982). The list closest to the Buddhist model is found in the sixth-century *Scripture of Karmic Retribution*. A set of ten items of goodness, it consists of prohibitions against killing, stealing, sexual misconduct, greed, anger, and frivolity, as well as against lying, bad speech, double-tongued speech, and fancy language. The text, in accordance with dominant Numinous Treasure doctrine, specifies the karmic punishments in hell and rewards in paradise that await people who either violate or follow the precepts (4.2a-3a). Supplemented by an additional two precepts that prohibit lack of filial piety to the parents and

---

[8] The four *Vinaya* collections translated were:
   1. The "Ten Chapter Vinaya" of the Sarvastivadins (*Shisong lü* 十誦律), translated in 404-409 in Chang'an under the guidance of Kumārajīva.
   2. The "Four Part Vinaya" of the Dharmaguptas (*Sifen lü* 四分律), translated 410-12 in Chang'an by Buddhayasas from Kashmir.
   3. The "Mahāsaṇghika Vinaya" (*Mohe sengqi lü* 摩訶僧祇律), translated by Faxian 法賢 in 416-18.
   4. The "Five Part Vinaya" of the Mahīsāsakās (*Wufen lü* 無分律), translated by Faxian in 422-23.
      See Hirakawa 1960, 115-55; Nakamura 1964, 56-61; DeGroot 1969, 2-3; Foulk 1991; Yifa 2002, 5-8.
   For a translation of the Pali text, see Rhys-Davids and Oldenberg 1965.

loyalty to the ruler, the same list with details on karmic consequences also appears in the *Twelve Highest Precepts of Admonition*, a sixth-century development of Numinous Treasure rules.[9]

A similar set of ten rules called the "ten precepts" appears in the *Precepts against the Roots of Sin* (*Zuigen pinjie* 罪根品戒, DZ 457), a text of the early Numinous Treasure canon. This set prohibits jealousy, intoxication, debauchery, contempt, slander, greed, killing, contentiousness, and deception. It has only one admonition, which encourages followers to maintain an even and focused mind (1.6ab). The list is further supplemented by a set of ten evils avoided by obeying the precepts. They are killing, intoxication, greed, lustfulness, lack of kindness and filial piety, and also include several forms of devotional misbehavior, such as despising the teachers, reciting the scriptures carelessly or in an abbreviated form, raging in anger against the four ranks (monks, nuns, lay men and women), disrupting scriptural instructions, or failing to believe in karma and retribution (1.6b-7a).[10] The precepts claim to save people in all parts of the universe, bringing them enough merit to be reborn in the heavens—not only by themselves but together with their ancestors of seven generations.

Moving even further beyond the Buddhist model, the most frequently used set of ten precepts in medieval Daoism, called Ten Precepts in capitals to distinguish them from the many other lists, are first found in the *Scripture on Setting the Will on Wisdom* (*Zhihui dingzhi jing* 智慧定志經, DH 10; DZ 325), a work of the early Numinous Treasure corpus that can be dated to the first half of the fifth century. In the sixth century, these ten precepts are formulated in a text of their own, the *Scripture of the Ten Precepts* (*Shijie jing* 十戒經, DH 31, 32; DZ 459), which appears in numerous Dunhuang manuscripts and is frequently cited in medieval texts. The rules consist of the five precepts, plus five self-admonitions to act in harmony and with compassion. The latter are:

6. I will maintain harmony with my ancestors and family and never disregard my kin.
7. When I see someone do good, I will support him with joy and delight.
8. When I see someone unfortunate, I will support him with dignity to recover good fortune.
9. When someone comes to do me harm, I will not harbor thoughts of revenge.
10. As long as all beings have not attained the Dao, I will not expect to do so myself. (1ab)

Followers who take these Ten Precepts are held to support living beings in various situations of life and to avoid strife for personal salvation unless all beings have attained it. To bring this message home, they are accompanied by a set of fourteen principles of self-control (*chishen* 持身), also found in *Precepts against the Roots of Sin* (1.5a). They are personal resolutions that guide

---

[9] With some variations, the list is also found in the *Scripture of Great Offerings* (DZ 37, 26b-27a) and in the *Esoteric and Secret Collection of Perfection* (*Neibi zhenzang jing* 內秘真藏經, DZ 4, 6.6a-7a), a philosophical expansion of the *Scripture of Karmic Retribution* that probably dates from the seventh century. The *Great Offerings* list appears various in later materials, e.g., in WSBY 46.8ab; *Essentials for Pervading the Mystery of the Great Dao* (*Dadao tongxuan yao* 大道通玄要, DH 97); and *Essential Rules and Observances* (*Yaoxiu keyi* 要修科儀, DZ 463, 5.3ab).

[10] The complete set of these precepts and evils also appears in the *Scripture of Causation Through Former Actions* (*Benxing suyuan jing* 本行宿緣經, DZ 1114, 2b-3a), another ancient text of Numinous Treasure, and in the *Explanation of the Merit and Karma of the Eight Simplicities* (*Basu gongye jue* 八素功業訣, DZ 1321), a Highest Clarity apocryphon. A variant list of the ten evils, closer to the Buddhist list (see Demiéville 1929, 1:20), is found in *Jade Book of the Great Empyrean* (*Taixiao langshu* 太霄琅書, DZ 1352, 8.5a); *Highest Scriptural Precepts* (*Taishang jingjie* 太上經戒, DZ 787, 13a); and YJQQ 38.14a.

practitioners to behave graciously and with kindness in various social situations. For example: "When I speak with another's lord, I shall feel gracious toward his country;" "When I speak with another's father, I shall feel kind toward his son;" "When I speak with a stranger, I shall feel protective about his country's borders;" and "When I speak with a slave, I shall feel concerned about his affairs" (1b). The rules teach practitioners to be sympathetic and identify with the plights and loyalties of others in many different situations. They create a conscious awareness of the feelings and views of others, encouraging harmonious communities and an altruistic mind-set.

Lay practitioners could take the Ten Precepts in an ordination ceremony to receive the rank of Disciple of Pure Faith (*qingxin dizi* 清心弟子), an advanced status which came with a formal transmission of the *Daode jing* and certain related texts. The title is adopted from Buddhism and denotes a fully initiated yet still beginning Daoist who has spent some time as an "officer of the Dao" (*daoguan* 道官) but has not yet entered the higher levels of ordination (Kusuyama 1984; 1992, 114-35). To take this level of ordination was very common under the Tang, as numerous Dunhuang manuscripts document (see Schipper 1985; Benn 2000). The precepts were understood to guarantee eventual liberation from rebirth and ascension into Heaven. As the *Scripture of the Ten Precepts* says:

> Following these guidelines, you will never fall behind. Instead you will attain complete liberation of the five realms of suffering and the three bad rebirths. You will be protected by the heavens and supported by the myriad gods. Keep on performing the purgations and honor the precepts, and naturally you will go beyond the world. (2a)

Even more inward-focused and cited most commonly in medieval sources is yet another set, the so-called Ten Wisdom Precepts of Numinous Treasure. They appear first in the *Jade Instructions on the Texts Written in Red* (*Chishu yujue* 赤書玉訣, DZ 352), a commentary to Ge Chaofu's first Numinous Treasure scripture,[11] and are most prominent in the *Great Precepts of the Highest Ranks* (DZ 177), a major classic on Numinous Treasure cosmology and behavior (Yamada 2000, 239-40; Ōfuchi 1979a, 30-37).

Set in a Mahāyāna-style pattern, the latter text describes how the Heavenly Worthy transmits the precepts to the Lord of the Dao with the purpose that all living beings may realize the Dao and be free from the eight difficult conditions, never fall into the hells, and be reborn speedily on the human plane. For that, they should practice the Ten Wisdom Precepts. As the Ten Precepts, they contain the five precepts plus five more psychologically oriented guidelines. However, unlike the classic list, they add admonitions to every single precept and focus more strongly on the development of compassion. For example:

1. Let there be no evil or envy in your heart, and never give rise to dark thieving thoughts. Be reserved in speech and wary of transgressions; in your imaginings remain mindful of the divine law.
2. Maintain benevolence and do not kill, instead feel sympathy and support for the host of living beings. Be compassionate and loving, and widely rescue and benefit all.
3. Maintain chastity and be withdrawing and yielding, neither lascivious nor thieving. Always practice goodness and mindfulness, disregarding yourself to support other beings. . . .

---

[11] On the text, see Soymié 1977, 7; Bokenkamp 1983, 479; Ren and Zhong 1991, 266-67; Kleeman 1991, 172-73.

9. Do not create quarrels and confusion through your mouth and tongue or criticize and debate the four ranks. If you create blame and hatred among the celestial community this harms and diminishes your spirit and *qi*.

10. In all conduct and interactions be of even and unified mind. Be harmonious among people and reverent toward the gods, acting always to maintain this state. (2ab; Bokenkamp 1989, 18-19)

In addition, the text warns against passions and desires, bad and flowery language, intoxication, jealousy, and self-aggrandizement, as well as criticism and debate.

Like the classic set, the Ten Wisdom Precepts have a supplement. In this case it is a set of twelve dedications, called "desirable attitudes" or "things to follow" (*kezong* 可從; Kleeman 1991, 172). They encourage practitioners to develop strong intention and faith in the Dao, compassion for all beings, respect for the teachers, as well as a mind of goodness, rebirth in a sagely environment, proper purity, and never-tiring efforts for salvation. They begin:

1. Seeing the perfect scriptures and the orthodox divine law, I will open salvation for all. For this I will bring forth a strong intention for the Dao and in my mind pray that in later generations I may rise to be among the great sages.

2. I will constantly practice a compassionate mind and pray and be mindful that all beings equally get to see the divine law. May their salvation be wide and far and never have any hindrances or obstacles.

3. I will love and delight in the scriptural teaching, surveying and penetrating it deeply and widely. With my intention and will firm and clear, I will open education for all those in ignorance and darkness. (3a)

Unlike the admonitions described so far, these rules are less directed toward society in general but focus on protecting the lineage and promulgating the Daoist teaching. Practitioners vow to obey their teachers, have faith in the Dao, honor the scriptures, participate in the purgations, keep their bodies and minds pure, and "give rise to a mind of goodness, without depravity or falseness, free from jealousy and ill-will, evil and envy" (9a). The attainment of a harmonious society and universal mind that will eventually open the path to immortality is increasingly linked with obedience to the religious hierarchy and the performance of Daoist rituals. It is thus not surprising that the Ten Wisdom Precepts are recited frequently in a ritual context and form part of the Mud and Ashes purgation, the Golden Register purgation, and the rite of nocturnal annunciation.[12]

LATER LISTS

From the Tang dynasty onward, and particularly since the Song, lists of ten precepts have proliferated in the Daoist tradition. Using the Numinous Treasure rules as their basis, they serve ei-

---

[12] The ritual use of the precepts is documented in the *Observances for Lamps, Spells, and Vows* (DZ 524, 8a-9a), as well as in various sources cited in WSBY, including the *Scripture of the Great Precepts* (*Dajie jing* 大戒經, 35.6b-7b; 50. 3b-4a) and the *Scripture of the Golden Register* [*Purgation*] (*Jinlu jing* 金籙經, 48.5a-6a). In the following centuries, the Ten Wisdom Precepts appear as follows: in the eighth century, in Zhang Wanfu's *Observances for Ordination* (*Chujia chuandu yi* 出家傳度儀, DZ 1236), 8b-9a; *Essential Rules and Observances* 5.1ab; in the tenth century, in Du Guangting's 杜光庭 (850-933) *Observances of Precepts Transmission for the Golden Register* (*Jinlu shuojie yi* 金籙大齋說戒儀, DZ 486), 4b-5b; and in the eleventh century, in the YJQQ under the heading "Ten Precepts Observed to Practice Purgations and Pursue the Dao" (39.18a-19a)

ther as membership formalities for lay followers or to prepare them for participation in rituals. Three sets survive from the Tang.

First, from the seventh century there is the *Scripture of Jade Clarity* (*Yuqing jing* 玉清經, DH 72; DZ 1312). Revealed by the Heavenly Worthy to the Lord of the Dao and the host of perfected in the Heaven of Jade Clarity, it contains an integrated discussion of karma and retribution, and outlines the performance of purgations and activation of spells against demons (Ren and Zhong 1991, 1033-34). It also has a presentation of heterodox or foreign practices (Eskildsen 1998, 129), showing that despite their imitation of Buddhist models Daoists were also concerned with establishing a strong delimitation of their creed.

The text presents two major sets of precepts in a section entitled "Transmitting the Precepts" (1.33a-40b), which also contains details on how to perform audience rites to the Dao, enter the sacred area, and undergo purifications. All evil thoughts have to be eschewed, and practitioners are to take cleansing baths in facilities carefully separating men and women. Its ten precepts summarize guidelines for communal harmony, such as rules against offending one's parents, killing living beings, plotting against the government, debauching women, and exposing oneself to the Three Luminants (1.8b-9a).[13]

A separate list of fifteen rules prohibits committing the ten evils and five contrary behaviors. They include rules against killing, stealing, and intoxication as found in the five precepts together with warnings that closely resemble the *180 Precepts of Lord Lao*, which prohibit disobedience toward father and lord, exposure of nakedness, living in separation from one's kin, disregarding others, harming the poor and orphaned, cheating the old and sick, destroying nests and killing animals, trading for profit, getting involved with the military, and removing hair or other things from corpses on the battlefield (1.33a).

A second Tang-dynasty set appears in the *Ten Precepts of Initial Perfection* (*Chuzhen shijie wen* 初真十戒文, DZ 180), a text first mentioned in Zhang Wanfu's 張萬福 *Collected Precepts of the Three Caverns* (*Sandong zhongjie wen* 三洞眾戒文, DZ 178) and dated to around the year 700. It contains the classical five precepts together with warnings against disloyal and unfilial behavior, ruining others for gain, slandering religious worthies, interacting with impure folk, and speaking carelessly or frivolously. The rules are initial guidelines for those who have made the decision to dedicate themselves to the Dao, using both prohibitions and prescriptions. For example: "Do not speak or laugh lightly or carelessly, increasing agitation and denigrating perfection. Always maintain seriousness and speak humble words, making the Dao and its virtue your main concern." The set is of particular importance, because it later became foundational for Complete Perfection (Liu 1990, 133-36).

A list of ten items of goodness, formulated as instructions to be mindful and listed after the classic five precepts, appears in the *Record of Purgations and Precepts* (*Zhaijie lu* 齋戒籙, DZ 464, 2a), another eighth-century work which contains a concise summary of the major Daoist purgations (see Yoshioka 1967; Malek 1985). It too emphasizes the need to be filial and loyal, then encourages followers to be compassionate, forbearing, critical of evil, dedicated, nurturing, caring, and generally act in a selfless and devout manner. It specifies various concrete measures they hope

---

[13] The same precepts are also found in *Highest Scriptural Precepts* (*Taishang jingjie* 太上經戒, DZ 787, 1a-2b) and YJQQ 38.1a-2b. See Liu 1990; Yoshioka 1961a, 59-60.

to perform for the sake of all beings, such as planting fruit trees, establishing shelters and wells, creating prosperity, and furthering Daoist education. Used as a guideline toward the proper Daoist attitude, the rules focus more on the mindset of the believer than on specific devotional or communal actions.

Beginning with the Song dynasty, precepts appear mostly in the context of specific rituals where they serve to establish the attitude and purity necessary for efficacious success. The two earliest examples concern the salvation of the dead and form part of the *pudu* 普度 ritual of universal salvation (see Boltz 1996; Orzech 2002). One appears in the *Wondrous Precepts of Ninefold Perfection* (*Jiuzhen miaojie* 九真妙戒, DZ 181) as part of a ritual that activates talismans for salvation of beings from hell.

The text begins with a description of the Heavenly Worthy residing in the Palace of the Three Primes. He explains the realities of the universe to a host of deities, including the Lord of the Dao and Lord Lao. He opens the golden registers of life and death and shines a bright radiance through the cosmos and particularly the hells, of which a detailed description follows, then praises the good works of the Ten Worthies Who Save From Suffering (Jiuku tianzun 救苦天尊)— deities who first appeared in the seventh century and rose to prominence in the late Tang and Song dynasties (see Yūsa 1989).

Next, the Northern Emperor (Beidi 北帝), the ruler of the realm of the dead at Fengdu 酆都 (see Mollier 1997), asks a question about rules to aid people in salvation from hell. In response, the Heavenly Worthy gives the "Nine Precepts of Wondrous Perfection," which include the basic rules against killing, stealing, lying, and lasciviousness together with three injunctions against anger, pride, and lack of resolution also found in the Buddhist ten items of goodness, plus two rules encouraging loyalty and filial piety (5a-6a) (see Kleeman 1991, 177; Ren and Zhong 1991, 133). Some rules are not merely prohibitions but come with positive admonitions. For example:

4. Do not engage in lasciviousness but behave properly in relation to all beings.
5. Do not steal but follow righteousness and give of yourself.

The same precepts also play a role in the school of the Heavenly Heart (Tianxin 天心), where they are listed in the *Great Methods of the Jade Hall* (*Yutang dafa* 玉堂大法, DZ 220, 20.10b-11a), dated to 1158 (see Boltz 1987, 36-37). As in the *Wondrous Precepts of Ninefold Perfection*, they are essential for the activation of efficacious talismans to liberate people from hell. But they are also useful to prevent disasters, to dissolve the roots of evil, to get rid of the Three Deathbringers, to control the unruly material souls, and to avoid all danger and disease, thus aiding the ascent to perfection (Yoshioka 1961a, 63-65).

Another set of precepts administered to the dead in a ritual of universal salvation that is still performed today (Ōfuchi 1983, 418-19; Saso 1975, 14.4012-14; Maruyama 2002) appears in Jin Yunzhong's 金允中 *The Great Rites of Highest Clarity and Numinous Treasure* (*Shangqing lingbao dafa* 上清靈寶大法, DZ 1223, 44.11b-12b), dated to 1221-1223. First the sufferers are fed and relieved of their grievances, then they are urged to accept the ten precepts which will prevent them from doing any further harm to the living and thus stop their creation of bad karma. More specifically, the rules prohibit ghosts from creating havoc among the living in various ways, by moving about at odd hours, throwing sand and casting stones, and bringing pestilence and epidemics into the world. For example:

Do not leave and enter at odd hours, collide with the living, wantonly go among people, continuously create havoc, cause people to have strange dreams and imaginings, or upset the multitude of harmonies. Only pray that all spirits of darkness be easy at heart and receive salvation. (Boltz 1996, 211)

Ghosts must not occupy people's trees and flowers, burn down their homes and lodges, hunt for meat, or haunt the living through various deviant elements, such crows or magpies, foxes, curs, dogs, or rodents. There should be no harming of people's domestic animals, scaring horses into galloping off, or any other stirring up of misfortune or causing of sickness and terror among people. Instead, the ghosts should develop goodwill and compassion, "praying that all spirits of darkness be easy at heart and receive salvation."

Precepts for the living in preparation of ritual activity became dominant in compendia from the Yuan and Ming dynasties. For example, the *Great Rites of Universal Salvation* (*Duren dafa* 度人大法, DZ 219, 71.25b-26b), a Yuan-dynasty collection (Boltz 1987, 28-29), presents several lists of precepts and good attitudes to which practitioners swear in a ceremony of Numinous Treasure. They are written down in a formal document and submitted to the gods, binding the participant to good behavior and proper actions in the Dao. The rules involve several sets of ten:

-- ten pledges to avoid harmful tendencies, such as anger, greed, dissolution, bad company, resentment, unseemly haste, disturbance of or irreverence toward sacred writings, and other acts that might anger the gods;

-- ten positive pursuits, such as sympathy for the old, compassion for the poor, succor for the spirits of the dead, respect for all beings, the recitation of scriptures, the holding of purgations, and generally the "release and redemption of all living creatures;"

-- ten prayers, expressing the desire to be strong in determination; to transcend death; to gain awareness of the body; to support the salvation of all beings; to join perfection; and to aid in the establishment of Great Peace, the awakening of all beings, and the immortality and liberation of their ancestors.

A simpler set, reminiscent of the *Ten Precepts of Initial Perfection*, is found in *A Corpus of Daoist Ritual* (*Daofa huiyuan* 道法會元, DZ 1220, 154.5ab), a major ritual compendium of the fourteenth century (see Loon 1979; Boltz 1987, 47-49). Like the earlier set, the rules begin with an emphasis on filial piety and loyalty and from there move on to prohibit lasciviousness, greed, and intoxication. In addition, they also admonish practitioners not to get involved in worldly litigation or to boast that they have reached perfection. Followers are not to be lax in their practice, to compromise their virtue, or to exert any sort of negative influence on their surroundings.

A yet different version of the ten precepts occurs in the *Great Complete Collection of Rules and Models for Daoist Followers* (*Daomen kefan da quanji* 道門科範大全集, DZ 1225) from the fifteenth century (Ren and Zhong 1991, 966-67). Here the ten precepts are used in rituals to activate the power of the phase fire and the Northern Dipper with the purpose of ensuring long life, prosperity, and good fortune. According to the accompanying description, the officiant presents a memorial extolling the power of the deities and asking for their protection. He then asks the participants to approach the altar and reads the precepts to them. They begin with: "Do not upset or disturb your body and spirit (equanimity)." Following this, the rules demand the abstention from attitudes like pride, contempt, slander, impurity, lasciviousness, and laxity; they admonish followers to cultivate reverence, faith, respect, purity, self-control, steadfastness, diligence, truthfulness, and modesty. Once read, the priests asks the participants whether they are able and willing to uphold these rules. The participants answer: "We shall uphold [them]." Following this, they are promised full support by the Four Heavenly Kings and are encouraged to perform rites at regular intervals and remain mindful of the Dao (30.4a-5a; 54.4a-6a).[14]

In a slightly different application, there is also a set of ten precepts used as an *aide-memoire* for followers of the school of Pure Brightness, Loyalty, and Filial Piety (Jingming zhong- xiao dao 淨明忠孝道), a Southern Song group that integrated Confucian doctrine and morality into Daoist practice (see Boltz 1987, 70-78; Akizuki 1978). Its *Rites of the Flying Celestials of Pure Brightness* (*Jingming feixian fa* 淨明飛仙法, DZ 563) specifies ten rules to remember major aspects of the teaching, such as the "eight ultimates" (loyalty, filial piety, modesty, diligence, openness, generosity, forgiveness, forbearance); the daily record or ledger of merit and demerit to be kept by all members; adjustment and refinement, i.e., matching activities to the patterns of yin and yang and purifying bodily energies; and economy and frugality, which means to limit oneself to keeping only the essential necessities for daily living. The school also encourages members to care for the sick and the poor, to honor teachers and fellow followers, to recite the scriptures, and to cultivate inner nature and destiny. The program expressed in the shorthand of the ten precepts thus covers a wide range of Daoist activities integrated with socially responsible living in the world.

Not only for ritual and membership purposes, moral rules in Song Daoism were also essential for the preparation of inner alchemical transformation. Thus, the *Wondrous Scripture of Exterior Daily Practice* (*Wai riyong miaojing* 外日用妙經, DZ 645) lists forty-seven rules of conduct which allow the dissolution of desires necessary before beginning the great interior work—described in its partner text on "Interior Daily Practice" (DZ 646).

Moving in concentric circles, the text ranges from "respect for Heaven and Earth" and the sun and the moon to "fear of the law of the land," obedience to "father and mother," and the correct behavior toward superiors and inferiors. Adepts are to honor social relations and obey state laws, to do good and eschew evil, to stay away from the debauched and learn from the perfected. They are to give up luxury, to devote themselves to perfection, to befriend the wise, and to keep away from sounds and sights. "Always battle your ego and never give in to jealousy and hate" (1b). The text combines Daoist cosmological concerns and renunciation with the traditional Confucian vision, in which human behavior is determined largely in the context of obligation to family and society (see Kohn 2000b).

A similar tendency is also found in two sets of ten admonitions by early masters of Complete Perfection (see Komjathy forthcoming). Ma Danyang's 馬丹陽 (1123-1183) set appears in the thirteenth-century collection *Recorded Sayings of the Perfected Immortals* (*Zhenxian yulu* 真仙語錄, DZ 1256; Boltz 1987, 169). It warns against worldly involvement and encourages humility, calmness, perseverance, and allegiance to the teaching (2.18b). The second set is associated with Liu Chuxuan 劉處玄 (1147-1203) and appears in the *Collection of Immortal Joy* (*Xianle ji* 仙樂集, DZ 1141; JY 205; Boltz 1987, 162-63). It insists that followers should "not offend the laws of the country," but should instead give up all sensory and emotional entanglements with the world. They

---

[14] The precepts are the same in both chapters of the text, but in *juan* 54 they are accompanied by more extensive explanations and appear in a slightly different order: 2-3-4-5-6-10-8-7-9-1. In each case, the precept is followed by the virtue to be developed through its observation.

should live simply, joined by fellow practitioners, and strive to be humble and serve all beings, "lessening themselves and benefiting others" (1.8b-9b).

The ten precepts in Daoism combine admonitions to behave with proper virtue as already spelled out among the early Celestial Masters with Mahāyāna sets of ten precepts and items of goodness. They represent a different stage of ethical development in that they go beyond the control of concrete behavior and social context, focusing instead more on the internal mind-set of practitioners and their attitude toward other beings. They are distinct in their formulation in that they commonly combine prohibitions with admonitions and in some cases even personal dedications and resolutions. But even the sets that are phrased purely as prohibitions are sometimes called "ten items of goodness," indicating that the focus is not on abstention or avoidance but on the inner unfolding of goodness.

Taking these different admonitions together, it becomes clear that altruistic morality and consideration for others are key factors in the adept's growth toward Daoist salvation. This level of Daoist ethics promotes compassion, empathy, and kindness. It encourages a mind set that places followers into the shoes of others and makes them look at reality from a different perspective. Built on the restraint of bad behavior in the behavioral prohibitions, their goal is to raise awareness to a wider social and eventually cosmic level. Admonitions help practitioners to come out of their limited individual and selfish thinking and grow into a mind that approaches the Dao. They express ways of interacting and thinking both within the Daoist community and the larger society and form the basis for further, even more specific rules that govern Daoist organizations and encourage forms of pious behavior in support of masters, scriptures, and institutions.

CHAPTER FIVE

Forms of Community

Building on clear prohibitions and sets of admonitions to do good, Daoist communities created rules and prescriptions that regulated their organizations. The earliest records surviving are fragments from the *Scripture of Great Peace*, which was conceived in the second century C.E., lost after the Yellow Turban rebellion in 184, and reconstituted in the sixth century. It describes nine categories of human beings and lists various sins and crimes against the community together with descriptions of the ideal state and methods for its achievement. Among the early Celestial Masters, the *180 Precepts of Lord Lao* details instructions on social interaction, correct use of speech and writing, ways to preserve and protect the environment, and how to relate to outsiders. The community emerges as a close-knit joining of people who work and live together and carefully preserve their special status both within and without. Each member had to contribute consciously to the success of the enterprise, ensuring the harmony and peace of the entire organization in the ordinary acts of day-to-day life.

Succeeding Celestial Masters communities also emphasized the importance of personal actions in the creation of communal harmony. The northern Celestial Masters of the fifth century outline their vision in works associated with Kou Qianzhi and his northern theocracy, while their sixth-century southern counterparts specify the rights and duties of priests in texts like the *Statutes of Mystery Metropolis*. In addition to remonstrating with followers to obey the rules, these texts allow some insight into the division of ranks, ordination procedures for priests, and enhanced responsibility and duties of the latter.

A similar division into lay followers, ordained priests, and monastics also applied in the other major schools of medieval Daoism and the integrated organization of the religion in the Tang dynasty. Lay followers, in several sets of admonitions and items of goodness, were to give donations, to honor the masters, to recite the scriptures, to attend purgation ceremonies, to serve the ruler, and to propagate their families and fortunes. Leaders, on the other hand, underwent extensive ordination procedures and were held to higher standards of behavior. Joined together in the great enterprise of creating a harmonious community of the Dao on earth, they equally strove to create states of joy and peace.

Looking at the different forms of community and their various organizational rules, it becomes clear that much of the early millenarian patterns, with their clear hierarchy of administrators, lists of precepts, social boundaries, and specific duties survived into the lay organizations and even in monastic institutions. Lay groups continued some closed struc-tures and internal patterns, yet they were also more open to new practices and varied behavioral guidelines. Their priests, moreover, came to be trained in monastic institutions, which served as specialized and segregated centers of Daoist power. Priests underwent ordinations which retained the patterns of early initiations as well as the formalities of blood covenants from Chinese antiquity. Daoist communities, however different at first glance, show a remarkable continuity through the ages.

EARLY COMMUNITIES

The earliest surviving records on Daoist community organization are found in the *Scripture of Great Peace*, parts of which go back to the second century. According to this, in high antiquity human society used to be perfectly balanced as each individual had the place that suited him and fulfilled his tasks according to his capacities (Kaltenmark 1979, 21). Since then, a steady decline occurred, and morals became increasingly depraved, leading to complex government structures, irregular worship, and manifold sins. The Great Peace movement saw this world going further into decline and meeting its eventual destruction, and prepared its members for the new world to come by increasing their moral and energetic purity and creating a smoothly functioning community.

To this end, they strongly prohibited four pernicious kinds of conduct: lack of filial piety, failure to procreate, eating manure and urine, and begging (Kaltenmark 1979, 35). Six sins in two sets, moreover, characterized their social awareness: personal accumulation of Dao, virtue, and wealth, as well as failure to practice Dao, virtue, and work. In each case, the text insists that members had to share their knowledge, material goods, talents, and strength with others, thereby keeping the circulation of *qi* going on all levels of society and creating cosmic harmony (Wang 1979, 241-42; Kaltenmark 1979, 34). The ultimate vision of the text consists of "utmost pervasion" (*dongji* 洞極), a state when everything, "both the good and the bad, is in perfect communication and union with the yin and yang of Heaven and Earth in such a way that there is response throughout the universe and each being obtains his proper place" (Kaltenmark 1979, 25).

There were, moreover, nine different kinds of human beings, each responsible for a certain portion of the cosmic enterprise: formless spirit men ruling primordial *qi*, great spirit men governing Heaven, perfected beings in charge of Earth, immortals supervising the four seasons, men of the Great Dao managing the five phases, sages in charge of yin and yang, ordinary people who govern the cultivated plants, and slaves who manage merchandise and trade (Wang 1979, 222; Kaltenmark 1979, 31). Each type had to maintain the *qi* at to utmost harmony, so that it flowed smoothly and created prosperity, long life, and good fortune. In concrete terms this meant that members participated in purgations and the taking of precepts. They were advised to eat moderately, abstain from alcohol, undergo medical healing, harmonize their minds with music, and practice meditations such as concentration on the One (Kaltenmark 1979, 41-44). Priests submitted regular reports to Heaven, indicating the state of the community in its creation of an ideal life on earth.

Further concrete guidelines on behavior in the early communities are found among the early Celestial Masters. Their *180 Precepts of Lord Lao* contains rules regarding many different areas of life and experience, apparently in no specific order or arrangement. Various attempts have been made to classify them. For example, Kristofer Schipper establishes fourteen categories, including rules on diet, sexual behavior, and personal conduct; precepts that demand respect for seniors, juniors, servants, slaves, animals, nature, and personal possessions; prohibitions regarding ritual activities; and rules for interaction with lay followers, ordinary people, and the state (2001, 84-85).[1]

As is obvious from this classification, the rules cover all contingencies of community life, from interaction among members through the consumption and treatment of food to personal integrity and spiritual propriety. They prohibit abortion and musical entertainment, the forming of cliques and political parties, ownership of slaves and cruelty to animals. They also pay close attention to personal and environmental interaction. For example, members must not spy into the affairs of others, use fancy or ambiguous language, scold others in anger, discuss the faults of others, criticize the teachers, claim great merit and virtue, or use words in other unseemly ways.

They are also held to honor the natural environment, to avoid cutting trees, picking flowers, startling birds and beasts, disturbing worms and insects, and burning fields or forests. They should generally live in a low-impact manner, be conservative in their use of food and drink, keep the roads and wells free from obstructions, and abstain from throwing harmful substances into public supplies of water and food. Their building of houses, graves, and roads should match the *qi* of the natural surroundings, and they should respect natural marshes and waterways, only minimally interfering with the topography of the land. In terms of outsiders, they are to maintain their separate identity as people of the Dao, to avoid all contact with worldly officials and members of the military, to limit their travels to the absolutely necessary, and to abstain from serving in ceremonial or astrological functions for people of the world.

Taken together, the rules in the *180 Precepts of Lord Lao* give a thorough outline of what is unacceptable Daoist behavior in order to raise social awareness and enhance group cohesion. The text clearly reflects the concerns of an agricultural community of people who need to preserve and manage the land to their best advantage and who live closely together, joined in the mutual enterprise of creating harmony in a difficult world. The text also conveys a strong feeling of opposition against outsiders or common people, with whom contact was to be limited and who must never be made partial to texts and in-group secrets. The rules thus served both to create a harmonious life within the Celestial Masters and to protect their identity by delimiting their special nature against all other organizations and especially against the lay population of so-called demon-worshipers.

Again, there is a central concern with *qi* or cosmic energy, which not only keeps individual life together but also determines the social network and the interaction patterns with Heaven and Earth. Essential on all levels—nature, state, and family—*qi* must never be lost but always be guarded, preserved, strengthened, and cultivated. Because each level depends on the other, moreover, there is a basic need of harmony in each; failure of harmony on one level leads to disruptions on another. The community rules of the *180 Precepts* emphasize the creation and maintenance of harmony and good *qi* on all levels of life, making it clear that nobody ever stands alone but that all life is always embedded in a multitude of networks and energetic constellations which need to be nurtured to the utmost. Moral action in this context becomes the creation

---

[1] The leaders of Orthodox Daoism of America also list the *180 Precepts* in "Part Three" of *The Blue Book* and divide them into eight categories (O.D.A. 1998). Heinrich Hackmann, on the basis of the 180 precepts as contained in the *Precepts of Medium Ultimate* has seven categories with subdivisions (1931, 46-48).

and continuation of the most essential, fundamental web of life, the proper way of relating to everything around one— whether human or nonhuman, animate or inanimate.

LATER CELESTIAL MASTERS

A similar emphasis on the harmonious interaction of beings and different levels of existence is found in the community rules associated with Kou Qianzhi and the theocracy of the northern Celestial Masters. Traditional sources, such as the *History of the Northern Wei* (*Weishu* 魏書, ch. 114; see Ware 1933), describe how Lord Lao ordered Kou "to persuade men and women to erect altars and shrines where they could worship morning and evening" (Liu 2001, 54). Through regular devotions followers were to open the channels of communication with the gods and spirits and to learn the methods of immortality (Yang 1956, 48).

The texts of Kou's revelation detail these instructions further. They originally consisted of twenty *juan*, but survive only in fragments: a firmly identified part consisting of thirty-six rules on initiations, purgations, and proper priestly behavior in the *New Code* (*Laojun yinsong jiejing* 老君音誦誡經, DZ 785; see Yang 1956; Tang and Tang 1961) and a more tentatively ascribed doctrinal discussion of community conduct in the *Precepts and Observances Taught by the Celestial Master* (*Tianshi jiao jieke jing* 天師教戒科經, DZ 789).

The latter provides a doctrinal overview of medieval Daoist worldview and social expectations. It can be divided into twelve sections that discuss the basic state of harmony, the effects of good and bad actions, the five precepts, as well as ways to serve the Dao and extend life. In all cases, the social context is of utmost importance. Practitioners are to maintain harmony with Heaven and Earth, the state, and the family, and perform good actions that involve all these entities— beginning with veneration of the Dao and moving on to service of masters, parents, and political authorities. The Dao manifests itself in the political sphere of imperial China, so that the virtues and social behaviors associated with political correctness directly relate to religious endeavors.

Evils and sins are tendencies that involve social violations—aggression, sensuality, intoxication, and greed—which lead to power mongering, deception, favoritism, bribery, dependence, and the bartering of official positions (5a). Punished supernaturally by the celestial administration as they would be on earth by imperial officials (3a), they ultimately originate in the human mind, which is why the five precepts are directed at mind-control through the avoidance of licentious ideas, anger and violence, poisonous thoughts, intoxication, and greed (3b-4b). "You must control your will for extended periods; you must be firm in your strong efforts; you must concentrate your thoughts," the text says (10a).

Models for good behavior, moreover, are the wise (*xianzhe* 賢者) who realize the deeper connection of all things and the importance of the Dao.

> For the wise even in poverty and humility there is no need to forcefully pursue wealth and honor. They understand that this would only labor their essence and thinking and cause their self-containment to end. They know that pride and contempt confuse the will, causing people to forego long life. (6a)

> The wise guard the Dao with an upright mind and never allow themselves to be lazy or remiss. Rather, they are diligent and solid, showing the ignorant how to control themselves and to serve [the Dao] correctly. They cultivate the great Dao with diligence, knowing that it is utterly venerable and lofty, with none higher. (7b)

Teaching ordinary or "ignorant" people how to live in harmony with the Dao through being in line with family, state, and cosmic patterns, the wise are the leaders of the new state-wide Daoist community. They encourage all followers, known as "comrades" (*tongzhi* 同志), "fellow followers" (*tongfa* 同法), "fellow congregants" (*tongyi* 同義), or "people of the Dao" (*daoren* 道人), to come together in worship, to chant the scriptures and precepts, to attend meetings in the lodge of tranquility (*jingshe* 静舍), and to join the assemblies in the community hall (*tang* 堂) (8b). Unlike the "prayers and sacrifices of wine and meat to demons and spirits" undertaken by ordinary people, which are essentially ineffective, this will lead to peace and prosperity in family and society, as well as to personal longevity and good fortune (9a).

The *Precepts and Observances* provides an outline of the basic worldview and concerns of early medieval Daoists. It is somewhat exceptional since it does not use Buddhist concepts or terms and does not mention the confession rituals or festivals of the Three Primes central among the earlier Celestial Masters. Nor does the text refer to libationers, household registers, or kitchen feasts. However, this shortcoming is more than made up for in the *New Code*, where they form the central concern.[2]

The *New Code* consists of thirty-six rules that each end with the ritual formula: "Be very clear and careful about them [the precepts], honor and practice them in accordance with the statutes and ordinances," an adaptation of the traditional Celestial Masters spell "Swiftly, swiftly, in accordance with the statutes and ordinances." *New Code* rules begin with conditions for membership in the ranks of the Dao and ordination procedures (nos. 1-3), recount Kou's original revelation and place it in the Celestial Masters' history (nos. 4-5), and outline the evils of the time in terms of political and social disharmony, closely echoing the *Precepts and Observances* and using certain similar expressions (no. 6).

Following this, the rules become more concrete, specifying libationers' methods of offerings, community banquets, and assemblies (nos. 7-14), providing guidance for relating to official authority (nos. 15-17), and giving details on how to present petitions (nos. 18-20, 26). The text concludes with a series of specific rules on how libationers are to move about in public; to enter and leave the oratory; to interact with slaves, women, and the sick; to relate to ancestors and other spiritual figures; and are to be buried. Some of these derive from the Buddhist *Vinaya*, imitating the behavior of monks in public and in relation to women and other beings.[3]

Unlike the *180 Precepts of Lord Lao* and the *Precepts and Observances*, the *New Code* does not contain moral injunctions and community regulations, but instead provides a glimpse of the ritual concerns and specific organizational patterns of the theocracy. For example,

> Lord Lao said: If among the people of the Dao there is sickness or illness, let it be announced to every home. The master shall first command the people to light the incense fire. Then with the master in the oratory, the people on the outside should face west with their hair unbound, knock their heads to the ground, and confess and unburden all their sins and transgressions. The master shall command them to tell all—nothing is to be hidden or concealed—and to beg for clemency and pardon. . . . (16a)

---

[2] The *New Code* is reprinted with annotation in Yang 1956, 38-54. For discussions, see Kobayashi 1990; Mather 1979; Ren and Zhong 1991, 565; Kleeman 1991, 178; Kohn 1998a, 93-94; 2000a, 290.

[3] Especially rule no. 21 (on walking about in public) is clearly adapted from the *Vinaya* (T. 721, 17.348c). See Mather 1979, 114; Yang 1956, 50.

The text also contains the earliest descriptions of a ceremony attached to the transmission of Daoist scriptures, spelling out the rudiments of Daoist ordination. It says:

> Officers of the Dao and register disciples, when they first receive the precepts and statutes, should perform eight bows to the scripture of the precepts, then stand up straight before the text. Whether master or friend, hold the scripture and make eight obeisances, then recite it to the proper melody. The recipients then prostrate themselves and recite the scripture [mentally] in their intention, scroll by scroll. Thereafter they formally request it and give eight more bows. If there is someone who cannot recite it to the melody, he or she should just plainly recite it, and that is all. (1a)

This rite seems to involve the presence of a group of masters and recipients, formal bows and obeisances, and the ritual chanting of the precepts as presented in the scripture. The precepts are at the center of the ceremony, and the text explains that they "must always be venerated and treated with great diligence" and should not be transmitted except with the prescribed methods (1a).

Some additional details are described in the following:

> Officers of the Dao and register disciples, when copying the scriptures, precepts, and statutes, must never omit, misspell, add, or alter anything, not even one single character. If in drafting and writing copies of the precepts, they fail to state the proper scroll heading on the second or third page, then the rules and statutes are not complete, and great disasters will befall their bodies. These rules and precepts of mine naturally have officials that supervise and manage them; they follow the scripture and its precepts closely and keep inspecting how it is being treated. Therefore, be very clear and careful about them, honor and practice them in accordance with the statutes and ordinances. (1b; Kohn 2003b, 385)

This shows that the text of the precepts, once received in a formal ceremony, had to be copied by adepts and was protected by a series of deities assigned to serve as guardians. The written word was essential, and the exact text had to be preserved in order to avoid punishment by the resident gods and cosmic powers. The belief expressed here reflects the emphasis placed in Daoism on the written word (see Robinet 1993) and indicates the medieval understanding that all ritual objects had to be treated very carefully since they were guarded by special deities.[4]

Following the theocracy, ritual rules of similar detail have survived in the southern work *Statutes of Mystery Metropolis* from the sixth century.[5] It begins with thirteen desirable states such as emptiness, nonbeing, purity, and tranquility that will lead to perfection. Then it lists forms of good and bad fortune accumulated through various numbers of good or evil deeds. Following

---

[4] A similar ceremony of transmission is also described in the preface to the *180 Precepts of Lord Lao*, a later addition to the collection that was recovered from Dunhuang (DH 78). Adepts purify themselves by bathing, abstention from the five strong vegetables, and changing into fresh clothing. Bowing to their master, they receive the rules by reciting them three times and vowing to observe them. When the transmission is over, adepts obtain the text of the precepts and make one copy for personal use (Maeda 1985; also *Essential Rules and Observances* 5.14a-19a).

[5] Ed. DZ 188; trl. in the "Supplement." A lay-centered text of rules for priests, the text is cited in the seventh century in the monastic manual *Rules and Precepts for Worshiping the Dao*, the Daoist encyclopedia *A Bag of Pearls from the Three Caverns* (*Sandong zhunang* 三洞珠囊, DZ 1139), and the Buddhist polemic *In Defense of What Is Right* (*Bianzheng lun* 辯正論, T. 2110, 52.489c-550c) by Shi Falin 釋法琳 (dat. 622). Thereafter the text is mentioned in the ritual compendium *Essential Rules and Observances* of the eighth and the YJQQ of the eleventh centuries. For discussions, see Kobayashi 1990, 206-7; Ren and Zhong 1991, 137-38; Robinet 1984, 2:280; Nickerson 2000, 263-64.

this, the text presents twelve rules on concrete ritual practices, such as the visualization of the gods, the chanting of scriptures, the eating of sacrificial food, as well as the ritual schedule and attitudes toward teachers and family. The section also has a list of undesirable attitudes of a deceiving nature, such as taking evil for good, crooked for straight, or pure for turbid. Each statute, moreover, is associated with a particular punishment, such as the subtraction of 400 days or five years from the life expectancy.

Next come one hundred entries focusing on the idea of sickness and healing. They begin by mentioning the celestial administration, specifying that the Director of Transgressions (Siguo 司過) reports all misdeeds while the Director of Fates shortens life. Virtue is defined as the physician of the human condition, and religious practice as the medicine. All good deeds and devotional attitudes then listed are described as one potent remedy each, while all evil actions are defined as sicknesses. In addition, the latter are also responsible for physical diseases, which the supernatural agencies send down as punishments.

The last two sections are closest to the *New Code* (Yang 1956, 25-28). Section five has twenty-seven items of communal and ritual import, specifying subtractions from the life expectancy for various improper actions, such as not following the inheritance procedures when taking over community leadership from one's father; squabbling over the transmission after the death of a master; failure to attend assemblies or pay the right amount of tax; seeking fast promotion; making mistakes in setting out banquets; creating disturbances during the Three Assemblies; failure to worship properly, at the right times, or in a state of uncleanliness; and so on. For example:

> Any leader among the male and female officers should arrange for the offerings for the kitchen-feasts in rice and other taxes to be spread out properly on the days of the Three Assemblies. The host of officers should organize the hundred families to make offerings at the Assemblies. Anyone not doing this in harmony with the rule books and in contradiction to the divine law will be punished by a one-period reduction in reckoning. (13a)

The text concludes with sixteen items that focus on the presentation of ritual petitions in the communal worship hall. It describes how to enter the sacred space on the right day and at the right hour, properly purified and attired in ritual vestments. Officials should perform the rites for the sake of the entire community and not for personal gain. In each case, failure to comply with a given statute results in a demotion in rank by one or two levels, a reduction of life expectancy, or a visitation by sickness for a given number of days. For example:

> When entering a parish hall to present a petition, in all cases be of upright posture and quickened gait, take your place on the right and left according to rank and exhibit seriousness and devotion. Do not allow men and women to intermingle or stand in the wrong place. Do not let them look around idly, chatter noisily, push and shove, or advance and retreat either too quickly or too slowly. Offenders in positions of authority will be demoted by one rank. If they are not demoted, they will be fined three ounces of jade and punished by a two-period reduction in reckoning. (19b)

The later Celestial Masters thus follow the early movments in both their general doctrine and specific rules. They too emphasize the need for continuous harmony among family, society, and cosmos. However, their rules also have a distinct political dimension, extending the community concerns of the early groups to a larger entity but not changing them in principle. Where the early millenarians saw an opposition between their in-group and outsiders, protecting the secrets and practices of their followers, the leaders of the later Celestial Masters focused on society at large, distinguishing the wise from the ignorant, i.e., those who recognize the workings of the Dao and act accordingly from those who still worship with blood sacrifices and pursue wealth and honor. The rules provide more detail, the doctrines are formulated more extensively, but the fundamental tenet remains that the Dao governs the cosmos, society, and personal lives with perfection, and to take part in this perfection one has to act with moral goodness and ritual propriety. As the *qi* flows on all levels of life in purity and harmony, one will experience good fortune and long life—not only in oneself but also in the community.

LAY ACTIVITIES

Among the other Daoist schools of the same period, lay followers were held to demonstrate their allegiance to the Dao less by paying taxes and attending assemblies than by giving donations, sponsoring temples and monasteries, honoring the masters, and generally supporting a holy and beneficial lifestyle. Unlike the rules of the Celestial Masters who provided detailed instructions for community organization and the behavior of priests, the precepts in Numinous Treasure were directed mainly toward devout lay followers, who strove to transform their sensory experience into a perception of the Dao. The rules closely follow the Buddhist pattern, aiming at the realization of Dao-nature through the attainment of perfect wisdom and the development of good karmic merit, which in due course will lead to immortality and a celestial position. The precepts mirror Mahāyāna ideals and impose control on the senses and passions, while also demanding the development of compassion and the effort to save all beings.

An early set of ten items of goodness that describes the activities of Numinous Treasure followers and gives a sense of community cohesion is found in the *Precepts against the Roots of Sin* (1.4ab). It contains general instructions to reject death and protect life, to help the sick and poor, to serve the preceptors and sacred writings, to follow the cultivation and purgation schedule, and generally to maintain propriety, educate the ignorant and always follow the divine law. Doing so, practitioners attain good karma and gain the merit that can make them a flying celestial.

Another set of admonitions that specifies communal activities is the "Ten Admonitions to Do Good," found in the *Great Precepts of the Highest Rank* (8b-9b). These rules guide disciples to serve the preceptors and the Three Treasures, to carefully copy the scriptural writings, to support the building of facilities for the Dao, to aid the supply of incense and lamp oil, to serve ruler and parents, to practice meditation and purgations, to develop compassion and benevolence, and to give liberally to the Dao.[6] For example, the text says:

> The First Admonition: Always assist the preceptors in the veneration of the Three Treasures and presentation of offerings, so they can cause people in every generation to become full gentlemen, wise and filial and of superior ability. Glorious and noble, they will be lofty and born as sages among humankind, their families and followers illustrious. . . .

---

[6] These rules also appear in the *Precepts of the Highest Ranks* (*Shangpin jiejing* 上品戒經, DZ 454) 3a-4a; the *Great Precepts of Original Prayers* (*Benyuan dajie* 本願大戒, DZ 344) 9b-10b; and the *The Fifty-Eight Prayers of Great Clarity* (*Taiqing wushiba yuanwen* 太清五十八願文, DZ 187) 4a-5a. In various later collections, they are cited in WSBY 46.13a-14a, *Highest Scriptural Precepts* 11a-12a, *Essential Rules and Observances* 5.2ab, and YJQQ 38.11b-12b.

The Third Admonition: Always assist those who erect lodges for meditation and purgations, so they can cause people in every generation to be born in high and noble families, their bodies rising up the heavenly halls. They will nourish on spontaneity itself and always dwell in nonaction. . . .

The Fifth Admonition: Always assist the preceptors and wearers of religious garb, so they can cause people in every generation to be tall and elegant, wandering freely through the Middle Kingdom. They will never fall among the border tribes or barbarians, and both male and female will be upright and proper as they don the formal headgear and wear the ritual jade pendants from their belts. (8ab)

A similar set of admonitions, formulated more tersely and listed in a group of twenty-five, is also found in the *Scripture of Prohibitions and Precepts* (DH 34). Followers should observe the precepts, repent their sins, join the purgations, support the institution, and strive for the salvation of all. The text says:

Always greatly establish merit and virtue on behalf of the country's ruler and the kings among men, so their sage rule may flourish and be lofty without limits.

Always create fields of blessedness for the people in all-under-Heaven, the men and women of the hundred families.

Always strive on behalf of those in the three bad rebirths and five realms of suffering, indeed of all living beings, that they may leave behind all suffering and afflictions and complete the Dao of immortality. (l. 24-26)[7]

Lay followers were thus encouraged to serve the Three Treasures by propagating the teachings, giving offerings, and making donations. They should sponsor the copying of scriptures and venerate the holy texts, making sure they were not transmitted to the wrong people. Followers should honor and support the religious leaders and masters, providing them with vestments and ritual utensils and helping them when old and sick. They should provide for the erection and maintenance of lodges, halls, and monastic centers; give ample amounts of incense, lamp oil, and art supplies; and by supporting the poor and orphaned in their community set an example of compassionate and Dao-conscious living. As for their schedule, they were held to perform devotions at home twice a day and to commit themselves to observing special fast days or retreats.

These retreats or *zhai* 齋 were popular both in Chinese Buddhism and Daoism (see Soymié 1977; Tsuchihashi 1964). They occurred in groups of six, eight, or ten days per month, centered around the new and full moons. The six *zhai* days were the 1st, 8th, 14th, 15th, 28th, and 29th of every month. The eight *zhai* days added the 23rd and 24th, and the group of ten days, known as the "ten days of uprightness" (*shizhi* 十直), involved practice also on the 18th and 28th. Going back to the Indian Buddhist practice of bimonthly confession and chanting of precepts (see Prebish 1975; Yifa 2002), these fast days were used by lay followers to behave with increased purity and can be described as a form of "temporary renunciation" or retreat. Practitioners would take additional precepts and offer prayers to the deities, especially to the Great One, the Northern

---

[7] A similar list of twenty-four rules, formulated as prohibitions but also specifying concrete actions to be taken within the Daoist organization, is found in the *Twenty-four Precepts for Followers* (DZ 183). The first section of the *Precepts of the Three Primes* (DZ 452) echoes the same idea. The *Precepts of the Highest Lord Lao* describes daily activities for followers, including recitations while burning incense, the observance of several fast days each month, and some longer periods of more intense religious practice during the year. See Kohn 1994, 195-96.

Dipper, and other central cosmic administrators who inspected their earthly charges on those days (*Essential Rules and Observances*, DZ 463, 8.4a; see also Min 1990, 94).

Beyond this, practitioners attended several major annual festivals, such as those of the Three Primes on the fifteenth of the first, seventh, and tenth months, and those honoring the Eight Nodes (*bajie* 八節) at the beginnings and high points of the four seasons. In addition, large-scale purgations were also scheduled at special occasions, such as the Golden Register Purgation for cosmic and political harmony, the Yellow Register Purgation for universal salvation, the Purgation of the Luminous Perfected for learning and scholarly achievement, the Purgation of Spontaneity for internal self-cultivation, and the Purgation of Mud and Soot for the confession of sins and prevention of bad fortune (Yamada 2000, 248-50; Benn 2000, 319-20).

Confession rituals focused on the repentance of sins and pleaded with the celestial authorities for mercy and lenient treatment. Often enacted in dramatic detail, they had devotees tying themselves up and hanging themselves upside-down with tears streaming down their faces (Chappell forthcoming). Influenced by Buddhist practices (see Yifa 2002; Kuo 1994), these confessions also continued practices of the Celestial Masters and ancient rituals for the pacification of the dead.

For purposes of special devotion, lay Daoist followers moreover sponsored the creation of steles and sacred images, hoping to lure the spirits down for closer communication, to expiate sins, to demonstrate their faith, and to increase their dedication to the creed and their moral stamina in the face of worldly temptations (Liu 2001, 53; 2003, 55). These images could be exposed on mountain sides for greater efficacy or used in private shrines at home, where believers would make offerings, pay homage to the gods, and perform daily rites of refuge and offering (see Abe 1997; Bokenkamp 1997b; Kamitsuka 1998). Some devotees also donated statues and steles to religious temples and monasteries, where they would form part of a larger pantheon of Daoist deities, aiding the donors in the creation of greater merit and a closer connection to the divine (Liu 2001, 54).

All this activity required a healthy material cushion, and followers of Numinous Treasure were accordingly encouraged to expiate their sins, to pray for good fortune, to do well in business, to observe filial piety, and to have numerous offspring. They were to provide for the religious institution and serve the state to the best of their abilities, creating an integrated, morally upright, and just society through their efforts. In their prayers, finally, they were to include all beings, expressing their hope for universal salvation.

INTEGRATED ORDINATION

The leaders of these lay Daoists, then, were formally ordained priests who went to monastic institutions for their training and often remained among the celibate clergy, dedicating themselves to a life of the Dao. They began their career by undergoing an initial ordination to the rank of Disciple of Pure Faith through the transmission of the ten precepts as contained in the *Scripture of the Ten Precepts*.

As described in the *Rules and Precepts for Worshiping the Dao* (Kohn 2003c, 389-91; 2004, sect. 18),[8] candidates were carefully chosen and underwent extended periods of ritual and scriptural training under the guidance of an ordination master and with the active support of their families and community sponsors. As the time of ordination approached—determined through cosmic calculation and by imperial permission—the candidates went to a large teaching monastery for their ceremony. There they secluded themselves for purification, while the masters made sure the guarantors and officiants were ready and all materials were prepared correctly. As described further in the *Transmission Formalities of Scriptures and Precepts* (Chuanshou jingjie yi 傳授經戒儀, DZ 1238), usually a ceremony involved three masters—the Ordination Master (*dushi* 度師), the Registration Master (*jishi* 籍師), and the Scripture Master (*jingshi* 經師; see Benn 1991, 40)[9]—five to ten witnesses, and a group of officiating priests, divided according to their role as cantors, purgation overseers, incense attendants, lamp attendants, and scripture attendants.[10]

Not only the responsible officiants but also all material objects had to be in good order, including an ordination platform and the preparation of the scriptures and precepts to be handed over. Last-minute arrangements or temporary stop gaps were discouraged. For example:

> If the chosen date arrives and the time comes close but the scriptures and methods are not all ready, some masters have their ordinands receive blank sheets of paper or a roll of plain silk. This is an insult to the sacred scriptures and a fraud. (*Rules and Precepts for Worshiping the Dao*, in DH 39; Kohn 2004, sect. 20)

Once all was properly set, the festivities went on for several days. On the evening prior to the central rite, the officiant presented a memorial to the gods to announce the great ritual step to be taken (Schipper 1985, 132). The main event, then, began with the ordinands lining up in the courtyard before the altar platform. First,

> they face west to bid farewell to their parents and give thanks to their ancestors, bowing twelve times. Then they turn to face north and bow to the emperor four times. The reason for this is that, once they have donned the ritual vestments of the Heavenly Worthies, they will never again bow to parents or worldly rulers. Therefore, when anyone joins the Daoist community, he or she must first bid farewell and give thanks. (*Rules and Precepts* 6.9b)[11]

Thus the ordinands leave their old life behind, get ready to step into the otherworldly community of the Dao, and formally undergo separation from the ordinary world. They then enter the liminal phase of the rite and surrender to the Dao:

---

[8] An abbreviated description of these ordination procedures is also found in the *Rules and Observances for Students of the Dao* 1.20b-21a. For more on the "Disciple of Pure Faith," see Kusuyama 1984. The ordination ritual was common in the Tang. See Schipper 1985, 135-37.

[9] These masters were also called the Master of Orthodoxy, the Master Supervising the Ordination, and the Master Testifying to the Covenant. See *Transmission Formalities* 7a. A similar group of masters still preside over Orthodox Unity ordinations today. See Lai 2003, 422; Li 1993, 125-26; Kohn 2003b, 185.

[10] Lesser ceremonies might require only one of each, but more elaborate ordinations would have groups of them—five cantors, six overseers, seven incense, eight lamp, and nine scripture attendants, plus the three essential masters making a total of thirty-eight officiating priests. See *Transmission Formalities* 5b, 7a; Benn 1991, 40-41; Kohn 2003a, 185.

[11] This part of the rite closely echoes Buddhist ordination ceremonies. See Misra 1969; Prip-Møller 1967; Buswell 2000; Matsunaga and Matsunaga 1976; Loori 1998; Chen-Hua 1992.

The ordinands stand erect with their hands folded over their chests. Still facing north, they surrender to the Three Treasures, bowing three times to each. They say:

With all my heart I surrender my body to the Great Dao of the Highest Nonultimate.
With all my heart I surrender my spirit to the Venerable Scriptures in Thirty-Six Sections.
With all my heart I surrender my life to the Great Preceptors of the Mysterious Center. (*Rules and Precepts* 6.9b)

After the surrender, ordinands received the insignia of their new status: religious names, formal titles, vestments, and headdresses. As described in the *Transmission Formalities*, further necessities were provided later: hut, rope-bed, awnings, coverlet, dishes, book case, writing knife, ink, and so on (11b-12a). To show their new affiliation, ordinands also tied their hair into a topknot, unlike Buddhists who shaved theirs. Also unlike in Buddhism, where nuns had to observe many more rules than monks and were given a lower status, women in Daoism were treated equally and underwent the same ceremonies (Despeux and Kohn 2003, 120-21).

In exchange for their new status, ordinands made a solemn declaration to follow the Dao and to work to uphold it. This declaration involved the pledge of lavish gifts of gold, silk, and precious objects to the master and the institution, as well as the formal oath to follow the rules and to support the goals of the organization.[12] Following this, ordinands bowed to the masters and chanted a set of stanzas on the development of true wisdom, succeeded by taking refuge in the gods of the ten directions. Then they formally received the ten precepts and their related scriptures and ritual tokens.

These tokens usually consisted of various contracts, talismans, registers, ordinances, and methods. According to the *Scripture of Dignified Observances of Orthodox Unity* (*Zhengyi weiyi jing* 正一威儀經, DZ 791), they were essential in establishing the Daoist's status in the otherworld. Contracts, for example, were needed so that the officials of Heaven and Earth knew the ordinand's new rank. Talismans and registers served to make the divinities descend, to gain divine protection, and to ensure that the memorials would reach their proper destination. Ordinances ascertained that the Daoist could move freely through the mountains and rivers of the nine provinces, while ritual methods (spells, incantations, sacred gestures) helped to prevent demons and spirits from blocking roads or bringing sickness and harm (1ab). Much like the precepts but more focused and more concrete in their application, the tokens protected against disasters and dangers and ensured the Daoist's cosmic power (11a).

The transmission of scriptures, precepts, and tokens concluded the main part of the rite. Afterwards ordinands bowed once again to the masters and patriarchs and chanted the final "Hymn to the Precepts." It says:

Honoring the precepts without a moment's relapse,
For generations we create nothing but good karma.
With concentration we are mindful of the Great Vehicle,
And soon embody the perfection of the Dao.

---

[12] *Rules and Precepts* 6.9b-10a. A list of preferred pledge objects is also found in *Transmission Formalities* 10b. According to the *Essential Rules and Observances*, the pledge was divided into three parts: two tenths were given to the ordination master, two tenths went to poor hermits, and the remainder was given to the institution (1.7b-8a; Benn 1991, 37). For more details on medieval ordination procedures, see Benn 2000, 327-31.

(Rules and Precepts 6.10a-11a)

For three days after the ceremony, ordinands made copies of their scriptures, especially of precepts and ritual manuals, so that one set could remain in the institution for safekeeping and the other could be used in daily ritual.[13] No mistake was permissible, and every character and heading had to be done just perfectly. Once this was complete, the final part of the ordination took place. Ordinands donned their new vestments and performed a thanksgiving ceremony, "presenting offerings to the great sages, masters, and worthies of the various heavens" (6.11a), while the masters prepared a detailed record.

HIGHER RANKS

The ceremony just described provided the fundamental blueprint for all Daoist ordinations in the middle ages. It followed after a series of initiations into ranks of the Celestial Masters, now formally called Orthodox Unity (Zhengyi 正一), which included the register disciple, demon soldier, Dao official, and libationer. Each of these came with registers containing the names of protective spirit generals. Anyone holding registers of as many as 150 generals, as described in Lu Xiujing's *Abbreviated Rules for Daoist Followers* (*Daomen kelue* 道門科略, DZ 1127), had to be good, loyal, simple, careful, prudent, diligent, and utterly dedicated to the Dao, since he or she was part of the organization's vanguard (Nickerson 1996, 356; see Schippper 1985, 131-35).

From the initiate level, practitioners could move on to the rank of Disciple of Pure Faith, above which there were five further ordination ranks in medieval Daoism that each came with specific sets of rules:[14]

Rank	Precepts Texts
Spirit Cavern	*Sanhuang jing, Badi jing*
Mystery Ascension	*Shengxuan jing*
Mystery Cavern	*Shangpin dajie, Zuigen pinjie, Mingzhen ke, Sanyuan pinjie*
Perfection Cavern	*Guanshen dajie*
Three Caverns	all precepts

As ordinands attained the higher levels, the requirements became more intense, monastic status was essential, and ceremonies grew to greater levels of intricacy. The ordination of the two Tang princesses Gold-Immortal (Jinxian 金仙) and Jade-Perfected (Yuzhen 玉真) held in February 711 is a fine example of a Mystery Cavern ceremony. Described in Zhang Wanfu's *Synopsis of Transmission* (*Chuanshou lueshuo* 傳授略說, DZ 1241, 2.18a-21a; Benn 1991), it established Daoist status for the two daughters of Lady Dou, third consort of Emperor Ruizong (r. 710-712).

For their ordination into the rank of Mystery Cavern, a three-tiered altar, 3.5 meters high was set up in the Monastery of Refuge in Perfection (Guizhen guan 歸真觀) in the Inner Palace. Supported by golden pillars, it had ornate gates marked by purple and gold tablets and surrounded by blue-green silk cordons (Benn 1991, 22). Its tamped-earth floors were covered with brocade

---

[13] The personal copy would never leave the Daoist and would be buried with him or her eventually. See *Rules and Precepts* 5.3ab.

[14] This outline follows *Rules and Precepts for Worshiping the Dao* 5.4a-8a. A similar list of ranks is also found in *Rules and Precepts Regarding Ritual Vestments* (*Fafu kejie wen* 法服科戒文, DZ 788, 4b-5b). See Benn 1991, 72-98; 2000, 313-22.

cushions and intricate mats: its ramparts were lighted by seventeen types of lamps and four different kinds of candles, often giving forth special effects, such as "purple-flaming orchids" or "thousandfold moonbeams" (1991, 27-28). Each level had at least three tables: one for incense burners, made from jade or gold and burning aromatic woods, like aloeswood, frankincense, sandalwood, cloves, and camphor (1991, 29); another to be used as a lectern for the officiant's recitation of the memorial and the precepts; and a third on which the pledge offerings were placed. Each table, moreover, had a scarlet kerchief and a blue-green cover, seen as substitutes for smearing the lips with blood and cutting off a lock of hair in the sealing of the oaths—recovering the essence of ancient blood covenants (1991, 31; see Lewis 1990, 44; Kohn 2003c, 380-82).

More ornamentation was also present in the wrappers, cases, and bags used for the scriptures. They were all made from precious substances and bedecked with designs of celestial kings, immortals, mountains and rivers, clouds, dragons, phoenixes, and other sacred figures (Benn 1991, 31). The pledges—understood to appease the gods of the five directions and to ward off malign influences during the delicate transition—were extensive: 72 lengths of variegated silk net, 240 lengths of purple silk net, 480 lengths of coarse silk, 240 strings of cash, 200 ounces of gold, 25 lengths of five-colored brocade, 120 catties of incense, 500 ounces of blue-green silk thread, 24,000 sheets of memorial paper, 12 scraping knives, 38 knives and kerchiefs, 6 gold dragon plaques, and 54 golden buttons (Benn 1991, 32-35).

Such enormous wealth given to the institution is, of course, exceptional and occurs especially in ordinations held for members of the imperial family and other high-ranking aristocrats. But the overall impression remains that entry into the higher levels of the Dao required a full commitment, not only personally and socially but also materially and through observation of the proper forms. These forms, moreover, required that the ceremony, accompanied by many festivities, should last up to nine days, and that the full contingent of thirty-eight officiants be present. The ordination, then, while maintaining the basic pattern described above, consisted of entire sequences of preparations and the transmission of different levels of precepts and groups of scriptures, each preceded by a proper memorial sent to the gods, executed with great attention to detail, and concluded with the bestowal of rank to the new initiates (Benn 1991, 39-71).

Similarly splendid and impressive ceremonies were also performed for imperial relatives in later dynasties. An example is the ordination of Empress Zhang (1470-1541), the sole consort of the Ming emperor Hongzhi (r. 1488-1505) as Daoist priestess though the Celestial Master Zhang Xuanqing 張玄慶 (d. 1509) in 1493. Obtaining a high rank in the order of Orthodox Unity, she underwent a series of rituals and received an extensive group of scriptures, talismans, and registers (Little and Eichman 2000, 208). Her ordination is documented in an ornate scroll, 54 centimeters wide and over twenty meters long, that is now in the San Diego Museum of Art.

It shows the empress "floating on a cloud in the heavens, accompanied by an entourage and a large group of deities and adepts," including the Director of Fates, the Dark Warrior, the God of Literature, the first Celestial Master, celestial generals, zodiac deities, jade maidens, and many more (2000, 208). The inscription makes it clear that through the ceremony the empress is expected to receive a title and rank in the celestial administration, gaining the power to control spirits and demons, to activate the scriptures, and to perform efficacious rituals (2000, 213).

Like their medieval predecessors building on this as a first level, Complete Perfection Daoists created a system of ordination that centered on the transmission of monastic precepts in accordance with Neo-Confucian ethics and as supported by the Qing court. It was standardized by Wang Kunyang 王崑陽 (1622-1680), abbot of the White Cloud Monastery, who also formalized the establishment of the Longmen 龍門 lineage (Kubo 1951, 37; Esposito 2000, 629; Mori 1994).

As described in the *Precepts of Initial Perfection*, ordinands had to present themselves before a quorum of masters and examiners, then they took the three refuges, the five precepts of Lord Lao, and the ten precepts of initial perfection. They also vowed to behave with propriety and to observe all the regulations of the order.

Upon completion of the ceremony, they received an ordination certificate which gave the ordinand's name, age, place and date of birth as well as a list of the masters present to witness and document the ceremony. It also states the name of the ordination master and the various deities who preside over the formality and guarantee the newly created covenant (see box). Ordinands usually received two or three ranks at the same time, depending on their standing and preparation:

(1) Master of Wondrous Practice 妙行師 — *Precepts of Initial Perfection*
(2) Master of Wondrous Virtue 妙德師 — *Precepts of Medium Ultimate*
(3) Master of Wondrous Dao 妙道師 — *Great Precepts for Celestial Immortals*

The same ceremony is still performed today. It was revived in 1989 after a long hiatus under Communist proscription, when seventy-five Daoists, including thirty nuns, were ordained at the White Cloud Monastery in Beijing in a ceremony that was cut back to twenty days from the original one hundred. Participants, who had all lived in Daoist institutions for several years, were ordained into all three ranks and received all precepts texts (Lai 2003, 420; Goossaert 2003; Li 1993, 121-23). A second ceremony reviving traditional ordination took place in November of 1995 at the Celestial Master's Grotto (Tianshi dong 天師洞) on Mount Qingcheng in Sichuan. Ten senior monks presided over the formal induction of over 400 new Daoists into the order (Lai 2003, 420-21).

The numbers of Daoist monastics today are still comparatively low. In the century between 1808 and 1927, the White Cloud Monastery saw thirty-one ordination ceremonies that inducted 5,460 monastics (Yoshioka 1979, 236; Hahn 1989; Esposito 2001), while during the same period eight ceremonies in Shenyang ordained 1,740 monks and nuns (Lai 2003, 419). Only 6,450 Complete Perfection monastics were registered in 1996, but 133 regional Daoist associations were popularizing the institutions and working to increase the performance of rituals and popularity of the tradition (see Goossaert 2000). Still serving the creation of greater harmony on earth, Daoist leaders today dedicate themselves to a life of the Dao by honoring the precepts and by working for the salvation of all beings.

Certificate of Ordination into
Complete Perfection[15]

The disciple receiving the precepts Liu Yuxi, at the age of 39 years, who was born in the Guisi year [1833], 7th month, 14th day, *wei* hour [1-3 pm], now receives the Great Grace:

The Great Sage of Central Heaven, the Star Lord of the Sixth Palace of the Northern Dipper, by the name of Beiji Wu Quji, presides over and illuminates his body and destiny.

Originally from Shandong province, Laozhou prefecture, Chimo district, he left the house-holder's life in his home town at the Jade Emperor Temple [Yuhuang miao] on Crane Hill [Heshan] under the guidance of ordination master Hu Liangjing.

Today, in the capital of Beijing, at the White Cloud Monastery [Baiyun guan], at the holy al-tar of statutes of the Complete Perfection school, he bows down and, under the discipline master Zhang Yuanxuan, 19th generation successor of the lineage of celestial immortals, re-ceives the Precepts of Initial Perfection. To the end of his life he shall honor and venerate the precepts, never going against them or acting in their violation.

Present at the altar:

Master to witness the covenant:	Yang Yongsheng
Master to correct the observances:	Li Minghe
Master to oversee the precepts:	Ye Yongren
Master to promote the rules:	Li Yuankui
Master to guarantee the elevation:	Liu Yongmo
Master to present the registers:	Gao Mingyang
Master to arrange the rites:	Chen Yongxiang
Master to elicit the request:	Qu Mingting

The Perfected Lord of Dao Transformation, of Highest Prime
The Perfected Lord of Guarding Rightness, of Middle Prime
The Perfected Lord of Stabilizing the Will, of Lower Prime

Presiding at the altar: Zhang

Declared in formal acknowledgment and undertaken with deep veneration.

---

[15] As collected by Heinrich Hackmann in 1911. The text is the same for all three levels of ordination. See Hackmann 1920, 146-47; 1931, 6-7. The translation is based on the form used for the ordination using the "Precepts of Initial Perfection."

CHAPTER SIX

Monastic Discipline:
Changing Body and Behavior

Ordained Daoists who reached higher ranks tended to be monastic practitioners who lived in enclaves set apart from ordinary society and other religious organizations. The monastic institution arose in the late sixth century on the basis of the priesthoods of the Celestial Masters and Numinous Treasure (Schipper 1984, 201; Kohn 2003a, 39-42). It was also supported by the presence of Buddhist institutions of varying size as well as by small Daoist centers or "abodes" (*guan* 館), which were deeded to individual masters and their followers by devout emperors or aristocrats.[1] Monasteries came fully into their own around the time of unification, and flourished especially in the Tang dynasty, then underwent a renewed revival in the late twelfth century with the arising of Complete Perfection (Yao 1980; Tsui 1991).

In both cases, local or private temples that housed only a few practitioners existed side by side with large, state-sponsored institutions, which served as training seminaries for advanced practitioners, storehouses of books and art, and the location of grand ceremonies that benefited emperor and country. The main purpose of monasteries was and is to create an environment of separation and tranquility for advanced followers of the religion, a community that would allow practitioners to cultivate themselves and to attain higher states. Their organization and rules accordingly focus on the transformation of the individual, restructuring body conception and everyday behavior.

As the *Pure Rules, Mysterious and Marvelous* (ZW 361, 10.598-605) of the Complete Perfection school describes it, full-time monastic practitioners represent the "highest vehicle" of the religion. They "cultivate perfection and nurture inner nature," their minds firmly set on the mystery and their hearts participating in the Dao. They pattern their lives on Heaven and Earth, give up ordinary life to accumulate the merit of perfection, and dedicate themselves to meditation and the practice of inner cultivation to eventually transcend the Three Worlds and gain positions among the immortals. As perfected in the pure world of the Dao, they ride on cranes, float on clouds, and assemble near the golden towers and turquoise ponds of paradise (10.614).

Beyond this main goal of the monastic institution, however, it also serves religious devotees and supporters, enabling them to participate in the great endeavor of the Dao. Thus those belonging to the "middle vehicle" of followers are lay people who, with sincere heart and strong devotion, practice the recitation of scriptures and the performance of rituals, chanting the name of the Heavenly Worthy and dedicating their lives and efforts to the proper establishment of rites and ceremonies. They "purify their minds and bodies, are always aware of the divine law, and find

---

[1] On Buddhist institutions in medieval China, see Twitchett 1956; 1957; Zürcher 1959; Wang 1984; Foulk 1987; 1993; Gernet 1995. For a discussion of Daoist proto-monasteries, see Bumbacher 2000a; 2000b.

protection by good spirits" (10.614). They attain a celestial rank and are venerated by the people. Their path is greatly aided by the monastery which becomes a focal ground for devotional activities.

The same also holds true for the third group, those of the "lesser vehicle," i.e., people who sponsor the religion with material goods. They "erect temples and monasteries, have scriptures copied and statues cast" (10.615), give ample donations, and generally observe the moral rules. Mainly concerned with ordinary life, they visit monastic institutions on special occasions, making efforts that will grant them rebirth among the rich and noble. This in turn enables them to give amply and to sponsor religious activities, which in the long run may well lead to a life of monastic dedication.

As outlined in the *Pure Rules, Mysterious and Marvelous*, the role of the monastery in Chinese society was therefore not limited to providing an opportunity for a select few to practice esoteric and intense forms of inner cultivation in relative calm and detachment from ordinary affairs but afforded a stage for the performance of rituals and an opportunity for sponsorship. By joining the monastery temporarily, devotees could enhance their spiritual progress; by giving to monastics, people's material goods—otherwise a fetter to the world and a potential source of anxiety and suffering—were put to good spiritual use. On the other hand, this also created a strong pressure for monastic practitioners to fulfill the trust placed in them by people and the state— whose officials traditionally used monasteries as focal points of Great Peace and ritual venues to the divine. Placed in a special place in the larger human community, monastics in every aspect of their physical and spiritual behavior had to be models of purity and divinity in the world (Kohn 2003, 48-53).

They did so by wearing vestments, using special utensils, following a tight liturgical schedule, and controlling every aspect of their being, whether fulfilling ordinary tasks or engaging in religious ceremonies. In all activities striving to be pure, divine representatives of the Dao, monastics observed numerous injunctions that controlled their behavior and conditioned their bodily actions. This reflects what Marcel Mauss has described as "body techniques" or *habitus*, i. e., "ordered, authorized, tested actions" as opposed to *habitude*, a set of "habits or customs of the individual" (1979, 101-02). *Habitus* implies that one "cannot take the body for granted as a natural, fixed, and historically universal datum of human societies" (Turner 1997, 17). Rather, it describes the body as "an assemblage of embodied aptitudes" and indicates a form of bodily competence that is learned and "habituated to a certain level of being" (Asad 1997, 47).

Pierre Bourdieu, in his development of this notion, characterizes *habitus* further as "systems of durable, transposable dispositions, structured structures predisposed to function as structuring structures" (1990, 53). *Habitus* is "an infinite capacity for generating products—thoughts, perceptions, expressions, and actions—whose limits are set by the historically and socially situated conditions of its production" (Bourdieu 1990, 55). The various body techniques, therefore, learned and habituated in a culturally determined and structured manner, create a specific set of feelings, conceptions, and expressions that both reflect the culture and society that instilled them and gives them enduring structure (see Kohn 2001b, 156-57). The Daoist community on this level creates an even higher awareness of purity and oneness with the Dao, one that is, moreover, realized on a more physical and practical level.

HOLY VESTMENTS

The transformation toward this higher oneness begins with dressing in special garb, known as the "holy vestments" (*fafu* 法服) of the religion. In the middle ages, as described in the *Rules and Precepts for Worshiping the Dao* (3.6a) and the *Essential Rules and Observances* (9.2a), Daoist robes were mostly of yellow coloring, with women wearing gowns with a light green trim. The full set of vestments consisted of a lower garment described as a "skirt" (*qun* 裙), which was usually a wrap-around cloth, sewn from three or five panels and tied at the waist; a gown (*he* 褐), which covered most of the body and was held together with a sash; and a cloak or cape (*pei* 被), a large, flowing garment of translucent silk with open front and long sleeves that often contained multiple folds and intricate ornamentation. It measured 4.9 *chi* 尺 [feet] in width to match the four seasons, and 5.5 *chi* in length to follow the pattern of the five phases and divided into a varying number of folds, both in its main body and its sleeves, depending on the rank of the wearer.

On all ritual and formal occasions Daoists also wore a headdress (*guan* 冠), a word also translated as "cap" or "crown" and carrying connotations of our "tiara" or "diadem" (Schafer 1978, 11). On their feet they wore stockings of plain silk and shoes showing the design of yin and yang. The same pattern was also visible in their sashes, from which they hung various pendants that contained sections of scriptures, precepts, talismans, or registers (*Rules and Precepts* 3.7b).

Aside from showing patterns of yin and yang, each of these items of clothing also carried its own symbolism. As the *Rules and Precepts Regarding Ritual Vestments* (*Fafu kejie wen* 法服科戒文, DZ 788) of the early eighth century points out, *guan* for "headdress" indicates *guan* 觀, "to observe," and refers to the inward observation of one's own self while outwardly looking at all beings with detachment. Wearing a headdress, therefore, meant that the Daoist was free from inner desires and outward attachments, leading a life of heavenly dimensions. The lotus flower often depicted in the headdress, moreover, shows the purity of the Daoist in the world, while emblems depicting stars represent his or her standing among the divine (5b-6a).

Similarly, *pei*, "cape," is related to *pei* 披, "to open." It indicates that the Daoist opens himself to utmost purity while expanding the Dao and its virtue to everyone, serving to open enlightenment for all beings (6a). *He*, "gown," connects with *e* 遏, "restraint," and symbolizes the Daoist's utter control over inner passions and desires, as well as over outer attractions and afflictions. Complete restraint of the senses, moreover, means twofold forgetfulness and total dedication to the Dao (6a). Finally, *qun*, "skirt," is linked with *qun* 群, "multitude," and indicates that the Daoist has cut off the multitude of errors within and the host of entanglements without, thus attaining complete liberation (6b) (Kohn 2003a, 148-49).

The three garments—skirt, gown, and cape—plus the headdress, therefore, stood for the Daoist's purity, cosmic attainment, and elevated status. They connected their wearer with the larger universe; the headdress with its lotus or planetary imagery and dark color symbolized Heaven; the skirt with its five panels in imitation of the five phases and five sacred mountains represented Earth; and the gown with its 36 *chi* of cloth matched the 360 days of the year. The cape, finally, with its varying number of folds symbolized the continued interchange of yin and yang. Beyond this overall symbolism, Daoist ritual vestments were also inhabited by various protective deities and imitated the fashion of the gods above (2b).

As described in a set of forty-six rules found in the *Rules and Precepts Regarding Ritual Vestments* (7b-9b), also contained in the *Precepts of Initial Perfection* of Complete Perfection, all vestments had to be treated with great respect. They were consecrated before first use, hand-washed with great care, and ritually burned when worn out. Vestments had to be donned for all formal ritual occasions, travel in the world, and interaction with commoners, but taken off for all ordinary tasks and personal hygiene activities. The list begins:

1. Unless attired in ritual vestments, a Daoist must not ascend to the holy altar, enter the oratory, bow in prayer, make announcements or requests, confess transgressions, or seek kindness.
2. Unless attired in ritual vestments, a Daoist must not approach the scriptures and precepts, lecture or explain, recite or chant them.
3. Unless attired in ritual vestments, a Daoist must not perform rites of purgation and precepts, accept other people's obeisances, eat or drink holy food.
4. Unless attired in ritual vestments, a Daoist must not pay obeisance to the venerables, masters, and priests of extensive virtue or accept the obeisances of disciples.
5. Unless attired in ritual vestments, a Daoist must not enter or leave any dwellings, travel among people, or be seen by ordinary folk. (7b)

Given that medieval monastics performed rites to the Dao at six different times in the course of the day and had a steady stream of visitors from the faithful, they were putting their vestments to good use, always conscious of the presence of the gods in the robes and their own close communication with the divine in their ritual activities.

Both monks and nuns wore the same vestments, with the one exception that nuns had a more elaborate headdress. Both also owned a more utilitarian outfit for common tasks. This pattern in still true for monastics of Complete Perfection today, who have colorful robes for their formal services and a separate set of clothes for daily tasks. The latter are dominantly blue in color. As the *Pure Rules, Mysterious and Marvelous* says,

> Blue matches the direction of the east, the *jiayi* 甲乙 cyclical sign, the phase wood, and the position of the trigram Tai. It also corresponds to the *qi* of the green dragon and of life and growth. Thus it matches the descent lineage of the Imperial Lord of Eastern Florescence. (10.599)

In addition to this basic, dark blue robe, which is held together by a wide yellow sash, practitioners in daily life are to wear a yellow kerchief on their heads, which can be tied in a number of different styles:

> 1. Tang kerchief, 2. joint harmony, 3. wide and grand, 4. free and easy wandering, 5. purple yang, 6. the character "one," 7. threaded kerchief, 8. three teachings, 9. nine yang.

Among these nine styles, those who only use the "Tang kerchief" style tend to be followers of Patriarch Lü Chunyang of the Tang dynasty. That is why they only wear their headgear in Tang style. They are called the heirs of Chunyang.

Older monks often use the "joint harmony" style; younger monks tend to prefer "free and easy wandering." In cold weather, people often wear their head scarves in the "good fortune kerchief" style; in snow, they prefer the "wide and grand" mode. Most commonly the "purple yang" and "character one" styles are worn by upper-level practitioners, while those who have just taken initial precepts tend to wear the "threaded kerchief" together with the Crescent Moon headdress.

Those who already have taken the precepts of Medium Ultimate can wear the "three teachings" style with the Three Terraces headdress, while those who have reached the level of the precepts of the Celestial Immortals wear the headdress of the True Form of the Five Sacred Peaks. (10.598; Min 1990, 26-27)

While the kerchiefs thus allow the expression of specific ranks, lineages, and personal preferences, the robes for daily wear are uniform and standardized. So, in addition, are the items allowed for personal use, especially when away from the monastery. Here the text lists seven items, which it calls the "seven treasures," encouraging practitioners to keep them meticulously clean and in good repair, and to treat them as valuable aids to the monastic life. They are:

1. a rush mat, to purify demons from outside;
2. a quilted robe, to support mind and inner nature;
3. a single calabash, to contain proper food and drink;
4. a palm-leaf hat, to keep off wind and rain, frost and snow;
5. a palm-leaf fan, to brush off worldly affairs;
6. a blue satchel, to store the cinnabar scriptures;
7. a flat staff, to point to the great Dao, pure wind, and bright moon. (10.598)

The rules regarding vestments, therefore, express the tight control and strict organization of the monastics' life, limiting personal expression and encouraging a pervasive uniformity throughout the community while at the same time creating a visible, active presence of the divine. Opening the individual's awareness of the body and its garb, the vestments create the inner space necessary for the focus on spiritual goals and attainment of the Dao.

DAILY ROUTINE

The day of the monastery is tightly scheduled and filled with liturgical and spiritual tasks. In the middle ages, it was governed by six periods of worship (*liushi* 六時): cockcrow, dawn, noon, dusk, early evening, and midnight. These six periods were adapted from Buddhism, where they served to schedule hymns chanted to the buddhas (see Pas 1987; Yifa 2002, 12). In Daoist communities, as described in the Tang code *Rules and Observances for Students of the Dao*, at each period the bell was rung twelve times for several sequences, each beginning slowly and sonorously and moving into increasing speed and intensity (1.16b). The bells called the community to holy office so they could manifest their purity, express their good intentions, and receive encouragement to practice diligently (1.17a).

The day began with a minor rite at cockcrow to move on to the morning audience at dawn (3-5 a.m.). Breakfast was served afterwards, around 6 a.m., then there was unscheduled time for work or self-cultivation. Around 11 a.m., the main meal of the day, called the noon purgation, was held. It was accompanied by the formal chanting of incantations, thanksgiving for the food, repentance formulas, and an orderly exit and clean-up. This was followed by more time for work or meditation. At dusk, the evening audience was held. It was followed by lesser rites in mid-evening and at midnight (1.19a; see also Min 1990, 36-38).

The scheduling of various ritual activities during the night-time hours matches the continuous religious activities prescribed for monks in other traditions but stands in contrast to the traditional Chinese division of time into four periods—morning, day, evening, and night—among which the latter was strictly reserved for sleep and rest. In worldly communities, the gates were closed at night, and all moving about was prohibited; any activities during the dark hours were considered frivolous and lascivious, detrimental to social integrity and personal health (Richter 2001, 98-101). The active denial of the civil division of time and refusal to rest as ordinary people is another expression of the separation and special nature of the monastics (Kohn 2003a, 175).

Among the six periods of worship the daily services or "regular audiences" (*changchao* 常朝), celebrated at dawn and dusk, were most important. They involved the formal assembly of all recluses in the sanctuary, the presentation of offerings, and the extensive recitation of prayers and scriptures. They can be traced back to the morning and evening audiences with the parents, prescribed for filial children in the *Book of Rites* (10/1.4; Legge 1968, 1:450-51; Knapp 2004) and also echo imperial audiences held in the early morning.

In both cases, children or supplicants presented food and offerings, which appears in Daoism as the "presentation of offerings" (*gongyang* 供養), a term also prominent in Chinese Buddhism where it is used to translate the Indian term *pūjā*, the ceremony of hosting the deity. Daoists who had left their native families regarded the gods of the Dao as their true father and mother and venerated them accordingly—at the same time also recognizing their standing in the celestial administration and paying political-style homage, as is suggested in the term "audience" for the rites. The services thus joined traditional rules of filial piety with ancient court rituals and transposed them into a religious, celestial setting.

Before attending an audience service, Daoists had to purify themselves by washing their hands and faces. They donned ritual vestments and applied their insignia of divine standing, such as the ritual tablet and appropriate talismans. Assembling in order of ritual rank, they entered the sanctuary through the door closest to their proper place, bowed, and sat down. As is made clear in the Tang manual *Ten Items of Dignified Observances Shishi weiyi* 十事威儀, DZ 792), it was highly improper to assume a seat that was not one's own, the only exception being a case of late arrival (6b). The ceremony included homage to the Dao, confession of diligence, prayers for the forgiveness of sins, various chantings of hymns to the Dao, the scriptures, and the immortals, and a set of twelve prayers for the well-being of all beings, from yin and yang to the imperial family, all sentient beings, and those "suffering in the three bad rebirths and five realms of suffering" (*Rules and Precepts for Worshiping the Dao* 6.2b-4a).[2]

Complete Perfection practitioners, too, engage in morning and evening services and are subject to a tight schedule in the course of the day. As described in the *Pure Rules of Complete Perfection* (*Quanzhen qinggui* 全真清規, DZ 1235; Min 1990, 100-04) of the Yuan dynasty,[3] the day begins at 3 a.m. with the sounding of the plank, indicating that the "non-movement" period is over. Everyone washes his face and rinses his mouth and assembles for morning services to pay homage to the perfected and sages. Between 5 and 7 a.m. a light breakfast is served, followed by a period of group meditation practice. After 9 a.m. members are free to pursue personal cultivation or fulfill administrative and other duties.

The main meal or noon purgation takes place at 11 a.m., as was the case in the medieval institution. It is followed by another round of group meditation and more personal or duty time. At 5

---

[2] Similar patterns also apply in Buddhist services, which place a strong emphasis on confession and penance. See Yifa 2002, 19; Kuo 1994; Chappell forthcoming.

[3] For more on the text, see Kubo 1951; Yoshioka 1961, 67; Kleeman 1991, 186-87.

p.m. everyone assembles for the evening services, followed by more group meditation until 9 p.m. when the "non-movement" period begins. Another time of devotion is scheduled for the hours around midnight when the new yang begins to arise. Ideally at this time adepts work on inner cultivation and chant poems to enable them to resist the "sleep devils" (5b-6a; Yao 2000, 589).

In both the medieval and the modern monastery, therefore, time is dedicated entirely to the pursuit of the Dao, and the individual has little opportunity to go beyond the mold or to upset the organizational framework. All is subsumed under the great task to be accomplished, and the community takes precedence over all personal and individual needs.

BODY CONTROL

The sense of submission to a higher goal is also obvious in the degree to which physical movements of the body are controlled in the monastic environment. Monks and nuns are to behave with decorum and humility at all times, an attitude expressed most obviously through bows and obeisances. As the *Ten Items of Dignified Observances* says:

> It is hard to know how respectful the mind is, but the formally bent body can be clearly seen. For this reason, we must perform obeisances of the body in a diligent and attentive manner, so as to give expression to the worthiness and sincerity of the mind within. Thus humbling oneself, one expresses respect. (3a)

Monastics accordingly bow a lot, performing obeisances with dignity and proper posture, lest they betray an impious attitude—especially before the sacred statues and the senior masters (Kohn 2003a, 132-35).[4]

Their obeisances come in two major types: bows and prostrations. A bow is performed standing upright with either palms joined at chest level or the ritual tablet held tight, the head and torso bowed forward at an angle of about 45 degrees (3b). A prostration, in contrast, is performed from a kneeling position. Keeping one's back straight, one places the hands before the knees and lowers the head to the ground between them, in the classical formality of kowtow or "touching the head to the ground" (Suzuki 1965, 18). The texts describe this as "kneeling straight and putting all five limbs [legs, arms, and head] to the ground, without however bending the back" (3b).

Bows and prostrations are stationary as opposed to moving obeisances, during which one bows while advancing or retreating (Ōfuchi 1983, 219). Both types are further combined in a number of sequences so that, for example, when taking leave of one's master to travel outside of the institution or when expressing formal congratulations or condolences, the monk "always gives three bows, then kneels formally and kowtows to again pay his respects" (3b, 4a).

The *Essential Rules and Observances* makes a further distinction between bodily and mental obeisances. The former involves obeying the various rules and regulations and deals with the proper physical setting of obeisances, while the latter indicates that in certain ritual contexts or under special circumstances Daoists may bow in mind and not in body (9.5a). To do so,

---

[4] The same also holds true for Buddhist communities. See Yifa 2002, 93; Reinders 1997.

sit up straight, facing in the proper direction. Then close your eyes and clap your teeth as if you were in a real audience rite. In your mind imagine yourself turning to the different directions and bowing to the gods while mentally reciting the proper incantation. (9.5b)

This form of obeisance is also applied in formal rituals. According to the *Ten Items of Dignified Observances*, "the grand master mentally bows to the scriptures and statues, with all disciples following suit, while the lay followers just stay quietly in their places" (6a). Mental obeisances are further used when one is tired and exhausted or too sick to perform physical bows. The argument is that while mind and body should always work together, it is better to remain unmoving on the outside and pay one's respects internally than the opposite, moving the body while "being lazy and uninterested in the mind" (9.6a).

While obeisances serve to express the humble position of monks, an attitude of respect and apology should also be maintained when in a higher position. As the *Ten Items of Dignified Observances* says, "Whenever receiving an obeisance from someone, stand with hands raised and palms together to express your apologies for assuming a high position and accepting veneration" (4a). This humility is, moreover, necessary in various other situations, including the expression of shame, repentance, and expiation of guilt, as well as paying homage to virtue, the divine law, the deities, and future sages (3a). Bows are also commonly used when meeting a senior master, attending upon a master for instruction, encountering a friend who happens to be one's senior, or meeting a fellow disciple (3b).

Formal bows establish the proper relationship between two sides, be they human and human or human and divine. Thus, the *Rules for a Thousand Perfected* (DZ 1410) points out that whenever a disciple goes to attend on his master to receive instruction or for any other reason he must first don proper garb, put on the right headdress and shoes, then walk with dignity and elegance up to the master's residence (16b). If the master's door is closed, a soft knock or slight cough may be given three times. Should the master not reply, the same triple knock may be repeated twice; if not admitted after that, the disciple must quietly retreat (27a).

Once in the master's room, the disciple carefully closes the door in exactly the position it was in, advances slowly and in a straight line, his eyes never straying to the right or left and his demeanor dignified and serene. He gives a bow and formally announces his name in a clear voice. He remains standing at attention, keeping his hands in his sleeves and his posture straight and erect, "never leaning against a platform, a wall, or anything else," and only speaking when expressly asked to do so and then in a low voice, quietly, and with circumspection (*Rules and Observances for Students of the Dao* 1.1ab). He only sits down when so ordered, and even then he "waits until the order has been repeated three times" and first "touches his head to the ground, apologizing [for his rudeness]" (Kohn 2003a, 135).

In Complete Perfection, too, the proper conduct of monastics is specified in detailed rules that prescribe physical discipline and social interaction. Generally, as the *Pure Rules, Mysterious and Marvelous* says,

> all physical postures, walking, standing, sitting, and lying down have rules in the Complete Perfection community. All asking, answering, speaking, and talking have their proper beginning and end. In all activities, move as gingerly as a crane stepping. Thereby you will develop the bones of the Dao and the airs of an immortal.

Sit like a sturdy rock, sleep like a drawn bow, walk like the clear wind, and stand like a green pine. Issue sounds as softly as a sick person or a tender, young girl. Offer all activities like an elegant gentleman or a poor scholar. Ask in due turn, answer in due turn, and rely on the cinnabar scriptures for your choice of words, using their passages to point out errors and never engaging in common talk.

Then again, there are those who walk like a willow in the wind or sit like a drooping lotus; those who presume to talk about the military affairs of the country or critically discuss the Chan practice of the Buddhists. There are members who constantly question the great Dao, creating confusion for others; others again cheat and confuse the ignorant by praising themselves as venerable and full of learning. All those we call fellows without teacher or direction. (10.599; Kohn 2003b, 22)

Proper monastic conduct, therefore, begins with the physical control of the body, its posture and movements, and from there it extends to general patterns of politeness, proper speech, and decorum in one's actions. Thus, monks and nuns are supposed to stand erect and straight, not leaning on one foot; they are to stand up whenever they face a master or a guest and when performing a rite. Even then, the movement should not be abrupt and they should not lean toward the master or infringe on his space (10.604).

Similarly, monastics are to sit with their backs straight, mostly kneeling on their heels but also using the cross-legged posture, especially for meditation exercises (being careful not to touch their neighbors' knees or elbows). It is considered rude to remain seated in the presence of a master or a guest and is regarded an invitation to immorality to sit alone with a lady Daoist, be she a lay woman or a female disciple. The sleeping posture, too, is prescribed: on one's side with the legs bent. One must not sleep in the nude, even during the heat of summer, and during sleep periods must refrain from talking. One must never lie down on the same mat or even in the same room as one's master, and one cannot retire before the master does so himself. It is also prohibited to lie down during the day, after a meal, or with one's head towards the fire. In getting up, monks—belonging to cosmic yang energy—should place their left foot down first (10.604).

Like the resting poses of the body, so all movements have to be executed gingerly and consciously, with a constant awareness of all body parts and all social situations. One must not step in front of someone reciting a scripture or bowing in prayer, but tread carefully in all areas that house sacred activities. One must never run or walk in haste, swing one's arms wildly while walking, walk about with lay followers, or go near women or outcasts. When walking with one's master, one must remain a few steps behind him, keeping the head low in an attitude of service and unwavering devotion (10.604).

Just as the outward actions of the body have to be carefully monitored and controlled, so must the various senses. One should neither look at unwholesome or sensually stimulating sights nor read improper texts, those of lay origin or representing other teachings. When walking inside the monastery or its halls, one must guard one's eyes by looking only straight ahead, neither right nor left. When walking in the outside world, one must not look at pleasant sites and landscapes, entertainments and amusements, or girls and colorful folk. One must also guard one's ears and not listen to news or gossip, jokes or chatter, music or drama. Even if one has picked up some bits and pieces by coincidence, after returning to the monastery one must guard one's speech and not gossip about them or any worldly events that have come one's way (10.604).

Speech in general is a major issue in the texts, both ancient and modern. They all prohibit loud or boisterous vocalization as much as gossip and idle chatter. All speech is to be calm, quiet, and circumspect, and many topics are to be excluded completely. They include the faults and mistakes of others, the affairs of state and the common world, matters of women and marriage, Daoist rules and laws (unless at the proper occasion), jokes and fictional stories, as well as esoteric alchemical techniques, secret talismans, magical spells, and the practices of other religious groups. Sleep periods, meals, and hours of rest are times of complete silence, and only words of prayer and recitation are to be uttered in the halls of worship. One's master has to be addressed with utmost softness and politeness, and only in words suitable to the holy and honorable occasion (10.603).

RESPECT FOR MATERIAL OBJECTS

Beyond the masters and the gods, Daoist monastics also developed respect for everything, especially the material objects that were part of their institution and thus sanctified by the Dao. Among these, aside from vestments, the most important were the statues and scriptures, immediate reservoirs of cosmic power and divine energy. They deserved special care; as described in the last section of the *Ten Items of Dignified Observances* on "Safekeeping," they had to be regarded as holy, kept free from defilements and harm, and placed far away from "impure people or those of impure body and impure breath" (14a). The text says:

> Do not place other things on the same racks, put them together with discarded objects, or allow people to handle them carelessly. If there is nobody else and you have to handle and place them yourself, first wash your hands and wipe the scripture racks, equally on top and bottom. If you touch any other object in between, you have to wash your hands once more.

> Do not keep scriptures and sacred images in your residence. Only those contained in wrappers of black lacquer or the like placed in a special bookcase can expediently be stored in residences or bedrooms. Scriptures collected in wrappers of plain silk, even if placed in a bookcase, must not be so stored. (14ab)

Similarly, all other objects of practical and ceremonial use were considered of sacred importance and were part of the celestial realm created on earth—be they the bedstead, table, bench, and scripture box that furnished the cells; the robes, capes, headdresses, and shoes that made up the ceremonial vestments; the paper, ink stones, ink, and writing brushes used in the scriptorium; or the incense burners, gongs, bells, banners, curtains, and draperies that adorned the halls of worship.

Even the dishes used during the ceremonial meal were part of the cosmic vision. They consisted of three bowls of different sizes, holding five, three, and one pint(s) respectively, plus chopsticks and a spoon (9a); they came in two sets, one used in the monastics' residences or when traveling, the other reserved strictly for refectory use. The latter dishes are, as the *Rules and Precepts for Worshiping the Dao* states,

> to be kept separate from other ware and must never be used for other purposes. Instead, they should be maintained clean and pure at all times. They are called the "refectory set." After each use, wash and wipe them, then store them on a special dish rack. Never mix them with other dishes. Failure to comply carries a subtraction of 280 [days of life]. (3.9b; Kohn 2003a, 126)

Any harm or defilement done to any of these objects accordingly carried the most dire consequences. For example, the *Scripture of Karmic Retribution* says:

> Anyone who steals vessels, implements, or other objects used for offerings or festivals, in this life will become a lowly beggar who will never be satiated. Anyone who desecrates the statues and images of the Great Dao in this life will be like the mangy dogs and poisonous snakes, hungry and cold without respite and forever unable to find food. Having passed through this, he will be born among monkeys. (2.5b-6a)

These as other rules for monastic practitioners served to create a lifestyle in harmony with the rhythm of the Dao and in accordance with the celestial administration. They provided detailed instructions for daily activities, bodily discipline, and social interaction, and they gave followers a network of set guidelines that kept them safe and encouraged them to develop a greater spiritual dimension in their lives. The network formed a safeguard against the passions of the body and temptations of the senses and laid the foundation for the attainment of an otherworldly orientation and increasing oneness with the Dao. As the *Ten Items of Dignified Observances* says:

> Using and reciting the ten items [of the text] and their many rules, practicing them diligently—this is what we call keeping yourself safe from all violations. Teaching them to others, moreover, brings good karmic fruits too numerous to count. The host of living beings will look up to you with joy; the various celestials will be blushing with shame [in comparison].

> A person who behaves like this in this life will receive ten kinds of good fortune, virtue, honor, and respect. . . . And afterwards he does not appear again in this [level of] existence but enters the ranks of the sages. (16ab)

PUNISHMENTS

The proper behavior of monastic Daoists was also subject to various sets of punishments. Since monastics represented the highest purity of the religion and created an open line of communication with the divine, they were considered of particular importance by the state who had a strong interest in their continued propriety and setting a good example. As a result, beginning with the Tang dynasty, all ordained monks and nuns of both Buddhism and Daoism were subject to special state laws. They had to carry an official certificate at all times (Gernet 1995, 40) and had to comply with official behavioral codes. The earliest codes are found in two sets of sources, one a special code for the clergy known as the *Rules for Daoists and Buddhists* (*Daoseng ke* 道僧科) of the year 637, the other Tang legal codes, such as the *Six Departments of the Tang* (*Tang liudian* 唐六典) and the *Supplementary Interpretations of Tang Laws* (*Tang lü shuyi* 唐律疏義). The former, unfortunately, is lost but has been recovered partially from its Japanese counterpart, the *Regulations for Monks and Nuns* (*Sōni ryō* 僧尼律), written soon after its first conception and representing the same basic outlook (Ch'en 1973, 95).

According to these sources, monastics were not supposed to ride horses, possess military books, form cliques, solicit donors, stay for more than three days among lay families, participate in musical or other entertainments, or behave in any way rudely or abusively to elders or those of higher rank (Ch'en 1973, 102-3). Punishments for transgressions were harsh, and offenders had to be handed over to the secular authorities for all serious crimes. For example, if recluses partook of improper foods or liquor they could be condemned to hard labor; if they wore clothes of fine silk or aristocratic colors, they could be defrocked and sent to hard labor. Similarly, if they stole or desecrated sacred objects, they could be punished by imprisonment, hard labor, or exile. If they engaged in fortune telling and faith healing they faced reversion to lay status and, if they still continued their charlatanery, were threatened by strangulation (Ch'en 1973, 96-102; Kohn 2003a, 68).

Within the institution, moreover, misbehaving practitioners were punished by having to offer incense or a certain number of prostrations. Thus the *Rules for a Thousand Perfected* says:

> Some people create disturbances among the monastics. They do not follow the rules but drink alcohol and get intoxicated then ridicule and insult those above and below them. People like these should be punished by having to pay a fine. Some may also have accumulated excess goods or wealth which they enjoy and keep for later days: they should be punished with a beating. Then again, some steal money and silk from the offerings, while others destroy the plants and trees of the earth, harming the Daoist community. If these elements cannot be controlled, hand them over to the worldly authorities for punishment according to the law. (4a)

And the *Rules and Precepts for Worshiping the Dao* has:

> Anyone who violates the rules must be punished in accordance with the divine law, by offering incense and lamp oil, sounding the bell, and paying obeisance. Anyone who repeats the violation without showing penitence must be controlled more severely by being made to work hard repairing the monastery [buildings] on the inside or strengthening bridges [in the outside world]. Anyone, finally, who still does not comply is judged by the rules of the divine law, expelled from the order, and returned to his or her original [lay] state. (2.14b)

Beyond this, the monks' bad deeds were counted by the celestial administration and led to a reduction in life expectancy. For example, failure to observe the proper order of rank during rituals carried a deduction of 3,600 days or ten years from one's life as did the granting ordination without authority. Seven or eight years of life were taken off for not holding a thanksgiving rite after ordination, failing to obey the rules, wearing the wrong ritual vestments, and handing out blank scrolls during ordination. Even ordinary shortcomings carried a heavy toll: not keeping the outhouse or the well clean, sleeping in the company of others, protecting one's privacy with screens or curtains, getting angry, behaving with arrogance, or passing others without greeting each were punished by four months of reduced lifetime (Kohn 1998c, 856-57).

The same holds also true for Complete Perfection practitioners, who were subject to both internal and state punishments for their violations. An early outline is found in the *Pure Rules of Complete Perfection* under the heading "Ten Items of Punishments According to the Founder, the Imperial Lord Chongyang" (11b-12b), which goes back to Buddhist materials of the Song period. Especially the *Pure Rules of Baizhang* (*Baizhang qinggui* 白丈清規; see Collcutt 1983; Yifa 2002, 28) presents the same kinds of punishments for approximately the same offenses using a somewhat different terminology (Kubo 1951, 35). Later taken up in the *Pure Rules, Mysterious and Marvelous* (10.612), the same code was still in active use in the 1940s, as observed by Yoshioka Yoshitoyo during his stay at the White Cloud Monastery (1979, 240-41).

The most serious infractions among Complete Perfection were theft, sexual misconduct, grand larceny, and fraud. Since these actions harm the entire community, they are punished by having the offender's registration burned and handing him over to the local magistrate. The next set of violations, punished by caning and expulsion, involve actions that harm other people, both monastic and lay. They include an overall disobedience to the rules, the hoarding of personal property, taking advantage of one's monastic status to gain benefits from ordinary people, and lecturing on alchemy to lead the general populace astray.

Caning and temporary exile from the community are the regulation punishment for infractions of the third level, which tend to involve a lack of self control. It applies in cases of violations against rules of diet (wine and meat), speech (harsh words), respect (toward parents and elders), and humility (assuming greater authority). Fourth, there are infractions involving claims to personal greatness and a higher rank, which are suitably punished by demotion in rank. Constant engagement in foolish talk or deceitful speech, public speeches to the laity while dressed in nonmonastic garb, and the selfish cultivation of outside connections and accumulation of material goods all fall into this category.

The vast majority of infractions listed in the *Pure Rules, Mysterious and Marvelous* are minor behavioral shortcomings, punished by a prostration for the time it takes to burn one stick of incense. They include engaging in foolish talk or deceitful speech; laughing and joking in the sanctuary; smoking in the hall; failing to bow or appearing dirty at the morning and evening services; missing services, lessons, or other obligatory ceremonies and assemblies; entering the refectory in improper garb; speaking during meals or dropping eating utensils; carrying personal belongings into the refectory or smoking in it; eating selfishly and without sharing; using community food to entertain personal guests; sleeping in the nude; using dirty water or defiled firewood in the kitchen; using kitchen fire for burning incense or going to the sanctuary in one underwear; losing one's belt or cap; leaving the monastery without proper permission; disturbing the patterns of quiet and action; refusing to rise at the end of the rest time; reading repository scriptures privately; wasting useful materials; and in general failing to aid the official business of the monastery (10.613; see Min 1990; Kohn 2003b).

These and other actions infringed on the harmony and dignity of the monastic community and had to be controlled as much as possible. The behavior of the individual monastic was as much part of the communal success as the general administration and financial support of the institution. It was thus essential for monastic Daoists to behave with propriety and circumspection, to keep their bodies and actions under tight control, and to give their utmost to the Dao. Much more so than their lay and priestly counterparts, monastics were regulated in every aspect of their lives, their very bodies becoming expressions of holiness and transcendence. The injunctions and regulations concerning the monastic life accordingly present Daoist morality at its most concrete, providing a detailed outline of the transformative ethics of the Daoist religion and placing the Daoist life firmly into daily routine and bodily control.

CHAPTER SEVEN

From Community to Cosmos

The highest form of Daoist ethics goes beyond prohibitions, admonitions, and injunctions, moving the practitioner from community to cosmos and creating a mind at one with the Dao. Accessible to both lay and monastic practitioners, it reorients practitioners' thinking away from personal, ordinary concerns and toward oneness with the Dao through the creation of a desire for universal salvation, the well-being of all, and the harmony of the cosmos. For this, Daoists encourage adepts to work with resolutions and mindful intentions, making them the root of their thinking and identity.

Unlike most other rules, they are formulated in the first person. They plant good fortune for self and others through the right attitude and are expressed as good intentions, positive prayers, and vows in one's heart. The key term here is *yuan* 願, literally "wish," "resolve." In Buddhism, it renders *pranidhāna* and expresses the vow, commonly undertaken by bodhisattvas, to be firm and resolute in seeking liberation and to do everything in one's power to assist all beings in their spiritual efforts (Nakamura 1975, 200). In Daoism it occurs first in Numinous Treasure texts, meaning "vow" or "resolution" (Bokenkamp 1989).

In monastic manuals, such as the *Rules and Precepts for Worshiping the Dao*, the term is used either to encourage practitioners to develop good intentions (sect. 24) or to introduce a communal chant or prayer on behalf of all beings (sects. 15-18; see Kohn 2004). In the latter sense, it may also express a formal ritual action and appear in the compound "announcement and prayer" (*qiyuan* 啓願), which is still used today (Lagerwey 1987, 146). Experimenting with various English terms, I found have "prayer" most appropriate, especially when used in its traditional Christian sense as "the development of an attitude that is concentrated and contemplative," a sense of being blessed by the deity (Teasdale 2002, 35; Kohn 2003a, 172-73).

The practice of continued mental prayers and good wishes leads adepts to assist and save all beings. It teaches them to act morally, to give donations, and to participate in activities of the Dao. Educators in the Dao, they achieve a state of inward-looking mindfulness which allows them to live by a vision that centers on the cosmos rather than the community. Adepts reaching higher stages go beyond social concerns and behaviors and actively visualize the gods both in their bodies and in the greater universe. They ecstatically travel to the heavens and interact with the immortals, finding their true home in the great expanse of the pure realm of the Dao. As they become more familiar with the celestial realms, they gain heavenly status and, assisted by jade lads and jade maidens, join the ranks of the sages, perfected, and immortals in the entourage of the Heavenly Worthies. Thereby they transform into celestial immortals and come to lead an everlasting life of ease and divine splendor.

PRAYERS AND COMPASSION

The earliest set of resolutions in the Daoist tradition is a group of mental intentions found among early Numinous Treasure texts in *The Fifty-Eight Prayers of Great Clarity* (*Taiqing wushiba yuanwen* 太清五十八願文, DZ 187). Expanding on self-admonitions like the fourteen principles of self-control that accompany the Ten Precepts and the twelve desirable attitudes that go with the Ten Wisdom Precepts, the text specifies various situations in which followers are to think positive thoughts. But unlike these admonitions, which encourage practitioners to put themselves into one other person's place and to think kindly toward him or her, the resolutions take all sorts of situations and turn them into opportunities for a radical change of thinking, from the personal to the universal. The text begins:

1. When I encounter wives and children living in their homes, I shall pray that all may soon emerge from their prison of love, concentrate their intention, and observe the precepts.
2. When I encounter people drinking wine, I shall pray that all may control their gates of destiny and be far removed from bad fortune and disorder.
3. When I encounter young girls, I shall pray that all may guard their passions, restrain their sensuality, and set their wills and wishes on becoming wise.
4. When I encounter people engaging in licentiousness, I shall pray that all may get rid of their depraved thoughts and elevate their minds to the level of the prohibitions and precepts. (1a)

Both ordinary situations, such as the encounter or "seeing" (*jian* 見) of wives, children, and young girls, and the confrontation with potentially harmful activities, such as drinking and licentiousness, are used to transform the mind of the practitioner from a limited and maybe critical assessment toward good wishes for all beings. This universality of the mind to be cultivated elevates the practitioner beyond the boundaries of communal life. Each person and every situation becomes a reminder of what the Daoist should be like and how the world could look if all followed the rules of cosmic harmony and created peace.

The text continues by going through a whole gamut of possible types of people one may encounter: perfected, ordinary folk, good and bad, poor and rich, noble and humble, and those of numerous different ranks, from the emperor and his lords to the wise, recluses, and others. Having exhausted this list, the text moves on to different places: large states and small countries, busy marketplaces and quiet cottages, or high mountains and wide oceans, as well as to different activities people undertake. They could be performing religious observances, wandering about, talking to others, or eating and drinking. They could be hunting and fishing, ailing and growing old, or singing and dancing. Then again, there could be various natural phenomena one may encounter, such as snow and rain, wind and sunshine, or star light and rivers. All different situations trigger thoughts of universal salvation and good wishes for all beings. Adepts transform mentally to become as pure as the driven snow and as nurturing as the pouring rain, while their desires and sensory pleasures are scattered as if before a hard-blowing wind (3a).

Having a mind of good wishes and prayers for all beings comes close to realizing the Dao in this life. *The Fifty-Eight Prayers* points out that the path begins with the observation of elementary moral rules. Followers are to practice being "filial to kin, loyal to ruler, compassionate to servants, and open to friends" (6a). This creates an atmosphere of mutual trust which provides the basic personal and social security necessary for the practice of goodness and the gradual relaxation of egoistic goals. Firm in their openness to the Dao, practitioners can "give up all sex and wine, sound and sights, jealousy and envy, killing and harm, luxury and greed, pride and laziness" and desist from eating the five pungent vegetables, rich meats, and other luscious tastes (6a).

"Next, they stop taking grains in their meals, venerate and observe the great precepts, control and strengthen their diligence and will, undertake gymnastics and embryo respiration, practice breathing exercises and harmonize the inner fluids, and generally cultivate and build up their merit and virtue" (6b). Having reached this level of refinement, they become increasingly one with the subtler *qi* of the universe and more sensitive toward the needs and feelings of others, so that their mind naturally turns toward helping and supporting all beings in their needs. The resolutions prescribed in *The Fifty-Eight Prayers*, then, serve as a guideline for the right kind of thinking to be cultivated in an advanced practitioner who already has moved far away from ordinary life and mentation.

The same basic understanding is also found in the *Rules and Precepts for Worshiping the Dao*, which contains a section entitled "Dao Rules for Compassionate Assistance" found in a Dunhuang manuscript (DH 39; Kohn 2004, sect. 24). All other sections of the text outline ways to erect buildings, maintain statues, copy texts, chant scriptures, and perform rituals. In each case they list cosmic punishments for noncompliance in the form of subtractions of days from the life expectancy. This section, in contrast, prescribes positive ways of thinking and behaving in the world and specifies additional days of life to be gained. It begins with a general admonition to be pure in mind and heart, encouraging Daoists "always to make compassion foremost and in each affair to serve with your whole heart and always to bring forth loving mindfulness. Whether walking, sitting, lying down, or resting, constantly think of being of assistance in the salvation [of all]" (l. 26-28).

Following this, like *The Fifty-Eight Prayers*, the text outlines a number of different situations in which Daoists may find themselves that could give them an impulse to think positively toward universal salvation. For example, if Daoists are in uninhabited mountains or on winding roads, they should develop the good intention to build free lodges for the protection of all travelers (l. 30-32); if they encounter an impassable river, blocked road, or broken bridge, they should wish for all beings to be free from obstacles and obstructions (l. 33-35); if they wander through the countryside, they should develop the good intention to dig wells and plant fruit trees, so that all beings can quench their hunger and thirst (l. 36-40).

In all cases, instead of wishing for better roads and facilities for themselves and complaining about the hardships of the journey, Daoists are to use the opportunity provided by each and every experience to create a mindset of helpfulness and compassion. They should develop a social awareness of need and an inner urge to support life in all its forms. This awareness is particularly pronounced when they encounter people suffering from imprisonment, slavery, sickness, poverty, abandonment, and old age. These situations should lead to an even stronger intention to create fields of blessedness and to find ways to distribute charity, radiate purity, and provide medicines. Each thought is to end in the wish: "May they all attain good fortune without measure!" If practiced with dedication, this leads to an extension of longevity by a year or more, providing a concrete reward in this world matched only by the cosmic sense of oneness with the Dao.

DAILY VERSES

This oneness with the Dao, however, is not only found in great compassionate thoughts during encounters with others, but can also be achieved by raising the awareness of ordinary, daily functions with the help of special chants. For example, opening the eyes after a night's sleep, monastic Daoists are to think: "I pray that all living beings leave the path of error and enter awakening, bright and open like this bright morning." Upon hearing the bell that orders them to rise, they reflect: "May the great sound of the bell wake all to truth and perfection!" (Min 1990, 107). Verses like these accompany all daily activities of Daoists, creating a sense of cosmic connection and universal well-wishing even during the most mundane of acts. They appear variously in medieval texts, are prominent in the rules of Complete Perfection, and still play an important role today.

For example, the *Ten Items of Dignified Observances* has two chants for cleaning the teeth, one on using a willow branch, another for ground ashes. They are:

> The great yang [of the sun] harmonizes its energy
> To let spring arise and make the willow grow.
> Breaking it off, I take one branch,
> So I can clean my body and my mouth.
> Studying the Dao and cultivating perfection,
> May I go beyond the Three Worlds of existence!
> Swiftly, swiftly, in accordance with the statutes and ordinances!
> (8b; also *Rules for a Thousand Perfected* 30a)

And:

> Washing with ashes to remove the dirt,
> Using the ashes as a primary means,
> May foulness go and perfection arise.
> Cleansing the heart and cleaning the mouth,
> Realizing the Dao and saving others,
> Heaven is great and Earth everlasting!
> Swiftly, swiftly, in accordance with the statutes and ordinances! (8b)

In both versions, the act of cleaning the teeth with a natural substance is elevated to a cosmic purification of body and mind. It becomes the occasion for a wish of universal power and transcendence, while the very body of the Daoist turns into the field in which realization and cosmic oneness take place. Both chants, moreover, reappear in modern times, listed together with many others in the *Precepts of Initial Perfection* of the Complete Perfection school and in modern outlines of Daoist rules (Min 1990, 107-8). They also echo Buddhist practices as outlined in the *Vinaya* (Beal 1871, 226; Horner 1992, 2:391) and verses first found in the *Flower Garland Sūtra* (e.g., Cleary 1984, 318).[1]

Other chants are more specifically Daoist. One sanctifies combing the hair and tying the top-knot. It involves an imploration of various deities of the hair and head to take care of practitio-

---

[11] Similar verses are still used in Zen today (Kennett 1976, 302), where their authority is based on Dōgen's 道元 (1200-1253) *Eye of the Treasury of the Right Dharma* (*Shōbō genzō* 正法眼藏). See Yokoi 1986, 594-95.

ners and to give them protection. The chant, found first in the *Rules and Observances for Students of the Dao* of the early seventh century, runs:

> May the Great Emperor spread numinous power [to me];
> May the Five Elders recover spirit [for me].
> May the [gods of] Niwan and of Mysterious Florescence
> Preserve my essence and [grant me] long life.
> On the right I hold the shadow of the moon,
> On the left I pull the root of the sun.
> As the six harmonies are pure and refined,
> May the hundred spirits extend their kindness [to me]. (1.12b)

This elevates the grooming of the head to a cosmic activity. Following ancient Chinese models, which saw hair as an expression of the person's essence and placed special significance on its grooming (see Ōgata 1995; also Hiltebeitel and Miller 1998), the chant invokes first the Emperor of Heaven and the Five Elders, deities associated with the five phases in the five directions, to create a general cosmic connection. It then turns to the god of the Niwan Palace, who represents the center of the head and resides in the upper cinnabar field, a key location for communication with the divine, and the Lord of Mysterious Florescence, a deity more specifically associated with hair.

The chant was sung while using a special comb known as the Comb of Mysterious Florescence, adepts groomed their hair at cock crow each morning. They took the comb out of its special box and ran it through their hair while facing north. Grooming properly was very important since, as the *Rules and Observances for Students of the Dao* points out, a disheveled look made one appear like a commoner in grief, a sick or suffering person, someone poor and destitute, or just lazy and wayward. Women, moreover, should avoid putting their hair up in the fashion of the world and should not use ornaments from precious metals. Also, any hair combed out should be kept in a clean place and burned in secret within nine days of the combing (1.12a-13a).

Among more recent chants, found in the *Precepts of Medium Ultimate* of the Complete Perfection School, there are several regarding the sacred robes, tablet, shoes, and headdress. To give one example, the chant for vestments runs

> The scarlet robes of the precepts
> Are my body's ornaments.
> Cloudy skirts save from distress,
> Auroral pendants lift coveting inclinations.
> All hundred limbs fully covered,
> Never dare I not behave with gravity. (36b-37a)

Here the vestments of the Dao are described as divine agents of protection against distress and signs of the formal dignity of the Daoist. Symbolizing the precepts and the importance of the Daoist mission in the world, the robes encourage the strong determination to maintain the seriousness of the Daoist enterprise and always to behave with gravity. Similarly, the ritual tablet is described as symbolic of the Daoist's dignity and propriety, encouraging reverence and deep respect, while the shoes become the central focus of various protective deities who stand by the Daoist and walk everywhere with him. The headdress, finally, contains myriad images and allows yin and yang to shine forth freely (37ab).

Incantations for concrete activities even reached to the point of death. Accepted as part of the natural transformations of the body and seen as an opportunity to rise spiritually to the gods in an existence unfettered by physical limitations, death was approached with calmness and control in the Daoist environment (*Rules and Observances for Students of the Dao* 2.16a). As the end drew close, the dying person was moved into the Transformation Building, ideally located in the northwest corner of the monastery and equipped with a statue of the Heavenly Worthy. "Seated on a lotus throne, the god points skyward with his left hand. Make the dying person face the deity and focus on his or her impending transformation" (*Rules for a Thousand Perfected* 20b).

This echoes Buddhist practices in the so-called Impermanence Building (Tuzuki 2002, 68), where the dying were encouraged to prepare themselves by putting on clean, formal garb and by sitting up in meditation posture to consciously experience their passing (Prip-Møller 1967, 163; Foulk and Sharf 1994). It also reflects similar activities in ancient China where, according to the *Book of Rites*, "the sufferer lay with his head to the east" and his clothes were changed for the arrival of death (19/1.1; Legge 1968, 2:173). Along the same lines Complete Perfection Daoists are guided to mentally chant the "Incantation for Handing in the Registration." The *Precepts of Medium Ultimate* has:

> *Om*! As ordered, my body will now rest
> On the seat of the Seven Treasures,
> Ascend to the seat of Fivefold Radiance,
> And become a perfected king of the divine law.
> Wondrous, I am worthy to control all;
> Pure spirit, I visit the Jade Capital. (37b)

To the very end of life, Daoists are thus encouraged to think in cosmic and universal terms, seeing themselves as divine spirits and helpers of suffering humanity, their very physical existence an expression of celestial purity and cosmic oneness.

CELESTIAL COMPANIONS

Like the chants for everyday life, so the activation of celestial companionship through mental resolutions and mindfulness practice is important in both medieval and modern Daoism. Formulated in a set of eighty-four precepts as part of *The Great Precepts of Self-Observation* in the sixth century and recouped in the *Precepts of Medium Ultimate* of Complete Perfection, they guide practitioners to the cosmic mindset appropriate and necessary for higher Daoist attainments. Not only compassionate toward all beings and aware of the cosmic relevance of daily activities, Daoists were also to create internal resolutions to lead a life of purity and good karma, to encounter sages and divine beings, and to travel ecstatically to the gods.

Ecstatic visions of deities have formed part of advanced Daoist practice ever since the revelations of Highest Clarity in the mid-fourth century. Learning about the organization of the thirty-six heavens and receiving instructions on how to practice visualizations and ecstatic meditations in order to experience the higher planes, adepts of Highest Clarity inspired the Numinous Treasure school and later formed the highest rank of the integrated ordination hierarchy, only topped by those with comprehensive control over all Three Caverns.

Highest Clarity practice firmly placed practitioners into a cosmic context and made them see the gods and heavens as more real than the body and human society. Creating a representation of the universe, of the body, and of themselves, Daoists made this representation come alive and then proceeded to join it, becoming one with the universe at large and establishing themselves in its center (Robinet 1989b, 159). By joining the representation of the universe and ecstatically traveling to the higher reaches of the heavens, Daoists developed from ordinary people into cosmic beings. No longer limited to their earthly environment, they increasingly made the heavens their true home, wandered freely throughout the far ends of the world, and soared up into the sky. Full residents of heaven, they strove to get their names transferred from the registers of the living to those of the immortals, thereby excising any entry that might still be found in the ledgers of the dead. Eventually they achieved a proper position in the heavenly hierarchy.

The Great Precepts of Self-Observation and its modern counterpart, the *Precepts of Medium Ultimate*, set the framework for the moral, behavioral, and spiritual behavior of advanced Daoists. The texts claim celestial origin for the rules, stating that "the great precepts of self-observation in wisdom originally were floating rays of light, diffused and overflowing, radiating through the great void" (1a). Only after an extensive period did they coagulate into words, thus ready to be transmitted by the Heavenly King of Primordial Beginning to the Highest Lord and Lofty Sage of the Dao, who in turn passed them on to the Heavenly Emperor of Great Tenuity and the Perfected of Great Ultimate, the main revealing deities of the scripture.

Before listing the precepts, the texts present the "Hymn to Wisdom" in three stanzas, allegedly composed by the Emperor of Great Tenuity out of pure delight at receiving the precepts. These stanzas appear frequently in the literature and are typically recited during ordination ceremonies. They begin with a glorification:

> Wisdom arises from original nonbeing,
> Brightly it illuminates the ten directions.
> Combined in the void, formed in the mysterious empyrean—
> It pours from the various heavens as flowing fragrance.
> Its wonders are beyond belief,
> Its empty impulse truly beyond the real.
> It is right there, yet it is not—
> It is not there, yet nothing is without it.

Next, both texts present the precepts in an arrangement that follows the model of the Three Primes. The list begins with 180 elementary prohibitions addressed to those under the supervision of Lower Prime. Here the greatest degree of variation appears, the *Precepts of Medium Ultimate* leaving out numerous rules beginning with "Do not instruct anyone to" and instead integrating more rules from the *180 Precepts of Lord Lao*. Next, both texts present thirty-six partly prohibitive, partly prescriptive rules for followers of Middle Prime. They include rules of social politeness and tranquility of mind. The last division contains eighty-four precepts for disciples of Higher Prime and focuses on resolutions and the mindset of advanced practitioners.

The latter include various kinds of mental encouragements, beginning with the simple resolution to "maintain vegetarian food as my regular diet" (no. 217) and to "be at peace in poverty while reading the scriptures and practicing the Dao without tiring" (no. 220). Next, it directs practitioners to develop proper desire for Daoist practice, such as "burning all kinds of famous incense" (no. 221), "carefully listening to wondrous instructions" (no. 222), "diligently present-ing offerings to the Three Treasures" (no. 223), and the like. Then come wishes to save all beings, to repay the kindness of parents and teachers, to aid the purity of the state, and to help peace in the land (nos. 224-228). An altruistic thought similarly to a bodhisattva vow is listed: "May I place the myriad beings first and not attain the Dao only for myself" (no. 229). It is followed by the desire to be far removed from sensory enticements and the negative impact of ghosts and demons, doubts and errors, ambitions and passions (nos. 230-237).

After several more prayers for the well-being and the salvation of all beings, the sageliness of the emperor, and the heavenly ascent of one's ancestors (nos. 240-246), the text presents guide-lines for advanced meditation and visualization practice, moving the level of resolutions and mindfulness toward active companionship with the divine. It says:

265. May I ascend to the immortals and go beyond the world, riding in cloudy carriages drawn by dragon steeds. . . .
269. May I participate in celestial feasts and the fare of spontaneity, never even imagining the feeling of hunger and thirst.
270. May I join the celestials and perfected in serenity and nonaction.
271. May I command immortal lads and jade maidens.
272. May I wander to the east, to the eastern florescence with its green woods.
273. May I wander to the south, to the southern florescence with its great cinnabar.
274. May I wander to the west, to the western florescence with its peaceful nurturing.
275. May I wander to the north, to the northern florescence with its azure network.
276. May I wander to the northeast and save all the men and women of the hundred families there. May I give them these admonitions and precepts and save them through the gate of the northeast, allowing them to attain entry into the sphere of nonaction. (*Self-Observation* 15ab)

These resolutions create a mind in the practitioner that is still set on saving all beings but no longer looks to ordinary daily situations for its activation. Rather, it goes far beyond the experi-ences of daily life and the encounter of various people and situations, reaching into the heavens and cultivating the practitioner's divinity. The Daoist mind at this stage joins the Dao by over-coming the limitations of personal, sensory impressions, set irrevocably on the attainment of ce-lestial visions and the experience of realms beyond earthly levels. Empowered by the contact with the divinities and the experience of wandering to the far reaches of the universe, the Daoist becomes an even stronger guide for ordinary people, giving them precepts and instructions from a celestial perspective.

A further resolution is accordingly to "wander to many purgation halls, there to lecture and pre-sent the sagely Dao, to elucidate and explain its deepest obscurities" (no. 281). Beyond this, the advanced Daoist even wishes to "convert the great demon kings" and with their help to have his name "entered into the ranks of the immortals, far removed from the record of the [underworld] springs" (no. 290) while his "mind becomes the Dao" (no. 299).

A full partner of the gods above, he or she cavorts among the celestial palaces, moves freely in all directions, enjoys celestial music, and floats on the lotus blossoms of the heavenly pools. As a vivid image of heavenly existence is formed in the practitioner's mind through the steady recita-tion and remembrance of these resolutions, so his or her mind is made purer and more un-worldly, transcending the limitations of ordinary existence and even going beyond the desire for universal salvation and the betterment of the world. The Daoist becomes a pure, celestial being, returned to the Dao in mind and body and forever free to move about the heavenly spheres in ultimate nonattachment and cosmic openness.

THE PERFECTION OF VIRTUE

On a different plane, this celestial purity makes the realized Daoist a representative of perfect virtue, someone whose mind is no longer determined by thoughts, wishes, or even resolutions. Instead, the person becomes an embodiment of the highest virtues. This state is outlined in the *Great Precepts for Celestial Immortals* (*Tianxian dajie* 天仙 大戒, JY 291; ZW 403), the highest text of Complete Perfection precepts. Briefly summarized by Hackmann (1920, 169), this work shares with the other Complete Perfection texts that it is prefaced by a formal ordination certificate. However, unlike them it does not contain a list of rules. Instead, it gives general encouragement to develop wisdom, selflessness, and compassion. It also presents the text of the *Scripture of Purity and Tranquility* (*Qingjing jing* 清靜經), frequently recited at Complete Perfection services, as well as passages from the *Daode jing* and a number of other medieval texts, together with various holy verses (*gāthas*) and hymns of praise.

The text begins with the Heavenly Worthy of Primordial Beginning seated on a lotus throne in a celestial hall, answering the question of a dedicated perfected who already has the *Precepts of Initial Perfection* and knows about those for celestial immortals, but has not received them. The Heavenly Worthy outlines the nine ranks of immortals, the first three of which are strictly otherworldly, including the Golden Immortals of Chaos Prime and Nonbeginning, the Golden Immortals of Great Initiation and Pervasive Prime, and the Perfected Immortals of Creation and Numinous Prime. The remaining six ranks are accessible to human practitioners; among them the Celestial Immortals rank first, followed by Earth Immortals, Water Immortals, Spirit Immortals, Human Immortals, and Ghost Immortals (3a).

After this, the Heavenly Worthy and the celestial host chant a song of praise, then various medieval scriptures are adduced to emphasize the importance of controlled behavior. Next, the Lord of the Dao steps forward to present the ten virtues necessary for the attainment of celestial immortality and their practical application. These ten virtues are adapted from the ten bodhisattva virtues of Buddhism (see Soothill and Hodous 1937, 267; Keown 1992, 130). Three (marked with an asterisk) match the Buddhist model literally, three can be linked with similar ones, and four are replaced by new virtues. The list is as follows:

The system thus uses the first six of the classical Buddhist *pāramitās* while replacing the last four, i.e., expedient means (*upaya, fangbian* 方便), good resolutions (*pranidhāna, yuan* 願), strength of purpose (*bala, li* 力), and knowledge (*jnāna, zhi* 知) with more specifically Daoist traits (Soothill and Hodous 1937, 51).

Celestial Virtue	Buddhist Pāramitās
1. wisdom (*zhihui* 智慧)*	wisdom (*prajnā, hui* 慧)
2. compassion (*cibei* 慈悲)	charity (*dāna, shi* 施)
3. forbearance (*hanren* 含忍)*	forbearance (*ksanti, renxun* 忍尋)
4. controlled behavior (*xinggong* 行功)	moral conduct (*sila, jie* 戒)
5. mind-cultivation (*xiuxin* 修心)	calmness (*dhyāna, chan* 禪)
6. good karmic deeds (*shanye* 善業)	
7. efforts (*jingjin* 精進)*	efforts (*viriya, jingjin* 精進)
8. self-concealment (*shishen* 飾身)	
9. removal of passions (*yiqing* 遺情)	
10. universal mind (*puxin* 普心)	

Incorporating these ten virtues into his life, the budding immortal of Complete Perfection pursues twenty-seven actions, listed in a formulaic pattern, in each case repeating the formula for each virtue (9a-30a):

1. Through wisdom, compassion, forbearance [and the other virtues], I remove all dharmas of physical action, immeasurable and indescribable.[2]
2. Through . . . I separate myself from all dharmas of verbal transgressions, . . .
3. Through . . . I abandon all dharmas of thinking evil, . . .
4. Through . . . I give up all dharmas that entangle the root, . . .
5. Through . . . I abolish all dharmas of sound and sight, . . .
6. Through . . . I control all dharmas of love and desires, . . .
7. Through . . . I release all dharmas of playfulness and frivolity, . . .
8. Through . . . I wash off all dharmas of dirt and foulness, . . .
9. Through . . . I am free from all dharmas of darkness and delusion, . . .
10. Through . . . I do not give rise to any dharmas of lascivious imagination, . . .
11. Through . . . I do not give rise to any dharmas of doubt and vagueness, . . .
12. Through . . . I equalize all dharmas of liking and disliking, . . .
13. Through . . . I do not give rise to any dharmas of wrong recompense, . . .
14. Through . . . I always reside in the dharmas of nonbeing, . . .
15. Through . . . I abolish all dharmas of mental imagining, . . .
16. Through . . . I practice the dharmas of changing intention, . . .
17. Through . . . I become skillful at blocking the dharmas of words, . . .
18. Through . . . I do not give rise to any dharmas of confused transmigration, . . .
19. Through . . . I do not give rise to any dharmas of thoughts of enlightenment, . .
20. Through . . . I do not give rise to any dharmas of thoughts of others, . . .
21. Through . . . I do not give rise to any dharmas of thoughts of anxiety, . . .
22. Through . . . I become free from all dharmas of constant fixation, . . .
23. Through . . . I become free from all dharmas of constant purpose, . . .
24. Through . . . I become free from all dharmas of constant care, . . .
25. Through . . . I do not give rise to any dharmas of pursuing and longing, . . .
26. Through . . . I do not give rise to any dharmas of planning and predicting, . . .
27. Through . . . I learn to bear the dharmas that cannot be borne, . . .

---

[2] The text repeats the formula for each of the ten virtues. All lines, moreover, end with the words "immeasurable and indescribable."

Practitioners of this level of Complete Perfection perfect the altruistic application of the ten virtues in all dimensions of life. Doing so, they become free from sensory entanglements, foulness, wrongness, and delusion, and attain a level of comprehensive concern for all beings that matches the purity, kindness, and equanimity of the Dao. By going beyond even ecstatic excursions and celestial ranks, which were the highest goals of Daoist practice in the middle ages, Complete Perfection practitioners realize a morally pure and karmically refined state of universal-mindedness that closely follows Buddhist models yet is also solidly based in the world of the Dao. Their mind at one with the purity of the ten virtues, they are no longer able to commit any of the sins or shortcomings of ordinary thinking. Instead, they turn into pure representations of virtue, acting and thinking only in complete harmony with the cosmic flow. This makes them free from ordinary mentation, dissolving even minor inklings of tension, selfishness, worry, and concern. A mind of emptiness, of floating purity—this is the Dao at its ultimate level, a pure presence of virtue, wisdom, selflessness, and compassion.

To get to this level, and even to the mental freedom of conversing with the gods in the heavens, adepts have to develop yet another form of resolutions in their minds. They have to be willing to sacrifice themselves and many things precious to them for the attainment of the Dao. A set of resolutions of this nature, more determinations than prayers or exercises in mentation, is found in the *Scripture of Prohibitions and Precepts* of the early Tang dynasty. Here we have:

> I would rather be violated in my body and have it become minute, subtle dust than ever violate the scriptural precepts of the Heavenly Worthies.
> I would rather be harmed by wild tigers and poisonous snakes than ever harm the rules and prohibitions of the Heavenly Worthies.
> I would rather be killed in this body and have my life cut short than ever not fulfill the covenant and my pledges to the Heavenly Worthies.
> I would rather lose the sight of both eyes in my body than ever lose the dignified observances of the Heavenly Worthies. (l. 41-44)

In other words, practitioners need to be ready to overcome their inherent instincts of self-preservation. They must be willing to sacrifice their lives, selves, and senses for the greater good of the Dao, giving up anything rather than straying from the path toward universal oneness. They must also develop detachment to their bodies and lives in favor of obedience to the precepts and the duties of the Dao, thereby learning to sustain an inner dialogue that prefers violent bodily harm to any infraction of the rules:

> I would rather enter a great fiery pit than ever join the company of the impure and those outside the divine law.
> I would rather be eaten by wild animals and consumed by fire than ever eat the food of those outside the divine law.
> I would rather let a thousand pints of blood from my body than ever let words against the divine law out of my mouth.
> I would rather fall into the defilement of the outhouse than ever be defiled by the various passions and desires. (l. 45-50)

The various resolutions, intentions, and assertions of determination, therefore, create a form of universal ethics that involves a deep sense of well-wishing for others and an alignment of the practitioners with celestial purity and cosmic virtue. Through mental resolutions Daoists develop total dedication to the universe and the salvation of all beings. They effect a fundamental transformation of the self, from a limited if well-meaning personal and social entity into a floating universal being, at one with the greater flow of the universe. Their community has become the entire cosmos, whether they start out as lay followers or as monks and nuns. The latter is easier, and more monastic rules focus on the mental state of practitioners, but in all cases they go beyond the reverberations of karma, ritual purity, and bodily harm to align themselves fully with the heavens and to become as inherently good and as immortal as the Dao.

CONCLUSION

The perfect community in complete harmony with the cosmos is an essential ideal of the Daoist religion. Developing the age-old Chinese vision of Great Peace, Daoists envisioned the Dao as the fundamental force of creation ordering both the human world and the universe in complete wholeness (Eichhorn 1957). It pervades all equally, joining the different levels of existence into one: cosmos, nature, state, and body. Any action on one plane for them has reverberations on all the others and influences the entire system. State government, personal cultivation, and natural cycles are different aspects of one and the same system that, if all was as it was meant to be, should work together for the benefit of all.

As a philosophical position, this is most clearly expressed by the philosopher Guo Xiang 郭象 (d. 312) in his commentary to the *Zhuangzi (DZ 745)*. He insists that the universe exists by itself and of itself. It is perfect as it is, and nothing can be added to or subtracted from it. As Isabelle Robinet says, for Guo Xiang "the world is like the absolute" (1983).

Inherently perfect and unfolding in spontaneity, the universe is yet not without structure. It is organized through principle (*li* 理) and share or allotment (*fen* 分). Principle is a cosmic power that makes everything be what it is and appears in people as their destiny (*ming* 命). "Each individual has principle as much as each and every affair has what is appropriate to it," Guo Xiang says (3.14b). It is inescapable and determines the particular way of being of each individual, group, and natural constellation. Similarly allotment is a cosmic necessity, which in people appears as their inner nature (*xing* 性). It means that any concrete existence is only possible through obtaining some share in the Dao. This allotment determines the person's position in the larger cosmos, while principle is responsible for the particular way in which this position is filled (see Knaul 1985).

The ideal universe or state of Great Peace is reached when all people realize themselves by doing that for which they are naturally suited, creating personal contentment, social relevance, and an overarching harmony. While setting limitations on people's activities, Guo Xiang's system is not deterministic. Rather, society and human life are the arena in which people live up to their inborn abilities and opportunities and realize themselves fully. This utmost perfection involves also a natural ethics in reflection of the goodness of the cosmos and the inherent harmony of human community.

In religious Daoism, this ideal is played out in three different forms of community—millenarian groups, lay organizations, and monastic institutions, which historically grew out of each other and developed different yet interrelated forms. They each worked with basically four different kinds of moral and ethical guidelines—prohibitions, admonitions, injunctions, and resolutions, which can also be described as moral rules, supererogatory guidelines, instructions for daily living, and altruistic thoughts and prayers.

These rules set Daoists apart from ordinary people and the declined state of the world. They form the basis of community membership and create a separate sphere of power and efficacy which increasingly unfolds into an ideal world. Moral and ethical rules provide the elementary backbone strength that allows practitioners to banish demons, to command spirits, to control nature, and generally to act as a member of the celestial realm. Vowing to observe these rules places the person into the cosmic community and transfers allegiance from family and society to the Daoist organization, the host of the sages, and ultimately the cosmos itself.

While formulating moral and ethical guidelines, Daoists through the ages have used and transformed other traditions. They integrated Confucian virtues and demands of social cooperation; popular concepts of reciprocity between people, gods, and demons; as well as Buddhist notions of bodhisattva altruism, karmic retribution, and the perfection of virtue. Although formulated in various terms, Daoist rules are unmistakably Daoist because they work in relation to the *qi*-constellations of the human body, the workings of the celestial administration, and the supernatural forces of the universe.

It is thus not surprising that some of the major guidelines include resolutions of visualizations and ecstatic excursions, that the banishing of demons is never far away from the pronouncement of moral rules, and that sets of ten precepts are used to control hungry ghosts and other wayward spirits. As the *Scripture of Prohibitions and Precepts* says:

> The ones who scrupulously observes the precepts need not fear Heaven or man, need not fear demons and spirits. Instead in this life, the lads of the various heavens, the spirit kings of the diamond network, the five emperors of the Three Worlds, the spirit immortals, the soldiers and cavalry [of Heaven], the generals and strongmen—all the 1,200 [divine] personages come to attend and guard him.

> They will steer him clear of the host of misfortunes and disasters, official involvement and slander, capture and punishment, evil demon kings and nasty demons, water and fire, swords and weapons, tigers and wolves, scorpions and snakes, as well as all diseases and afflictions. (l. 61-63)

And yet, this magical empowerment also has a moral dimension in the sense that the Daoist cosmos is inherently good and can be approached by practicing goodness. The *Great Precepts of Self-Observation* says:

> The essentials of the Dao lie in practicing in accordance with the luminous rules and in accumulating goodness. Only on this basis can one traverse the realm of the Dao. . .

> The Dao is within me; it does not come from elsewhere. Just kindness, just love, just forbearance, just bashfulness—if you can practice these four virtues, you are getting closer to the Dao. (23a)

Daoist ethics is thus a conduit for the power and energy of the cosmos as it works in and through practitioners, both individually and communally. The rules lay the foundation of an attitude that realizes universal interconnectedness in everything one is and does. Practitioners' conduct is not isolated in the human sphere and separated from nature but is located in the larger context of the cosmic flow. Specific rules are not as important as the sense of the codex as a whole. As a result, behavioral guidelines are neither foundational nor separate but constitute a key aspect of Daoist practice that affects the nourishing powers of Heaven and Earth and leads to the creation of integrated communities that best allow the transformation of the individual into a fully realized cosmic being.

While all Daoist rules work toward cosmic harmony, they are also highly specific and appear differently not only among the three major kinds of community but also in the various ordination ranks and in different ritual contexts. This links back to Guo Xiang's notion of principle and allotment, acknowledging the unique nature of individuals and situations in the larger cosmic context. Sets of rules need to accommodate the variety of possible constellations of character, preparation, inner energy, and outer circumstances, leading to a tremendous variation in ethical guidelines over time and among schools.

Despite this, there is a strong continuity in the precepts throughout Daoist history, most obvious in the 180 precepts that existed from an early period among the Celestial Masters and have, with variations, continued down to Complete Perfection today. But also the ten precepts are highly persistent, with the elementary five rules as a baseline and various forms of supplementary injunctions. Once rules of filial piety and loyalty were added into the set of ten in the sixth century, they remained and are still at the top of the list. Even modern monastic rules are traditional, from the verses chanted to elevate ordinary activities, to the detailed rules on the treatment of vestments, and to concrete prescriptions for using the body. Throughout, the development of virtue and the practice goodness as appropriate for specific individuals and communities create an increased cooperation of all things and beings in the universe.

Moral perfection, of course, is not the prerogative of Daoists. If seen from a wider, cross-cultural perspective, what kind of ethical thinking or moral doctrine does this involve? How does Daoist doctrine compare with the ethics of other cultures and religions and with ethics theory today?

Ethics and moral actions are interpreted variously. Ideally, as Immanuel Kant demanded (1959), being morally good should be a goal in itself and bring its own reward. One should be good for its own sake, behaving morally should be the rational thing to do, and morality should not need an exterior motive. The argument is that basic moral rules are so self-explanatory, so logical, and so universal, that any thinking and feeling individual would follow them no matter what (Green 1987, 96). Still, even Kant admitted to the need for supraempirical beings "because of the severity of the rational dilemma raised by moral obedience" (Green 1978, 74), the fundamental conflict between the natural instincts of self-preservation, and the need to submit to the rules or the service of others, between inclination and duty (Kant 1960). There has to be a level of benefit and well-being beyond preserving the self and one's material existence if moral action is to be logically defensible. This level can only be of a supernatural, divine, or cosmic nature; it could be the belief in justice, God, karma, or ancestral wrath (Green 1978, 76, 109).

Other theories of moral behavior include utilitarianism (or prudence) and soteriology (divine command). The utilitarian or prudential position claims that people act morally because it is useful for them and for society. "It is, by and large, advantageous to be a morally upright person and disadvantageous to be an immoral one" (Green 1987, 95). The cost for breaking rules and precepts, both on the psychological and social (material) levels, is enormous. It is thus easier, and more useful, to comply. Modern penal codes and prison systems rely on this concept, imposing harsh punishments for misdeeds in the hope that people will see their uselessness.[1] Along similar lines, the ancient Buddhist propagation of the five precepts included a distinct set of benefits for laymen, such as wealth, good repute, self-confidence in public, an untroubled death, and rebirth in heaven (Gombridge 1971, 247; Obeyesekere 1968, 28; Keown 1992, 44-45).

---

[1] For more on the utilitarian model, see Mabbott 1969, 15-30; Hare 1965, 112-36; Baier 1958; Richards 1971; Williams 1980. For readings from original texts, see Taylor 1972, 136-95. A summary of all the different Western positions on ethical motivation is found in Becker and Becker 1992.

Unlike this explanation of moral behavior, the soteriological viewpoint, also known as divine command morality, emphasizes the belief in a superior deity or law. People act morally not because it is logical or because it gives them advantages but because a divine agency, a root power of the universe, has so decreed. The rewards of morality, despite all apparent futility on this earth, are of a higher nature; the purpose of the rules is beyond the limited faculties of human reason and perception to comprehend. Problems with this particular approach arise when the deity demands actions that are not only incomprehensible but even cruel and repulsive. At this point the devotion to the divine has to be tempered with human reason, and conflict arises (see Idziak 1980; Outka and Reeder 1973).

Religiously based morality tends to be soteriological. Within this framework, however, modifications apply. Buddhist ethics, for example, has been identified as an ethics of intention, as a form of moral determinism, and—especially in its Mahāyāna form—as a system that promotes altruism over all other considerations.

Intention in Buddhism is considered the central factor of all actions, whether mental, vocal, or physical (Tokuno 1991). "By the law of karma, every intention good or bad will eventually be awarded or punished" (Gombrich 1971, 246), often independent of the actual outcome of any given deed. A classical example is the case of the masturbating monk as opposed to one who has seminal emission during a dream. The former is guilty and punishable according to the *Vinaya*, the latter is not.[2]

The goal of the Buddhist path with all its disciplines and meditations accordingly is to create a "choosing will" (Horner 1936, 280) that is based on right knowledge and will always opt for actions in accordance with the best intention and the purest mind. "One wills to act because his actions are in conformity with his own inward state that has been cultured by awareness derived from right knowledge" (Holt 1981, 67). It is the purity of mind and moral quality of intention that brings about the desired soteriological results, i.e., improvement of karma and the eventual complete release from the chains of conditioned existence (Varma 1963, 41).

In terms of moral determinism, Buddhist ethical thinking assumes that the life and good fortune of the individual are determined by his or her moral actions, that there is "a law of just recompense in the world" (Varma 1963, 26), which will make sure one reaps exactly as one sows. This viewpoint stands in contrast with materialistic accidentalism, according to which everything happens at random and is due entirely to chance. It is also significantly different from divine election or fatalism, which maintains that decisions about one's life and fate are made on a supernatural plane and have nothing to do with one's actions or intentions (Varma 1963, 26).

Moral determinism takes into account three factors: the motivation or intention for one's action, the physical and instrumental steps taken to carry it out, and the consequences resulting from it (Varma 1963, 27; Obeyesekere 1968, 22-24). Aside from providing a reasonable answer to fundamental questions of fate and good fortune, it also encourages social conservatism (since social status is due to previously gained merit) and individualism (since one is fully responsible oneself) (Varma 1963, 42-46).

---

[2] For a discussion, see Holt 1981, 53-55; Sadhatissa 1970, 74; Sasaki 1956; Pachow 1955.

A third characteristic of Buddhist ethics its orientation toward altruism, defined as "a willingness to act in consideration of the interests of other persons, without the need of ulterior motives" (Nagel 1970, 79; Munroe 1996, 6). It can be motivated by various emotions—benevolence, sympathy, love, compassion—or it can be pure, an act done for its own sake and the welfare of others (Nagel 1970, 80). The key to altruism is perspective and cognition. It involves a different way of looking at the world, regarding oneself as merely a person among others, finding identity as part of a larger whole, imagining oneself in the situation of others, and seeing fellow human beings where ordinary people see strangers. As a result of this perception, altruists typically state that their unselfish actions are entirely natural and that they do not have a choice over whether or not to help someone (Munroe 1996, 9-14, 197-216; Nagel 1970, 82-83, 100-02). In Buddhism, especially vows and resolutions serve to create this kind of mindset, a bodhisattva way of looking at the world as a whole and seeing every creature as a suffering being striving to realize buddhanature.

Seen in this larger framework, Daoist ethics presents a mixture of the soteriological and utilitarian positions, with a strong Buddhist influence. Ultimately Daoists act morally because Heaven and Earth demand it, but doing so also brings distinct advantages in this life and creates greater harmony in the world. Daoist ethics, like Buddhist, is a form of moral determinism, since everyone will receive their just rewards on the basis of exact record-keeping by the celestial administration and the workings of karma. It is also an ethics of intention, but less so than in Buddhism, since the physical execution of an action and its social consequences are also taken into account.

Ultimately the Daoist ethical vision comes down to two central concerns: control over fate and its vicissitudes and the emergence of the fully conscious human being in transcendental freedom and oneness with Heaven and Earth. The problem of control becomes clear when examining the question of "moral luck." That is to say, however morally correct a person may act, there are always circumstances over which he or she has no control and that may seriously influence the outcome of his or her actions. For example, as Thomas Nagel points out:

> There is a morally significant difference between reckless driving and manslaughter. But whether a reckless driver hits a pedestrian depends on the presence of the pedestrian at the point where he recklessly passes a red light. (1979, 25)

Or again, there may be a careful driver who runs over a child just because she happened to run out into the street at that particular moment (Nagel 1979, 28-29). In other words, the outcome of our actions is determined not entirely by our intentions but is also limited by opportunities and factors beyond our control. It is subject to a broad range of external influences that are coincidental and can only be described as lucky or unlucky. Ascribing guilt to people on the basis of such external circumstances "amounts to holding them responsible for the contributions of fate as well as for their own" (Nagel 1979, 31)—and that is precisely what Daoists are doing.

Following Daoist rules prevents all sorts of unhappy events, be they negative emotions, sickness and disease, failure to prosper, disharmony among one's kin, trouble with the law, encounters with demons, or natural disasters. A person in good moral standing will feel at peace within and step only into positive situations. Favored by the celestial administration, he or she will be in good luck at all times, while someone who violates the rules will be haunted by misfortune—the direct result of bad karmic connections, medical violations, ritual failure, and celestial punishments. Obeying the precepts is thus a way to control the vagaries of fate and to afford the ultimate control over things commonly associated with sheer luck.

Besides serving as the ultimate control mechanism for the vicissitudes of fate, moral and ethical rules in Daoism are also the key factor in the creation of the fully conscious individual, one who has ultimate personal and transcendental freedom—in the sense that, as John Silber says in his discussion of Kant's *Religion Within the Limits of Reason Alone*,

> by telling us what we *ought* to do regardless of what our inclinations and desires may bid us do, the moral law forces us to be aware of ourselves as agents rather than as mere creatures of desire. (1960, lxxxvii)

In other words, the active adoption and observance of the precepts raises the person from an entity driven largely by desires to a conscious, considerate, and thoughtful human being, an individual in the fullest sense of the word as an independent agent with clear intention and complete responsibility. This entails a sense of freedom from drives and desires and an inherent liberty to fulfill the ideal of the universal human—the perfected. On the other hand, the commitment of evil is an act of bondage and the result of a failure to evolve. John Silber writes:

> Not even a wicked man wills evil for the sake of evil. His evil consists in his willing to ignore the moral law and to oppose its demands when it interferes with his non-moral incentives. His evil consists in his abandonment of the conditions of free personal fulfillment in favor of the adoption of the conditions of his fulfillment as a natural creature of desire. This represents the ultimate point in the abnegation of personality. (1960, cxxiv)

The *Ten Items of Dignified Observances* closely echoes this statement:

> Sinful people, obstructive and evil, are close to animals—they may have entered the human realm but have failed to obtain a human heart. In vain they engage in human relationships. Utterly polluted, they may listen to the divine law of the sages, yet their entire inclination is like that of animals kept in a dark pen. Even if all living beings were liberated, they would still not be awakened. With intentions of their low nature, they would only desire to return to their original bodies. (16b)

People without the precepts are blind and lack the ability to see; they are continuously hungry and remain forever starved for the Dao. They are not fully human and, by choosing to follow their lesser instincts rather than the call to moral purity, actively forego all chances of perfection and Daoist realization. Ethics and morality, therefore, form both the essential foundation and the overarching network of the Daoist enterprise, the line that divides the merely outwardly human from the fully perfected and transcendentally free. They open the alignment of humanity with Heaven and Earth in their cosmic goodness and thus allow access to the Dao, the force at the root of all self-transformation and spiritual realization.

Translation

of

Original Sources

THE TEXTS

There are over seventy texts on behavioral rules in the Daoist canon and its supplements, including later collections and manuscripts from Dunhuang. Many of these are discussed in this volume, and a large number are translated either here or in the "Supplement." To give a comprehensive survey of the materials, they are best divided into five distinct groups, following their chronological and sectarian appearance. The five groups are:

1. materials pertaining to the early communities of the Great Peace movement and the Celestial Masters, from the 3rd to the 6th centuries;
2. works addressed mainly to lay followers, linked with the major medieval schools, Numinous Treasure, Highest Clarity, and others, from the 5th and 6th centuries;
3. guidelines for members of medieval monastic institutions, from the 7th and 8th centuries;
4. lists of rules in various texts of the Song through Ming dynasties, largely connected with ritual instructions;
5. Complete Perfection texts that specify the modern ways of the monk together with detailed prescriptions of conduct and instructions on mental attitudes.

The following presents the texts in the order of the five groups. In each case, the title in English, followed by *pinyin* romanization and Chinese characters. Then available editions, a brief note on content and history, and references to translations and scholarly studies are listed. All texts contained in the Daoist canon are summarized and discussed in Ren and Zhong 1991, whose work is not mentioned in each instance. Titles printed in boldface are of works translated below. Those marked with an asterisk are translated in the "Supplement;" those with two asterisks are rendered in full.

EARLY COMMUNITIES: THE CELESTIAL MASTERS

3rd-4th c.: The earliest materials on ethics and community structure are found in documents remaining from the Great Peace movement of the second century. Among the Celestial Masters, founded in 142 C.E., texts focus either on general guidelines of behavior based on the *Daode jing* or on specific rules regarding ritual, communal, and exorcistic activities. Both provide good insight into the early communities and are important for our understanding. Neither has had a strong influence on the later tradition.

Scripture of Great Peace (*Taiping jing* 太平經), ed. DH 86; DZ 1101; Wang 1979. Based on divine words allegedly revealed by the Yellow Lord Lao (Huanglao jun 黃老君) to Gan Ji 干吉, the oldest layer of this complex text dates from about 140 C.E. A first version was presented to the Han emperor Xundi (r. 125-144) and a memorial on the text was submitted to Emperor Huandi in 166. The text was lost after the defeat of the Great Peace movement in the Yellow Turban rebellion of 184, surviving in various fragments but not listed in bibliographies or cited in other materials. In the sixth century the Highest Clarity Daoist Zhou Zhixiang 周智響 reconstituted it and presented it to Emperor Xuandi of the Chen dynasty (r. 568-582). Later the text fragmented again, so that of the 170 chapters listed in a Dunhuang manuscript many are lost (chs. 11-34, 38,

52, 56-64, 73-85, 87, 94-95, 115). Scholars divided the text into various layers, depending on grammar and content. For relevant studies, see Michaud 1958; Kaltenmark 1979; Kandel 1979; Mansvelt-Beck 1980; Petersen 1989-90; Hendrischke 2000, 143-45.

Xiang'er Commentary to the Laozi (*Laozi xiang'er zhu* 老子想爾注), ed. DH 56; Rao 1992; trl. Bokenkamp 1997. The main surviving fragment of this text does not contain the precepts. They are found in sixth-century collections, such as the *Scriptural Statutes of Lord Lao* (*Laojun jinglü* 老君經律, DZ 786, 1a-2a) and in *Highest Scriptural Precepts* (*Taishang jingjie* 太上經戒, DZ 787, 17b-19a). Ascribed to Zhang Lu, the grandson of the Celestial Masters' founder, they may well go back to the third century. The text also contains instructions on worldview and practices. Further studies include Boltz 1982; Mugitani 1985a; 1985b; Boken-kamp 1993; Ōfuchi 1991, 251-57; Kleeman 1991, 188; Min 1990, 111-12. A modern adaptation of the precepts is found in O.D.A. 1998, Parts 1-2.

Demon Statutes of Nüqing (*Nüqing guilü* 女青鬼律), ed. DZ 790. A fourth-century demonography of the Celestial Masters, this describes ways to identify demons and provides spells for their neutralization. This text is associated with the chief of all underworld demons, a shadowy figure called Nüqing. In its third scroll, the text has a section entitled "Prohibitions and Taboos in the Daoist Statutes." See Nickerson 2000, 266-68; Lai 2002a.

5th c.: Having metamorphosed into an organized religion, the Celestial Masters in the fifth century reorganized themselves to accommodate the demands of political correctness and an increasing Buddhist presence. Both northern and southern groups strove for structural reform; the north saw the emergence of the Daoist theocracy and the Louguan center with its adaptation of the five precepts; the south evolved integrative patterns with other schools and developed a more spiritual vision of the precepts.

The 180 Precepts of Lord Lao (*Laojun yibai bashi jie* 老君一百八十戒). This text survives independently in a Dunhuang manuscript (DH 78). It is also found in the sixth-century *Scriptural Precepts of Lord Lao* (DZ 786, 2a-12b), the eighth-century *Essential Rules and Observances* (*Yaoxiu keyi* 要修科儀, DZ 463, 5.14a-19a), and the eleventh-century encyclopedia *Seven Tablets in a Cloudy Satchel* (YJQQ, DZ 1032, 39.1a-14b). A more recent re-edition appears in *Daoist Books Outside the Canon* (*Zangwai daoshu* 藏外道書, ZW 765). It is translated in Hendrischke and Penny 1996. Its 180 precepts provide a good understanding of the Celestial Masters community. They were also essential for the later tradition and many of them are still part of the rules as used in Complete Perfection today. For studies of the text, see Schmidt 1985; Penny 1996; Schipper 2001.

**Precepts and Observances Taught by the Celestial Master* (*Tianshi jiao jieke jing* 天師教戒科經), ed. DZ 789. A fifth-century document, this contains several texts, including also the *Rules Governing the Family of the Dao* (*Dadao jia lingjie* 大道家令戒), discussed and translated in Bokenkamp 1997, 149-85. The *Precepts and Observances* is linked to Kou Qianzhi's theocracy and may represent part of his revelations in 415 and 423, but it may also be of southern origin and represent a different strand of medieval Daoism. The text outlines the theoretical framework of Daoist moral and communal practice, presents the five precepts with a psychological slant, and relates health and moral integrity to the presence of the body gods.

New Code, lit. *Scripture of Lord Lao's Recited Precepts* (*Laojun yinsong jiejing* 老君音誦誡經), ed. DZ 785. Another remaining fragment of Kou's revelations. It contains thirty-six precepts on proper behavior and community organization, many of which were taken up later in the *Statutes of Mystery Metropolis*. See Yang 1956; Mather 1979.

Precepts of the Highest Lord Lao (*Taishang Laojun jiejing* 太上老君戒經), ed. DZ 784; trl. Kohn 1994. A document of the northern Celestial Masters at Louguan 樓觀, this is set at the transmission of the *Daode jing* to Yin Xi 尹喜. It begins with three stanzas of scriptural chant, then contains five questions to Lord Lao on the precepts and their application. In response, Yin Xi receives a detailed explanation of the rules in terms of cosmology, practical application, ordination procedures, and hellish consequences of nonobservance. See also Jan 1986; Min 1990, 112-13.

Transmission Formalities of Scriptures and Precepts (*Chuanshou jingjie yi* 傳授經戒儀), ed. DZ 1238. A manual on ordination, associated with Louguan and based on the *Daode jing*, this describes attainment of the rank of Preceptor of Eminent Mystery through receiving twenty-four texts. See Kohn 2000, 291-92.

***The Five Precepts of Orthodox Unity** (*Zhengyi wujie* 正一五戒), ed. WSBY 46.16b-18a. This is a short outline of the five precepts and their cosmological connection as seen by the Celestial Masters.

Abbreviated Rules for Daoist Followers (*Daomen kelue* 道門科略) ed. DZ 1127; trl. Nickerson 1996. Compiled by Lu Xiujing 陸修靜 (406-477) in the mid-fifth century, this describes the dire straits of the Celestial Masters community at the time and recommends improvements. For more discussion, see Kobayashi 1990.

6ᵗʰ c.: As the empire prepared for unification, Daoist and Buddhist schools began to integrate their teachings and consolidate their organization. For the Celestial Masters, two texts describe this more complex structure, outlining overall values, community organization, and detailed behavioral guidelines. There are also several texts that integrate Celestial Masters teachings with Highest Clarity, presenting rules based on Highest Clarity texts or visions and addressing libationers and lay disciples. They focus on the correct handling of sacred materials and proper community arrangements.

***Statutes of Mystery Metropolis* (*Xuandu lüwen* 玄都律文), ed. DZ 188. This sixth-century work contains six sections on rules for the Celestial Masters community, including general guidelines, prescriptions for ritual practices, lists of undesirable attitudes, good and bad deeds, as well as various items of communal organization, such as inheritance patterns, assembly attendance, and rules for joining communal worship. For more on the text, see Kobayashi 1990, 206-7; Robinet 1984, 2:280; Min 1990, 113-16.

Dignified Observances of Orthodox Unity (*Zhengyi weiyi jing* 正一威儀經) , ed. DZ 791. A list of 132 entries under a total of thirty headings, this contains concrete instructions on the behavior of the followers of the Celestial Masters. Dated to the late sixth century, it is an immediate precursor of the monastic rules, many of which it shares. See Kohn 2003a, 209-10.

Numinous Register for the Protection of Residences (*Zhenzhai linglu* 真宅靈籙), ed. DZ 674. Ascribed to the Highest Clarity visionary Jin Ming 金明 or Qizhenzi 七真子, this goes back to a revelation of a highly potent register of numious generals in 552. The text outlines the register's powers and activation; it also contains forty rules, addressed to lay disciples, that prescribe the right moral attitude when using the register. See Yoshioka 1976, 105; Kohn 2004.

Precepts of Great Perfection (*Taizhen ke* 太真科), surviving in fragments, ed. Ōfuchi 1997, 409-505. The earliest fragment, nine rules on scriptural transmission, is found in the fifth-century Highest Clarity work *Jade Book of the Great Empyrean* (*Taixiao langshu* 太霄琅書, DZ 1352, 5.6a-10b). Later fragments are from the sixth century. They contain rules on transmission, petitions, purgation rites, registers, assemblies, parishes, and many more, indicating a Celestial Masters context.

LAY ORGANIZATIONS: MAJOR SCHOOLS AND OTHER LINEAGES

4th c.: The earliest materials on precepts outside of the Celestial Masters go back to lineages of longevity seekers and alchemists. Both describe the dominant worldview at the time, outlining the connection between long life and good deeds, and encouraging people to behave in an ethical manner for the sake of both the community and their own spiritual attainment.

Essential Precepts of Master Redpine (*Chisongzi zhongjie jing* 赤松子中戒經), ed. DZ 185. The text contains a dialogue between the Yellow Emperor (Huangdi 黃帝) and Master Redpine (Chisongzi) on the cosmology of human life, including the importance of good deeds and the effects of bad ones. It dates from the fourth century and survives in a Song-dynasty edition. For a study, see Kohn 1998c.

*Book of the Master Who Embraces Simplicity (*Baopuzi* 抱朴子), ed. DZ 1185; trl. Ware 1966. By the would-be alchemist Ge Hong 葛洪 (ca. 280-340), this is a major work on operative alchemy and concrete procedures for the attainment of immortality. Chapter 6 contains a set of behavioral guidelines called "Precepts of the Dao" that are presented as part of individual self-cultivation while essentially concerned with social relations. For more on Ge Hong and his text, see Sivin 1969; Sailey 1978.

5th c.: With the emergence of the Numinous Treasure school, Daoist behavioral guidelines enter an entirely new dimension. Numerous texts appear with many different kinds of precepts, often listed in groups of ten; rules evolve from being dominantly prohibitions to also include admonitions and resolutions; the cosmology expands to integrate visions of kalpas, hells, and karmic retribution; and new levels of communal ritual grow to accommodate the needs of a flourishing organized religion. The Buddhist impact is enormous, and many rules as much as their justification are adapted from the foreign religion. Many texts are listed among the earliest Numinous Treasure catalog (abb. LB) and thus date from the first half of the fifth century; they are later recouped by other works that pick up their rules in a tightened, abbreviated format.

Jade Instructions on the Text Written in Red (*Chishu yujue* 赤書玉訣), ed. DH 2; DZ 352 (LB 2). An early text of the ancient Numinous Treasure corpus, this presents a commentary to Ge Chaofu's 葛巢甫 *Perfect Tablets in Five Sections, Written in Red* (*Wupian zhenwen chishu* 五篇真文赤書, DH 1, DZ 22), the very first Numinous Treasure text. Among an outline of the new cosmology, it contains the ten precepts of wisdom and twelve desirable attitudes, classics of Numinous Treasure. See Soymié 1977, 7; Bokenkamp 1983, 479; 1989; Kleeman 1991, 172-73.

Great Precepts of the Highest Ranks (*Shangpin dajie* 上品大戒), ed. DH 7; DZ 177 (LB 13). Also part of the early corpus, this text specifies various sets of rules to be observed by adepts as they attain higher ranks, including the ten precepts of wisdom and twelve desirable attitudes as well as a set of ten items of goodness, based on Buddhist models.

Precepts of the Highest Ranks (*Shangpin jiejing* 上品戒經), ed. DZ 454. An alternate version of the *Great Precepts of the Highest Ranks*, with much the same cosmology and many of the same rules.

Observances for Lamps, Spells, and Vows (*Dengzhu yuan yi* 燈祝願儀), ed. DZ 524. Ascribed to Lu Xiujing and dated to the mid-fifth century, this presents the ritual context for the ten precepts of wisdom and twelve desirable attitudes.

***Precepts Against the Roots of Sin* (*Zuigen pinjie* 罪根品戒), ed. DZ 457 (LB 12). A two-*juan* outline of the unfolding of the world and the development of the Daoist teaching, this text forms part of the early canon. It contains several lists of ten precepts, ten items of goodness, ten evils, and resolutions for aspiring immortals.

Essentials for Pervading the Mystery of the Great Dao (*Dadao tongxuan yao* 大道通玄要), ed. DH 97; ZW 792. A later Numinous Treasure work that contains the same precepts as the *Precepts Against the Roots of Sin*.

Scripture of Causation Through Former Actions (*Benxing suyuan jing* 本行宿緣經), ed. DZ 1114, based on DH 17. Another Numinous Treasure text that has similar rules as the *Precepts Against the Roots of Sin*. See Kusuyama 1982.

Scripture on Setting the Will on Wisdom (*Zhihui dingzhi jing* 智慧定志經), ed. DH 10; DZ 325 (LB 16). Another early Numinous Treasure work that focuses on setting the correct determination for the Dao, this is the earliest source of the ten precepts, the most widely cited and most commonly used set in the Tang.

Scripture of the Ten Precepts (*Shijie jing* 十戒經), ed. DH 31, 32; DZ 459. The abbreviated, condensed version of the previous entry, this provides an ordination speech with ten precepts and fourteen rules of self-control as used in Tang ordination. See Schipper 1985.

The Precepts of the Three Primes (*Sanyuan pinjie* 三元品戒), ed. DH 15; DZ 456 (LB 18); WSBY 43; trl. Kohn 1993, 100-6. The most elaborate list of precepts in the early corpus, this contains 180 rules for Numinous Treasure practitioners, focusing on interaction with the master, protecting the scriptures, and proper forms of communal behavior. It adapts many rules from *The 180 Precepts of Lord Lao* and is a classic in medieval literature.

Great Precepts of Original Prayers (*Benyuan dajie* 本願大戒), ed. DH 16; DZ 344. Also known as *Highest Precepts to Dissolve Evil* (*Xiaomo dajie shangpin* 消魔大戒上品), this is part of the secondary Numinous Treasure corpus associated with Ge Xuan 葛玄. Dated to the fifth century, it contains a list of prayers, i.e., positive mental resolutions, made by Daoists to develop the perception needed for compassionate behavior, thus leading to altruistic ethics.

The Fifty-Eight Prayers of Great Clarity (*Taiqing wushiba yuanwen* 太清五十八願文), ed. DZ 187. The abbreviated, condensed version of the *Great Precepts of Original Prayers*, this focuses entirely on the fifty-eight prayers.

6th c.: As the schools continued to unfold and the Daoist religion became a more sophisticated and intricate organization, texts on behavioral guidelines flourished among all the different schools, showing increasing signs of integration and broadening in appeal and perspective.

Numinous Treasure: Daoists of this school continued to fine tune their rules, specifying lists of ten, twelve, and twenty-four precepts that integrated a growing number of karmic consequences and civil virtues, such as loyalty and filial piety.

**Twelve Highest Precepts of Admonition (*Shier shangpin quanjie* 十二上品權戒), ed. DZ 182. Revealed by Ge Xuan, the Perfected of Great Ultimate to the Immortal Lord on the Left, this probably dates from the sixth century. It specifies twelve prohibitions of unruly behavior after an introduction, a lament of the human condition, and encouraging verses.

**Twenty-four Precepts for Followers (*Ershisi menjie jing* 二十四門戒經), ed. DZ 183. Also revealed by Ge Xuan and of sixth-century origin, this lists the punishments in the hells and presents the exploits of the highest deity, the ritual schedule, and various practical guidelines. See Min 1990, 94-97.

*Scripture of Controlling Karma and Original Conduct (*Jieye benxing jing* 戒業本行經), ed. DZ 345. A short text of twenty-five pages, this presents a systematic description of the predominant medieval Daoist worldview in lists of ten—precepts, items, stages, directions, worlds, etc. It claims revelation by the Heavenly Worthy.

Scripture of Great Offerings (*Daxian jing* 大獻經), ed. DH 23; DZ 370. Revealed by the Heavenly Worthy of Primordial Beginning to the Lord of the Dao and the great sages of the ten directions, dates from the sixth century. It has a set of ten precepts focusing on ritual activities.

Highest Clarity: This school's early materials were not much concerned with rules but focused on instructions for ecstatic excursions and the nature of divine cosmology. In the sixth century, it evolved to the pinnacle of the Three Caverns and created a comprehensive set of 300 precepts that included earlier rules in combination with instructions for advanced visualization practice. It also presented several shorter lists of precepts and taboos, adapting Celestial Masters' guidelines, the Buddhist five precepts, and Numinous Treasure models.

The Great Precepts of Self-Observation (*Guanshen dajie* 觀身大戒), ed. DZ 1364; WSBY 45, *Essential Rules and Observances* 6. Containing the full set of 300 precepts and associated with the Highest Clarity school, this text is transmitted to ordinands of the rank of the Perfection Cavern. Like its predecessors, the *180 Precepts of Lord Lao* and the *Precepts of the Three Primes*, it contains a basic set of 180 precepts on orderly conduct plus a 120 rules of supererogation and ecstatic, visionary practice.

**Immortals' Taboos According to the Purple Texts Inscribed by the Spirits (*Lingshu ziwen xianji* 靈書紫文仙忌), ed. DZ 179; trl. Bokenkamp 1997, 362-66. Related to the *Purple Texts Inscribed by the Spirits* (*Lingshu ziwen* 靈書紫文), which appeared as part of the Highest Clarity revelations in the mid-fourth century, this dates from the fifth century. It contains a set of ten rules and taboos on the proper conduct of aspiring immortals. See also Min 1990, 93.

Jade Book of the Great Empyrean (*Taixiao langshu* 太霄琅書), ed. DZ 1352. This fifth-century text of Highest Clarity provenance contains similar lists as the *Precepts Against the Roots of Sin*. See Kusuyama 1982; Kobayashi 1990; Min 1990, 109-10.

Explanation of the Merit and Karma of the Eight Simplicities (*Basu gongye jue* 八素功業訣), ed. DZ 1321. A Highest Clarity apocryphon of the sixth century, this picks up rules from the *Precepts Against the Roots of Sin*. See Robinet 1984, 2:E6

Other Lineages: Various secondary schools and lineages evolved in the middle ages, with various materials on precepts. The school of the Three Sovereigns (also known as Spirit Cavern) created sets of three, five, and eight precepts; the lineage of Ascension to the Mystery, a side branch of Numinous Treasure that furnished its own ordination rank in the Tang, developed different sets of precepts; and the Jade Clarity line, described in a text of the same name, systematized the Daoist teachings and developed rules for lay followers.

Scripture of the Eight Emperors (*Badi jing* 八帝經), ed. DZ 640. One of the key texts of the Three Sovereigns school, this emphasizes personal integrity through following a set of eight precepts patterned on Buddhism which included the five precepts plus abstention from various luxury activities. The text also notes that Daoists are well advised to avoid any exhibition of vulgarity, as well as excesses in eating, drinking, heat, cold, gazing, listening, crying, shouting, thinking, and anger. All these activities harm the *qi* and body gods and disturb the purity of life, thus preventing the activation of talismans. For more on the text, see Andersen 1991, 54-57.

Precepts of Spirit Cavern (*Dongshen jiepin* 洞神戒品), ed. WSBY 46.14a-16b. Ascribed to the Yellow Emperor, this contains a set of three general guidelines, five precepts of sensory control, and eight precepts based on the "Hongfan" chapter of the *Book of History* (*Shujing* 書經).

Scripture of Ascension to the Mystery (*Shengxuan jing* 昇玄經), ed. DH 41; DZ 1122; ZW 742; Yamada 1992. A long and complex text of the sixth-seventh centuries, this can be described as a Numinous Treasure off-shoot with strong integrative tendenxces. In content, it presents a Mahāyāna-style exposition of the Daoist teaching by Lord Lao to Zhang Daoling 張道陵, the first Celestial Master. It emphasizes the philosophical dimension of the Dao together with the systematic and gradual practice necessary to attain it. In this context, it contains various sets of behavioral instructions.

Scripture of Jade Clarity (*Yuqing jing* 玉清經), ed. DH 72; DZ 1312; JY 37. A sixth-century text in ten scrolls that addresses various issues of the Daoist teaching, this contains ten precepts addressed to lay followers. Also reprinted in *Highest Scriptural Precepts* (DZ 787), they summarize the main guidelines found in the Celestial Masters. See Liu 1990; Yoshioka 1961a; Eskildsen 1998.

Collections: The integrative tendencies of the time also found expression in the creation of comprehensive collections, among them a multi-text assembly of various materials on precepts, an integrated presentation of all different rules with karmic consequences, and an extensive outline of karma and retribution as applied to different segments of the population, from emperor to commoner. Monastic and lay rules were formulated and the interaction among different branches of the religion was redefined.

Highest Scriptural Precepts (*Taishang jingjie* 太上經戒) ed. DZ 787. A sixth-century collection of various precepts texts, this includes the *Scripture of Jade Clarity*, the *Jade Book of the Great Empyrean*, the *Fifty-Eight Prayers*, and others. For a discussion, see Kusuyama 1982.

Scripture of Prohibitions and Precepts (*Jinjie jing* 禁戒經), ed. DH 35. A short, concise text of the early Tang on the different forms of rules in Daoism, this also outlines their effectiveness and the dire consequences of going against them.

Scripture of Karmic Retribution (*Yinyuan jing* 因緣經), ed. DH 27; DZ 336. A long text on various rules and methods concerning both monastic and lay practice, this dates from the Sui dynasty. It contains a similar list of precepts as the *Twelve Highest Precepts of Admonition*. On the text, see Yoshioka 1976; Nakajima 1984; Kohn 1998b; Kohn 2003a, 215-17.

Esoteric and Secret Collection of Perfection (*Neibi zhenzang jing* 內秘真藏經), ed. DZ 4. The text consists of ten *juan*. It contains an extensive discussion of the karmic effects of human actions. Following in the wake of the *Scripture of Karmic Retribution*, it dates to the seventh century.

MONASTIC INSTITUTIONS: INJUNCTIONS FOR CONCRETE BEHAVIOR

7th c.: In the early Tang dynasty, the monastic institution evolved to its full development. Monasteries were build widely, the imperial court supported the creation of large temples and seminaries, monks and nuns proliferated, and new rules were established for the physical layout and administrative structure of the institutions and also for the specific behavior of monastics amongst themselves and in lay society. Some texts are better organized than others, but they tend to create a fairly well integrated image of Daoist monastic life. There are, moreover, several works that specialize in prescribing concrete conduct in regard to food and clothing.

Rules and Precepts for Worshiping the Dao (*Fengdao kejie* 奉道科戒), ed. DH 39; DZ 1125; trl. Kohn 2004. An extensive presentation of the establishment and organization of Daoist monasteries, this work dates from the early Tang dynasty. Its eighteen sections deal with karma and retribution, monastic buildings, statues, scriptures, living quarters, formal paraphernalia, ritual garb, and ordination ranks. It also describes daily and annual rituals, such as the recitation of scriptures, morning and evening services, meal-time ceremonies, and ordinations. See Kohn 2003a, 217-19; 2004.

Ten Items of Dignified Observances (*Shishi weiyi* 十事威儀), ed. DZ 792. Dated to the mid-seventh century, this expands the *Rules and Precepts for Worshiping the Dao* by focusing on concrete aspects of Daoist monastic conduct: handling the seat cloth and the water pitcher, making obeisances, proper ways of coming and going, sitting and rising, washing and rinsing, and receiving the divine law. See Kohn 2003a, 221-22.

Rules and Observances for Students of the Dao (*Daoxue keyi* 道學科儀), ed. DZ 1126. Ascribed to a deity of the Numinous Treasure pantheon, this contains guidelines for monastic Daoist behavior in thirty-five sections. In style and outlook close to the *Rules and Precepts for Worshiping the Dao*, it deals with proper speech, physical movements, daily grooming, food taboos, and vestments, as well as with ritual implements and specific activities, including mourning. See Kohn 2003a, 220-21.

Rules for a Thousand Perfected (*Qianzhen ke* 千真科), ed. DZ 1410. Linked with Ge Xuan of the Numinous Treasure school, this goes back to the early seventh century. It presents 109 rules that appear in no particular order but can be divided into five categories: interaction with outsiders, etiquette in the community, treatment of food and resources, prohibitions of disruptive behaviors, and proper attitudes. See Kohn 2003a, 214-15.

Scripture of Behavioral Observation (*Guanxing jing* 觀行經), ed. DH 40. This fragmentary work consists of an itemized list of rules regarding monastic conduct. Much of it is close to the Buddhist *Great Sūtra of Three Thousand Dignified Observances for the Monk* (*Da biqiu sanqian weiyi jing* 大比丘三千威儀經, T. 1470, 24.912c-26a), ascribed to An Shigao 安世高 of the second century, but more likely dating from the fifth century (Hirakawa 1960, 193-96). See Akizuki 1960; Ōfuchi 1978, 121-22; Kohn 2003a, 211-14.

***Prohibitions and Precepts Regarding Ceremonial Food* (*Fashi jinjie jing* 法食禁戒經), ed. DH 80. An early Tang text revealed by Lord Lao, this describes the Daoist philosophy of food, emphasizing that the ultimate is to eat *qi* and be independent of earthly nourishment. While still eating, however, Daoists are to observe thirty-eight rules that prescribe ritual observances at meals, consideration for other people, and avoidance of all uncleanliness and impropriety. See Kohn 2003a, 219-20.

***Rules and Precepts Regarding Ritual Vestments* (*Fafu kejie wen* 法服科戒文), ed. DZ 788. Written by Zhang Wanfu 張萬福 around the year 700, this divides into two parts. The first is a dialog between the Highest Lord and the Celestial Master on the flowing robes of pure transformation worn by the celestials in heaven, dividing them into nine distinct ranks. The second part contains a list of forty-six rules on the proper treatment of vestments given by the Celestial Master. The latter is later recouped in the *Precepts of Initial Perfection* of the Complete Perfection school. See Benn 1991, 143-44; Kohn 1993, 335-43; Kohn 2003a, 223.

8th c.: On the basis of an established monastic institution and large numbers of trained religious followers, a formal ordination hierarchy for both monastics and priests was established. Trained in monastic seminaries, Daoists underwent lenghty ordination ceremonies and were ranked in a complex system that is described variously in the texts. People who wished to express their support for the organization without committing to extended training or monastic discipline, moreover, could take the ten precepts for lay followers, new versions of which also began to evolve. In addition, new collections of ritual requirements, purgation ceremonies, and repentance procedures appeared, comprehensively presenting the integrated structure of the religion.

Synopsis of Transmission (*Chuanshou lueshuo* 傳授略說), ed. DZ 1241. By the ritual master Zhang Wanfu, this has a detailed description of the major ordination ranks of the Daoist hierarchy, specifying the rules applicable for each. It also includes a minute account of the ordination of two Tang princesses into the rank of Numinous Treasure in 711. See Benn 1991; Kohn 2003a, 222-23.

Collected Precepts of the Three Caverns (*Sandong zhongjie wen* 三洞眾戒文), ed. DZ 178. Another work by Zhang Wanfu, this specifies the kinds of precepts to be used for the different ordination ranks. See Benn 1991; Min 1990, 91-92.

Observances for Ordination (*Chujia chuandu yi* 出家傳度儀), ed. DZ 1236. Also by Zhang Wanfu, this describes the rituals necessary for different ordination levels. Among others, it contains the ten precepts of the *Scripture of the Ten Precepts*, most commonly used for lay ordination to the rank of Disciple of Pure Faith. See Benn 1991.

Observances of Precepts Transmission for the Golden Register (*Jinlu shuojie yi* 金籙大齋說戒儀), ed. DZ 468. A ritual text ascribed to Du Guangting 杜光庭 (850-933), this specifies ceremonies associated with the Golden Register Purgation. To undergo this rite, adepts had to take the ten precepts. See Yoshioka 1961a.

*Ten Precepts of Initial Perfection (*Chuzhen shijie wen* 初真十戒文), ed. DZ 180. Dated to around the year 700, this contains an alternative set of ten precepts for lay practitioners, made up from the classic five plus rules against unloyal and unfilial behavior and other social misbehavior. The rules later became the key precepts given to novice monks of Complete Perfection.

*Record of Purgations and Precepts (*Zhaijie lu* 齋戒錄), ed. DZ 464. This eighth-century work contains a concise summary of the main purgations of the Daoist calendar. It also has a list of the five precepts and ten items of goodness. See Yoshioka 1967; Malek 1985.

Essential Rules and Observances (*Yaoxiu keyi* 要修科儀), ed. DZ 463. An extensive ritual compendium in 16 *juan*, this work was compiled by Zhu Faman 朱法滿 in the eight century. It is encyclopedic and provides descriptions of many practices and citations of earlier materials. It deals with the transmission, recitation, and lecturing of scriptures, with the proprieties between master and disciple, the retribution of sins, and ritual procedures. It also has lists of the precepts used among the various schools and ranks. See Ōfuchi and Ishii 1988, 188-99; Zhu 1992; Tuzuki 2000; Kohn 2003a, 223-35

Repentance to Dissolve Disasters and Avoid the Realm Ninefold Darkness (*Xiaozai jiuyou chan* 消災九幽讖), ed. DZ 543. An extensive compendium on rites of confession in ten scrolls, this has a preface by Li Hanguang 李含光 (683-769) and dates accordingly from the mid-eighth century. It discusses internal meditations and purification exercises as well as moral forms of behavior, including family responsibilities and efforts to save the dead and all beings. The first scroll, moreover, contains a set of ten vows for proper cultivation and the salvation of all beings. See Chappell 2004.

LATER RULES: SONG THROUGH MING

In the later dynasties, no great compendia on behavioral guidelines were composed, nor do we see major collections of rules or cosmological treatises on moral actions. Most Daoist texts focus on inner alchemy or the performance of rituals, and do not deal with rules and precepts. Those that do tend to be among the ritual group, and most commonly the rules are listed as part of the preparation for the ritual. They take up only the tiniest amount of space in these sometimes enormous collections, indicating that daily goodness was accepted as a preparation but did not merit special mention or elaborate discussions.

Song dynasty

Seven Tablets in a Cloudy Satchel (*Yunji qiqian* 雲笈七籤), ed. DZ 1032. A major encyclopedia of the early eleventh century, this contains numerous lists of precepts, recouping earlier texts and materials. See Schipper 1980.

*Wondrous Precepts of Ninefold Perfection (*Jiuzhen miaojie* 九真妙戒), ed. DZ 181. A Numinous Treasure text of the late Tang or Song, this contains instructions by the Heavenly Worthy to the Northern Emperor (Beidi 北帝) of the realm of the dead at Fengdu. It focuses on nine precepts that include the four basic Buddhist precepts plus three injunctions against anger, pride, and ir-resolution also found in the Buddhist ten items of goodness, as well as two rules encouraging loyalty and filial piety (5a-6a). See Kleeman 1991; Min 1990, 93-94.

Great Methods of the Jade Hall (*Yutang dafa* 玉堂大法), ed. DZ 220. A key text of the Song school of the Heavenly Heart (Tianxin 天心), this dates from 1158. Here the Precepts of Ninefold Perfection are activated in a ritual to exempt people from disasters and take them out of suffering. See Yoshioka 1961a; Boltz 1987.

**Wondrous Scripture of Exterior Daily Practice (*Wai riyong miaojing* 外日用妙經), ed. DZ 645. A text associated with the practice of inner alchemy, this was revealed by Lord Lao and comes with a matching work on "Interior Daily Practice" (*Nei riyong miaojing* 內日用妙經, DZ 646), which desribes the transformation of inner energies to higher levels of subtlety. In preparation for this great work, however, adepts are encouraged to follow forty-seven rules of conduct which allow the dissolution of desires and establishment of harmony. See Kohn 2000b.

*The Great Rites of Highest Clarity and Numinous Treasure (*Shangqing lingbao dafa* 上清靈寶大法), ed. DZ 1223. Another large ritual compendium, compiled by Jin Yunzhong 金允中 around 1220, this has a set of ten precepts to be recited as part of the *pudu* ritual of universal salvation. The rules prohibit ghosts from creating havoc among the living in various ways. See Boltz 1996; Orzech 2002.

*Rites of the Flying Celestials of Pure Brightness (*Jingming feixian fa* 淨明飛仙法), ed. DZ 563. Dating from the Southern Song, this text contains moral instructions of the school of Pure Brightness, which integrated Confucian doctrine and ethics into Daoist practice. Its ten rules focus on the performance of essential virtues, such as loyalty, filial piety, modesty, diligence, generosity, and so on. See Boltz 1987, 70-78; Akizuki 1978; Kleeman 1991.

Yuan-Ming

*Great Rites of Universal Salvation (*Duren dafa* 度人大法), ed. DZ 219. A Yuan-dynasty collection of Daoist ritual in 72 *juan*, this describes a series of precepts and good attitudes that practitioners swear to in a ceremony of Numinous Treasure. They are all written down in a formal document and submitted to the gods, binding the candidate to good behavior and proper actions in the Dao. See Yoshioka 1961a; Boltz 1987.

*A Corpus of Daoist Ritual (*Daofa huiyuan* 道法會元), ed. DZ 1220. A major ritual compendium of the fourteenth century, this has a set of ten rules that focus on filial piety and loyalty, then move on to prohibit debauchery, greed, and intoxication. In addition, the text admonishes practitio-

ners not to get involved in worldly litigation, boast that they have reached perfection. and virtue or exert any sort of negative influence on their surroundings. See Loon 1979; Boltz 1987.

*Great Complete Collection of Rules and Models for Daoist Followers (*Daomen kefan da quanji* 道門科範大全集), ed. DZ 1225. This is a Ming-dynasty collection of Daoist rules and rites in 87 *juan*. It contains a set of ten precepts (*juan* 30, 54) used in rituals to activate the power of the phase fire and the Northern Dipper that serve to ensure long life, prosperity, and good fortune. See Yoshioka 1961a.

MODERN MONASTICS: RULES OF COMPLETE PERFECTION

The school of Complete Perfection is an ascetic and monastic school that arose under the guidance of Wang Chongyang (1113-1173) in the late twelfth century. With the support of the Mongol rulers, it soon grew into the leading Daoist school of China, and to this day has remained its major monastic organization. Since communal living was essential to the school, it placed a strong emphasis on rules and behavioral guidelines. Several works document the early stages of communal organization, however, its major precepts texts, which are still transmitted in ordinations today, emerged only in the seventeenth century. They consist of three texts, matching the three main ordination ranks. Two out of the three recoup medieval materials, revealing a strong continuity of Daoist ethics and behavioral models.

**Chongyang's Fifteen Articles on Establishing the Teaching (*Chongyang lijiao shiwu lun* 重陽立教十五論), ed. DZ 1233; trl. Yao 1980; Reiter 1985; Kohn 1993, 86-92. The fifteen rules here give basic guidelines to Complete Perfection practitioners. Attributed to the founder himself, they can be divided into three sections: rules for concrete monastic settings and behaviors, practices of inner cultivation, and the attainment of transcendence. For more on Complete Perfection, see Yao 2000.

Recorded Sayings of the Perfected Immortals (*Zhenxian yulu* 真仙語錄), ed. DZ 1256. A thirteenth-century collection of materials pertaining to the Seven Perfected and Five Patriarchs, this also includes a set of ten admonitions associated with Ma Danyang 馬丹陽 (1123-1183), warning against worldly involvement. See Boltz 1987, 169.

Collection of Immortal Joy (*Xianle ji* 仙樂集), ed. DZ 1141; JY 205. A collection of numerous poems by Liu Chuxuan 劉處玄 (1147-1203), one of the Seven Perfected, this also contains a list of ten admonitions that focus on the proper attitudes of Complete Perfection practitioners. See Boltz 1987, 162-63.

Pure Rules of Complete Perfection (*Quanzhen qinggui* 全真清規), ed. DZ 1235. Attributed to Lu Daohe 陸道和 of the thirteenth century, this contains twelve sections, the first six of which detail concrete behavioral guidelines, while the second six consist of essays on goals of the school and the practices advocated by various masters. See Kubo 1951; Yao 2000; Yoshioka 1961a; Kleeman 1991.

Precepts of Initial Perfection (*Chuzhen jie* 初真戒), ed. JY 278, 292; ZW 404; trl. Hackmann 1920. A long text that contains several sets of precepts and numerous behavioral rules, this was edited by the Longmen 龍門 patriarch and White Cloud Monastery abbot Wang Kunyang 王崑陽 in the mid-seventeenth century. It is the text first-level practitioners of Complete Perfection receive. See Min 1990, 67-73.

***Precepts of Medium Ultimate* (*Zhongji jie* 中極戒), ed. JY 293; ZW 405; trl. Hackmann 1931. Also edited by Wang Kunyang, this represents the precepts for the medium rank of Complete Perfection. It consists of 300 rules and closely resembles the *Great Precepts of Self-Observation* of the middle ages. See Min 1990, 73-86.

Great Precepts for Celestial Immortals (*Tianxian dajie* 天仙大戒), ed. JY 291; ZW 403. The text used for ordinands of the highest level of Complete Perfection, this does not contain a list of rules but provides general encouragement to develop wisdom, selflessness, and compassion, using lists of ten qualities to be developed in different aspects of life. The ten closely resemble the bodhisattva virtues of Buddhism. The work also contains the text of the *Scripture of Purity and Tranquility* (*Qingjing jing* 清靜經) for recitation and other ritual materials and hymns. See Hackmann 1920; Min 1990, 86-88.

Pure Rules, Mysterious and Marvelous (*Qinggui xuanmiao* 清規玄妙), ed. ZW 361. Also known as *Rules One Must Know* (*Guiju xuzhi* 規矩須知), this was collected in manuscript form by Heinrich Hackmann from Daoists on Mount Lao in Shandong. It contains practical behavioral guidelines, daily chants, description of monastic offices, punishments for misbehavior, and some more philosophical discussions of Daoist monkhood. Its rules have remained influential until today. See Min 1990; Kohn 2003b.

Taken together, these numerous texts show clear patterns of the development of the Daoist institution. From the closed communities of the Celestial Masters through the lay organizations and monasteries of the middle ages to the ritual structures and celibate institutions of late imperial China and today, Daoist rules have played an important role in the tradition. They have defined who Daoists were and where they fit into the greater network of society, world, and cosmos. There have been tremendous changes in the course of the millennia and many rules have appeared in a variety of different guises. However, there has also been an enormous continuity, especially documented in the two initial ordination texts of Complete Perfection, which bring together much earlier materials.

The selection of texts translated below reflects their importance in the tradition, hoping to show the appearance of the different forms of rules—prohibitions, admonitions, injunctions, resolutions—in the Daoist context. Besides lists of rules I have included texts that describe the Daoist cosmological and psychological worldview as it relates to ethics and practical behavior. In addition, I thought it important to translate texts completely, rather than provide only glimpses and snippets, many of which I included in the "Supplement." Almost all texts are, therefore, translated in their entirety. Footnotes are limited to necessary explanations and cross-references to other texts. Much of what could be said in commentary to the texts is already present in the discussion above, and should not need repeating. Further materials, other important texts that have had not quite the same central status in the tradition or show the rules in the same representative manner, could not be included here. They are found in the "Supplement," which is easily available in electronic format.

TEXT ONE

The 180 Precepts of Lord Lao

INTRODUCTION

The 180 Precepts of Lord Lao (*Laojun yibai bashi jie* 老君一百八十戒) appears first in the sixth-century collection *Scriptural Statutes of the Lord Lao* (*Laojun jinglü* 老君經律, DZ 786, 4a-12b). Following this, the text is found with variations and abbreviations in *Essential Rules and Observances* 5.14a-19a and in YJQQ 39.1a-14b. The text is translated in Hendrischke and Penny 1996. It has been studied in Schmidt 1985; Kobayashi 1992; Penny 1996; and Schipper 2001.

The collection has been dated variously and on occasion linked to the Buddhist *Pratimokṣa*. A few things are known about it with certainty:

— It appears in the three editions listed above, dating from the sixth, eighth, and eleventh centuries.
— Among medieval sources it is cited clearly and by title three times, twice in the fifth and once in the sixth century.[1]
— The preface, which survives in a Dunhuang manuscript (DH 78), is a later addition. It links the text to the early *Scripture of Great Peace* and is no earlier than the mid-sixth century.[2]
— The text divides into 140 prohibitions and forty admonitions, following the typical pattern for other, similar codes.
— The most outstanding characteristic of the text is its haphazard organization and frequent repetition of similar precepts (e.g., killing in general, birds, and animals, eating meat, eating animal flesh, and so on). This indicates that, as Schipper suggests, some of the rules are extremely old and go back far into the dawn of Daoist communal history (2001, 79).
— The text is seminal in Daoist history. All other extensive community codes recapitulate its rules in one form or another, from the *Precepts of the Three Primes* of the Numinous Treas-

---

[1] The earliest citation appears in the *Dignified Observances in Laying Out Purgations* (*Fuzhai weiyi jing* 敷齋威儀經, DZ 532), a text of the Ge Xuan section in the ancient Numinous Treasure corpus (Bokenkamp 1983, 484; Kobayashi 1990; Yamada 2000, 235). Here it is mentioned as the defining code for all libationers (17a; Schipper 2001, 89-90; Penny 1996, 4). The second reference is in the commentary to the *Abbreviated Rules for Daoist Followers* (DZ 1127), by Lu Xiujing, a text commonly dated to the 450s, but whose commentary may be later. The *180 Precepts* is mentioned as essential to the Daoist priesthood (17b; Nickerson 1996, 257). The third citation occurs in Zhen Luan's *Laughing at the Dao* (*Xiaodao lun* 笑道論, T. 2103, 52.143c-52c), an anti-Daoist polemic of the year 570. Here it is mentioned once, with the statement that Laozi's precepts are so powerful they will cause trees to wither and animals to die (sect. 22; Kohn 1995c, 113).

[2] The text divides into three parts: an account of the appearances of the Dao of Great Peace and Laozi's exploits during his western journeys; a dialogue between Laozi and Gan Ji 干吉, the alleged recipient of the *Scripture of Great Peace*; and an introduction on value of the precepts in the form of an ordination ceremony. Only the third section may have been part of the text before 550 C.E. See Maeda 1985.

ure school through the *Great Precepts of Self-Observation* of the sixth century to the *Precepts of Medium Ultimate* of Complete Perfection.

While there are no questions regarding these basic points, controversy has ensued over two issues: the degree of Buddhist influence and the exact dating of the text. As regards the first, Zürcher asserts that there is no Buddhist influence in the text (1980, 29), while Penny identifies a number of Buddhist-inspired areas, notably three rules directly copied from the *Pratimokṣa*: nos. 66, 116, and 74, prohibiting urination while standing and over plants as well as aggressive begging. All these appear in the *Precepts for Monks* (*Sengqi jieben* 僧祇解本, T. 1426), translated by Buddhabhadra in 416, as nos. 64, 65, 66 (Penny 1996, 11; also Hirakawa 1960, 218). In addition, Penny suggests that the overall arrangement of the text into prohibitions and admonitions, as well as several rules against killing, eating meat, taking pungent vegetables, eating alone, picking the best morsels, and engaging in close interaction with women are taken from the Buddhist text (1996, 11-12).

However, unlike the first three rules mentioned, all these can also be found in other Daoist sources and have their own Daoist rationale. I would, therefore, suggest that there is Buddhist influence and that Penny is right in saying that "the appearance in China of Buddhist precepts inspired Daoists to write precepts of their own" (1996, 2). However, I also think that the rules of *The 180 Precepts of Lord Lao* are for the most part indigenous and only in their codification were inspired by Buddhist models.

This codification, moreover, probably only occurred in the fifth century after the many new translations of Buddhist texts under Kumārajīva and other major translators greatly increased the awareness of precepts, rules, and *Vinaya* collections in China. Also around this time, the southern Celestial Masters were hard pressed to establish themselves as politically reliable and supportive of the newly risen Liu-Song dynasty. However undeniably ancient the rules themselves may in fact be, their formal listing in *The 180 Precepts* is not mentioned before the mid-fifth century and, as an effort at standardization and codification, fits in perfectly with other legitimizing texts of the period, such as the *Inner Explanation of the Three Heavens* (*Santian neijie jing* 三天內解經, DZ 1205; see Bokenkamp 1997, 186-229), and with the reorganization of the priesthood attempted at the time and documented in Lu Xiujing's *Abbreviated Rules for Taoist Followers* (see Nickerson 1996). Contrary to Penny's suggestion (1996, 9-10), I see no evidence that would link the text to the earlier and no longer extant *Pratimokṣa* translation by Dharmakāla in 251 and thus no reason to date it prior to the early fifth century.

TRANSLATION

1. Do not keep many animals, slaves, or concubines.

2. Do not debauch other people's wives or daughters.

3. Do not steal other people's goods.

4. Do not kill or harm any being. [4b]

5. Do not wantonly take other people's goods, even if worth only one piece of cash.

6. Do not wantonly burn or destroy other people's goods, even if worth only one piece of cash.

7. Do not throw foods into the fire.

8. Do not raise pigs or sheep.

9. Do not wrongly pursue the material possessions of other people.

10. Do not eat garlic or the five strong vegetables.

11. Do not write to others in cursive script.

12. Do not frequently write to communicate with others.

13. Do not use drugs to effect an abortion.

14. Do not burn fields, wild lands, mountains, or forests.

15. Do not use gold and silver for eating utensils.

16. Do not pursue learning about military and state affairs nor divine their good and bad fortune. [5a]

17. Do not wantonly get intimate with soldiers or brigands.

18. Do not wantonly cut down trees.

19. Do not wantonly pick herbs or flowers.

20. Do not have frequent audiences with the emperor or high officials nor wantonly get intimate with them.

21. Do not slight and despise your disciples or cause disorder by wrongly favoring one over another.

22. Do not covet or begrudge material goods.

23. Do not wantonly speak in fancy language, create divisions, or arouse jealousy.

24. Do not drink alcohol or eat meat.

25. Do not accumulate material goods and despise the orphaned and poor.

26. Do not eat alone.

27. Do not buy or sell slaves. [5b]

28. Do not seek knowledge about other people's marriages.

29. Do not, by emphasizing the long and short of an affair, increase the resentment and hatred of people.

30. Do not engage in dancing or music.

31. Do not speak about other people's faults or guess and suspect a hundred different issues.

32. Do not speak about other people's hidden and private affairs.

33. Do not speak about the origin and status, or good and bad deeds, of other people's parents.

34. Do not praise other people to their face yet in a different place discuss their faults.

35. Do not employ foul objects to fool with people.

36. Do not throw poisonous drugs into wells, ponds, rivers, or the ocean.

37. Do not be alone with your clan leader to cultivate personal closeness.

38. Do not slight or be rude to other people's worthies.

39. Do not engage in killing.

40. Do not encourage others to kill.

41. Do not cause a separation among other people's families. [6a]

42. Do not kill another in hatred.

43. Do not distribute writings that slander others.

44. Do not claim to be skilled.

45. Do not claim to be noble.

46. Do not take pride in yourself.

47. Do not wantonly dig holes in the earth and thereby destroy mountains and rivers.

48. Do not slander, yell at, or curse anyone.

49. Do not step on or kick the six domestic animals.

50. Do not deceive others.

51. Do not refuse to cure diseases.

52. Do not have great expectations for the things of others.

53. Do not drain waterways or marshes.

54. Do not discuss or criticize your teachers.

55. Do not expose your body or bathe in the nude. [6b]

56. Do not slight and despise the teaching of the scriptures.

57. Do not despise old people.

58. Do not watch the six domestic animals copulate.

59. Do not fool about with others.

60. Do not rely on awe and power for advancement.

61. Do not form a clique on the basis of your family.

62. Do not carry knives or staffs. Note: Army members are excepted from this rule.

63. Do not live in a separate homestead or household.

64. Do not give rise to anger and rage.

65. Do not scold others as if they were slaves.

66. Do not urinate standing up.

67. Do not brand the faces of your slaves.

68. Do not cast spells so that other people die or suffer defeat.

69. Do not delight in other people's death or defeat. [7a]

70. Do not travel everywhere in wide confusion.

71. Do not gape at people.

72. Do not stick out your tongue at people.

73. Do not obliquely pursue other people's goods.

74. Do not disturb the hundred families by begging vigorously.

75. Do not act as a tax inspector for ordinary people.

76. Do not act as a ritual chief for ordinary people.

77. Do not landscape mountains, erect graves, or build houses for others.

78. Do not practice astrology, star divination, or analyze the cycles of heaven.

79. Do not fish or hunt and thereby harm and kill the host of living beings.

80. Do not separate husband and wife through licentiousness.

81. Do not view any of your disciples in a partial or one sided way. Note: View them as your own children. [7b]

82. Do not take away other people's night fires.

83. Do not rush among worldly people to condole with or ask about their bereavement. Note: It is suitable to commiserate privately.

84. Do not join a group or party with ordinary people, then engage in mutual abuse.

85. Do not denigrate others' accomplishments and merits and speak only of your own virtue.

86. Do not select the best accommodation or room and most comfortable bed to sleep.

87. Do not slander the things of others as being bad.

88. Do not praise your own things as being good.

89. Do not startle other people, causing them to be scared and afraid.

90. Do not comment on others' food or drink as to its being good or bad.

91. Do not speak badly about the comings and goings of other people.

92. Do not use your connections with district officials to harm other people. [8a]

93. Do not, when traveling among ordinary people, discuss and evaluate the straight or crooked quality of their affairs.

94. Do not forcefully take other people's things and distribute them in charity.

95. Do not in winter dig up insects hibernating in the earth.

96. Do not travel for fun or without permission, rushing about for days and months.

97. Do not wantonly climb trees to plunder nests and destroy birds' eggs.

98. Do not catch birds or beasts in cages or nets.

99. Do not bore holes into the walls of other people's houses to spy on their families and womenfolk.

100. Do not throw anything filthy or defiled into public wells.

101. Do not block up ponds or wells.

102. Do not cheat or deceive the old or young.

103. Do not wantonly read other people's writings.

104. Do not entice free people and make them into slaves. [8b]

105. Do not accumulate and hoard material goods and treasures, thereby inviting bad luck and misfortune.

106. Do not covet or hanker after a nice residence.

107. Do not hide and bury vessels or other objects.

108. Do not destroy or ruin coins.

109. Do not light fires on the plains.

110. Do not obstruct roads with thorns and spikes.

111. Do not talk too much and exert your mouth and tongue.

112. Do not throw away anything with writing on it or bury it in front of the outhouse.

113. Do not pay obeisance to other people's ghosts and spirits.

114. Do not keep commoners' books on divination or the *Chart of the Eight Gods* and do not practice them.

115. Do not make friends with soldiers.

116. Do not urinate on living plants or into water that people will drink. [9a]

117. Do not speak or walk about with a woman alone.

118. Do not sacrifice to the ghosts and spirits in search of good fortune.

119. Do not set up numerous taboos and taboo names for others.

120. Do not set up numerous taboos and taboo names for yourself.

121. Do not wantonly or lightly enter rivers or the ocean to take a bath.

122. Do not wantonly borrow things from others, then use them as presents or bribes.

123. Do not serve as a guarantor for others, contract sales, or traffic in real estate and slaves.

124. Do not come and go among irresolute and lascivious folk.

125. Do not concoct poisonous drugs and keep them in vessels.

126. Do not make loud, harsh sounds, but always keep smiling.

127. Do not engage in litigation on behalf of others or concern yourself with official affairs. [9b]

128. Do not acquire writings on secrets and plots or read such things.

129. Do not wantonly whip the six domestic animals.

130. Do not ride a horse or drive a carriage without good reason.

131. Do not collect food or leftovers with your hands or selectively eat all the rare items.

132. Do not startle birds and beasts.

133. Do not criticize or discuss the good or bad qualities of what others eat and drink.

134. Do not wantonly open up dammed in lakes.

135. Do not advertise yourself as a healer of the sick. Note: Only go if invited by the family of the sick person.

136. Do not travel alone. Note: Always go with someone else. [10a]

137. Do not plot ways to personal profit on behalf of others.

138. Do not widely pursue precious objects.

139. Do not go with a woman into the mountains. Always use a separate path and stay in different quarters.

140. Do not reject the root [major foundations] and pursue the branches [minor details].

141. Always present offerings in accordance with your ability; do not take on many hardships.

142. Always be mindful of purity and remember the divine law, honor the pure and wise, and [sparingly] eat like a deer and drink like cattle.

143. Always be careful where you take lodging. Note: Inspect it first before you act, and never startle or offend anyone.

144. Always stay true to Orthodox Unity and do not get involved in worldly practices.

145. Always keep the great intention and maintain determination [of the Dao]; do not in confusion violate or go against the teaching and orders of the Three Worthies.[3] [10b]

---

[3] These are either the gods of the Three Primes, the lords presiding over heaven, earth, and water, or the Celestial Masters of the first three generations. They are not, as Hendrischke and Penny suspect (1996, 26), the

146. Always diligently avoid enmity and suspicion; do not use your parents' familiarity and kindness in serving your ruler.

147. Always diligently pursue long life; do not tire day or night.

148. Always diligently avoid evil places. Do not covet higher income or illicitly strive for glory and profit.

149. Always diligently nourish on *qi* and abstain from grain as part of the Dao of long life.

150. Always diligently avoid being cruel to others; do not abandon or turn your back on your friends.

151. Every time you eat or drink, take it all in one turn; do not angrily pronounce the beauty or bad qualities [of the meal].

152. Every time you burn incense, always pray for the good of the myriad families and Great Peace in all under heaven; do not pray merely for yourself.

153. Every time people address you as libationer, take care to establish awe in them; do not act lightly or hastily and become their laughing stock.

154. Every time you receive food from someone, cast a spell of good wishes to the effect that the donor may attain good fortune and be always full and satisfied. [11a]

155. Unless there is a special affair, do not assemble a large crowd of people to eat and drink to excess.

156. Unless there is a special affair, do not wantonly receive many obeisances and respects from others.

157. Whenever you enter another state, first ask about the wise and good people, then pay your respects to them in person.

158. Whenever you enter another state, first ask about the local prohibitions and taboos.

159. Whenever you enter anyone's home, first ask about personal and taboo names of the family venerables and elders.

160. Whenever you enter anyone's home, do not expect the common people to provide food and drink.

161. Women: Do not travel together with a man.

162. Men: Do not, in a dark room, talk with a woman. [11b]

163. Men and women: Do not own more than three sets of clothes.

164. Men and women: Do not sit together to eat and drink or touch hands when giving or receiving anything.

Three Purities or the Three Treasures, concepts that arose only in the fifth and sixth centuries and were not part of Celestial Masters doctrine.

165. When heaven brings disasters, calamities, floods, droughts or other disharmonies, do not resent or hate them.

166. When among worldly people you find many bad ones and few good, do not grow anxious. The Dao will protect its divine law.

167. If someone scolds you, merely submit; do not answer back.

168. If someone slanders you, concentrate on cultivating the great Dao; do not let yourself be sad and depressed, thus lessening your essence and spirit

169. If someone harms you, be doubly good to him. Note: Goodness drives out evil as water extinguishes fire.

170. If someone gives something to one person and nothing to you, do not hate the person for not giving you anything. [12a]

171. If someone sings your praises, do not get overjoyed; if someone offends or abuses you, do not get angry.

172. If someone kills birds and beasts, fish or other living beings for you, do not eat them.

173. If something has been killed for food, do not eat it.

174. If something smells rank, do not eat it.

175. If you do not know where something came from, you can eat it but do not think of it as wonderful.

176. To be able to cut out all meat of living beings and the six domestic animals is best; without doing this, you will violate the precepts.

177. To be able to eat only vegetables is most excellent; should it be impossible, match [your food to] the ruling constellation.

178. If you are able to honor the wise, give importance to the sages, and practice wisdom, I will take you beyond to where you will encounter perfected and immortals.

179. During travels, if you do not have proper lodging or family, you can take shelter under trees and rocks; then recite the 180 precepts, and the spirits will come to stand guard over you, three layers deep. No soldier, brigand, demon, or tiger will dare to come close.

180. Practice these precepts without violation, and if you violate one make sure you repent properly. Then change your behavior to cultivate them better in the future and encourage others to worship and receive them. Always think of the precepts, never think of evil, and widely pursue the salvation of all beings. Bow to the gods and perfected: they will help you be complete!

Lord Lao told his disciples:

In the old days, all the wise ones, immortals, and sages attained the Dao following these 180 precepts. The Dao is originally shapeless and can only be attained with the help of a teacher. The Dao cannot be transcended; the teacher cannot be taken lightly. As disciples, therefore, knock your heads and bow repeatedly to receive their orders.

TEXT TWO

Precepts of the Highest Lord Lao

INTRODUCTION

The *Precepts of the Highest Lord Lao* (*Taishang Laojun jiejing* 太上老君戒經, DZ 784) is a short text of twenty-nine pages, including ample commentary, contained in the Daoist canon. Parts of the text are also cited in YJQQ 39.14b-16b. The text is not complete but has a short note in the end stating that the last part is lost. It is studied and translated in Kohn 1994. Its connections to Buddhism were first pointed out in Jan 1986.

In content, the *Precepts of the Highest Lord Lao* concentrates on listing and explaining the five classical Buddhist precepts in a Daoist setting. It begins by narrating the story of Laozi's emigration from China and the transmission of the *Daode jing* to Yin Xi 尹喜, the Guardian of the Pass. This invokes the classical biography of the ancient philosopher in the *Record of the Historian* (*Shiji* 史記) by Sima Qian 司馬遷 (154-80 B.C.E.), which describes how Laozi transmitted the text before leaving for the west. It also echoes the *Scripture of Western Ascension* (*Xisheng jing* 西昇經, DZ 726; trl. Kohn 1991a), a text associated with the northern Celestial Masters at Louguan 樓觀 and dated to the late fifth century.

The *Precepts of the Highest Lord Lao*, too, belongs in this context. It was compiled at a time when Daoism was already firmly established as an official religion, encompassing several schools and including both specialized and lay followers. In fact, the text clearly refers to the school of Highest Clarity and calls it the "Great Vehicle," for which it hopes to lay the moral and devotional foundation. The five precepts in their cosmological setting as described in the text were, moreover, adapted from the Buddhist apocryphon *Sūtra of Trapusa and Bhallika* (*Tiwei boli jing* 提謂波利經), whose second scroll survived in Dunhuang (S. 2051) and whose first scroll remains in fragments (see Makita 1968/1971). Dated to the mid-fifth century, the text was ascribed to the monk Tanjing 曇靜, a follower of Tanyao 曇曜, who developed the saṇgha-household system under the Toba-Wei dynasty (Lai 1987, 13).

Conceived to restore the Buddhist church to strength after it lost its position under the Daoist theocracy, saṇgha-households consisted of families who paid taxes in the form of grain to the Buddhist community but were exempt from all other state duties. The saṇgha would store the grain for redistribution during famine or sell it to satisfy their own needs. The variant form of Buddha-households included freed criminals or slaves who did manual labor in the monasteries, putting state offenders to religious use (see Ch'en 1964, 153; Sargent 1957). In this context, the *Sutra of Trapusa and Bhallika* offered simple instructions on basic Buddhist practice for ordinary lay followers.

Just as the *Precepts of the Highest Lord Lao* consists of a dialogue between Lord Lao and Yin Xi, so the *Sūtra of Trapusa and Bhallika* presents an interview of the Buddha by the two gentry devotees

145

Trapusa and Ballika. Both texts are thus placed near the first source of the teaching and are attributed high authority. Both begin with an introduction that sets the stage, then present the five precepts and praise their power, relating their effects to the activities of the five phases, five planets, five sacred mountains, and five Confucian virtues. They are heavily imbued with popular Chinese religious thinking, referring to devotional activities at the times when the celestial administrators update their records and prescribing special observances of the eight nodal days of the year, days of "kingly *qi*" when the "gods of Heaven and Earth, all the forces of yin and yang interact and mingle with each other" (Makita 1968, 147).

The *Precepts of the Highest Lord Lao* is divided into eight sections, for the most part introduced by a question from Yin Xi. The questions are:

1. What are the exact words of the precepts?
2. Why are there five?
3. How can one ever lose them?
4. What is their deepest root?
5. How does one receive the precepts?
6. What violations are their in worshiping the scriptures?

The text explains the nature and origins of the precepts, outlines the proper procedures for receiving them, and details the necessary devotional activities to keep them active. It places a heavy emphasis on cosmology and celestial connections, providing a framework for good human behavior that matches the worldview of medieval China

TRANSLATION

[1a] Lord Lao went west, planning to go to India. On his way he transmitted the *Daode jing* to Yin Xi, the Guardian of the Pass. Yin Xi duly received the text, then begged for more instructions on proper self-control and the divine ways of venerating the scripture.[1] [1b] Lord Lao, thereupon, went on to give Yin Xi the essential precepts. He instructed him to uphold all of them so as to go beyond the world.

Thus he recited the following song in three stanzas: [2a]

Enjoy the divine law as if it were your [dear] wife![2]
Love the Scripture like a precious piece of jade! [2b]
Uphold the precepts to control all the six passions!

---

[1] The same story appears as the mythological framework narrative of the *Scripture of Western Ascension* (Kohn 1991, 57-80), which is based on the *Scripture of the Conversion of the Barbarians* (*Huahu jing* 化胡經). For a detailed discussion, see Kohn 1998a, 275-90. The commentary here adds that although the precepts are already contained in the *Scripture* they are subtle and intricate and not obvious to a beginner. Therefore Yin Xi requests more explicit instruction.

[2] The commentary reads this statement in two ways. First literally, it emphasizes that the relation between humanity and the Dao is like that between yin and yang, one of mutual need and support. The ideal yin/yang relationship, furthermore, is that between husband and wife, from which also the creation of life begins. Second, the commentary explains the word "wife" through the same character, written with the "tree" radical. This word means "resting place," "abode." With this imagery, practitioners are encouraged to place themselves in a position of the Dao, to make it their place of security in this world of passion and uncertainty.

Be mindful of the Dao and give up all desires! [3a]
In deep serenity, good *qi* assembles,
In calm reverence, the spirit is at rest.
Celestial kings with care give their protection, [3b]
For generations, you find great blessedness.

Exuberant and growing, family and state develop,
Ever more, the scriptures and Dao flourish. [4a]
Celestials and humans join in the common vow,[3]
Whirl away and enter the Great Vehicle.
Heart set on course, plant fields of blessedness, [4b]
Ever so slowly rise up through the law's wheel.[4]
My seven ancestors are reborn in the halls of heaven,
Myself, I ascend in the broad light of day. [5a]

The Great Dao pervades mystery and emptiness,
Be mindful and you will have universal impulse![5]
Purify your being, join immortal perfection,
Obtain a cosmic diamond body for yourself! [5b]
Go well beyond the hardship of the Three Worlds,[6]
Be free forever from the five sufferings of the hells, [6a]
Take full refuge in the highest *Scripture* [*Daode jing*],
And for silent recitation bend your head in prayer.

Thereupon Yin Xi, listening carefully until the song had ended, knocked his head to the ground. Then he stood up again and asked formally to be given the words of the precepts.

Lord Lao said:

The first precept is to abstain from killing.
The second precept is to abstain from stealing.

---

[3] Celestials and humans (*tianren* 天人) here refers to the two major kinds of beings in the Daoist universe, adopting the Buddhist notion of *deva*. They interact, according to the commentary, on the basis of virtue and support each other. In earlier Daoist texts, the same term is also used to refer to the followers of the Dao, the "celestial brotherhood." In popular Buddhism of the time, the reverse, *rentian* 人天, is used to denote the lay movement that taught "the performance of good deeds for the sake of better rebirth as humans or in heaven as gods" (Lai 1987, 15).

[4] *Falun* 法輪, the "wheel of the dharma" (*dharmacakra*) is a Buddhist image for the continued teaching of the Buddha and the truth of the Buddha which is able to crush all evil (Soothill and Hodous 1937, 273). Here it is understood as the eternal cycle of rebirth and transmigration and is used as an image for the ladder of ascent toward residence in the highest heavens.

[5] The commentary explains this statement as the effect of oneness with the Dao. Since the Dao is placed above all else and governs the world, it can exert its impulses (*gan* 感) on everything, and all beings respond (*ying* 應) to it. An adept in the position of the Dao will similarly have the power to control his destiny by giving out the right impulses. For a broader discussion of the concept of *ganying*, see Le Blanc 1992; Brokaw 1990.

[6] These are the worlds of desire, form, and formlessness, a total of twenty-eight heavens Daoism adopted from Buddhism. See Zürcher 1980.

The third precept is to abstain from licentiousness.
The fourth precept is to abstain from lying.
The fifth precept is to abstain from intoxication.

These are the five precepts. [6b] All male and female Disciples of Pure Faith, once they have taken these five precepts, must never violate them as long as they live. Then they are truly Disciples of Pure Faith!

Lord Lao said: The precept to abstain from killing means that you must not kill any living being or anything that contains vital energy, be it flying or merely wriggling. [7a]

Lord Lao said: The precept to abstain from stealing means that you must not take anything that does not belong to you, be it owned by someone or without obvious owner, even as little as one single copper coin.

Lord Lao said: The precept to abstain from licentiousness means that you must not make sexual advances to any person, male or female, unless they are your lawful wife or husband. If you are a recluse, you must never marry or take a wife.

Lord Lao said: The precept to abstain from lying means that you must not make any statements to other people about anything unless you have perfectly understood it in your mind, and especially not if you have neither heard nor seen the thing yourself. [7b]

Lord Lao said: The precept to abstain from intoxication means that you must not drink any alcohol unless you are physically sick or do so for ritual purposes.

Lord Lao said:[7] These five precepts are the foundations of self-control, the basis of maintaining the divine ways. [8a] All good men and women of the Dao, as they vow to follow the divine ways, receive them to uphold. They should never violate them as long as they live. Thus they become Disciples of Pure Faith, receive the scriptures, attain the divine ways, and forever realize the perfection of the Dao.

Thereupon Yin Xi, listening carefully until the exposition had ended, [8b] bowed again and asked: "Why are there five?"

Lord Lao said: The five precepts control all evils, just as Heaven has five essences which control all spiritual powers of the universe; [9a] just as Earth has five phases which control the host of living beings; just as human beings have five inner organs which control all spirit radiance.

The five precepts are barriers to abstain from all evil. Make sure you do not lose them! If people lose them and are without barriers, the three deepest hells [of fire, blood, and swords] will be full to overflowing, while the heavenly halls, will be empty and deserted. [9b] Thus there are these five.

"Great indeed," Yin Xi said with awe, "are the precepts! How could one ever lose them?"

---

[7] Here begins the part also cited in YJQQ 39.14b.

Lord Lao said: Once you have firmly taken them, there will be no more loss.[8] But even if you have lost a precept once, you can still retake it. Then there will be no permanent loss either.[9]

[10b] Yin Xi asked, "May I dare to inquire about their deepest root?"

Lord Lao said: I shall indeed speak to you about their deepest root. Listen truly, listen carefully! Once you have grasped them properly, you spread them so that all will know!"

Yin Xi bowed again deeply, then stood up, reverently bent to listen.

Lord Lao said: The five precepts began together with Heaven and Earth and have existed together with the myriad beings. [11a] Those who uphold them encounter good fortune; those who lose them are plagued by misfortune. Those who have perfected the Dao in the past all did so by following the precepts. Through them the twenty-five body gods [five organs times five precepts] are deeply at peace. This is what the *Scripture of the Dao and the Virtue* tells.

[11b] Lord Lao said:[10] The five precepts of Heaven are the five planets.[11] As soon as the Dao of Heaven loses its precepts, there are natural catastrophes.

[12a] For Earth, they are the five sacred mountains.[12] As soon as the Dao of Earth loses its precepts, the hundred grains can grow no longer.

Among the seasonal patterns, they are the five phases. [12b] As soon as the five seasons lose their precepts, fire and water fight each other, and metal and wood do each other harm. In government, they are the five emperors.[13] As soon as the five emperors lose their precepts, dynasties topple and rulers perish.

[13a] In human beings, they are the five inner organs. As soon as the five inner organs lose their precepts, inner nature goes mad.

[13b] Lord Lao said: The five precepts are at odds with some directions and in line with others. [14a] The precept to abstain from killing belongs to the east. It embodies the *qi* of Germinating Life and honors natural growth. People who harm and kill living beings will receive corresponding harm in their livers.

---

[8] YJQQ interrupts its citation of the text here, but includes the commentary. This is the only place where it does so (39.15b).

[9] According to the commentary, this means that anyone who has taken the precepts already in an earlier life will have no problem maintaining them now. But even if one begins now and falls short of one or the other, one can always confess one's sins and make another effort. Also, since people are originally endowed with the Dao, and the precepts contain the essence of the Dao, there can ultimately be no real loss.

[10] The following is again found in YJQQ 39.15b-16b.

[11] Jupiter, Venus, Mars, Mercury, and Saturn. They rule the energies of the five directions, maintaining their "constancies." The commentary here uses the word *chang* 常 commonly used for the five Confucian virtues. The basic system is the same as the standard correspondence pattern of the five phases. See Eberhard 1933.

[12] Taishan, Hengshan, Huashan, Hengshan, and Songgao shan. They govern the energies of Earth and rule the weather, gathering and dispelling the clouds. Making the wind and rain come at the right moment, they guarantee good harvests. On sacred mountains in China, see Chavannes 1910; Soymié 1956.

[13] Taihao, Yandi, Shaohao, Zhuanxu, and Huangdi. Mythical rulers, they governed the land in perfect harmony and accordance with the phases. On ancient Chinese mythical rulers and their later integration into Han-dynasty cosmology, see Karlgren 1946.

The precept to abstain from stealing belongs to the north. It embodies the essence of Great Yin and presides over the resting and storing of nature. People who steal will receive corresponding calamities in their kidneys.

[14b] The precept to abstain from licentiousness belongs to the west. It embodies the material power of Lesser Yin and preserves the purity and strength of men and women. People who delight in licentiousness will receive corresponding foulness in their lungs.

The precept to abstain from intoxication belongs to the south and the phase fire. It embodies the *qi* of Great Yang and supports all beings in their full growth. People who indulge in drink will receive corresponding poison in their hearts.

[15a] The precept to abstain from lying belongs to the center and the phase earth; its virtue is faithfulness. People who lie will receive corresponding shame in their spleens.

These five virtues all supplement each other. They must never be cut short or destroyed.

Lord Lao said: If among these five you lose just one, your life expectancy will not reach fulfillment. [15b] Thus, not to kill means that you must not even entertain the idea of killing. [16a] Not to steal means that you must not even touch something that is not your own. Not to engage in licentiousness means that you must not even entertain improperthoughts. [16b] Not to get intoxicated means that you must not even have the slightest inclination to drink. Not to lie means that you must not allow yourself even the slightest indiscretion. [17a] Practice all the precepts like this and you can truly fulfill them![14]

Lord Lao said: Among the actions prohibited by the precepts, especially licentiousness and intoxication can give rise to all five evils.[15] [17b] The precepts are precepts against evil. It is only in a world full of evils that men and women mingle in free sensuality and thus come to harm their flesh and blood. They are rude to their superiors and cruel to those beneath them; they destroy and splinter the virtue of Heaven.

Dead drunk, they get into disputes and quarrels, bringing misfortune to their lives and shame on themselves. Lying and cheating all around, they lose all guidelines they could follow. [18a] Stealing even from their six relations, they grab from all, not just from strangers. Killing off a

---

[14] The commentary explains all these in some more detail. First, it says that one should not even "cause others to kill, encourage others to kill, observe others as they kill, or order others to kill." In any of these cases, although no physical killing is undertaken, the mind is infested by evil and the precept is broken. Stealing, too, should be avoided even to the point of a small uncontrolled taking. Even taking what is public for one's private use, bending the law to grab hold of more possessions, cutting plants or trees from public land, or pretending ignorance of rules to enrich oneself—all these are breaches of the rule. Next, it says that any wish even to release sexual desire, forgetting self and family, leads into sin. Even if one leads an irreproachable life of the Dao on the outside but within is seething with fantasies and wishes, one is not pure, not following the rule. Also, intoxication is like a fire that has gotten out of control. Any wish for it will weaken the mind and lead to disaster.

[15] The commentary specifies: Licentiousness leads to luxury, luxury leads to extravagance, extravagance leads to greed, greed leads to theft, theft leads to cheating, cheating leads to fear, fear leads to killing. Thus all evil deeds arise from one single source. Intoxication, in turn, leads to loss of control and loss of control leads to licentiousness, precipitating the same sequence.

host of living beings, they are only interested in giving satisfaction to their mouths and stomachs.

[18b] Like this, people of all kinds and ranks, as they come back to life with newly received karma, forever find themselves fallen upon terrible hardships. Worse, once started on the five evils, there is no end or stopping them!

Emerging to yet another life, they end up among the fringe people and barbarians, with a short life expectancy and much suffering [due to their killing]. Living with a husband or a wife who is ugly and cruel, they are forever separated from purity and contentment [Comm: because of their licentiousness]. [19a] Poor and destitute, cold and exposed, they will find no peace anywhere they live. And whatever wealth and lifestock they may acquire is stolen by others [because of their own stealing]. Whatever they say, nobody will believe them. None will wish to be their kin [Comm: due to their lying]. Their minds dull and their thinking full of blockages, everybody makes fun of them or treats them with contempt [Comm: because of their intoxication].[16]

[19b] Lord Lao said: Male and female Disciples of Pure Faith, on the other hand, who uphold and obey the precepts will find the world a happy place and never know sorrow nor distress. Respected and well honored by all others [Comm: due to being always chaste] they will bring cheer and joy to anyone they meet [Comm: because they never killed]. They will always be sustained and well nurtured throughout their lives [Comm: since they did not commit any theft]. [20a] All will look up to them and come to them for help [Comm: because they never lied], their wisdom profound and full of subtlety [Comm: due to never being intoxicated].

Such people live in pure and quiet places, where the four great elements are regular and stable. Doing so, they are in a condition to cultivate the divine ways and eventually reach the perfection of the Dao.

[20b] Yin Xi bowed again and said, "May I dare to ask how to receive the precepts?"[17]

Lord Lao said: If a certain man or woman, upon hearing of the divine ways, develops faith, he or she should take refuge in the Three Treasures. [21a] At this time, forehead to the ground, he or she recites:

> I take refuge in the Great Dao with my body! I take refuge in the Great Dao with my spirit! I take refuge in the Great Dao with my life![18] [21b] I, the man or woman so-and-so, hereby renounce all the false teachings of the world and vow to uphold and honor the proper precepts [of the Dao]. [22a] To the end of my body, to the end of my life, I shall never break any of them for ever and ever!

---

[16] Here ends the part also found in YJQQ.

[17] This section deals with the concrete procedure of ordination. An equivalent section is also found in the *Sūtra of Trapusa and Bhallika* (Lai 1987, 26-27).

[18] According to the commentary, the body has good and evil, the spirit has hope and dread, and life has longevity and early death. They are three and yet ultimately only one. By taking refuge in the Dao, the body will be strong and have no more bad karma; the spirit will be clear and no longer fear the demons; the life expectancy will be long and no longer subject to untimely death. Properly speaking, the second refuge (of spirit) should be taken in the scriptures and the third (of life) in the teachers of the Dao. See *Rules and Precepts for Worshiping the Dao* 6.9b.

Then the novice should chant the precepts. Thus, with heartfelt commitment, he or she receives them.

Lord Lao said: If again there is a man or woman who, after having received the proper precepts, continues to progress and in addition wishes to receive the *Scripture* [*Daode jing*] and divine ways, [22b] he or she must first receive another, more appropriate set of precepts and vow to uphold them firmly, every single one, in perfect purity.

Then he or she can receive still further teachings. Morning and evening, she recites the scripture with heartfelt commitment, never missing the proper times. Every month, moreover, she observes ten fast days, [23a] and every year, three major rites. Reciting the *Scripture* ten thousand times, she can then ascend to the stars in broad daylight.[19]

If such a follower furthermore explains the teaching to others, widely spreads its wondrous meaning, and thus turns into a great beneficiary for the host of living beings, then he or she will forever be free from the three bad rebirths and all kinds of suffering. [23b] With such merit and virtue the Daoist can completely cut off karma and retribution and extirpate its uncountable roots. Ascending thus to Highest Clarity, he will never again fall back into the karmic cycle.

Lord Lao said: Male and female Disciples of Pure Faith, be they householders or recluses,[20] once they have received the *Scripture* and the divine ways, shall vow to take delight only in spiritual immortality. Day and night they recite and study, ever pursuing the wondrous meaning [of the Dao].

[24a] Getting rid of all agitation and confusion, they harmonize their minds and control their inner natures. With soft countenance and benevolent *qi*,[21] they admonish all men and women to do likewise. Getting far away from the five evils and firmly upholding the five precepts, they continuously worship the Three Treasures. [24b] Accepting the commands [of the Dao] and working to fulfill them, they are not choosy about what may be sweet or bitter. Upholding all the great precepts, they go through hardship with firmness and zeal. They give freely with indulgence and sacrifice themselves to save all beings.[22]

[25a] As they further leave the world, wander about alone and live in dark seclusion, they meditate to reach serenity so that the host of troubles cannot touch them. Thus they are bound to attain nonaction.

---

[19] The commentary explains this with Laozi's words in the *Scripture of Western Ascension*: "With complicated phrases and words of marvel, inner intention cannot be revealed. Recite the scripture 10,000 times, and attain sincerity in your essence and pervasion in your mind" (4.6-7; Kohn 1991, 236).

[20] The commentary explains that both forms of the religious life are acceptable, but that the householder's way is superior. Life in the seclusion of the mountains should only be a crutch, used while the mind is still agitated and society still causes confusion and anxiety. The superior adept practices right in the middle of worldly life. This relates closely to the primarily lay-oriented concern of the *Sūtra of Trapusa and Bhallika*.

[21] According to the commentary, anyone with a defiled mind has a harsh face and forbidding expression. When the intention is fierce, the speech is rude. People who purify themselves and pursue the Dao become softer in their expression, facial and vocal.

[22] Giving freely is an important part of the Dao, just as the virtue of *dāna* or charity is central to Buddhist practice. In Daoism, a set of seven "rules about giving freely" is found in the *Great Precepts of the Highest Ranks* 13b-14a.

Yin Xi asked again: "Are there violations in worshiping the scriptures? [25b] — Lord Lao said: Indeed, there are ten and three.²³ —Yin Xi queried: "What are they?" [26a]

Lord Lao said: Listen now with great care! These ten and three are made up of the six defilements and the six senses together with the mind, from which they all spring forth. [26b] Thus there are licentiousness and greed, jealousy and anger,²⁴ stealing and cheating, [27a] lying and deception, fancy talk and dishonesty, cajolery and self-righteousness—the sexes mingling in defilement, the divine ways are broken everywhere. [27b] This, indeed, is not being a Disciple of Pure Faith!

The network of Heaven never loses anything; life and death can never be escaped. [28a] People like this, denying their inborn wisdom, thus defile the perfect ways and destroy all roots of goodness. They will forever be outside all awareness of the good. [28b] For however many bodies yet to come, they will be planted deep in the mire of passions and desire.²⁵ With no hope to ever get away, they will always be full of terror and of fear.

[29a] In hell, they will feel the five pains without interruption. Coming to life, they will find themselves in hardship and in evil. Beings so deep in evil, [29b] they cannot be saved or healed again. The wheel of life and death [*samsāra*] turns, neither hearing nor seeing. All events arise from a single thought and go on to produce innumerable thoughts and responses without end.²⁶

---

²³ This is a reference to *Daode jing* 50: "Three out of ten are companions of life;/Three out of ten are companions of death." While commonly read this way, some commentators also explain the "three and ten" as thirteen. Hanfeizi, for example, says that they refer to the four limbs and nine orifices as factors that sustain life and death (chap. 30). The text here follows this reading, explaining the thirteen as the six defilements plus the six senses, plus the mind/heart as their ruler and origin.

²⁴ The commentary constructs these four in causation: Licentiousness leads to greed, greed leads to more licentiousness and to greed for fame and wealth. Wanting it all for oneself, one cannot bear another to be better and develops jealousy. This, in turn, causes anger and aggression against others.

²⁵ According to the commentary, this kind of an existence is like being a chicken or a dog, i.e., a helpless victim of passions, instincts, and impulses. Human beings should rise above this state and learn control with the help of the Dao.

²⁶ A note in the text states that the remainder of the original is lost.

TEXT THREE

The Essential Precepts of Master Redpine

INTRODUCTION

The Essential Precepts of Master Redpine (*Chisongzi zhongjie jing* 赤松子中戒經, DZ 185) is a classic on the connection of moral behavior and the universe. It consists today of one scroll in eleven pages, and is cited first in Ge Hong's *Book of the Master Who Embraces Simplicity* (6.5a). This shows that the text goes back to the fourth century, when it was available in south China. However, in its extant edition it dates only from the Song dynasty (Ren and Zhong 1991, 135-36).

The Song-dynasty edition is described in the preface which features the story of the Song official Xue Yuan 薛瑗 and the Daoist master Gongming Zihao 公明子昇. The official has ten sons, all afflicted with various sicknesses, deformities, or disabilities, which no physician can cure. Upon the Daoist's advice to change his lifestyle to a more altruistic pattern, the problems of his children improve dramatically (pref. 1a-2a; Yoshioka 1960, 730). The text is mentioned in various Song catalogs (Loon 1984, 110) and cited in works of that period, such as the well-known *Treatise on Impulse and Response* (*Ganying pian* 感應篇, DZ 1167), by the scholar-official Li Changling 李昌齡 (fl. 1127-1150).[1] To the present day, the *Essential Precepts* forms a part of popular retribution culture and has inspired numerous ledgers of merit and demerit (see Brokaw 1990).

In terms of doctrine, *The Essential Precepts of Master Redpine* is yet entirely free of Buddhist influence, its pattern of retribution being strictly limited to natural agencies and the celestial administration. It mentions the underworld realm of Fengdu 酆都 (5b), which came to play an important role in the cosmology of Highest Clarity (see Robinet 1993), and is not unlike the *Scripture of Great Peace* (ed. Wang 1979) in its link of people's fate with the position of the stars (Penny 1990; see also Staal 1984) and in its emphasis on the notion of inherited evil as an explanation for the suffering of infants and other innocents (see Hendrischke 1991).

The text thus combines the doctrines and ideas of various early schools. Its only trace of Song-dynasty thinking is found in the emphasis placed on the "constellations of the Three Terraces and the North Culmen" (2a), which are the central deities in the Song school known as the Heavenly Heart (Boltz 1987, 33-38; Drexler 1994, 85-94). As these constellations also appear earlier and much of the text's content is otherwise found in various Six Dynasties' scriptures, the work can be placed in the fourth century.

In content, *The Essential Precepts* presents a dialogue between the Yellow Emperor and Master Redpine, both classical figures in the Daoist tradition described in the *Immortals' Biographies* (*Liexian zhuan* 列仙傳, DZ 294) of the Former Han dynasty (Kaltenmark 1953, 50 and 35). The

---

[1] On the *Treatise*, see Hervouet 1978, 370-71. It is translated in Suzuki and Carus 1973. Its printing history is discussed in Bell 1992; for its relation to the *Essential Precepts*, see Yoshioka 1960, 731; 1970, 220.

154

Yellow Emperor, in particular, is the classical student who learns from the Master of Wide Perfection (Guangchengzi 廣成子) in the *Zhuangzi* (ch. 11), from Zhibo 值伯 in the medical textbook *Inner Classic of the Yellow Emperor* (*Huangdi neijing* 黃帝內經), and from the Pure Woman in the sexual manual *Classic of the Pure Woman* (*Sunü jing* 素女經). Master Redpine, on the other hand, is closely associated with various dietary and gymnastic practices (Yamada 1989, 104). A highly inspiring immortal who has lived both in the heavens and on earth for a very long time, he is famous for his reliable reports on the workings of the universe.

The dialogue between them consists of nine questions posited by the Yellow Emperor, which Master Redpine answers in varying degrees of detail. The questions are:

1. Why are people different in their fortunes?
2. How long is a typical human life?
3. Why are there miscarriages and the deaths of infants?
4. How can one improve one's lot?
5. Which sins are punished by subtractions from the life expectancy?
6. Do sins and punishments match one another?
7. How can one dissolve the sins already accumulated?
8. Can one find the Dao even in ordinary human life?
9. What types and ranks of wise ones are there?

Answering these questions, Master Redpine presents an outline of how human fortune comes about and the various ways to control and improve it. His key points are five:

1. The stars govern human life through the celestial administration and the gods in the body.
2. Sins and good fortune are inherited within families.
3. Certain numbers of good or bad deeds bring specific results in terms of health, fortune, and length of life.
4. The celestial administration effects subtractions from the life expectancy for specific misdeeds.
5. Moral rectitude will alleviate harm and even lead to salvation.

In explaining the role of human actions in the greater universe, the text places the central control over human life and fate in the stars above. The execution of the stars' judgment lies both in the immediate response of Heaven and Earth, which surround people with good or bad *qi*, and in the hands of the celestial administration, whose members keep track of human behavior and effect subtractions from the life expectancy. People's fates and activities are intimately interconnected with the workings of the cosmos, and Heaven and Earth are forever closely present in all that human beings think and do.

TRANSLATION

[1a] Xianyuan, the Yellow Emperor, knocked his head to the ground and asked Master Redpine: I have seen the myriad people receive life, but why is it not equal? There are those rich and noble, there are those poor and humble. There are those with a long life, there are those with a short life. Some are met by obstruction and troubles and undergo punishment in the cangue [punishment board]; others again suffer from extended illness and have their bodies all tied up. Some die suddenly without apparent disease, others live a long life with good emoluments. Like this, people are not equal. I pray you, sir, to explain the situation to me.

Master Redpine said: People coming to life are all in isolation, each depending on one particular star. There are big stars and small, each governing a specific person's longevity and shortness [of life], decline and prosperity, poverty and wealth, death and life. As for those who do good, good *qi* will cover them, good fortune and virtue will follow them, all nasty evils will leave them, the spirits and numinous forces will guard them, other people will have respect for them, and all misfortunes will stay far away from them. As for those who do evil, bad *qi* will cover them, disasters and misfortunes will follow them, all lucky and auspicious signs will avoid them, baleful stars will shine on them, other people will detest them, and all sorts of unpleasant and disastrous affairs will crowd around them.

[1b] Day or night, whatever people do in their actions and minds, all the good and evil they commit, whether they secretly violate the prohibitions and taboos of Heaven and Earth, or give rise to personal blame and the accumulation of sins, is not the same at all. Day or night, whenever people do evil, the body gods and the Director of Fates [Siming] will submit a report to the stars and constellations above. They in turn will effect a subtraction from the sinners' lives, so that the [light] *qi* of Heaven will leave them and the [heavy] *qi* of Earth will cluster around them. This is why they go into decline.

The Yellow Emperor asked: Altogether, how long should a human life expectancy be?

The Master replied: When people first come to earth, Heaven endows them with a life expectancy of 43,800 days, that is 120 years of life, each of which corresponds to one calendar year. So people originally receive a total life expectancy of 120 years. But if they violate the prohibitions and taboos of Heaven and Earth, certain amounts of time are subtracted from it and it will come to an end.

The next question was: On occasion there are those dying while still in the womb or those who only live to see a few years. They have not yet done anything in the world, so what prohibition or taboo could they have violated?

Master Redpine explained: Things like these happen because the sins of the ancestors and forebears bequeath calamities upon their descendants. Ever since antiquity, heroes and wise men have established a corresponding teaching, which has remained in the books of the immortals. [2a] They all admonish people to do good and to know the very incipience of evil, so that even in ten thousand ages they give nothing but good fortune to their numerous generations of descendants.

Now, human beings live between Heaven and Earth and are endowed with the two *qi* of yin and yang. Sovereign Heaven, although high, yet has its correspondence down below. Mother Earth, although low, yet has its correspondence far above. Heaven does not speak, yet the four seasons move in order. Earth does not speak, yet the myriad beings come to life. People reside right between the two. All their licentious intentions and passionate desires, whatever they do or do not do, Heaven and Earth know all about it. For this reason we say that Heaven has four-sided [all-round] knowledge.

Normally, people never say anything to recompense the grace Heaven and Earth have shown to them; on the contrary, they utter frequent complaints against them. Still, Heaven brings forth people and endows them with the trigrams Qian and Kun manifest in their father and mother, with the sun and the moon manifest in their two eyes, with the stars and constellations manifest in their nine orifices, and with the movement of wind and the power of fire manifest in their warm [body] *qi*. Then, when life ends, all these return to the soil.

In addition, Heaven houses the [constellations of the] Three Terraces and the North Culmen as well as the offices of the Director of Fates and the Director of Emoluments. They commonly take the perfected talisman of the Great One and place it on people's heads to examine if they are full of sins. In accordance with their finding, they make a subtraction from the life expectancy.

If the celestials subtract one year, the star [essence] above the person's head loses its luster and he or she runs into lots of difficulties. [2b] If they take off ten years, the star gradually fades and the person encounters disasters, decline, and various diseases. If they subtract twenty years, the star's radiance is reduced significantly and the person runs into legal trouble and is imprisoned. If they take off thirty years, the star dissolves and the person dies. If at this time, the subtractions are not complete and Heaven needs to ruin further years, they will be taken from the person's descendants, sons and grandsons. Should that not be sufficient either, they extend destruction to his married relations and retainers. The latter, of course, have no idea where they went wrong or what they violated; they can only say that they have a reduced life expectancy.

In this way Heaven never cheats on living beings but shows them its inclinations, like a shadow following its object, through day and night, light and darkness, thunder and lightning, rain and snow, intertwining rainbows, eclipses of the sun and the moon, and floating characters of wisdom. All these are signs given by Heaven. Similarly Earth never cheats on living beings but shows them its inclinations, like an echo follows the sound, by making rivers and streams dry up and bringing forth landslides and earthquakes, hurricanes and tornadoes, sandstorms and moving stones, floods and locust plagues, famines and droughts, epidemics and other disasters. All these are signs given by Earth.

[3a] The demons and spirits cheat on living beings either. They show them their inclinations through good and bad fortune, strange omens and auspicious signs. These are the signs given by demons and spirits. Nor does the ruler cheat on living beings. Rather, shows them his good inclinations by making sure that Heaven and Earth are in harmony, the stars and constellations follow their course, disasters and calamities end, all in the four directions take refuge, and the myriad people are at peace. These are the signs of a good ruler among men.

Typically people's actions, speech, and intentions do not make any reference to these activities of Heaven and Earth. For this reason the sages often say: Sovereign Heaven has no personal feelings, only virtue. This is just it. Thus people should be in awe of the mandate of Heaven, in awe of the great man, and in awe of the words of the sages.

Whatever good and evil people egotistically commit in their daily lives, Heaven and Earth know all about their inner feelings. Even if they secretly harm the life of another being, the spirits can clearly see it in their bodies. Also, whatever they say in body, speech, and mind, the demons always listen to their voices. Then, if they violate the prohibitions a hundred times, the demons take away their essence. If they violate them a thousand times, the Earth registers their form. It they commit nothing but evil every day, they will be imprisoned and put into the cangue. Such is the retribution enacted through yin and yang. Sovereign Heaven thus has its set of precepts and agreements, any violation of which will be punished by misfortune through either spirits and demons or Heaven and Earth.

[3b] **The Yellow Emperor asked again**: The signs of good and evil exhibited by the spirit immortals afford much blessing and good fortune. Could you please examine and explain them for me?

Master Redpine responded: The various methods of self-cultivation, life-preservation, and the control of one's inner nature, when undertaken regularly from the clear morning onward, will bring auspicious *qi* to concentrate in one's heart and be recorded in one's thoughts. Speaking good, doing good, and seeing good all day long will prevent the three karmic causes from arising. In three years Heaven will send down a special star of good fortune and in all cases will bring fortunate rewards.

Some people, on the other hand, speak evil, do evil, and see evil regularly from the clear morning onward; they even instruct others to do evil every day. In three years bad fortune and afflictions will haunt the person, his wealth will vanish and his mouth begin to rot. Earth will increase the *qi* of early death surrounding him, and the person will go into an irreversible decline.

The nine things Heaven detests are the nine greatest obstacles for humanity. Goodness in this context is the match of evil, while evil is the partner of goodness. Or, in other words, the good man is the teacher of the bad man, while the bad man is the material on which the good man works. Good fortune is the proof of bad fortune, while bad fortune is the remnant of good fortune. Thus, if a good man always encounters disasters and decline, frequently suffers from bad fortune and afflictions, then this is due to the surplus of his ancestor's ill fortunes.

[4a] Therefore, a person who cultivates goodness all his life has no need to select an auspicious hour or good day to do his business but can use any time and will naturally obtain good fortune even in the midst of difficulty. This is because the hundred numinous forces surround and protect him—how would the good spirits stay away from him? In the same vein, a person who does nothing but evil all his life vainly selects an auspicious hour or good day for his business yet he will naturally encounter bad luck even in the midst of a promising situation. This is because the evil spirits are harming him and all lucky spirits avoid him.

Thus, on anyone in the world who constantly cultivates goodness throughout life Heaven will naturally bestow an increased good fortune and longevity, surrounding him with harmonious *qi*. This is how Heaven's fortune follows the person's body like a shadow. If you want to avoid decline and destruction, join Heaven in maintaining the prohibitions and taboos, the gains and losses, of Heaven and Earth. As for the proper way of self-cultivation and life-preservation, I will now explain it in detail.[2]

If a person does one single good deed, his spirit and intention will be calm and at peace. 10 good deeds, and his *qi* and strength will be strong and vigorous. 20 good deeds, and his body will be free from affliction and harm. 30 good deeds, and all he pursues will come out as intended. 40 good deeds, and he will be rich and cheerful. 50 good deeds, and he will have a long line of sons and grandsons. [4b] 60 good deeds, and he will not encounter any cheating, violence, or evil people, nor will he get entangled in legal affairs. 70 good deeds, and he will excel and be noble in his studies. 80 good deeds, and he will obtain the benefits of the Earth. 90 good deeds, and the spirits of Heaven will come to protect him.

To a person of 100 good deeds, Heaven will provide a good emolument and help him encounter wise men and sages. 200 good deeds, and he will make himself a name for later generations and his descendants will receive good emoluments. 300 good deeds, and his sons and grandsons for three generations will be rich and noble, profitable and happy. 400 good deeds, and his sons and grandsons for four generations will be rich and noble, receiving outstanding official employment. 500 good deeds, and his sons and grandsons for five generations will receive fiefs and be raised into the aristocracy. 600 good deeds, and his sons and grandsons for many generations will be loyal and filial, rich and noble. 700 good deeds, and his family will bring forth wise men and philosophers for many generations. 800 good deeds, and his family will bring forth men of the Dao and the virtue. 900 good deeds, and his family will bring forth sages. 1,000 good deeds, and his family will bring forth immortals.

If someone, therefore, in antiquity behaved with goodness and propriety, he accordingly received a good emolument through the way of Heaven, attained an increase in this body's life expectancy, and ascended to the ranks of the immortals. His good fortune, moreover, reached out to his sons and grandsons, so that they would give birth to sages and wise men.

On the other hand, if someone commits one single evil deed, his intention will not be calm and at peace. [5a] 10 evil deeds, and his *qi* and strength will be hollow and declining. 20 evil deeds, and his body will be afflicted by many ailments and diseases. 30 evil deeds, and nothing he pursues will come to pass. 40 evil deeds, and he will be in constant difficulties, face decay and destruction, and have his affairs go awry. 50 evil deeds, and he will never find an equal partner. 60 evil deeds, and his line of descendants will die out. 70 evil deeds, and the demons of yin will plan to harm him. 80 evil deeds, and he will encounter disasters of water and fire, and come close to being burned or drowned. 90 evil deeds, and he will be poor and cold, in distress and weak, hungry and famished, and slowly go mad.

As regards a person of 100 evil deeds, the *qi* of Heaven will harm him and obstruct his affairs so that he is thrown into prison, punished by the law, and dies an ugly death. 200 evil deeds, and

---

[2] The following list reappears many times in later sources. See *Statutes of Mystery Metropolis* 2a-3a; the *Comprehensive Perfect Words* (*Zhiyan zong* 至言總, DZ 1033), 5.5b-6a, 9ab), Du Guangting's *Record of the Assembled Immortals in the Heavenly Walled City* (*Yongcheng jixian lu* 墉城集仙綠, DZ 783) 1.4a-5a (Kohn 1989, 88-89); and the supplement to the *Treatise on Impulse and Response* (DZ 1167), 11.2b-3b. For a comprehensive survey of all lists and their variants, see Yoshioka 1967, 294-99.

the *qi* of Earth will harm him, so that robbers and brigands come to hurt him. 300 evil deeds, and his family for generations will bring forth only humble and lowly people. 400 evil deeds, and his sons and grandsons for generations will be destitute and lowly, paupers and beggars. 500 evil deeds, and his sons and grandsons will cut off his family line. 600 evil deeds, and his sons and grandsons for generations will be blind and deaf, mute and mad. 700 evil deeds, and his sons and grandsons will be the five kinds of rebels, unfilial and criminal people. [5b] 800 evil deeds, and his family will bring forth rebellious ministers and unfilial sons that cause destruction and beheadings to the entire clan. 900 evil deeds, and his family will bring forth demonic and evil people who cause destruction to their own and other clans. 1,000 evil deeds, and his sons and grandsons for generations will be malformed and of crooked limbs looking like maimed animals or wild birds.

The bad destiny that comes from accumulating evil thus flows over so that the misfortunes strike for numerous generations. First the Director of Fates subtracts time from the sinner's life expectancy, then the star on his head tumbles and his body dies, then his soul is captured in the dark realm of Fengdu, and finally the misfortune hits his descendants of later generations.

The Yellow Emperor next asked: What kinds of sins do people commit that induce the Director of Fates to make a subtraction from the life expectancy?

Master Redpine replied: I submit that when the people of the world commit violations, bad actions, or faults, or again speak contrary words, Heaven's way is no longer even. Instead it is bent and loses its spontaneity. Getting furious and cursing upsets Heaven. Getting imprisoned and locked into the cangue upsets Heaven. Being hungry, poor, ill, and sick upsets Heaven. Unseasonable cold, heat, frost, and snow upset Heaven. Irregularities in the length of day and night upset Heaven. It upsets it even more when people do evil then come to pray and besiege Heaven [for help]; or if they go against the four seasons, disobey the five phases, expose their naked body to the Three Luminants, [6a] and then come to request a benefit at a shrine or temple of the Three Luminants or the various stars and constellations; or if people see eclipses of the sun and the moon with their own eyes, yet never for a moment stop being greedy for their own delight and pleasure.

They have no respect for Heaven and Earth or the demons and spirits.
They are unfilial toward their father and mother.
They curse the wind and the rain.
They reject and ruin the sages and the scriptural teachings.
They desecrate and destroy the shrines and temples to Earth and ancestors.
They dig up tombs and graves to steal the valuables of the dead.
They cheat the blind, the deaf, and the dumb.
They enter and defile other people's residences to steal gold and brocade.
They expose themselves in public, taking off their clothes.
They throw impure substances into all sorts of food and drink.
They bury good talismans deep within the Earth, silently cursing all living beings.
They raise nasty worms to prepare the *gu* poison, envious of the wise ones and jealous of those of high ability.
They kill and harm the lives of other beings, leaving them behind without heads or limbs.
They accuse and slander ordinary people to diminish and reduce them.
They spy on the private affairs of others.
They obstruct and block roads and paths.

They fill in and build up ditches and drains.

They steal other people's goods.

They throw away and cast off usable medicines.

They cut and chop off people's trees and bushes, herbs and grains, flowers and fruit, gardens and forests.

They injure and hurt the six domestic animals.

They pollute and defile wells and stoves, offices and observatories, temples and residences.

They clad themselves in the robes of filiality, then sing lewd songs and engage in merry making. [6b]

They set fire and burn mountain sides.

They destroy and despoil other people's products and efforts.

They dry up and exhaust pools and fish ponds.

They fish to catch water creatures, such as turtles and fish.

They go against contracts and pledges in their interaction with others.

They disregard and despise the way of the spirits.

They are crafty and devious, false and deceptive.

They say "yea" and think "nay."

They use bad language and speak slander.

They distort the partial and essential and bring much litigation and contention.

They instruct others to frequently complain to the officials.

They expose their nakedness to other people.

They loosen their hair when eating or drinking.

They diminish good and increase evil.

They enrich themselves and injure others.

They ardently believe heterodox teachers.

They teach others to go against the divine law.

They attack and kill the innocent.

They take what is right and twist it into falsehood.

They use and employ devious skills.

They present what is light and claim it as heavy.

They kill and cut things down in spring.

They destroy many lives in summer.

They see evil and do nothing about it in fall.

They dig the earth and open hollows in winter.

They leave other people's flesh and bones unburied.

They love killing and hate life.

They take themselves seriously and despise all others.

They cheat the orphaned and maltreat the lonely.

They defeat others to win for themselves.

They endanger others and take away their peace.

They borrow goods and do not return them.

They praise themselves and denigrate others.

They join with evil to pursue their power.

They sell and barter with the rights of others.

They secretly harbor poisonous [thoughts] yet show compassion on their faces.

They see killing and add to the fray.

They know of a transgression yet do not do anything about it. [7a]

They see good and do not follow it.

They turn their backs on their kin and approach strangers instead.

They despise the lofty and show pride to the lowly.

They do not accept the advice of their parents, teachers, and friends.

They let their wives and concubines bicker and fight.

They pick on the small and talk down to them.

They speak with contempt and abandon their flesh and bones.

They regret it if they ever commit an act of generosity or kindness.

They enjoy to point out the deficiencies of others.

They spy and penetrate others' secrets only to provoke and mock them.

They debauch the wives and concubines of others.

They do anything that is against the Dao.

They exploit the kindness and love of others.

They steal the goodness and service of others, yet say of themselves that it is their own.

They are burdened by heavy sins yet pull others in to testify on their behalf.

They slight and despise all above and below, never choosing whether they are noble or humble.

They depend on alcohol and constantly insult other beings.

They treat other beings with no regard for them.

They discard and throw away food and drink.

They disregard and maltreat clothes and garments.

They demand and strive without bounds, never staying away even from danger and death.

They obtain something new and promptly forget the old.

They discard the root and pursue the branches.

They receive kindness and do not pay it back.

They cheat, deceive, and generally insult all others.

There are over 800 items of transgressions and violations such as I just listed. They can only be described briefly. I cannot go into them in more detail. Still, whenever a person in the world commits any violation, he in all cases also violates his very own personal radiant star or constellation. [7b] A memorial will duly be submitted to the Highest Emperor, the seven stars [of the Dipper], the six pitch pipes, the four seasons, the eight winds, the nine palaces, and the five phases. They will then cause the Director of Fates to make an appropriate subtraction from the life expectancy, making the person short lived and having manifold misfortunes extend even to his sons and grandsons.

The Yellow Emperor then asked: When people violate the prohibitions and taboos of Heaven and Earth, they receive a certain subtraction from their life expectancy. What is the relationship between the exact measure of the subtraction and the sin committed?

Master Redpine replied: People are at the root of Heaven and Earth and should accordingly act in goodness and submit to their connections. People of the world may present an outward appearance of harmony and compliance, yet on the inside they often harbor thoughts of darkness and jealousy. In that case, they still violate the prohibitions and taboos and their sins accumulate and are not limited to just one. Now, whatever they do is registered and memorialized by the Director of Fates one sin after the next. In accordance with them, he orders punishments for people. Someone who killed, for example, will himself be caught up between two armies and suffer death on the battlefield. If he has killed only once, he will be harmed in his own body and that will even the score of his fate. If he has killed twice, then he will be caught between five armies and the Great One will come to slay him. Plus, the evil deed will continue to follow him further and create continued misfortunes for his descendants.

The Yellow Emperor asked yet another question of Master Redpine: I have now heard you speak about all the many evil deeds people commit in the world. It has robbed me of my peaceful sleep. Pray, tell me, how can one be liberated from all these sins?

[8a] The Master answered: Among sins there are some from which one can be liberated and others from which one cannot. If people of the world accidentally commit an act against the Dao and in their hearts offer repentance for their transgression, they can be exonerated. If they hear but do not believe, if they know they are at fault but do not change their ways and still commit evil, or if they change their course a lot and keep poisonous thoughts in their hearts, their sins cannot be exonerated.

Master Redpine said: When people practice the Dao of goodness, Heaven and Earth and the demons and spirits all give them good fortune and help them. Never engaging in anything evil, how could they not fulfill the Dao of goodness? All that people in the world need to do is honor and venerate Heaven and Earth and the Three Luminants, never violate the prohibitions and taboos, love and obey their fathers and mothers, maintain harmony with their siblings, be compassionate and empathic to the orphaned and lonely, save and support the poor and sick, and respect and honor their teachers and elders.

Ever since antiquity, the sages and wise men have taught and shown people how not to go against [the rules] but instead be humble and modest, reverent and respectful. Every time they encounter wind and rain, heat and cold, baleful stars and strange signs, halos around the sun and the moon, or disastrous eclipses, in all cases they should think only of goodness, respectfully keep away from the demons and spirits, and instead offer sacrifices to Heaven and Earth. As they thereby get their merit registered above, their reckoning is extended and their emoluments are increased. Seeing someone do evil, they should always admonish him or her to cultivate goodness.

[8b] If they encounter a good person, they should respect and follow him. If they meet with bad luck or danger, they should seek protection in their heart. If they find themselves in difficulty and distress, they should join others for stability and security. If they are involved only in easy affairs, they should take on the heavy duties of others. Also, they should admonish others not to get involved in official affairs or engage in verbal disputes and litigation. Rather, they should repair or build wells of righteousness, drains and ditches, and clear up and fix roads and paths. Never let a small matter be the reason to lose the bigger picture, nor allow a big affair be in the way of dealing with a minor matter.

Seeing people suffering loss should give them pain and a sense of urgency; seeing others win and gain should make them feel joyous. Supporting the emaciated and protecting the weak, they should be generous and kind, help and cherish the orphaned and poor, and honor and care for the lowly and humble. As they yield their emoluments to others, so Heaven records their merit, again increases their age and longevity, and grants protection and good fortune to their sons and grandsons.

Anyone with the genuine will and faith not to go against [the rules] who in his heart venerates the Dao and the virtue will have no need to avoid dangers and perils or be saved from drowning in rivers and lakes. Free from lascivious thoughts and outward sexual urges, he or she will never encroach on the residences, homes, or creations of others. Never going against principle and injuring or harming the life of any being, people like these love life and hate killing. Never losing their propriety and respect, they will always practice in accordance with the scriptures and sacred writings. In kindness never forgetting to recompense others, they are gentle with all and have no regrets.

[9a] Widely encompassing patience and forbearance, they exhaust loyalty and are fully filial. Never relaxing in [their performance] of the dignified observances, they have no use for material wealth and do not get attached to fanciful and ornate garments. In selecting food for themselves, they never unreasonably kill life. They are in all respects like the great ones of old who:

> were strangers to none;
> never thought themselves wise;
> never thought themselves good;
> never thought themselves free;
> never thought themselves rich;
> never thought themselves dignified;
> never thought themselves unique;
> never thought themselves praiseworthy;
> never thought themselves important;
> never thought themselves venerable;
> never thought themselves great;
> never thought themselves useful; and
> never thought themselves specially able.

Still, as the great [powers] recorded their earthly merits, they all received extended reckoning and longevity.

Again, those who will receive multiple extensions of their reckoning are people who exhaust their loyalty in serving their ruler, exhaust their filiality in serving their father, are never proud or arrogant, respect their teachers and elders, open enlightenment to the young, hide their brilliance and praise the transmission of the masters, always cultivate themselves, are modest and harmonious, make peace both with those above and below, are caring and loving and level-minded, never listen to slander or wrong words, and generally have an upright mind that they apply in all they do.

If female, they filially obey their mothers-in-law and respectfully obey their husbands. Pure and chaste, they act with clarity, drinking pure *qi* and swallowing sound. Reverent and alert from dawn to dusk, with harmonious expression and joyful mien, they venerate their superiors free from egotistic urges. For all this they receive an increase in reckoning, extended longevity, and enhanced emoluments. [9b] All disasters and obstacles are dissolved, and both men and women become very perceptive and wise.

On the other hand, people who experience reduced longevity and less good fortune are typically ministers who slay their rulers, sons who kill their fathers, disciples who serve their teachers but soon turn their backs on them or forget about them in pursuit of their own interests. Also, they are those who create rebellion and disorder, behaving without ritual propriety; those who do not properly distinguish between kin and stranger; and those who are only intent on pleasing themselves and engage in licentiousness.

Among women, they are those who turn their backs on their father and mother, behave without filiality towards their mothers-in-law, despise and humble their husbands, speak nothing but backbiting and slander, instigate fights and competition among the six relations, steal and grasp with an attitude of greed and indolence, and always judge their neighbors as being worse.

All these people will suffer from a deduction in life expectancy and good fortune, and will be tied up in bad situations and diseases as long as they live. In life they will be hated by all, in death they will fall deep into the hells.

The Yellow Emperor asked again: Still, there is also the wondrous Dao among humanity. How can one get to hear about it?

Master Redpine replied: Now, the good or evil people undertake and hold on to all originate in their minds. The mind contains the sprouts of the five robbers and the root of the myriad evils. Then, if people in their minds intend and practice goodness, even though the good deed may not yet be complete, the good spirits already respond to it. Similarly, if the mind brings forth evil, even though the evil act may not yet have germinated, the bad spirits already know all about it.

Therefore, if a gentleman does good for one thousand days, there is yet never enough goodness. [10a] If he brings forth evil even for a moment, there is already too much evil. This goes as far as the arising in the mind of secret greed and avarice. Each mental action has its gain and loss, matching the way of Heaven. Also, if someone creates an intention to harm another being, even before he has had a chance to actually do so, his life and death, decay and flourishing will already be impacted.

As the [unidentified] *Scripture* says: "Heaven has five robbers. Who recognizes them will flourish; who loses sight of them will perish. The teaching has five virtues. Who practices them will flourish; who disregards them will perish."

Practice these virtues to become kind, friendly, reverent, withdrawing, and modest. They are benevolence, righteousness, propriety, wisdom, and faithfulness. Turn your back on them and become evil and obstinate [subject to the five robbers]: greed and envy, killing and murder, aggression and violence, cheating and betrayal, deception and flattery.

People of the world more often than not practice the five bad behaviors and in their minds typically bring forth nine kinds of mentation [*nian*]:

— when they see another person prosperous and noble, they say that he ultimately came from wind and dust in the past and in their minds pray that he will become homeless and deprived;

— when they see another wealthy and noble, they laugh saying that he was poor and destitute in the past and pray that he will be destroyed;

— when they see another have money and rich silks in great abundance, they develop the intention to encourage others to steal from him;

— when they see another have beautiful wives and concubines, they develop the intention to commit adultery; [10b]

— when they see another live in a big home and large estate, they develop the intention to set fire to it and burn it down;

— when they are burdened by debt to someone, in their hearts they wish that the moneylender may die and the debt expire;

— when they cannot obtain the wealth and property of others, they develop a mind that is full of affliction and hatred;

— when they see another accidentally fall into danger, they say this is because of his wrongdoing in the past;

— even in relation to their father and mother who gave birth to them, they wish that they die early because they desire their house and goods.

These are nine typical thoughts of ignorant people. They are the reason why Heaven and Earth and the demons and spirits hate such folk, create lots of disasters and misfortunes for them, and drastically reduce their reckoning and longevity.

People who practice the five virtues, on the contrary, always harbor nine good thoughts or realizations [*si*]:

— when they see another prosperous and noble, they realize that their own karma for good fortune is still thin;

— when they see another having much grain and rice in his storehouse, they realize that they have not planted and sown diligently and with sufficient vigor;

— when they see another rich in gold and jade, they realize that this is not their property;

— when they see another have beautiful wives and concubines, they realize that their own partner does not create quarrels or upheaval;

— when they see another live in a big home and extensive estate, they realize that they have peace in their small and humble cottage; [11a]

— when they see someone who in the past was in debt to them run afoul of the officials, they develop an intention of helpfulness and support;

— when they hold someone's debt that is not being returned with interest, they realize how much pain and effort the debtor is expending and reward him for that;

— when they want to borrow someone else's money or goods [and have difficulty doing so], they realize their own earlier lack of kindness;

— when they see another serve his parents, they always think that they should spare no hardship or effort to repay their own parents' love.

If people in the world can practice these nine realizations and give up the previously listed nine bad thoughts, they will be full of highest wisdom and illumination. While alive in this world, they will always be surrounded by good fortune and happiness, and their blessings will even flow down to their sons and grandsons. All obstacles and misfortunes will evaporate, and disasters will be unable to reach them.

The Yellow Emperor then asked: You mentioned "men of wisdom." What kinds are they?

Answer: They come in three kinds, all full of benevolence and good will. Those of high wisdom understand the patterns of Heaven and have insight into the principles of Earth. Without studying they know, without being taught they understand. Silently they recognize all. They examine the tones and pitches and inspect wisdom and stupidity. Their minds are full of empathy and compassion, and they do not despise others. They recognize success and defeat [in good time], understand when to advance and withdraw, and clearly distinguish life and death. People like these, although they may be poor, will in the end be rich; although they may be humble for a time, they will be lofty in the end. Such are the people of high wisdom.

[11b] Those of medium wisdom deeply penetrate the scriptures and writings, are always conscious of ritual propriety and proper respect. They look up to the wise and think of order, support those in danger and rescue the weak. Gracious and generous, they have no regrets; loyal and filial, they suffer no failure. In their speech they do not harm other beings, in their behavior they are always humble and withdrawing, warm and modest. People like these may not study, yet they find awakening in the end; they may not stand out yet, but they will find full attainment. Such are the people of medium wisdom.

Those of lesser wisdom practice good deeds. They amend their past [habits], cultivate the future, pursue good actions, and think much of learning. Devoutly believing in the patterns of good and evil, they do not encroach upon the possessions of others but protect their own life and take good care of their body. Matching the principles of the Dao and recognizing the universal law, they spontaneously love the weak while inherently fearing disasters and decline. Like this making continuous efforts, they never undergo loss or failure, and never meet with obstructions or misfortune. Such are the people of lesser wisdom.

The Yellow Emperor said: Excellent! Most excellent, indeed! These words are too precious to be measured in terms even of merit and virtue. I will diligently follow what you have explained, and show its record to the multitude of people, thus creating a great passage [to transcendence] for all living beings. Humbly I knock my head to you and withdraw to practice in accordance with the teachings.

Text Four

Great Precepts of the Highest Ranks

INTRODUCTION

The *Great Precepts of the Highest Ranks* (*Shangpin dajie* 上品大戒, DZ 177) belongs among the original Numinous Treasure scriptures (LB 13; Yamada 2000, 234; Kleeman 1991, 175-76). The text is also found among Dunhuang manuscripts (DH 7; see Yoshioka 1961b, 935-37).

In content, it begins with a Mahāyāna-style setting and consists of the transmission of various sets of precepts given by the Heavenly Worthy of Primordial Beginning (Yuanshi tianzun 元始天尊) to the Highest Lord of the Dao (Taishang Daojun 太上道君). The goal is to help all living beings realize the Dao and thereby escape the eight difficult conditions, never fall into the hells, and be reborn speedily on the human plane. For that, they should first of all practice the ten wisdom precepts but also follow all other rules presented here.

The text claims to go back to a time when the world was first created by the Heavenly Worthy, a deity adapted from a combination of the all-encompassing Dao at the dawn of the universe with the truth-body (*dharmakāya*) of the Buddha. After the world first came into being, it was in its purest state and people were pure and simple and did not have evil minds. As a result they lived long and attained pervasive good fortune.

Over the following eons, the world went through several declining cycles until the present age arrived, known as the Highest Sovereign (Shanghuang 上皇) kalpa. A time of moral and religious disintegration, people are deluded and eager to harm each other, creating misfortune and early death. The Heavenly Worthy responds to this by providing extensive guidance through scriptures, talismans, spells, and precepts. He hopes to minimize damage and to assist people in transcending the world and attaining immortality.

His key assistant in this enterprise is the Lord of the Dao, also known as the Highest Lord and often named simply "The Dao." He functions as the mouthpiece of the creator and serves as the revealer of sacred scriptures and precepts, asking the Heavenly Worthy for guidance on behalf of all human beings. He is a bodhisattva-like figure who is close to the full attainment to the Dao, has spent a hundred million kalpas perfecting himself and yet does not retire to celestial splendor.

Instead, he entices the creator deity to provide assistance to suffering humanity, which takes the form of several sets of precepts, commonly listed in sets of ten and consisting of both prohibitions and admonitions, encouraging the development of altruism and compassion. They often echo the six *pāramitās* or bodhisattva virtues— charity, moral conduct, forbearance, effort, calmness, and wisdom. They lead adepts to pursue the "ten right actions" in proper vision, hearing, knowledge, and mindfulness; to develop the "ten good abilities" of controlling the senses; and eventually to become "followers of the ten cycles," a gradual ascent to the Dao that involves the observation of different levels of precepts and leads to complete freedom from sensory desires and the utter transcendence of all.

Except for the last set of seven rules, the precepts are also contained in *juan* 6 of the *Essentials of Pervading the Mystery of the Great Dao* (*Dadao tongxuan yao* 大道通玄要, DH 97). The text specifies various sets of precepts to be taken by adepts as they attain higher ranks. It contains a set of ten precepts based on Buddhist bodhisattva precepts and vows. The first list is, in fact, a mixture of the ten items of goodness required of the striving bodhisattva and the precepts of the *Brahma Net Sūtra*, a Buddhist apocryphon of the mid-fifth century that has exerted some influence on Daoist precepts. Individual sets of precepts, moreover, are found in numerous other contemporaneous and later sources.

TRANSLATION

[1a] The Heavenly Worthy of Primordial Beginning, on the first day of the seventh month of the first year of Opening Sovereign, at the noon hour, was in the Mulberry Forest of Floating Network, on the Mountain of Many Temples in Western Jade Country. There he transmitted to the Highest Lord of the Dao the "Text and Method of the Great Precepts of Wisdom of the Highest Ranks."

The Lord of the Dao received the precepts, stood up facing north, and prostrated himself, head and body, upon the earth. Turning to the east, he then bowed to all ten directions.

The Heavenly Worthy told the Highest Lord of the Dao:

From today on, widely spread the sounds of the divine law, awaken all living beings, and liberate all men and women from disasters and distress. On their behalf request good fortune, salvation, and the eradication of the roots of suffering. Make the living see the Dao and be free from the eight difficult conditions; make the dead rejoice and feast in the heavenly halls and be reborn early among humanity, transmigrating only among sages and kings.

For this cultivate the purgations and pursue the Dao, and in all cases maintain a unified mind. Request and venerate the Ten Wisdom Precepts, receive them with discernment and never forget them. With concentrated mind and collected mindfulness, deeply meditate on spontaneity, [1b] never giving rise to confused imaginings or otherwise disturbing or agitating the body and spirit. If you can do so, come and listen quietly. [1b]

The Heavenly Worthy then told him the Ten Wisdom Precepts:

1. Let there be no evil or envy in your heart, and never give rise to dark thieving thoughts. Be reserved in speech and wary of transgressions, and in your imaginings remain mindful of the divine law.

2. Maintain benevolence and do not kill, and instead feel sympathy and support for the host of living beings. Be compassionate and loving, and widely rescue and benefit all.

3. Maintain chastity and be withdrawing and yielding, neither lascivious nor thieving. Always practice goodness and mindfulness, disregarding yourself to support other beings.

4. Do not engage in passions or desires, never giving free rein to your mind. Be chaste and pure, and maintain prudence in all actions without flaws and disgrace. [2a]

5. Let there be no bad words in your mouth, and let your words not be flowery or ornate. Be straightforward within and without, never committing transgressions of speech.

6. Reduce the wine you drink, always using it in moderation and harmonizing your *qi* and inner nature. Make sure your spirit is not diminished or harmed, and never commit a multitude of evils.

7. Do not be jealous of others superior to yourself and never contend for merit and fame. In all things be retiring and withdrawing, putting yourself last and saving others.

8. Do not criticize and debate the scriptural teachings, nor revile and slander the sagely texts. In body and mind support the divine law, constantly acting as if you were facing the gods.

9. Do not stir up quarrels and confusion through your mouth and tongue or criticize and debate the four ranks. If you create blame and hatred among the celestial community[1] this harms and diminishes your spirit and energy. [2b]

10. In all your conduct and interactions be of even and unified mind. Be harmonious among people and reverent toward the gods, acting always to maintain this state. [2] [2b]

The Heavenly Worthy said:

Cultivate and venerate these precepts, in each case remaining attuned to the mind of Heaven. Always practice great compassion and pray that all beings may equally go beyond danger and the world. Be modest and yielding and venerate the teachings, never being lax or lazy. Rather maintain goodness and die than commit evil and live!

Doing so, you will never regress but can attain transcendence of the five realms and thus never again tread the three bad rebirths. Instead, you will be protected by the various heavens and respected by the myriad gods. Practicing extended purgations and venerating the precepts, you will naturally go beyond the world.

---

[1] This translates *tianren* 天人, literally "celestial people." The term indicates the community of Daoist believers who ready themselves for ascent into the higher spheres.

[2] The same set of Ten Wisdom Precepts is also found in the *Jade Instructions on the Text Written in Red* (DZ 352, 1.2b-4a), an early Numinous Treasure work on rules for purgations (Ren and Zhong 1991, 266; Soymié 1977, 7). For a translation according to this version, see Bokenkamp 1989, 18-19. Among later Numinous Treasure texts, the precepts are found in the *Observations for Lamps, Spells, and Vows* (DZ 524, 8a-9a). See Kleeman 1991, 179-80; Yoshioka 1961a, 65-66.

They also appear four times in WSBY: first, as "Wisdom Precepts of Mystery Cavern" (46.9a-10a), followed by the twelve resolutions, six precepts to control the passions, and six precepts for salvation (46.10a-12b); second, in the context of the Nocturnal Announcement as cited from the *Scripture of the Great Precepts* (35.6b-7b); third, in a ritual context from the *Scripture of the Golden Register [Purgation]* (48.5a-6a); and last, as part of the Rite of Mud and Ashes, again from the *Scripture of the Great Precepts* (50.3b-4a).

In later medieval literature, the Ten Wisdom Precepts appear in Zhang Wanfu's *Observances for Ordination* (DZ 1236, 8b-9a) and in *Essential Rules and Observances* (DZ 463, 5.1ab). After this, they are listed in Du Guangting's *Observances of Precepts Transmission for the Golden Register* (DZ 486, 4b-4b); and cited in YJQQ as the "Ten Precepts Observed to Practice Purgations and Pursue the Dao" (39.18a-19a).

The Highest Lord of the Dao could barely control his joy and delight. He knocked his head to the ground, paying respects to these instructions.

The Heavenly Worthy said:

Students of the Dao! Cultivate the purgations and perform rites to the Dao, thereby opening up salvation for all in the celestial community. Performing the various good deeds and merits, [3a] you should moreover adopt the Twelve Desirable Attitudes to fully attain salvation from this world. Following them correctly, you naturally attain right perfection and eventually enter nonaction. All you pray for will be fulfilled.

The Twelve Desirable Attitudes[3]

1. Seeing the perfect scriptures and the orthodox[4] divine law, I will open salvation for all. For this I will bring forth a strong intention for the Dao and in my mind pray that in later generations I may rise to be among the great sages.

2. I will constantly practice a compassionate mind, pray and be mindful that all beings equally get to see the divine law.[5] May their salvation be wide and far, and never have any hindrances or obstacles.

3. I will love and delight in the scriptural teaching, surveying and penetrating it deeply and widely. With my intention and will firm and clear, I will educate all those in ignorance and darkness.

4. I will respectfully[6] receive the instructions of my teachers, widely educating and encouraging others, causing all to enter the walls of the divine law and forever be far away from the paths of blindness. [3b]

5. I will have faith in the mystery and wonder [of the Dao], honoring and venerating the scriptures and oral instructions. I will recite and activate them morning and evening, never tiring or being lazy.

6. I will not serve glory and glamor but break the chain of karma and retribution in the ordinary world. Maintaining a focused mind and firm determination, all that I undertake will be for the divine law.

7. I will diligently recite the great scriptures, praying and being mindful that for all beings the bridge [of release] shall be wide open and that they shall establish good karmic connections in their future lives.

8. I will respectfully give rise to a mind of goodness, without depravity or falseness, free from jealousy and illwill, evil, and envy.

9. When entrusted to life, I shall always encounter a sagely generation, joining the divine law of Numinous Treasure and continuing the teaching without interruption. [4a]

---

[3] These twelve rules are also found in *Precepts against the Roots of Sin* 1.8a-9a.
[4] Following *Roots of Sin* and reading *zheng* 正 (orthodox) instead of *chu* 出 (issue).
[5] Following *Roots of Sin* and reading *fa* 法 (divine law) instead of *wen* 聞 (hear).
[6] Following *Roots of Sin* and reading *zun* 遵 (respectful) for *zun* 尊 (worthy).

10. I will cleanse my body, uphold the precepts, cultivate the purgations, and establish merit. I will widely rescue the host of living beings so they all can attain salvation and liberation.

11. Whatever field I study and read on widely I shall proclaim and make accessible to my fellows[7] in the divine law, thus preparing all in Heaven and among humanity to equally attain salvation.

12. I will always encounter enlightened teachers, life after life receive the teachings, and proclaim them widely to save innumerable people. May all develop a mind of goodness and attain the perfect Dao.

The Heavenly Worthy said:

Students who cultivate and practice the divine law always should follow these precepts of the Twelve Desirable Attitudes. Once they practice these good thoughts with a unified mind, they will encounter sagely texts life after life and their karma will be linked to the Dao. They will have friends[8] and acquaintances in the various heavens and in their lonely transcendence of the Three Worlds will be without obstacles or hindrances.

Forever they will be free from the three bad rebirths, the five realms of suffering, [9b] and the eight difficult conditions. The spirit luminants [of Heaven] will respect and protect them, while the gods of Earth will surround and guard them. Their homes will always be pure and dignified and the ten thousand disasters will not come near them. This we call "being upright and straightforward, and attaining the Dao!" Diligently undertake the exercises and recitations, and widely proclaim the teaching to your fellow students, causing them all equally to enter the gate of the divine law.

The Heavenly Worthy said:

The Dao is venerable and the divine law is wondrous. Humanity is also noble. Therefore the Dao reveals the divine law and dispenses the precepts and scriptural writings in order to save the human person. Once human beings have gone beyond, they ascend and become one with the Dao.

To do so, always practice keenly, uphold the purgations, and venerate the precepts. Concentrate your mind in tranquil serenity, make your will and thoughts clear and penetrating, and with unified intention take refuge and return [to the divine law]. Unify your imaginings so they are no longer dual, keep the six senses clear and clean. Whatever you pass through, do not taste it but keep inside and outside clear and empty, always matching spontaneity. On every purgation day offer incense and announce your prayers, presenting to the powers above in accordance with your heart. Then the supervising patrols of the Four Heavens and the dignified gods of the Ten Divisions will descend to be with you wherever you go. Observe and listen to their utmost sounds, let their brilliance be reflected in your mind and heart.

If you know how to perform rites to the Dao, you can amass merit in the various heavens. Good and bad fortune will become clear to you, and the Dao will not be a burden. Practice with dili-

---

[7] Following *Roots of Sin* and reading *tong* 同 (fellows) for *dong* 洞 (pervasive).
[8] Following *Roots of Sin* and reading *you* 友 (friends) for *nü* 女 (women).

gence and receive [the precepts] with discernment, never causing the demons to speak [against you]. [5a]

The Heavenly Worthy said:

If any good man or good woman develops an intention toward the Dao and spontaneity, comes to enter the gate of the divine law, receives the Ten Wisdom Precepts and practices according to the Twelve Desirable Attitudes, he or she becomes a Disciple Pure Faith of the Great Dao. The merit created thereby matches that of the valiant and fearless flying celestials. Such flying celestials who have not yet attained the Dao are called "Followers of the Ten Cycles." They can fly and wander through the void and harness the steeds of the various heavens.

A Disciple of Pure Faith still remaining on this earth can attain liberation from all sorrow and distress, and go beyond the multitude of sufferings. Their bodies will radiate a bright glow, and within they are pure and upright. Able to summon ghosts and control spirits, they can subdue all demons and specters. Going through the ten cycles, they eventually attain the highest level and become full flying celestials.

Beginning with the first cycle, if he practices keenly and with efforts, is never lax or remiss in the mind, performs only meritorious and virtuous actions, observes long purgations and austerities, and never tires of performing rites to the Dao morning and evening, he can become a flying celestial. From here he further progresses and eventually goes completely beyond the Three Worlds to become a perfected of Highest Clarity.

The Heavenly Worthy said:

When you receive my Ten Wisdom Precepts and Twelve Desirable Attitudes, you should knock your heads and become Disciples of Pure Faith. [5b] From the day when you receive the precepts, honor and practice them with all your heart. Never dare to be unfaithful for a moment, but always take refuge in them with your life.

Anyone in the ten directions who can do so will forever encounter splendid and prosperous families in which to be born and will be healthy and strong in body. The gods of Earth will serve as his guards, and the officers of the Three Worlds will receive him formally. The souls and spirits of such a person's ancestors up to seven generations will ascend to the Southern Palace, where they will be clothed and feted at heavenly banquets. They will all attain an early rebirth and inevitably return to the human plane, coming to life in royal families. Forever and ever, in every generation, their karma will be linked with the Dao.

The Heavenly Worthy said:

Set up purgations and perform rites to the Dao, then the Imperial Kings of the Four Heavens on your behalf will harness clouds and luminous chariots and enter radiant jade carriages. In their entourage, they will be followed by perfected and jade maidens, who will hold flowery banners in their hands. Before them goes the Phoenix Singer, behind them follows the Heavenly Equalizer. White cranes and wondrous lions will whistle and sing elegant melodies. They will burn incense and scatter flowers, floating through the air to come to you.

Look up with reverence during your rites to the Dao, observantly listen to the sounds of the divine law. Then the Heavenly Kings will descend before you, and the myriad numinous powers will pay their respects. Like this, how could you not fulfill the divine law?

For this, first of all receive the Ten Wisdom Precepts, [6a] then perform rites to the Dao and move ahead in an orderly and elegant fashion. Calm your mind and shutter your intention. Whether sitting, rising, lying down, or resting, never deviate from the rules and observances. The Heavenly Kings will rejoice in gladness and inscribe your name in Highest Clarity. This is called attaining the Dao. It all lies in the square inch of the mind.

The Highest Precepts of Wisdom to Block the Six Passions[9]

1. Let not your eyes gaze widely or be confused by flowery colors lest they lose their clarity and their pupils, no longer bright and penetrating, diminishing their radiance.

2. Let not your ears be confused in their hearing or obscured by the five sounds lest you harm spirit and destroy uprightness and come to hear bad sounds everywhere.

3. Let not your nose widely smell various vapors or be distracted by stench lest it become easily mixed and turbid and the body be no longer clear and pure. [6b]

4. Let not your mouth covet fancy tastes, all kinds of rich and savory foods lest turbidity pour into the five spirits and the inner organs and intestines become soaked with it.

5. Let not your hands commit any evil act or steal other people's goods lest greed and personal profit become part of your self and misfortunes arise before you even know it.

6. Let not your mind fill with [egoistic] love and passion or agitate the five spirits lest this harm your essence and destroy your *qi*, so the whole body go wild and be led astray.

The Heavenly Worthy said:

These six forms of consciousness are great afflictions to the personal body. Once one comes to be born as male or female, even though one receives a pure physical body, the six emotions cause it to be no longer pristine. Without seeing the scriptural teachings and hearing the sounds of the divine law, the physical body cannot become aware of itself [as pure] and will sink ever deeper into delusion and sin. Then the life expectancy is shortened and one cannot fulfill one's Heaven-given years. Forever stuck in the evil ways [of low rebirth], one is greatly to be pitied.

For this reason, I have explained these forms of consciousness and thereby opened salvation for all in the celestial community. With a heart full of goodness and true faith, [7a] direct your intention to take refuge with your life. Venerate and honor the sagely teaching and firmly close the door to all evil. Then your body will enter emptiness and the void, and you will attain the wisdom of the six pervasions.[10] The wisdom of the six pervasions includes the pervasion of sight,

---

[9] The same list is also found in WSBY 46.11b-12a.

[10] This translates *liutong* 六通, which in Buddhist texts is rendered "six supernatural powers," i.e., the powers of a buddha in the fourth *dhyāna*. They are universal vision, hearing, and knowledge of other minds as well as the ability to see one's former lives, multilocate, and to know the end of vicious propensities (Mochi-

hearing, the void [air, smells], emptiness [sound], clarity [objects], and the subtle [thoughts]. These six pervasions mean that nothing is left unpervaded. Through them the six passions are laid to rest and the inner spirits naturally return to you. The One naturally arises and your essence is naturally strong. You attain long life and eventually go beyond death altogether.

The Highest Precepts of Wisdom for the Salvation of All Living Beings[11]

1. If you see someone destitute and in extremes, close to the danger of dying, pray for him to have a bright life next time, with the strength to control his bad fortune and adversity. May his life be long and extended. May he meet auspicious generations without end.

2. If you see someone destitute and poor, hard pressed by hunger and cold, give of yourself in a generous manner so that others may be rich and noble. May their good fortune and reward multiply a myriad times. May they be happy generation after generation. [7b]

3. If among beings that contain blood, there is one on the warpath killing people, open up salvation for this being so that it may be saved from the danger of death. May it see a new life full of health and vigor. May it never again encounter adversity or evil.

4. Give wisely to the birds and beasts, to all species of living creatures. Take from your own mouth to feed them, let there be none left unloved or not cherished. May they be full and satisfied generation after generation. May they always be born in the realm of blessedness.

5. Save all that wriggles and runs, all the multitude of living beings. Allow them all to reach fulfillment and prevent them from suffering an early death. May they all have lives in prosperity and plenty. May they never step into the multiple adversities.

6. Always practice compassion in your heart, commiserating with all. Liberate living beings from captivity and rescue them from danger, so their merit may grow exceedingly. May all people in their lives find safety from danger, health out of sickness, wealth from poverty. May all find what they desire in their hearts.

The Heavenly Worthy said:

These six forms of consciousness are ways to make the mind pervasive and develop wisdom. Spread virtue of this kind and you act in harmony with spontaneity. [8a] Blessings and good fortune will forever rest with your personal body, while bad fortune and harm will eternally stay away from your door.

Perform good without stopping and accumulate good karma from generation to generation, and in the first cycle you will receive the reward of becoming a flying celestial. Continue to accumulate merit and go beyond the wheel of transmigration altogether, over nine cycles gradually entering the Great Dao. Then, in the tenth cycle, your religious name will be recorded in the various heavens and with your ancestors of seven generations you will ascend to be born in the heavenly halls, clothed and feasted in blessed virtue. After that, when again reborn among humanity, even while still within the wheel of rebirth, you will be a spirit king and forever live at fortune's gate.

---

zuki 1933-36, 5060a). See also *To Illustrate the Way* (*Yudao lun* 愈道論, T. 2102, 52.17c) and the *Flower Garland Sutra* (T. 278, 9.655a and T. 279, 10.300b).

[11] The same rules are also found in WSBY 46.12ab.

The Precepts of Admonitions for Assistance to Do Good[12]

The First Admonition: Always assist the preceptors in the veneration of the Three Treasures and presentation of offerings, so they can cause people in every generation to become full gentlemen, wise and filial and of superior ability. Glorious and noble, they will be lofty and born as venerables among humankind, their families and followers illustrious.

The Second Admonition: Always assist those who carefully copy the scriptural writing, so they can cause people in every generation to be perceptive and bright, able to hear even the most wondrous and obscure. [8b] They will always encounter a generation of sages, receive the scriptural teachings, and be able to recite each stanza and phrase.

The Third Admonition: Always assist those who erect lodges for meditation and purgations, so they can cause people in every generation to be born in high and noble families, their bodies rising up the heavenly halls. They will nourish on spontaneity itself and always dwell in nonaction.

The Fourth Admonition: Always assist those who replenish the supply of incense and lamp oil [for the altars], so they can cause people in every generation to be abundant and fragrant, pure and radiant with light. Their appearance and complexion will be exceptionally wonderful, and their heavenly bodies will be erect and splendid.

The Fifth Admonition: Always assist the preceptors and wearers of religious garb, so they can cause people in every generation to be tall and elegant, wandering freely through the Middle Kingdom. They will never fall among the border tribes or barbarians, and both male and female will be upright and proper as they don the formal headgear and wear the ritual jade pendants from their belts.

The Sixth Admonition: Always assist the country's ruler, all parents, subjects, and children in being loyal and obedient, so they can cause people in every generation to have numerous male and female heirs who will be wise and erudite and never suffer from the hardships of the world.

The Seventh Admonition: Always assist those who practice meditation and purgations and recite the scriptures, so they can cause people in every generation to avoid falling into the hells and instead to ascend to the heavenly halls. [9a] There they will pay respects to the host of sages, then speedily be reborn as human beings. They will be born in the families of kings as is their intention, dress in easy garb and comfortable shoes. Together with their ancestors of seven generations they will rejoice in their good karmic conditions. From beginning to end glorious and happy, they will move along with the wheel of the divine law and attain the Dao of immortality.

The Eighth Admonition: Always assist all Daoists and ordinary people who study the scriptures, so that they can cause people in every generation to be of penetrating wisdom and profound ability. Whether active or at rest, they will follow the dignified observances and will always serve as the teachers of humankind.

---

[12] This list of ten occurs also in a manuscript (DH 7; Ōfuchi 1979a, 30-38) and in the *Scripture of Precepts of Highest Rank* (DZ 454, 3a-4a). The rules area also found in the *Great Precepts of Original Vow* (DZ 344, 9b-10b) and the *Fifty-eight Vows of Great Clarity* (DZ 187, 4a-5a), translated in full below. Among collections, it appears in WSBY 46.13a-14a, *Essential Rules and Observances* 5.2ab, *Highest Scriptural Precepts* 11a-12a, and YJQQ 38.11b-12b.

The Ninth Admonition: Always assist all those who give liberally and remonstrate with contentiousness, so they can cause people in every generation to be long-lived and wise, wealthy and happy, always free from discontent and trouble.

The Tenth Admonition: Always assist all those who abandon jealousy and passion and instead firmly practice good deeds, so they can cause people in every generation to be happy and at peace, free from all misfortune and unrest. Then the sick will be healed and the loyal rewarded and honored by the masses. None will be left out of good fortune and blessings, and all families will be pure and noble. As heavenly beings they will all be loved, nurtured, honored, and held dear by all. [9b] Thus all will be born in the realm of blessedness.

The Heavenly Worthy said:

These admonitions to do good should not be practiced by anyone not a follower of the ten cycles of the great Dao. Anyone who can practice them obtains merit equal to that of a flying celestial. His mind realizing the wisdom of the six pervasions, he floats through emptiness and nonbeing. After this body, he will always be able to fly about the clouds, join the host of sages, and wander freely in the ten directions. If even after this he is not remiss, he will also attain an official rank and even become a king among immortals. His ancestors up to seven generations will be free to leave the realm of dark night and ascend to the Southern Palace, to be clothed and feasted at heavenly banquets. Receiving all the good fortune spontaneously, his divine law is lofty and wondrous, and he will save innumerable people. Eminent he is in his great transformations. It is hard to describe indeed.

The Heavenly Worthy said:

The wisdom of the six pervasions is as follows: Heaven corresponds to the pervasion of seeing; Earth corresponds to the pervasion of hearing; the east corresponds to the pervasion of the void; the west corresponds to the pervasion of emptiness; the south corresponds to the pervasion of clarity; the north corresponds to the pervasion of the subtle.

The six pervasions reach everything and everywhere without limits. They are unfathomable and never end. There is nothing they do not encompass, [10a] nothing they do not cover. They are the energies of the six kinds of awareness. If someone always continues to develop these six kinds of wisdom, he will eventually attain the six pervasions. Then the six kinds of awareness will be bright and open.

Just control and suppress the six passions, and you will naturally attain them. Get rid of the roots of evil and give rise only to thoughts of goodness. In your heart embody the six forms of grace, and naturally you will attain spirit immortality.

The Heavenly Worthy said:

To fulfill the foundations of the Dao and go beyond the ten sufferings and eight difficult conditions, you must receive the great precepts, cultivate the purgations, and establish virtue. Once you have built up various forms of goodness and merit, you will be praised throughout the Three Worlds and regarded with favor in the various heavens. None will not go beyond; no Dao will not be fulfilled.

However, as long as you do not receive the great precepts, you practice even long purgations in vain, even if you give up all worldliness, stop eating grain, and withdraw to the mountains and forests. As long as you pursue salvation in your body of flesh and do not practice the wisdom of the six pervasions, your merit will be lost and in vain, and you will have no base to develop.

Thus, you good men and good women, develop a dedicated mind, diligently pursue [perfection], and receive [the precepts] with discernment. For this, I reveal this scripture to you, so you can widely open the path to salvation. May the sounds of the divine law be heard all over the ten directions. [10b]

The Heavenly Worthy said:

Heaven corresponds to the pervasion of seeing. This means that with the eyes of Heaven understanding is lofty and wisdom pervades all without limits. Above and below, in the four corners and eight directions, nothing is not illuminated, nothing is not radiantly bright. Although we speak of the unified pervasion of wisdom, in fact all five colors are deeply penetrated. Heaven pervades the natural spontaneity of things, thus there is no harm, no loss. As long as people pattern themselves on Heaven, the bright pupils in the eyes will be able to freely follow the radiance of the five colors.

On the other hand, if people do not uphold the precepts, the energy of the six forms of awareness cannot enter people's orifices, and wisdom cannot be pervasive. Seeing the five colors, the eyes' pupils fly out to meet them, gradually darkening their radiance and causing people to go blind. For this reason, I deliver these precepts and open salvation for all in the celestial community, causing men and women to hear the sounds of the divine law and wishing that they may go beyond the world and extend their years. To do so, venerate the great precepts, practice them diligently and without forgetting. Always be careful about the multiplicity of colors and imaginings which squander the spiritual power of the eyes.

Keep yourself well restrained and continue to nurture the pupils of your eyes. Meditate on perfection and calm your thoughts, let wisdom pervade all and open your vision to emptiness and the void. Uphold the precepts and restrain yourself, then the five colors will return to you. When the five colors return, [11a] there will be no more loss or harm. Preserving your years, you can be without limits.

The Heavenly Worthy said:

Earth corresponds to the pervasion of hearing. With it, even remote wisdom can be heard, its sound corresponding to Heaven. Above and below, in the four directions, there is nothing that is not pervaded, nothing that is not distinctly heard. Although we speak of the universal pervasion of wisdom, in fact all the five sounds are equally perceived. Earth pervades the natural spontaneity of things, thus it brings forth the five sounds. There is none that does not reverberate with it. Thus there is no harm, no loss. As long as people pattern themselves on earth, there will be the gods of the five sounds inside their ears.

On the other hand, if people do not uphold the precepts, wisdom cannot be pervasive, and the tone of the five sounds cannot be heard except in confusion. Then the five sounds cause people's inner gods to fly off and scatter, the void inside the ears will be destroyed, and instead there will be an abundance of wailing and crying sounds. The five inner gods then cry and lament, eventually causing people to go deaf. For this reason, I deliver these precepts and open salvation for all in the celestial community, causing men and women to hear the sounds of the divine law and wishing that they to attain long life.

To do so, venerate the great precepts and restrain the gods of the ears. Do not do too much hearing of non-ritual noises, but listen to the wondrous scriptures in perfect tranquility, hear the stanzas of the divine perfected. [11b] Thus you will reach out to wisdom, be open to the sound of the Great Void. Uphold the precepts and restrain yourself, then the five sounds will return to you. When the five sounds return, your ears will be free from all evil sounds. Preserving your years, you can overcome all and find true eternity.

The Heavenly Worthy said:

East corresponds to the pervasion of the void, to the energy of rising yang. As this energy emerges from the void, wisdom is bright and vast. Thus we speak of the pervasion of the void. Far and wide there is no obstacle, no limit for ever and ever. Such is the energy of rising green [yang]. We speak of the universal pervasion of wisdom, yet in fact all the five energies are equally pervaded. There is nothing that the void does not encompass, thus there is no harm, no loss. Although people have a physical body, this body is yet also patterned on the void. As long as the nose is in yellow [central] harmony, it can avoid the bad spirits.

On the other hand, if people do not uphold the precepts, wisdom cannot be pervasive. Then people cannot match it and remain unable to leave the various smells and fumes of food behind. Smelly and foul energy will cause the inner gods of the nose to block and obstruct the passages, which in turn leads to an interruption in the natural transformations of things and causes the bright bridge to be unopened. For this reason, I deliver these precepts and open salvation for all in the celestial community, causing men and women to hear the sounds of the divine law and wishing that they go beyond all suffering and away from the eight difficult conditions. [12a]

To do so, venerate the great precepts and restrain the inner gods of the nose. Do not smell too many bad vapors and thereby overburden the bright bridge, but exercise vital energy and open yourself to radiant wisdom, pervade cosmic energy and enter the void. Uphold the precepts and restrain yourself, then the multitude of energies will return to you. When the multitude of energies returns, you can merge with them in oneness. Preserving your years, you can be without harm and defeat.

The Heavenly Worthy said:

West corresponds to the pervasion of emptiness, to the energy of lesser yang [yin]. As this energy emerges from emptiness, wisdom is clear and subtle. Thus we speak of the pervasion of emptiness. Emptiness is without solidity, pervading all far and wide without limits. Such is the energy of lesser yin. Although we speak of the universal pervasion of wisdom, in fact all the five tastes are equally pervaded. Emptiness and nonbeing cannot be entered; emptiness and nonbeing will never be obvious—and yet people in their selves are fully patterned on emptiness.

On the other hand, if people do not uphold the precepts, wisdom cannot be pervasive. As long as wisdom has not been entered, the five tastes are a great affliction. Pestered by greed for the taste of rich food, the five gods [of the mouth] cannot be at peace. Following one's lopsided inclination, one's years are bound to be short. For this reason, I deliver these precepts and open salvation to all in the celestial community, [12b] causing men and women to hear the sounds of the divine law and wishing to extend their life expectancy.

To do so, venerate the great precepts and restrain the five gods. Take care not to be too greedy for the five tastes or delight in rich food that will overburden the five inner organs. Always maintain purity and cleanliness within, and wisdom will arise in you. Then you can recognize the five tastes for what they are, and inside and outside will be in proper harmony. Then your life expectancy will not suffer harm.

The Heavenly Worthy said:

South corresponds to the pervasion of clarity, the energy of greater yang. As the energy emerges from clarity, wisdom is clear and open, and all the passageways are pervasive and clear. In the south the Red Emperor rules over his court of pervasive yang. He orders and refines the myriad beings. As you too receive his refinement, you become radiant.

On the other hand, if people do not uphold the precepts, wisdom cannot be pervasive. With wisdom unpervasive, the gods of the heart will be agitated and be subject to love and passions, leading people astray. This will ail the gods and harm the life expectancy, making longevity impossible. For this reason I deliver these precepts and open salvation to all in the celestial community, causing men and women to hear the sounds of the divine law and to develop a wish to attain long life and transcendence of afflictions. [13a]

To do so, venerate the great precepts and restrain the gods of the heart, do away with emotions and drive out desires, abandon worldly grime and enter purity. As you become pervasive and bright in wisdom, your six forms of consciousness will be open and overflowing and you can enter pervasive clarity and join the energy of spontaneity in your personal body. Preserving your years, you will attain eternal life.

The Heavenly Worthy said:

North corresponds to the pervasion of subtlety. As it arises from the dark, this wisdom is far-reaching and deep, subtly reaching to perfection. Softly examining both sin and good fortune, it controls the origin of all life. The hands are patterned on the four seasons and correspond to the Heavenly Pass above. As the Heavenly Pass revolves in a steady course, so the hands move below. Several great deities reside in the hands, connecting to life and always full. They relate people to the four great elements and observe their prosperity and decline.

On the other hand, if people do not uphold the precepts and wisdom is not pervasive, the heart will be agitated and the multitude of evils will arise. When the hands act without proper awareness, they steal greedily for their own gain. This in turn leads to a shortened life expectancy and a failure to live out one's years. For this reason I deliver these precepts and open salvation to all in the celestial community, causing men and women to hear the sounds of the divine law and to develop a wish to find long life and go beyond the roots of evil.

To do so, venerate the great precepts and restrain the gods of the hands. As you become pervasive and bright in wisdom, [13b] your heart will be naturally clear and your hands will no longer covet or steal. Then the roots of evil do not arise. Going along with the energy of Heaven, you can enter spontaneity in your personal body. Preserving an extensive life expectancy, you can attain eternal life.

The Highest Precepts of Retribution for Merit and Wisdom

1. Give freely to provide offerings for the Three Treasures and the sacred scriptures. For a donation of one coin and more, you will be rewarded 740,000 times. For 10,000 cash and more, you will receive merit uncountable. Your name will be entered into the ledgers of the various heavens. Your personal body will ascend on high. As a disciple of the ten cycles your ancestors up to seven generations will ascend also. You will be the guest and friend of all celestials.

2. Give freely for the vestments of the preceptors, the copying of sacred scriptures, and the building of oratories and halls. For a donation of one coin and more, you will be rewarded 320,000 times. For 10,000 cash and more, you will receive merit uncountable. Generation after generation you will be perceptive and bright, always encountering enlightened teachers. You will be born in noble families and your ancestors up to seven generations will be guests of the Highest Lord. [14a]

3. Give freely to the preceptor Daoist to help with incense, lamp oil, and sacred food. For a donation of one coin and more, you will be rewarded 240,000 times. As your merits grow numerous, your reward will multiply. Generation after generation you will be rich, never poor or destitute. Your ancestors up to seven generations will enjoy participation in celestial feasts.

4. Give freely to the mountain Daoists. For a donation of one coin and more, you will be rewarded 120,000 times. As your merits grow numerous, your reward will multiply. Generation after generation you will find sagely teachers and always encounter the teaching of the Dao and the divine law. Your ancestors up to seven generations will enjoy contact with the Five Emperors.

5. Give freely to the Disciples of Pure Faith to help with their incense, candles, and sacred food. For a donation of one coin and more, you will be rewarded 32,000 times. As your merits grow numerous, your reward will multiply. Generation after generation you will be joyful and happy, never encountering the various forms of suffering. Your ancestors up to seven generations will ascend to the heavenly halls, wander freely about in nonaction and always rest in blessedness. [14b]

6. Give freely to the poor among the celestial community. For a donation of one coin and more, you will be rewarded 12,000 times. As your merits grow numerous, your reward will multiply. Generation after generation you will be wealthy and noble, living in joy and happiness without end. Your ancestors up to seven generations will receive celestial feasts in the four directions and be fed and clothed by spontaneity.

7. Give freely to the host of living beings, even taking from your very own food. One coin and more, you and your ancestors up to seven generations will be rewarded 200 times. Generation after generation your sons and grandsons will form an illustrious family, rising to splendor for 6,000 years to come. They will never fall into the hells but always ascend to the blessedness of spontaneity.

The Heavenly Worthy told the Highest Lord of the Dao:

These items of wisdom and precepts of merit and virtue serve to develop spontaneity and an intention for the Dao in all men and women among the celestial community. By lessening their ego and giving freely, they widely open fields of blessedness and multiply their merit and virtue. The merit of giving one coin will be rewarded ten thousandfold.

The principle of retribution is as clear as the sun and the moon. Some will find it in this life, others will see it in the future. Still, the reward of good fortune is varied and not necessarily of one type. [15a] Some may accumulate merit to make up for earlier transgressions; others may take their virtue to pay off debts of sin; yet others may transfer it to exonerate their ancestors from their punishments. For this reason the rewards for good behavior may not be immediately obvious. Still, the Three Bureaus and Nine Offices record everyone's merits and transgressions meticulously—not missing even the slightest bit.

Then again, if one's earlier sins are already dissolved and one does not commit any new transgressions in this body, the later merit may not yet be apparent and one may seem no different from anyone else. This is because one has received some obstacle on the day of one's birth. But later, to be sure, the gods of the heavens will come to save one and produce the reward of pure blessings. Thus, even if you have already achieved the move of the souls of your ancestors up to seven generations to the heavenly halls, still good fortune may come to you later—but come it will, without a single error even in 10,000 cases.

Clearly tell all men and women, so they understand perfectly well the rule of cosmic retribution and perfect accordance. The Dao of Heaven does not move vainly—a good heart and sturdy faith together with diligent practice without laziness will certainly open up salvation and grant you blessedness without limit.

The Heavenly Worthy told the Highest Lord of the Dao:

In the various heavens, the highest sages, utmost perfected, great gods, divine sovereigns, and all the many people who have attained the Dao and gone beyond the grime of this world, [15b] all have attained their status through the virtue of giving freely and the merit of doing good deeds. As their merit was complete and their virtue sufficient, they attained the rewards of goodness. Revolving without interruption, they all found the perfection of the Dao, transcended the Three Worlds, and now wander about freely in the Forest of the Seven Treasures at the Mystery Terrace in the Jade Capital, located in the Heaven of Grand Veil in Highest Clarity. At this time they fully understand that the merit of giving freely is never lost but brings joy and happiness in spontaneity, continuing from generation to generation without measure. Even if the original gift was small, blessings and good fortune will come without end.

Now, in a declining world, falsehood and superficiality reign, and people's feelings are given to stinginess and greed. They only know how to gather and accumulate material goods, creating heavy burdens for themselves. None is able to open their hearts to create the merit and virtue [of giving]. As they fail to accumulate merit, sins and defilements grow daily, and the halls of blessedness are removed ever farther. Engulfed and submerged in the gathering of sin, they continue to transmigrate through the five realms and are born in the eight difficult conditions. Once having lost the realm of blessedness, they cannot expect to ever come back to it. Men and women increasingly get involved with each other, none recognizing how their fate has come about. Seeing [the condition of] their souls and spirit is painful indeed! It causes the deities in the various heavens to explain the prohibitions and precepts, causing men and women to hear the sounds of the divine law, and opening up salvation for the host of living beings in the hope of assisting their entry into the realm of blessedness. [16a]

The Heavenly Worthy said:

I once looked at the men and women in the various levels of hell, only to find that even those punished by imprisonment in darkness, with souls in terrible destitution, in their previous lives had encountered the bright precepts. Some had encountered but not practiced them; others had practiced but not properly honored them. So, in the course of various lives regretfully they had turned about and entered the gateway of sin. Some in their lives committed evil and never created any karma of good deeds; others did not know how to give freely and develop a mind conducive to establishing merit, widely creating fields of blessedness, and extracting the roots of fate. They only knew how to commit more sins and as a result have had to drag their tails through the three bad rebirths and eight difficult conditions. Thinking of their ignorance and foolishness, they are much to be pitied indeed.

For this reason I continue to deliver the precepts and open salvation to all in the celestial community, causing men and women to hear the sounds of the divine law. I hope that they will learn how to develop a mind of the Dao, establish the merit of goodness, uproot all forms of suffering, and create a good karmic connection with the Dao. May they all attain joy and peace and wander about freely in spontaneity!

The Highest Lord of the Dao received the precepts from the Heavenly Worthy of Primordial Beginning and proceeded to further open up salvation in the various heavens, the four directions, and all the different regions of the earth. As his merit and virtue were complete, [16b] he transmitted them further to the celestial kings of the various heavens, the great sages of the ten directions, the Sovereign Lord of Great Tenuity, the perfected of the four poles, as well as the residents of the Palace of Eastern Florescence, the great divinities of the various regions, the jade maidens, and the host of immortals.

Together they achieved the appropriate level of pervasion and set out to serve the salvation of all beings, including those born later, making them too hear the sounds of the divine law. At this time, none among the various heavens did not rejoice greatly. It is excellent! Most excellent indeed!

TEXT FIVE

Scripture of the Ten Precepts

INTRODUCTION

The *Scripture of the Ten Precepts* (*Shijie jing* 十戒經, DZ 459) is a short text revealed by the Heavenly Worthy of Numinous Treasure that also appears in Dunhuang manuscripts (DH 31, 32; see also Ōfuchi 1978, 108). It is discussed with regard to its various versions and Buddhist models in Yoshioka 1961b. It uses in Tang ordination are described in Schipper 1985.

Its ten precepts are the classical rules of medieval Daoism as they were applied when practitioners attained the rank of Disciple of Pure Faith. They appear first in the *Scripture on Setting the Will on Wisdom* (DZ 325, 7b-8a), a text of the ancient Numinous Treasure canon that goes back to the early fifth century (see Bokenkamp 1983; Yamada 2000; Ren and Zhong 1991, 341).

The same precepts, accompanied by fourteen principles of self-control, are further listed in WSBY 46.7ab, *Essential Rules and Observances* 4.9ab, *Highest Scriptural Precepts* 13b, and YJQQ 38.13b-14a. The *Rules and Precepts for Worshiping the Dao* has a detailed description of the ordination formalities accompanying transmission of the precepts (6.11ab).

TRANSLATION

[1a] **The Heavenly Worthy said:**

Oh, you good men and good women[1]! You were able to develop an intention for the Dao of spontaneity and have come to enter the river of the divine law. Now receive my ten precepts and fourteen principles of self-control to become Disciples of Pure Faith in the great Dao,[2] gaining courage and strength to fly to the heavens and increase your merit.

From here onward you will never slide back again but most certainly attain transcendence and go beyond the Three Worlds to become perfected of Highest Clarity. For this, now bow down and receive [the precepts], repeating them with truth in your hearts:

---

[1] This expression *shan nanzi shan nüren* 善男子善女人 is adopted from Buddhism.
[2] This title *qingxin dizi* 清心弟子 is an adaptation from Buddhism that applies to first-level ordinands who have taken the ten precepts. See Kusuyama 1984.

The Ten Precepts

1. Do not kill but always be mindful of the host of living beings.

2. Do not be lascivious or think depraved thoughts.

3. Do not steal or receive unrighteous wealth.

4. Do not cheat or misrepresent good and evil.

5. Do not get intoxicated but always think of pure conduct.

6. I will maintain harmony with my ancestors and family and never disregard my kin.

7. When I see someone do a good deed, I will support him with joy and delight.

8. When I see someone unfortunate, I will support him with dignity to recover good fortune. [1b]

9. When someone comes to do me harm, I will not harbor thoughts of revenge.

10. As long as all beings have not attained the Dao, I will not expect to do so myself.

The Fourteen Principles of Self Control[3]

1. When I speak with another's lord, I shall feel gracious toward his country.

2. When I speak with another's father, I shall feel kind toward his son.

3. When I speak with another's leader, I shall feel loving toward his followers.

4. When I speak with another's older brother, I shall behave as a younger brother should.

5. When I speak with another's minister, I shall feel loyal toward his lord.

6. When I speak with another's son, I shall feel filial toward his parents.

7. When I speak with another's friend, I shall feel trusting toward his companions.

8. When I speak with another's wife, I shall feel virtuous toward her husband.

9. When I speak with another's husband, I shall feel harmonious toward his family.

10. When I speak with another's disciple, I shall feel respectful toward his formalities.

11. When I speak with a farmer, I shall feel conscientious about agriculture.

12. When I speak with a senior Daoist, I shall feel orthodox about the Dao.

13. When I speak with a stranger, I shall feel protective about his country's borders.

14. When I speak with a slave or maid, I shall feel concerned about his or her affairs.

---

[3] These fourteen principles first appear in *Precepts against the Roots of Sin* 1.5ab.

The Heavenly Worthy said:

To cultivate and venerate the pure precepts [of the Dao], always keep your mind linked with Heaven and always act with great compassion.

[2a] Solemnly vow that you will strive for the liberation of all living beings of the world, humbly and modestly venerate the teaching, never allow yourself to be lazy or lax. Whatever happens, calmly stick to the good, thus you can die. Never do anything bad, thus you can live.

Following these guidelines, you will never fall behind. Instead you will attain complete liberation of the five realms of suffering and the three bad rebirths. You will be protected by all the heavens and supported by the myriad gods. Keep on performing the purgations and honoring the precepts, and naturally you will go beyond the world.

Concluding Verse

All you who practice cultivation and study properly

Vow to perfect the Dao of true realization.

Full of compassion, be mindful of the words of my precepts

And the very sound of the Dao will put an end to your vexation.

TEXT SIX

Precepts of the Three Primes

INTRODUCTION

The *Precepts of the Three Primes* (*Sanyuan pinjie* 三元品戒, DZ 452) consists of 180 precepts arranged according to the Three Primes. It can be dated to the fifth century as it appears in the ancient Numinous Treasure canon.[1] The complete text also appears in WSBY 43 and DH 15. In content, the rules are revealed by the Heavenly Worthy of Primordial Beginning for the sake of the Lord of the Dao and begin with a description of the offices of the Three Primes, i.e., the three central bureaus of Heaven, Earth, and Water that are in charge of life and death. Each bureau has specific administrative responsibilities and an extensive staff of 120 officials, named in each case with proper title and relevant duties.

Then the text details the sixty sins under each jurisdiction. The Highest Prime is concerned with the proper transmission of scriptures, relationships to the masters and preceptors, and harmony within the religious community. The text here only lists forty-three precepts, yet it claims that "these sixty [*sic*] precepts are supervised by the Twelve Officials of the Central Administrative Section of the First Office of Heaven" (24b).

The first twenty-two rules in this section address "all those who pursue the highest Dao." They focus on the proper ritual behavior among the higher echelons of the community. The following rules, as much as those under the jurisdiction of the Middle and Lower Primes, are concerned with rules for "students of the Dao and lay followers."

Followers should not engage in jealousy, greed, nasty schemes, or improper relations to women, outsiders, slaves, and animals, but rather perform basic social politeness and show respect among community members. The rules punish theft, slander, gossip, laziness, lack of filial piety and loyalty, and other egoistic faults. In each case, the formulation of the rules is against a certain sin. Many community rules recoup the regulations of the Celestial Masters, showing a strong continuity among Daoist precepts.

The translation below focuses on the precepts proper, i.e., pages 22a-31a. It is different from my earlier rendition (Kohn 1993, 100-06), which imitated the original in not numbering the rules and understood some instructions differently. In this version, I have added consecutive numbers to make reference and comparison to other lists of precepts easier. Also, I have modified the wording of the rules so that it matches that of other precepts texts.

---

[1] LB 22 (Yamada 2000, 235). See also Ōfuchi 1974, 52; Bokenkamp 1983, 483; Ren and Zhong 1991, 338-39; Kleeman 1991, 170-71.

TRANSLATION

[22a] All those who pursue the highest Dao! Do not commit the following sins:

1. The sin of disbelieving the scriptures and precepts, harboring doubts or being of two minds.

2. The sin of slighting the sage writings or criticizing the sacred scriptures.

3. The sin of slighting the teachers or going against the oath and covenant.

4. The sin of slandering the teachers and elders or failing to honor the righteous of heaven.

5. The sin of stealing the scriptural writings or practicing without the a teacher and lineage. [22b]

6. The sin of studying without a teacher or passing [the teachings] on to disciples.

7. The sin of collecting the scriptural writings illicitly and transmitting them to disciples.

8. The sin of obtaining any scriptures without the formal covenant and ordination through a teacher.

9. The sin of receiving the scriptures without relying on the scriptural rules or transmitting them in the wrong year or month.

10. The sin of transmitting scriptures to the wrong people.

11. The sin of receiving the lineage of a preceptor without having established the merit of ordination.

12. The sin of transmitting [teachings] to disciples without having the necessary merit.

13. The sin of transmitting announcements and memorials to the divine law not in accord with the tradition of the teachers.

14. The sin of transmitting the scriptures without sending an announcement or memorial to the five emperors.

15. The sin of receiving the scriptures without faith or while despising the Dao. [23a]

16. The sin of assuming merit and fame for yourself and abandon the road of the wise.

17. The sin of not paying obeisance to the teachers and worthies on new moon, full moon, and the days of the eight nodes.

18. The sin of not cultivating the purgations and [days of] uprightness.

19. The sin of being impure during the purgations and [days of] uprightness.

20. The sin of taking shortcuts in reciting the scriptures.

21. The sin of engaging in disputes and fights while traveling overland.

22. The sin of harboring anger and rage against your teachers or elders.

All students of the Dao and all lay followers! Do not commit the following sins:

23. The sin to attack or fight with a good person.

24. The sin to speak evil or with a bitter tongue.

25. The sin of criticizing the teachers, donors, or hundred families. [23b]

26. The sin to drink alcohol and lose your temper.

27. The sin to kill living beings or give rise to evil thoughts.

28. The sin to harbor greed and passion, pride and sloth.

29. The sin of befouling the divine law of the Dao.

30. The sin to curse and yell at demons and spirits.

31. The sin to kill or harm the host of living beings.

32. The sin to use fancy language, double-tongued, or faithless speech.

33. The sin to be lewd and lascivious, foul and turbid.

34. The sin to steal people's things.

35. The sin to be jealous of the wise or envious of their abilities. [24a]

36. The sin to refuse your teacher's kindness.

37. The sin to cheat on your teacher and turn your back on the Dao.

38. The sin to expose celestial writings.

39. The sin to defame and slander the divine law of the scriptures.

40. The sin to turn about in the middle of cultivating the scriptures.

41. The sin of being disloyal to your superiors.

42. The sin of being harsh to your inferiors.

43. The sin to cheat and deceive fellow students.

44. The sin to say good things while harboring evil in your mind.

45. The sin to speak about the transgressions and evils of others. [24b]

46. The sin of slighting the Three Luminants.

47. The sin of despising the ghosts and spirits.[2]

These sixty (*sic*) precepts are being supervised by the twelve officials of the central administrative section of the First Office of the Department of Heaven, by the fourteen officials of the central administrative section of the First Office of the Department of Earth, and by the fourteen officials of the central administrative section of the First Office of the Department of Water.

---

[2] This concludes the first section of these precepts. Numbers 48-60 are missing.

To all students of the Dao and all lay followers! You must not commit the following sins:

61. The sin of being jealous or envious of your fellow students.

62. The sin of speaking flowery words or lies.

63. The sin of coveting personal benefits, gathering them in without ever being satisfied. [25a]

64. The sin of amassing emoluments and pile up treasures without thinking of giving them away.

65. The sin of taking pleasure in grabbing the valuables of others for yourself.

66. The sin of wishing harm and defeat, homelessness and dispersal on others.

67. The sin of collecting knives, staffs, or other weapons.

68. The sin of slaughtering the six domestic animals or killing any living beings.

69. The sin of shooting down wild animals or flying birds.

70. The sin of burning mountain sides in order to hunt.

71. The sin of setting traps to catch fish.

72. The sin of using eating utensils made from gold or silver.

73. The sin of coveting lucrative appointments or serving a tyrannical government. [25b]

74. The sin of destroying material objects in order to create merit.

75. The sin of throwing food or drink into the water.

76. The sin of coveting rich and delicious flavors, fat, and meat.

77. The sin of coveting the five strong vegetables.

78. The sin of writing in a flowery style and with false intentions.

79. The sin of assembling large crowds.

80. The sin of harboring schemes toward another's wife or daughter.

81. The sin of discussing affairs of state.

82. The sin of harboring schemes toward another's material goods.

83. The sin of taking coarse objects and presenting them to others as fine things. [26a]

84. The sin of concerning yourself with the affairs of aristocrats, nobles, and kings.

85. The sin of wantonly talking about the cycles of heaven and the starry mansions.

86. The sin of burning fields, wild lands, mountains, or forests.

87. The sin of cutting down trees or idly picking flowers and herbs.

88. The sin of interacting with bad people or getting too close with strangers.

89. The sin of mixing with ordinary people or picking fights with them.

90. The sin of eating alone when among people, without thinking that they might be hungry too.

91. The sin of destroying marriages among the people of the world.

92. The sin of going out to engage in worldly dancing and music.

93. The sin of outwardly swearing allegiance to the people of the world while secretly setting out to ruin these good men. [26b]

94. The sin of speaking about the transgressions and faults of another person's elders or superiors.

95. The sin of exposing the secret evil or egoistic baseness of others.

96. The sin of attacking a good person or quarreling with him without end.

97. The sin of spying on others' writings or pry into their subleties.

98. The sin of speaking or walking with a woman alone.

99. The sin of staying among a group of mixed men and women.

100. The sin of eating in a group of mixed men and women or wrongly exchanging clothing with any of them.

101. The sin of giving instruction to a group of mixed men and women to no good effect.

102. The sin of thinking yourself noble and taking pride in yourself.

103. The sin of repaying public nobleness with resentment. [27a]

104. The sin of leaving [your family] and set up a separate household.

105. The sin of aborting children or harming the unborn.

106. The sin of being estranged from your ancestors and relatives, instead joining a strange family.

107. The sin of throwing poisonous drugs into fresh water and thus harming living beings.

108. The sin of developing a crush on a disciple.

109. The sin of assembling a crowd of people.

110. The sin of distributing writings that slander others.

111. The sin of presuming on yourself or develop a temper.

112. The sin of wantonly creating taboos and tabooed names.

113. The sin of having expectations of the things of others. [27b]

114. The sin of discussing the long and short of your teachers or friends.

115. The sin of despising the teaching of the scriptures and the words of the divine law.

116. The sin of belittling someone in old age or sickness.

117. The sin of rejecting beggars.

118. The sin of assuming power and dignity when guiding the people of the world.

119. The sin of forming a clique on the basis of your family.

120. The sin of living separate from your parents and brothers.

These sixty precepts are being supervised by the twelve officials of the left administrative section of the Left Office of the Department of Heaven, by the fourteen officials of the left administrative section of the Left Office of the Department of Earth, and by the fourteen officials of the left administrative section of the Left Office of the Department of Water.

[28a] To all students of the Dao and all lay followers! You must not commit the following sins:

121. The sin of harbor inganger and rage against any of your disciples.

122. The sin of raging against a good person.

123. The sin of not setting free the living and saving the dying.[3]

124. The sin of forgetting your teacher when in wealth and wellbeing.

125. The sin of observing the purgation days of the various heavens without being mindful of the Dao.

126. The sin of harboring anger and raging against your teachers and elders.

127. The sin of discussing other's transgressions and faults.

128. The sin of making fun of people if they are dull and dumb, poor and impoverished. [28b]

129. The sin of encouraging people to do evil.

130. The sin of preventing people from doing good.

131. The sin of delighting in the misfortunes and losses of others.

132. The sin of approaching or leaving anyone impolitely, with your back to them.

133. The sin of worshiping the five sacred mountains and three great rivers without holding the ritual tablet.

134. The sin of befouling the five sacred mountains and three great rivers.

135. The sin of taking away others' cherished possessions.

136. The sin of rushing among common folk or starting a quarrel with the people of the world.

137. The sin of congratulating or condoling people of the world or seeking pleasure among the common masses.

138. The sin of laying claim to another's merit in order to make it your own virtue. [29a]

---

[3] The idea of "setting free the living" (*fangsheng* 放生) is adopted from Buddhism. Today it commonly means taking animals, and especially fish or turtles, bound for consumption and bringing them back into a natural habitat.

139. The sin of speaking about the good or bad qualities of what others eat or drink.

140. The sin of startling the ailing or distressed among the hundred families.

141. The sin of startling birds and beasts or catch them by digging up the earth.

142. The sin of startling the old or young.

143. The sin of looking down upon officials and administrators.

144. The sin of evaluating the straight or crooked [ways] of the world.

145. The sin of wantonly discussing the rise and decline of the state.

146. The sin of pursuing stinginess while giving donations.

147. The sin of roaming about the country without ends.

148. The sin of climbing up high and falling down low. [29b]

149. The sin of imprisoning flying birds and running beasts in cages.

150. The sin of delighting in others' bereavement and misfortunes.

151. The sin of throwing thorns into people's paths.

152. The sin of paying obeisance to ghosts and spirits.

153. The sin of exposing your naked body to the Three Luminants.

154. The sin of raging at the wind and the rain.

155. The sin of borrowing things without returning them to their proper owner.

156. The sin of deceiving others with splendor and fancy words.

157. The sin of developing pride and disregard the Three Treasures or making light of the celestial worthies.

158. The sin of plotting against the lords, elders, teachers, or fathers of other people. [30a]

159. The sin of encouraging people to be unfilial toward their parents and brothers.

160. The sin of developing pride and calling yourself a perfected.

161. The sin of using the miscellaneous arts of heterodox cults or developing heterodox views.

162. The sin of studying without the proper scriptures or teachers, thus cheating and deceiving both people and spirits.

163. The sin of owning a surplus of clothes without giving them away to the poor.

164. The sin of copying the scriptures and precepts in secret or disclosing them lightly.

165. The sin of adorning your robe or gown with gaudy colors to be flowery and ornate.

166. The sin of ascending to the high seat with an unclean body.

167. The sin of despising the teacher and his school, completely lacking in reverence.

168. The sin of not offering purgations and prayers when your teacher is in mourning. [30b]

169. The sin of pursuing worldly prosperity and abandoning your teacher and father.

170. The sin of expecting to rise to splendor when your teacher attains noble rank.

171. The sin of not taking care of your teacher when he is sick or impoverished.

172. The sin of distancing yourself from the distress of others, just pursuing your own pleasure.

173. The sin of entering or leaving a household of the Dao without the proper announcements.

174. The sin of interacting wantonly and chattering with others when entering a household of the Dao.

175. The sin of performing purgations and prayers without transferring merit to the Three Bureaus.

176. The sin of wallowing in self pity for your own family or school, never thinking of the plight of others.

177. The sin of resenting the Dao or blaming your teacher if there is bereavement or sickness in your family.

178. The sin of claiming personal revelation of the Dao and scriptures if you have in fact received them from your teacher.

179. The sin of transmitting your teacher's divine law of the Dao without proper procedures, due covenant, and pledge.

180. The sin of not invoking the five emperors on the days of the eight nodes.

These sixty precepts are being supervised by the twelve officials of the right administrative section of the Right Office of the Department of Heaven, by the fourteen officials of the right administrative section the Right Office of the Department of Earth, and by the fourteen officials of the right administrative section of the Right Office of the Department of Water.

TEXT SEVEN

The Fifty-Eight Prayers of Great Clarity

INTRODUCTION

The Fifty-eight Prayers of Great Clarity (*Taiqing wushiba yuanwen* 太清五十八願文, DZ 187) is an abbreviated version of the *Great Precepts of Original Prayers* (*Benyuan dajie* 本願大戒, DZ 344) which contains the same list (4a-7a). Both texts go back to the fifth century and form part of the Numinous Treasure school (Ren and Zhong 1991, 137). Their central focus is on a long set of resolutions or mental prayers that turn people's minds away from personal concerns and desires and allow them to focus on the well-being and salvation of all beings.

The key term is *yuan* 願, which means "earnest wish," "vow," or "positive intention." In Buddhism, it renders *pranidhāna* and expresses the vow, commonly undertaken by bodhisattvas, to be firm and resolute in seeking liberation and to do everything in one's power to assist all beings in their efforts towards it (Nakamura 1975, 200). *Yuan* first appears in Daoism in the early Numinous Treasure texts, meaning "vow" or "resolution" (see Bokenkamp 1989). In institutional manuals, it is used either to encourage practitioners to develop good intentions or to introduce a communal chant or prayer on behalf of all beings (see Kohn 2004) and may also express a formal ritual action. As such, it can appear in the compound "announcement and prayer," which is still used today (see Lagerwey 1987, 146).

In *The Fifty-eight Prayers of Great Clarity*, *yuan* indicates a mental resolution to develop the perception needed for altruistic thinking and behavior, thus leading to the state of universal morality. Although *yuan* in this context does not imply the invocation and petition of a higher power as indicated in the Western term "prayer," in other places it does; even here, the idea is to develop a devout, prayerful mindset. Thus the word has been translated as "prayer," or "I pray."

TRANSLATION

1. [1a] When I encounter[1] wives and children living in their homes, I shall pray that all may soon emerge from their prison of love, concentrate their intention, and observe the precepts.

2. When I encounter people drinking wine, I shall pray that all may control their gates of destiny and be far removed from bad fortune and disorder.

3. When I encounter young girls, I shall pray that all may guard their passions, restrain their sensuality, and set their wills and wishes on becoming wise.[2]

---

[1] The word used is *jian* 見, literally "to see," but since some of the following situations involve other senses, I have opted for "encounter" instead.

[2] The word "wise" (*xian* 賢) is used to indicate a dedicated Daoist practitioner, as opposed to the "ignorant" who have not yet joined the Dao.

4. When I encounter people engaging in licentiousness, I shall pray that all may lose their depraved thoughts and elevate their minds to the level of the prohibitions and precepts.

5. When I encounter women, I shall pray that all may restrain and curb their fleeting beauty and instead enjoy the Dao and spontaneity.

6. When I encounter a perfected, I shall pray that all may walk in faith, be converted to the true way, and soon enter the gate of the divine law.

7. When I encounter the masses of the people, I shall pray that all may be yielding and free from struggles, embrace the Dao, and find peace in this world.

8. When I encounter a good person, I shall pray that all may curb their imaginations, develop worship, and hold on to the Dao.

9. When I encounter a bad person, I shall pray that all may do away with inauspiciousness and find only auspicious situations, never violating the laws of the king. [1b]

10. When I encounter a poor person, I shall pray that all may take from themselves to give generously and later receive great good fortune.

11. When I encounter a rich person, I shall pray that all may save and support the myriad beings, and in every generation receive ample emoluments.

12. When I encounter a noble person, I shall pray that all may pass on his teaching and instructions, and all may obey his lectures and guidelines.

13. When I encounter a humble person, I shall pray that all may diligently practice cultivation without being lazy, and each may attain what they deserve.

14. When I encounter an emperor or king, I shall pray that all may honor and trust the way of the king and be filial toward him like to their father and mother.

15. When I encounter a lord or minister, I shall pray that all may receive his teachings and orders, and that all in the four directions take refuge in benevolence.

16. When I encounter a soldier, I shall pray that all may be mindful of their benevolent hearts and all under heaven may yield to wisdom.

17. When I encounter a prince, I shall pray that all may sing daily of Great Peace, for the succession of the dynasty, and for the continuation of the [imperial] family.

18. When I encounter a wise person, I shall pray that all may walk in the practice of virtue and regard the Dao as the ancestor of the world.

19. When I encounter a Daoist or recluse, I shall pray that all may clearly understand salvation through the divine law, attain the Dao, and ascend to perfection. [2a]

20. When I encounter a mountain Daoist, I shall pray that all may encounter the gateway to the Dao and speedily become flying immortals.

21. When I encounter a teacher, I shall pray that all may personally receive the sagely teaching, become deeply erudite, and be known as sages.

22. When I encounter a sage, I shall pray that all may venerate and worship him, serving him whenever they see him, and that all countries may regard him with respect.

23. When I encounter an immortal, I shall pray that all may complete the Dao of perfection and fly up to the heavenly halls.

24. When I encounter a city or town, I shall pray that all may seriously work together to repair and adorn it and base their communal life on the Dao.

25. When I encounter a great state, I shall pray that all may treat it with veneration and fulfill virtue as naturally as water flows to the sea.

26. When I encounter a small state, I shall pray that all may know when to stop, live in purity and emptiness, and feel at peace in their homes.

27. When I encounter a marketplace, I shall pray that the crowd of wise ones be as thick as a hornets' nest, all widely spreading the orthodox Dao.[3]

28. When I encounter someone sitting in quiet observation, I shall pray that all may be eminent in merit and virtue, and all may realize their will as members of the celestial brotherhood.

29. When I encounter someone observing purgations and precepts or offering incense, I shall pray that all may be daily new in their Dao and virtue and be open and content well into their old age. [2b]

30. When I encounter someone reciting the scriptures, I shall pray that all may ascend to the high seat and listen to the scriptural instructions.

31. When I encounter someone teaching the scriptures, I shall pray that each and every one may receive lectures on them and practice the scriptural teachings with proper ritual.

32. When I encounter a monastery, I shall pray that all may penetratingly observe the ten directions, nothing being hidden or concealed.

33. When I encounter a high mountain, I shall pray that all may establish virtue like this and never again regress in transmigration.

34. When I encounter the sea, I shall pray that all may have wisdom without measure and support family and state.

35. When I encounter an academy, I shall pray that all may study eagerly to complete the Confucian curriculum and properly obey the explained teachings.

36. When I encounter someone purifying his hands, I shall pray that all may always hold the scriptural texts and never stop even for a short moment.[4]

---

[3] This classifies the Dao as *zheng* 正 or "orthodox," using a term that means "right," "true," "proper," or "in the right alignment." It refers to the best way things can be; the way they are meant to be by the Dao; and the natural, straightforward way of being. In Buddhism, *zheng* refers to *sāt*, "right," which indicates the correct way of doing things in order to alleviate the burden of karma and attain liberation as in, for example, "right action" or "right speech" (see Nakamura 1975, 697).

37. When I encounter someone using good speech, I shall pray that all may continue to recite the scriptures of the Caverns, daily new and never falling silent.

38. When I encounter someone moving his feet, I shall pray that all may go beyond the Three Worlds and fly up to Highest Clarity.

39. When I encounter someone sitting quietly on a mountain, I shall pray that all may destroy all conscious reflections and attain perfection, finding peace and leisure in empty serenity.

40. When I encounter someone eating and drinking, I shall pray that all may give up all bondage and enter tranquility, fully attaining the sweetness of the Dao. [3a]

41. When I encounter a great fire, I shall pray that all may be free from disasters and harm, instead creating only fields of blessedness.

42. When I encounter a sick person, I shall pray that all may use the Dao to find peace and avoid all suffering and danger.

43. When I encounter a dead person, I shall pray that all may study the Dao to live forever and go far beyond the three bad rebirths.

44. When I encounter someone hunting or fishing, I shall pray that all may no longer commit sins and filthy deeds and forever enter nonaction.

45. When I encounter a barbarian, I shall pray that all may be born as royal guests in the Middle Kingdom and never in the border regions.

46. When I encounter a young person, I shall pray that all may study in accordance with their time to become proficient and rich in their life expectancies.

47. When I encounter an old or sick person, I shall pray that all may use the Dao to hold on to life and never decay or grow old.

48. When I encounter the Three Luminants, I shall pray that all may be universally illuminated with numinous brightness, while all darkness and obscurity are being dispelled.

49. When I encounter clouds and rain, I shall pray that all may be soaked with kindness and full to overflowing, so there is nothing that does not grow.

50. When I encounter fresh snow, I shall pray that all may always live in purity and freely rest in spontaneous fulfillment. [3b]

51. When I encounter a numinous wind, I shall pray that all accumulated heaps of desire may be destroyed and scattered, so virtue can flow both near and far.

52. When I encounter clear water, I shall pray that all may wash off all dirt and be pure and empty, even calming their minds.

---

[4] The *Great Precepts of the Highest Ranks* has an additional prayer under this entry. This increases the total to 59. It says: "When I encounter a diligent student, I shall pray that all may study to become erudite and diligent and follow the various teachings."

53. When I encounter famous incense, I shall pray that all may receive beauty both fragrant and flourishing, and that the multitude of defilements may be dissolved.

54. When I encounter delightful luxury, I shall pray that all sensory pleasures may scatter into the various forms of sageliness, and all may come to love each other fully.

55. When I encounter a horse and carriage, I shall pray that all may attain the Dao and nonaction, to stride on a phoenix and ride a dragon.

56. When I encounter music and singing, I shall pray that all worldly games and fun may scatter and become the delights of the Dao.

57. When I encounter a fortunate feeding, I shall pray that all may be satiated and full, and in this world enjoy celestial banquets; that virtue may flow to leaders and people like rivers return to the sea; that generations of ancestors may have long lives, always resting in nobility and splendor; and that all in the world as well as the members of the four ranks are born into royal families.

58. When I encounter someone spreading charity, I shall pray that all bad fortune may dissolve in ninefold darkness and good fortune may arise in the ten directions; that virtue may be like the northern sea and rise and flourish everywhere; that all ancestors of seven generations may be reborn in heaven; that all sons and grandsons may be wise and loyal, wealthy and noble, eminent and lofty; that all they wish may always come to pass; and that all students of the Dao may become flying immortals, striding on clouds and riding off on dragons. [4a]

All Daoists, whether sitting or lying down, should always pray:

> May I and all others be in harmony with the virtue of the four great elements; bodily merge with the perfection of the Dao; forever live in Mystery Metropolis; spontaneously be united with friends and teachers; save all beings in the ten directions; help the world receive divine kindness; wander about freely in being and nonbeing; and penetratingly observe the gate of the mystery.

They should, moreover, carefully follow the **Ten Admonitions to Do Good**. . . .[5]

These ten are called the essential precepts of highest wisdom for admonition to progress. They are all contained in the first scroll of the *Great Wisdom Scripture*.[6]

The divine law transmitted them to the Perfected of Great Ultimate to regulate the practice of the Dao.[7] [5b] Anyone with the right karmic fortune who gets to see this text should venerate it in secret. Showing it to others wrongly and not believing in it will cause great misfortune in this life and lead to one's descent to the demons after death, being locked up in the deep hells,

---

[5] The Ten Admonitions are also contained in the *Great Precepts of the Highest Ranks* (DZ 177), translated above (p. 178-79). The *Fifty-Eight Prayers* lists it in full, but I do not repeat it here.

[6] This presumably refers to the *Great Precepts of Original Prayers* noted above. It may also intend a Daoist text on wisdom patterned on the Buddhist sūtra on "Perfection of Wisdom," but probably does not refer to the Buddhist text itself, since it does not contain the ten items of goodness.

[7] Perfected of Great Ultimate (Taiji zhenren 太極真人) is the religious title of Ge Xuan, the grand uncle of Ge Hong and alleged founder of the Numinous Treasure school, to whom the five talismans with explanations were transmitted. See Yamada 2000.

transmigrating only in the five realms of suffering, and in later lives never being able to attain human birth. Thus the Dao will be destroyed, and so will be the precepts of the scriptures.

The Perfected of Great Ultimate said: In doing evil, none is worse that jealousy, killing, greed, luxury, pride, and slander. Harboring even one of these in your mind will inevitably ruin your years and life expectancy. Holding on to any of them while trying to study spirit immortality—how can this not be vastly pitiful?

Daoists who observe the purgations, burn incense, practice purity, and recite the scriptures create prosperity for the world. They do not want to be obvious about it, so even if one sees them, it is as if they were not being seen.

The Perfected of Great Ultimate said: People of the world are greatly deluded. Far removed from the immortals, they compete in serving the demons and spirits, killing living beings in pursuit of life. Abandoning life—how can they not be far away from it? [6a] They never cultivate goodness, control themselves, or practice forbearance when harmed.

All they want is to receive a lavish funeral after death. But then their bones will not know whether their souls and self have been caught in the five poisons and dark prisons of the hells, suffering hardships in the three bad rebirths and transmigrating endlessly through the five realms of suffering. When they come to life, they again have no good opportunities [for the Dao] and instead strive to accumulate wealth and treasures. Never getting enough, they burden themselves with layers of possessions. Eventually their good fortune is exhausted and sin arrives, their body dies, their name perishes, and their wealth and treasures are scattered in the four directions—like an ill wind that blows about the dust.

The Perfected said: As regards the character of those who study the Dao, they should first of all be filial to their kin, loyal to their ruler, compassionate to their servants, and open to their friends. Trustworthy, they will be trusted in return; admonishing against evil and supporting the good, they know neither them nor us or the pursuit of private and egoistic goals. Never falsely joining any heterodox teachings, they can truly serve people as well as the Dao. Next, they give up all sex and wine, sound and sights, jealousy and envy, killing and harm, luxury and greed, pride and laziness. Then they cut off all foods that contain the five pungent vegetables, rich meats, and luscious tastes. After that, they begin to be mindful of the dark and mystical realm, and in their minds envision purity and emptiness. [6b] Next, they stop taking grains in their meals, venerate and observe the great precepts, control and strengthen their diligence and will, undertake gymnastics and embryo respiration, practice breathing exercises and harmonize the inner fluids, and generally cultivate and build up their merit and virtue.

The Perfected said: He who relies on others for his forbearance can never be truly forbearing; he who relies on others for his bearing harm can never truly bear harm; he who relies on others for his practice can never truly practice; he who relies on others for his residence can never truly have a residence; he who relies on others for his clothing, can never truly have clothes; he who relies on others for his food can never be truly fed; he who relies on others for his protection can never be truly protected; he who relies on others for his studies can never be a true student.

Thus carefully begin using numinous medicines and change your diet to include more cloudy sprouts. Then the Three Deathbringers will drown and be destroyed, the six inner palaces [viscea] will flourish, and the five inner organs will be at peace.[8]

Then you can undertake long purgations and extended meditations, quietly recite the scriptures of the [Three] Caverns, taste the multitude of wonders, and begin to nurture on cinnabar fluids. With a mind like this, how could you not attain the Dao and ascend to the immortals?

The Perfected said: Without cultivating the human Dao of serving one's ruler and kin, without giving up all sensual pleasures, sex and wine, greed and craving, luxury and pride, personal indulgence, and the cheating of the wise ones, whatever you give or loan out will not return to you. [7a] Others will not place themselves second if you behave like this. For a long time you will be unable to reform or control your mind, always being quickly engulfed by desires. Even if you appear to practice the purgations and precepts and study the Dao, your weak flesh will easily fly away from it. Is this not pitiful indeed?

People like this become long-term dwellers of hell, stepping among the five poisons, the mountain of swords, the tree of knives, the boiling cauldron, and the fiery furnace. As their five limbs are scorched and soaked, they wish for death but cannot find it. When hungry, all they get to eat is iron; when thirsty, all they get to drink is fire. Released from this, they are cast into cold and ice, which harm their flesh and break their bones. Eventually they transfer to the Three Bureaus who may decide to create a new mountain or ocean and have them lug heavy loads of earth and stones, whipping and flogging them in punishment. Thus they pass through the three bad rebirths and five realms of suffering, continuously going back and forth between the ten sufferings and eight difficult conditions.[9] Their misery is without measure; it cannot be described in words.

The Perfected said: These people in no way come close to those who have awakened on the outside and become wise. The latter venerate and cultivate the Dao of perfection, respect and trust the scriptures of the Dao, and only do good. In accordance with the transformations they come and go, changing and floating along with the times, wandering at ease about the walled realms, resting in purity and tranquility, and being utterly self-contented. [7b] When their life expectancy runs out, they enter the halls of blessedness and never pass through any prisons or bad rebirths. Or again, they may become demon [officers] and spirits. Later, they are born again as humans. Never losing their original good intentions, through transmigration they gain the root of faith and create the karmic connections necessary for becoming wise men. Then one day, their accumulated defilements are exhausted, and at last they can enter the immortal Dao.

---

[8] This passage refers to the refinement of the body through meditation and dietary changes. Instead of ordinary food, Daoists take refined herbs and medicines, then nourish on the *qi* of the five directions in the form of "cloudy sprouts." This destroys the Three Deathbringers, parasites who make people greedy and sick, and has an overall cleansing and lightening effect on the body, whose organs and viscera become pure and ready for the gods. See Kohn 1995b; Eskildsen 1998.

[9] The ten sufferings are hell punishments. In the eight difficult conditions it is hard to meet enlightened beings. Both come from Buddhism. In Daoism, see *Scripture of Controlling Karma and Original Conduct* (DZ 345).

TEXT EIGHT

The Great Precepts of Self-Observation

INTRODUCTION

The Great Precepts of Self-Observation (*Guanshen dajie* 觀身大戒, DZ 1364) goes back to the sixth century and is associated with the transmission of the scriptures and practices of Highest Clarity (Ren and Zhong 1991, 1078-79). Based on a series of revelations granted to the medium Yang Xi 楊羲 (330-?) in the 360s, the Highest Clarity scriptures were first written down by two brothers Xu, who duly spread the new teachings in the area (Robinet 1984, 1:108). They were welcomed by the local aristocracy who found in the newly discovered heavens a rank and nobility denied to them on this earth (Strickmann 1978a). After being lost and reassembled in the fifth century (Strickmann 1981), the Highest Clarity texts and their advanced practices of visualization and ecstatic excursions became the pinnacle of Daoist achievement.

The practices aimed at the individual's perfection in the Dao. Creating a representation of the universe, of the body, and of themselves, Daoists made this representation come alive and then proceeded to join it, becoming one with the universe at large and establishing themselves in its center (Robinet 1989b, 159). By joining the symbolic universe and ecstatically traveling to the higher reaches of the heavens above, they developed from ordinary people into cosmic beings. No longer limited to their earthly environment, they increasingly made the heavens their true home, wandered freely throughout the far ends of the world and soared up into the sky. Ultimately full residents of heaven, they strove to get their names transferred from the registers of the living to those of the immortals, thereby excising any entry that might still be found in the ledgers of the dead. Eventually, they believed, they would attain a position in the heavenly hierarchy above.

The Great Precepts of Self-Observation consists of 300 rules, also listed in WSBY 45 and *Essential Rules and Observances* 6, and further mentioned in the *Great Meaning of the Gate to the Mystery* (*Xuanmen dayi* 玄門大義, DZ 1124) of the Sui dynasty. It provides the framework for the moral, behavioral, and spiritual behavior of advanced Daoists. It begins with the statement that "the great precepts of self-observation in wisdom originally were floating rays of light, diffused and overflowing, radiating through the great void." Only after an extensive period did they coagulate into something resembling words and were transmitted by the Heavenly King of Primordial Beginning to the Highest Lord and Lofty Sage of the Dao, who in turn passed them on to the Heavenly Emperor of Great Tenuity and the Perfected of Great Ultimate, also known as the Heavenly King. The two main revealing deities of the scripture, their comments are appended after the precepts proper.

Before listing the precepts proper, the text provides the "Hymn to Wisdom" in three stanzas, allegedly composed by the Heavenly Emperor of Great Tenuity out of pure delight at receiving the precepts. These stanzas appear frequently in the literature and are typically recited during ordination ceremonies. Next, the text presents the precepts, in an arrangement that follows the Numinous Treasure model and divides them according to the Three Primes.

The list begins with 180 elementary and strictly prohibitive rules addressed to those under the supervision of Lower Prime (1a-10b). Next come thirty-six partly prohibitive, partly prescriptive precepts to followers classified as Middle Prime (10b-12b). They include rules of social politeness and tranquility of mind. The last division contains eighty-four precepts for advanced disciples of Higher Prime (12b-17b). They are prescriptions of certain thoughts to keep in mind, for example: "May I be at peace in poverty and recite the scriptures of the Dao without slackening." They also include reminders about ecstatic excursions and the various celestial regions to be visited, for example, "May I wander to the palaces and residences in the various heavens to ask about the Dao and discuss the scriptures with the perfected."

The rules of *The Great Precepts of Self-Observation* also appear in the seventeenth-century *Precepts of Medium Ultimate* (JY 293; ZW 405), translated in the "Supplement," where they provide guidelines for medium-level practitioners of Complete Perfection (see Hackmann 1931). The modern text has the same subtitle, "for self-observation in wisdom," and the same introduction and chant. The first 180 precepts appear in a slightly different order and with some textual variants—most conspicuously leaving out all repetitions, i.e., precepts with the prefix "Do not instruct anyone to . . .". The remaining 120 rules are identical to a large degree.

The last pages of *The Great Precepts of Self-Observation* are not taken up in the *Precepts of Mediurm Ultimate*. They present comments and admonitions on the precepts by their three divine recipients, the Heavenly King of Primordial Beginning (17b-19b), the Heavenly Emperor of Great Tenuity (19b-22a) and the Lofty Immortal of Great Ultimate (22a-24b). They each recount their experiences in receiving and following the precepts, show in glowing vivacity the delights that come from obeying them scrupulously, and picture the gory details of failure to do so. For example, they insist that the precepts reside essentially in heaven and "only rarely appear on earth." When received and used properly, they help practitioners to "observe all the various gods in the body, the numinous perfected of the three hundred joints and passes, and prevent them from leaving wantonly and creating demonic trials." Eventually,"a turquoise chariot of clouds and mists will spontaneously arrive and receive you; you ascend to heaven in broad daylight and bodily float about the waves of emptiness" (18a).

TRANSLATION

[1a] The great precepts of self-observation in wisdom originally were floating rays of light, diffused and overflowing, radiating through the great void. After 3,000 kalpas, they were assembled into this text. This was then given by the Heavenly King of Primordial Beginning to the Highest Lord and Lofty Sage of the Dao. Together they duly ascended to the halls of Perfection Cavern to explain and recite them. Later they transmitted them to the Heavenly Emperor of Great Tenuity and to the Heavenly King, Lofty Immortal of Great Ultimate. All this was only by word of mouth, never had the text been written down.[1]

---

[1] This introductory paragraph is also cited in WSBY 32.11b-12a.

When the Heavenly Emperor of Great Tenuity received the precepts, he composed a holy song [*gātha*]:[2]

Wisdom arises from original nonbeing,
Brightly it illuminates the ten directions.
Combined in the void, formed in the mysterious empyrean—
It pours from the various heavens as flowing fragrance.
Its wonders are beyond belief,
Its empty impulse truly beyond the real.
It is right there, yet it is not—
It is not there, yet nothing is without it.

In wisdom to constantly observe the body,
Is foremost in studying the Dao.
As I thereby imperceptibly enter the mysterious ford [to the Dao],
So spontaneously my spirit is registered above.
The Heavenly Worthies always give me protection,
[1b] The demon kings guard me with precious words.
Brilliantly shining in my diamond body,
I go beyond ever farther to stand before the Highest Lord.

Wisdom arises from the root of the precepts,
The Dao of perfection has the precepts as its key.
The Three Treasures all begin through them,
And they are honored and received even by lofty sages.
Floating in this boat of no-death,
I suddenly am saved in the [Heaven of] Great Existence.
When I then recount the precepts,
Celestials then come to knock their heads to me.

---

[2] This chant is also found in two sixth-century Numnious Treasure texts, the *Scripture on Observing the Body* (*Guanshen jing* 觀身經, DZ 350, 1b-2a), and the *Observances for the Purgation of Spontaneity of Numinous Treasure* (*Lingbao ziran zhaiyi* 靈寶自然齋儀), which remains as a Dunhuang manuscript (P. 3228; Ōfuchi 1979a, 142).

It occurs again, with minor character variations, in WSBY 35.5ab, 48.3ab, and 50.2b-3a, as well as in *Rules and Precepts for Worshiping the Dao* 6.10ab, *Essential Rules and Observances* 5.23b-24a, and in the *Golden Book on Rescue and Salvation* (*Jidu jingshu* 濟度金疏, DZ 466, 10.6b). The latter was originally compiled in twelve scrolls by Lin Lingzhen 林靈真 and dated to 1302, then expanded under the Yuan and Ming to 321 scrolls (Ren and Zhong 1991, 346-48). The last stanza of the chant is furthermore found in Du Guangting's *Precepts for the Golden Register Purgation* (DZ 486, 3a). See Ren and Zhong 1991, 358.

THE PRECEPTS[3]

Students of the Dao, you must not:

1. Kill any living beings, even the wriggling worms. (ZJJ 1)[4]

2. Instruct anyone to kill any living beings, even the wriggling worms.[5]

3. Drink alcohol. (ZJJ 3)

4. Instruct anyone to drink alcohol.

5. Use fancy language, double-tongued or faithless speech. (ZJJ 5)

6. Instruct anyone to use fancy language, double-tongued or faithless speech.

7. Engage in licentiousness or violate the wives and daughters of the hundred families. (ZJJ 8)[6] [2a]

8. Instruct anyone to engage in licentiousness or violate the wives and daughters of the hundred families.

9. Steal people's things. (ZJJ 9)

10. Instruct anyone to steal people's things.

11. Be jealous of another's wisdom or envy their abilities. (ZJJ 15)

12. Instruct anyone to be jealous of another's wisdom or envy their abilities.

13. Refuse your teacher's kindness and love. (ZJJ 14)

14. Instruct anyone to refuse their teacher's kindness and love.

15. Be disloyal to superiors. (ZJJ 16)

16. Instruct anyone to be disloyal to superiors.

---

[3] The precepts are not numbered in the original. To make them more accessible, I have added consecutive numbers. The same precepts also appear in the seventeenth-century *Precepts of Medium Ultimate* (JY 293; ZW 405), which also contains the same subtitle "for self-observation in wisdom" and the same introduction and chant. About two thirds of the first 180 preceptsvare identical in both texts. When this is the case, the corresponding number of the rule in the *Precepts of Medium Ultimate* is indicated by "ZJJ" (for *Zhongji jie*) in parentheses. Minor textual additions in the *Precepts of Medium Ultimate* are included in brackets. Textual omissions and more significant variants are described in footnotes, also using the abbreviation ZJJ. Precepts numbered 181-300 are generally identical and noted specifically only when there are variations in content or numbering.

[4] ZJJ formulates this differently: "Do not kill or harm any living beings or anything that has life" (Hackmann 1931, 8).

[5] This is both a warning not to allow others to do evil and a prohibition against doing things by proxy. More freely translated the rule might read: "You must not let anyone kill living beings on your behalf."

[6] Again, the later text has a variant: "Do not secretly spy on women or give rise to even a minor thought of licentiousness" (Hackmann 1931, 9).

17. Be harsh to inferiors. (ZJJ 17) [2b]

18. Instruct anyone to be harsh to inferiors.

19. Cheat or deceive fellow students or people who have not yet reached proper understanding. (ZJJ 19)[7]

20. Instruct anyone to cheat or deceive fellow students or people who have not yet reached proper understanding.

21. Treat your disciples with contempt. (ZJJ 21)

22. Instruct anyone to treat their disciples with contempt.

23. Speak good while mentally harboring evil. (ZJJ 28)[8]

24. Instruct anyone to speak good while mentally harboring evil.

25. Speak of others' transgressions and evils. (ZJJ 25)

26. Instruct anyone to speak of others' transgressions and evils.

27. Amass the seven treasures without giving freely to the four ranks. (ZJJ 30)[9] [3a]

28. Instruct anyone to amass the seven treasures without giving freely to the four ranks.

29. Enjoy other people's money, wealth, or miscellaneous goods or make that their responsibility.

30. Instruct anyone to enjoy other people's money, wealth, or miscellaneous goods or make that their responsibility.

31. Carry knives, staffs, or other weapons. (ZJJ 31)

32. Instruct anyone to carry knives, staffs, or other weapons.

33. Raise the six domestic animals. (ZJJ 33)

34. Instruct anyone to raise the six domestic animals.

35. Conduct lavish funerals and bury your kin with extensive gifts of food and drink in vessels of gold and silver. (ZJJ 43)[10]

36. Instruct anyone to conduct lavish funerals and bury their kin with extensive gifts of food and drink in vessels of gold and silver.

37. Covet pleasure, glory, and rich emoluments. [3b]

38. Instruct anyone to covet pleasure, glory, and rich emoluments.

39. Destroy the small and tiny creatures of the world by burning. (ZJJ 42)[11]

---

[7] The second part of this rule is omitted in ZJJ.

[8] ZJJ has: "Do not say "right" while thinking "wrong" or harboring hidden evil" (Hackmann 1931, 11).

[9] ZJJ has: "Do not amass numerous material goods without thinking of giving them away freely" (Hackmann 1931, 11).

[10] ZJJ reads: "Do not bury anyone with extensive vessels and objects" (Hackmann 1931, 12).

40. Instruct anyone to destroy the small and tiny creatures of the world by burning.

41. Throw food fit for use by the people of the world into water or fire. (ZJJ 41)

42. Instruct anyone to throw food fit for use by the people of the world into water or fire.

43. Covet the pleasures and tastes of the world. (ZJJ 44)

44. Instruct anyone to covet the pleasures and tastes of the world.

45. Covet eating the five strong vegetables. (ZJJ 4)

46. Instruct anyone to covet eating the five strong vegetables.

47. Write in fancy script. [4a]

48. Instruct anyone to write in fancy script.

49. Take coarse objects and present them to others as fine things. (ZJJ 45)

50. Instruct anyone to take coarse objects and present them to others as fine things.

51. Pursue knowledge of military or state affairs. (ZJJ 51)

52. Instruct anyone to obtain knowledge of or to plan any military or state affairs.

53. Devise schemes for power or subversion. (ZJJ 54)

54. Instruct anyone to devise schemes for power or subversion.

55. Have an audience with an emperor, king, or feudal lord [ZJJ: or aristocrat] without good reason. (ZJJ 55)

56. Instruct anyone to have an audience with an emperor, king, or feudal lord without good reason.

57. Divine [ZJJ: obtain knowledge of] the phases of Heaven or point out and discuss the stars and lunar mansions. (ZJJ 57) [4b]

58. Instruct anyone to divine the phases of Heaven or Instruct and discuss the stars and lunar mansions.

59. Burn fields, wild lands, or mountain forests. (ZJJ 67)

60. Instruct anyone to set fire to fields, wild lands, or mountain forests.

61. Pick flowers or herbs without good reason. (ZJJ 65)

62. Instruct anyone to pick flowers or herbs without good reason.

63. Establish close relations with bad people. (ZJJ 97)[12]

64. Instruct anyone to establish close relations with bad people.

65. Cut down trees without good reason.

---

[11] ZJJ has: "Do not burn or otherwise destroy created material objects" (Hackmann 1931, 12).

[12] ZJJ has: "Do not interact or make friends with bad people."

66. Instruct anyone to cut down trees without good reason. (ZJJ 66)

67. Chatter with people or indulge in the company of ordinary folk. [5a]

68. Instruct anyone to chatter with people or indulge in the company of ordinary folk.

69. Eat alone when among people. (ZJJ 69)

70. Instruct anyone to eat alone when among people.

71. Tell worldly marriage fortunes. (ZJJ 71)

72. Instruct anyone to tell worldly marriage fortunes.

73. Engage in [ZJJ: observe] worldly dancing or music. (ZJJ 73)

74. Instruct anyone to practice worldly dancing or music.

75. Reveal the secret faults of others or their personal coarseness. (ZJJ 75)[13]

76. Instruct anyone to reveal the secret faults of others or their personal coarseness.

77. Spy on others' books and writings. [5b]

78. Instruct anyone to spy on others' books and writings.

79. Speak or walk about with a woman alone. (ZJJ 80)

80. Walk together with a woman or, if unavoidable, take an elder along.

81. Sit together with a woman; instead always maintain the segregation of men and women.

82. Eat together with a woman or wrongly exchange clothing with her. (ZJJ 82)

83. Give private instruction to a woman. (ZJJ 83)

84. Speak about the good and evil of another person's ancestors. (ZJJ 84)[14]

85. Openly praise the people of the world. (ZJJ 85)[15]

86. Put poisonous drugs into wells, ponds, rivers, or the ocean. (ZJJ 87)[16]

87. Instruct anyone to put poisonous drugs into wells, ponds, rivers, or seas. [6a]

88. Be partial about your clan.

89. Be distant to those of other families.

90. Instruct anyone to abort a fetus. (ZJJ 90)

91. Instruct anyone to leave their families. (ZJJ 91)

92. Repay hatred with resentment. (ZJJ 92)[17]

---

[13] ZJJ omits the second half of this rule.

[14] ZJJ has: "Do not speak about the transgressions and faults of another person's family or elders" (Hackmann 1931, 14).

[15] ZJJ adds: "while secretly planning to destroy a good man" (Hackmann 1931, 14).

[16] The ZJJ variant is: "Do not carelessly throw poisonous drugs into [public] water."

93. Engage in a sexual or love relationship with one of your disciples.

94. Wantonly assemble a crowd of people. (ZJJ 94)

95. Instruct anyone to wantonly assemble a crowd of people.

96. Hand sacred books or eulogies over to the people of the world.

97. Instruct anyone to hand sacred books or eulogies over to the people of the world. [6b]

98. Think yourself noble. (ZJJ 99)

99. Instruct anyone to claim nobility for themselves.

100. Take pride in yourself. (ZJJ 99)[18]

101. Instruct anyone to take pride in themselves.

102. Think yourself right and give vent to your temper. (ZJJ 100)[19]

103. Instruct anyone to think themselves right and give vent to their temper.

104. Wantonly hold numerous taboos and avoidances. (ZJJ 105)

105. Instruct anyone to wantonly hold numerous taboos and avoidances.

106. Have expectations on the things of others. (ZJJ 106)

107. Instruct anyone to have expectations on the things of others. [7a]

108. Drain or block local ponds [ZJJ: waterways, or marshes]. (ZJJ 108)

109. Instruct anyone to drain the reservoir.

110. Discuss the long and short of your teacher's or friends' ability. (ZJJ 118)

111. Treat the sacred scriptures with contempt or abuse the words of the divine law. (ZJJ 121)[20]

112. Instruct anyone to treat the sacred scriptures with contempt or abuse the words of the divine law.

113. Despise the old and sick. (ZJJ 114)

114. Instruct anyone to despise the old and sick.

115. Reject beggars. (ZJJ 115)

116. Instruct anyone to reject beggars.

117. Presume authority to tower over the people of the world. [7b]

118. Instruct anyone to presume authority to tower over the people of the world.

---

[17] ZJJ has: "Repay public nobleness with resentment" (Hackmann 1931, 15).

[18] The precepts numbered 98 and 100 are joined together in ZJJ (no. 99).

[19] ZJJ reads: "Do not give vent to your temper and let yourself go" (Hackmann 1931, 15).

[20] ZJJ has a minor variant: "Do not despise the teaching of the scriptures and the words of the divine law" (Hackmann 1931, 16).

119. Form a clique on the basis of your family. (ZJJ 89)

120. Instruct anyone to form a clique on the basis of their family.

121. Join a homestead or household separate from your parents. (ZJJ 117)

122. Instruct anyone to join a homestead or household separate from their parents.

123. Develop anger or rage at your disciples.

124. Blame or rage against the [ZJJ: good] people of the world. (ZJJ 123)

125. Scold others as if they were slaves or animals. (ZJJ 124)

126. Mark slaves on the forehead or harm their four limbs.

127. Delight in the misfortunes and losses of others. (ZJJ 126) [8a]

128. Instruct anyone to delight in the misfortunes and losses of others.

129. In jest tell worrisome things to the people of the world.

130. Serve as ritual chief for ordinary people. (ZJJ 129)

131. Landscape mountains or build residences for others. (ZJJ 130)

132. Divine the good and bad fortune of the world. (ZJJ 132)

133. Instruct anyone to divine the good and bad fortune of the world.

134. Leave or approach anyone with your back to them.

135. Instruct anyone to leave or approach anyone with their back to them.

136. Live together with a crowd of people of the world.

137. See a noble in audience without good reason. [8b]

138. Ride horses or use carriages [ZJJ: or engage in travel without good reason]. (ZJJ 151)

139. Take away what others desire.

140. Rush among a crowd or start a quarrel with the people of the world. (ZJJ 138)

141. Congratulate or condole with the world or seek pleasure among common crowds. (ZJJ 139)[21]

142. Claim others' merit and fame as your own virtue. (ZJJ 140)

143. Sleep or rest on beds that are ornately carved or studded with gold and jewels. (ZJJ 152)[22]

144. Discuss the good or bad qualities of what others eat and drink. (ZJJ 153)[23]

---

[21] The second half of this rule is not found in ZJJ.

[22] ZJJ has: "Do not select comfortable accommodation, rooms, beds, or mats to sleep on" (Hackmann 1931, 19).

[23] This reading was amended with the help of ZJJ, using *lunren* 論人 (discuss other people) instead of *mingren* 名人 (famous people).

145. Startle the hundred families or cry danger without good reason. (ZJJ 170)

146. Startle birds and beasts or catch them by digging up the earth. (ZJJ 172)

147. Alarm the old or young without good reason. (ZJJ 169) [9a]

148. Look down upon officials or administrators. (ZJJ 146)

149. Predict affairs of the world or discuss what is straight and crooked about them. (ZJJ 147)

150. Be generous and gracious merely in pursuit of personal advantage.

151. Roam about the country without ends. (ZJJ 151)

152. Climb high towers without good reason. (ZJJ 150)[24]

153. Catch wild birds or animals in cages. (ZJJ 63)

154. Block up wells, ditches, or ponds. (ZJJ 107)

155. Delight in other people's bereavement or misfortune. (ZJJ 126)

156. Obstruct people's walkways with thorns and spikes. (ZJJ 155)

157. Instruct others to obstruct people's walkways with thorns and spikes. [9b]

158. Offer sacrifices to the spirits and earth gods. (ZJJ 156)[25]

159. Instruct anyone to offer sacrifices to the spirits and earth gods.

160. Pay obeisance to ghosts and spirits. (ZJJ 157)

161. Instruct anyone to pay obeisance to ghosts and spirits.

162. Expose your naked body to the Three Luminants or vainly yell at the wind and the rain. (ZJJ 159, 160)

163. Exchange goods with others without returning your proper due. (ZJJ 162)[26]

164. Destroy or harm the material goods of others.

165. Encourage people to do evil. (ZJJ 163)

166. Prevent people from doing good. (ZJJ 164)

167. Observe the precepts and purgation periods of the various heavens without being mindful of the Dao. (ZJJ 174) [10a]

168. Fail to observe the six annual purgations or pass up the mid-month purgation. (ZJJ 161)[27]

---

[24] ZJJ has: "Do not climb up high, then go close to the drop" (Hackmann 1931, 19).

[25] The variant has: "Do not pursue good luck by worshiping lascivious cults or offering sacrifices to the spirits and earth gods" (Hackmann 1931, 19).

[26] ZJJ reads: "Do not borrow any material goods or objects without returning them to their proper owner" (Hackmann 1931, 20).

[27] ZJJ has: "Do not fail to cultivate the purgations and days of uprightness, nor be lax during those days."

169. Fail to observe the rules, precepts, prohibitions, and statutes contained in the teachings of the scriptures.

170. Perjure yourself for others' sake.

171. Loudly discuss other people's evil.

172. Trust anyone who speaks in rage against the people of the world.

173. Make fun of people if they are dull and dumb, poor and impoverished. (ZJJ 171)

174. Willfully add anything to or subtract from the precepts of the scriptures. (ZJJ 168)

175. Pridefully disregard the Three Treasures or make light of the celestials. (ZJJ 173)

176. Encourage people to plot against their rulers, elders, teachers, or fathers.

177. Encourage people to be unfilial toward their parents and brothers. (ZJJ 175)[28]

178. Pridefully call yourself a perfected. (ZJJ 176)

179. Follow or use the miscellaneous arts of heterodox cults or develop heterodox views that are not true. (ZJJ 177) [10b]

180. Own a surplus of clothes or utensils [ZJJ: and not give them away to the poor]. (ZJJ 178)

— Bully people into studying the Dao.

— Study without the proper scriptures, thus cheating both people and spirits. (ZJJ 180)

The above are the precepts for self-observation in wisdom, numbers 1 to 180. They represent the Dao of the highest immortals and are known as the Precepts of Lower Prime, containing the wisdom of Jade Clarity.

Students of the Dao, you must not:[29]

181. Expect to receive obeisances and respect from others.

182. Secretly copy the scriptures and precepts of others.

183. Gaudily adorn your robe or gown [ZJJ: to be flowery and ornate]. [11a]

184. Ascend the high seat for reading the scriptures with an unclean body.[30]

Students of the Dao:

185. When walking with others, always let them go first.

186. When studying with others in the summer, volunteer to hold the stove for the presentation of food offerings.[31]

---

[28] The variant in ZJJ has: "Do not engage in relationships with unfilial or unbrotherly people" (Hackmann 1931, 20).

[29] The precepts from 181 to 300 are identical with those in ZJJ—with two exceptions, referenced in the footnotes.

[30] ZJJ omits "for reading the scriptures."

187. When studying with others in the winter, volunteer to hold the pitcher for offering the libation.[32]

188. When eating with others, always take the coarse and plain vegetables.[33]

189. When eating with others, always stop eating before everyone else.[34]

190. When studying with others, always be respectful to those who have overcome their selves and attained awakening before you.

191. When studying with others, always allow them to choose their place first.

192. When studying with others, always be mindful of the teaching and never be lazy.[35]

193. When studying with others, always ask them to precede you. [11b]

194. When doing evil by yourself and later receiving evil in return, do not harbor resentment.[36]

195. When [hurt,] do not harbor resentment, rage, or feelings of revenge.

196. When speaking with a woman, do not look straight at her face or exchange a smile with her.

197. When crossing a river together with a woman, do not raise your eyes to glance straight at her.[37]

198. When having lost something, do not suspect your fellow students or other people.[38]

199. When having lost something, always seek the main fault in yourself and regret your many sins.

200. When suffering calamity or sickness, always be compliant and blame only yourself, striving to be mindful to change past behavior and do better in the future.

Students of the Dao:

201. Always be ready to endure what others cannot.[39]

---

[31] ZJJ omits "for the presentation of food offerings."

[32] ZJJ omits "for offering the libation."

[33] ZJJ omits "and plain vegetables."

[34] This follows ZJJ, reading *zhi* 止 (stop) instead of *zheng* 正 (proper).

[35] This follows ZJJ, reading *lai* 懶 (lazy) instead of *jie* 解 (understand).

[36] ZJJ omits "and later receiving evil in return."

[37] ZJJ has a general rule here: "When crossing a river with others, do not struggle forward to select a good spot" (Hackmann 1931, 22).

[38] ZJJ omits "or other people."

[39] ZJJ has only four of this list (nos. 201, 205, 206, and 208) in sequence (i.e., nos. 201-04; Hackmann 1931, 23). The remaining four items are replaced with four rules based on the *180 Precepts of Lord Lao* (nos. 157-59, 168; see Hendrischke and Penny 1996, 26-27). It says:

    205. Whenever you arrive in any place, first ask about the wise and good people, then pay your respects to them in person.

    206. Whenever you arrive in any place, first ask about the local prohibitions and taboos.

    207. Whenever you enter anyone's home, first ask about the personal and taboo names of the family venerables and elders.

202. Always be ready to give up what others cannot.

203. Always be ready to wear what others cannot. [12a]

204. Always be ready to eat what others cannot.

205. Always be ready to learn what others cannot.

206. Always be ready to permit what others cannot.

207. Always be ready to accept what others cannot.

208. Always be ready to abandon what others cannot.

Students of the Dao, understand that:

209. Without scriptural training, you float about aimlessly in spirit and cannot penetrate the ideas of perfection.

210. With an unclean body, your spirit and material souls will depart.

211. With a strong personal mind, you cause the heavenly perfected to rise far away and the demon officials be unsupportive.

212. With strong family feelings, you cannot destroy the three poisons and the three perfected will not come to stay.

213. With a strong personal body, you cannot remove the various desires, and your essence and thinking will not be responsive. [12b]

214. Only with an empty mind can you be tranquil and serene and easily join the perfected.[40]

215. Only when at rest in the source of the mystery can you prevent vain agitation from shaking up primordiality.

216. Only by diminishing consciousness and containing all personal views can you attain perfected views.

The above are the precepts for self-observation in wisdom, numbers 1 to 216. They represent the Dao of All-Highest Orthodox Perfection and are known as the Precepts of Middle Prime, containing the wisdom of Jade Clarity.

Students of the Dao, cultivate the following thoughts:

217. May I maintain vegetarian food as my regular diet [ZJJ: and may all my volition be clear and frugal].

218. May I save others first and only then save myself.

219. May I reside in the dark tranquility of mountains and forests to meditate [ZJJ: on the utmost Dao].

---

208. If someone slanders you, concentrate on cultivating the great Dao. Do not let yourself be sad and depressed, thus lessening your essence and spirit.

[40] ZJJ has: "Settle your mind to be tranquil and serene, and the myriad worries will all be forgotten."

220. May I be at peace in poverty while reading the scriptures and practicing the Dao without tiring.

221. May I burn all kinds of famous incense, so that its fragrance can drift up to the various heavens and penetrate the realms of the demons. [13a]

222. May I be among the wise and carefully listen to their wondrous instructions.

223. May I request the scriptures of the Three Caverns and diligently present offerings to them.

224. May I establish merit to save others, never tiring to the end of kalpas.

225. May I repay the original virtue of my teachers and friends, never remiss to the end of kalpas.

226. May there be purity in the state and may the king make efforts toward Great Peace, so that none remain without the Dao.

227. May all neighboring states also follow the Dao, so that all maintain proper borders.

228. May I pray for the hundred families so they can always live in peace.

229. May I place the myriad beings first and not [ZJJ: pray to] attain the Dao only for myself.

230. May I remain far away from ghosts and spirits, treating them neither with undue respect nor with contempt.

231. May I remain far away from all heterodox arts and cults that are prohibited and tabooed.[41] [13b]

232. May I remain far away from all entertainments of sound and sight, singing and dancing.

233. May I remain far away from all people who have contacts with ghosts and spirits, all those who are enticing or false.[42]

234. May I venerate the origin and guard perfection [ZJJ: be steady in thought and never waver].

235. May my mouth never go against my mind nor my mind ever burden my body.

236. May I be free from doubts and errors regarding the sagely writings, neither adding to nor subtracting from the rules and the divine law.

237. May I be free from ambitions and passions.

238. May I be clear and open, always guarding perfection.[43]

239. May my mind be free from improper imaginings—just empty, just serene.

240. May all families have peace and harmony and may all be free from suffering and pain.

---

[41] ZJJ has: "May I remain far away from all heterodox arts and cults involving sacrifices and bad dreams."

[42] ZJJ writes "shamans and sorcerers" instead of "people who have contacts with ghosts and spirits."

[43] These two precepts are joined into one in ZJJ, resulting in a small change in numbering to number 257, then adding one rule: "258. May I gain penetrating insight into the ten directions and may nothing be hidden from my gaze."

241. May the miserable and suffering people of the world, entangled in sin and deep in distress, all attain the dissolution of their burdens. [14a]

242. May the emperor be bright in sageliness and spread the Dao, and may the imperial family prosper daily more.

243. May the lords and ministers be widely supportive, always protective, and filled with Dao.

244. May Heaven and Earth, the sun and the moon, the wind and the rain, the frost and the snow all be timely.

245. May my parents nurture me to good karma.

246. May my ancestors of seven generations and my parents all ascend to the heavenly halls.

247. May my teachers early attain ascension to salvation.

248. May my fellow students, who have not yet fathomed the deepest source of the Dao, become deeply immersed in the stanzas of the sacred texts.

249. May my comrades and I support each other in the teaching and help one another in entering the orthodox Dao.

250. May I never go against the texts that my mouth chants.

251. May I regard the parents of others as my own.[44] [14b]

252. May I regard the children of others as more important than my own.

253. May I regard the bodies of others as more important than my own.

254. May I regard the wounds and pains of others as more important than my own.

255. May I regard the shame and evil of others as more important than my own.

256. May my fate and karma be cut off at its roots.

257. May I never be born again in the world once the roots of my womb are cut. May I be close friends with those of similar karma.

258. May the tree of my life wither so my spirit can merge with Great Nonbeing. May I encounter the Dao and join perfection for kalpas without end.

259. May the road to the three bad rebirths be blocked and the hells be closed forever.

---

44 This entire set of five precepts about regarding "others like my own" is not found in ZJJ. Instead the text has five rules adapted from the *180 Precepts of Lord Lao* (nos. 146-50; see Hendrischke and Penny 1996, 26). They are:

   250. May I diligently nourish on *qi* and abstain from grain to attain the Dao of no-death.
   251. May I diligently pursue long life, day and night without tiring.
   252. May I diligently avoid suspicion and doubt, never getting entangled in affections or undue familiarity.
   253. May I diligently avoid afflictions and troubles, never carelessly coveting worldly glory.
   254. May I diligently avoid being cruel to others, never abandoning or turning my back on my friends. (Hackmann 1931, 27)

260. May I nurture my spirit while eating and avoid all rich and fancy foods. [15a]

261. May I be careful about the great divine law, always visualizing the Three Palaces and the perfected child therein.

262. May I look upon the world with the radiance of harmony, never becoming prideful towards ordinary people.

263. May I uphold the precepts and scriptures of the Three Treasures, constantly chanting them without slackening.

264. May I visualize the Female One, recite the *Scripture of Great Profundity*, and gaze off as if facing the gods.[45]

265. May I ascend to the immortals and go beyond the world, riding in cloudy carriages drawn by dragon steeds.[46]

266. May I always encounter people like my teachers, friends, and fellow students.[47]

267. May I encounter perfected and men of the Dao who practice cultivation of the divine law.

268. May I encounter sagely kings as rulers of the world, to whom even people from beyond the seas come to knock their heads, riding the wind and hoping to be converted.

269. May I participate in celestial feasts and the fare of spontaneity, never even imagining the feeling of hunger and thirst.

270. May I join the celestials and perfected in serenity and nonaction.[48] [15b]

271. May I command immortal lads and jade maidens.[49]

272. May I wander to the east, to the eastern florescence with its green woods.

273. May I wander to the south, to the southern florescence with its great cinnabar.

274. May I wander to the west, to the western florescence with its peaceful nurturing.

275. May I wander to the north, to the northern florescence with its azure network.

276. May I wander to the northeast and save all the men and women of the hundred families there. May I give them these admonitions and precepts and save them through the gate of the northeast, allowing them to attain entry into the sphere of nonaction.

277. May I wander to the southeast and save all the men and women of the hundred families there. May I give them these admonitions and precepts and save them through the gate of the southeast, allowing them to attain communion with the Dao as their basic karmic cause.

---

[45] ZJJ reads: "May I guard the Female and hold onto the One, seeing them as if facing the gods themselves."
[46] Instead of "riding in cloudy carriages. . .," ZJJ has: "benefiting and assisting the multitude of living beings."
[47] ZJJ has the variant: "May I and my teachers, friends, and fellow students together attain the fruits of the Dao."
[48] ZJJ has "ease" instead of "serenity."
[49] ZJJ reads: "May immortal lads and jade maidens come to serve me at a banquet of the divine law."

278. May I wander to the southwest and save all the men and women of the hundred families there. [16a] May I give them these admonitions and precepts and save them through the gate of the southwest, allowing them to attain entry into the Dao of nonaction.

279. May I wander to the northwest and save all the men and women of the hundred families there. May I give them these admonitions and precepts and save them through the gate of the northwest, allowing them to attain entry into the sphere of utmost perfection.

280. May I wander freely to the garrisons of Qin, to the lofty terraces, and to Mount Kunlun.

281. May I wander to many purgation halls, there to lecture and present the sagely Dao, elucidate and explain its deepest obscurities.

282. May I wander to the Golden Towers in Highest Clarity to pay my respects to the perfected and the Highest Lord.

283. May I wander to the Palace of Seven Treasures in Jade Clarity to pay my respects to the Three Primes and the Heavenly Worthies.

284. May I wander to the Palace of Cinnabar Mist in Jade Clarity to pay my respects to the Highest Lord and the twenty-four lofty sages.

285. May I wander to the Shady Jade Forest on the Floating Dawn Terrace of the Seven Treasures in the Highest Jade Capital to pay my respects to the Highest Lord, the Heavenly Worthies, the great sages of the ten directions, and all those who begin anew when a kalpa ends. [16b]

286. May I wander to the Palace of Purple Clouds to pay my respects to the thirty-nine lofty sages of the Perfection Cavern.

287. May I wander to the palaces of yellow gold in all thirty-six heavens to pay my respects to the imperial lords of Heaven.

288. May I wander to the palaces of golden glow in all nine heavens to pay my respects to the most-high utmost perfected.

289. May I wander to the palaces and residences in all the various heavens to ask about the Dao and discuss the scriptures with the perfected.

290. May I wander to the palaces of seven treasures in Six Heavens [of Fengdu] to encounter and convert the great demon kings and [with their help] have my talismanic ledger entered into the ranks of the immortals, far removed from the record of the [underworld] springs.

291. May I wander to the palaces and halls of the sun and the moon where their radiant brightness is shining forth to have audience with the kings of the sun and the moon, and there drink the florescence of the sun and the moon, partaking of their golden fluid.

292. May I wander to the palaces of floating light in the great Brahma Heavens to pay my respects to the four celestial emperors and there listen to the heavenly chanting of the wondrous odes of the empyrean. [17a]

293. May I wander to the forests of seven treasures in the various heavens which give forth a numinous fragrance that floats everywhere and goes even against the wind, and there listen to the cries and wing flapping of the lions and dragons, all ranging beyond 3,000 miles.

294. May I wander to the cleansing pools in the various heavens to sit peacefully on top of their lotus blossoms, whose fragrance is as pure as spontaneity and floats freely through the various heavens. May the hundreds and thousands of heavenly pools be like a single place to me and give happiness to all people.

295. May I wander to the various heavens to listen to the celestial music that is so unlike anything imaginable on earth.

296. May I wander to the heavens beyond the ten directions to pay my respects to the images of the great sages and the most-high true perfected.

297. May I wander to the celestial diamond palaces in the limitless depth below to pay my respects to all the perfected, primordial and ancient.

298. May I wander to the secret palaces and grotto chambers contained in the famous mountains of Heaven and Earth to pay my respects to the host of sages and to all those who have attained the Dao before me. [17b]

299. May my mind become the Dao and may I forever be free from wrong views and false thoughts. May my mind be empty and my intention be at peace—no yearning, no worrying, only thinking peacefully and in empty serenity.[50]

300. May I keep secret the appellations and taboo names of the celestials and perfected, and may they never issue form my mouth.[51]

The above are the precepts for self-observation in wisdom, numbers 1 to 300. They represent the Dao of the Highest Nonultimate and are known as the Precepts of Upper Prime, containing the highest wisdom of Jade Clarity.

The Heavenly King of Primordial Beginning said:

When the lofty wisdom scriptures of Perfection Cavern had not been proclaimed in the world, students who received them in transmission often became perfected. Thus the text is hard to encounter and hard to use fully—only rarely does it appear on earth. Its precepts are venerable and serious and cannot be properly expressed in words. Through them one can observe all the various gods in the body, the numinous perfected of the three hundred joints and passes, and prevent them from leaving wantonly and creating demonic trials. Never violate them! If you receive and chant these precepts, make sure not to go against them! Nor without their proper study issue them!

[18a] Due to this, one day a turquoise chariot of clouds and mists spontaneously arrives to receive you. You ascend to heaven in broad daylight and bodily float about the waves of empti-

---

[50] This rule is not found in ZJJ.

[51] This precept appears as no. 299 in ZJJ. It adds a general admonition as its last rule, again based on the *180 Precepts of Lord Lao* (no. 180):

> 300. Practice these precepts without violation, and if you violate one make sure you repent properly. Then change your behavior to cultivate them better in the future and encourage others to worship and receive them. Always think of the precepts, never think of evil. Widely pursue salvation of all beings in spontaneous accordance with the spirits and perfected. Then all good fortune will be yours and you can preserve yourself and realize perfection. (Hackmann 1931, 33)

ness. You bring forth a round radiance from the top of your head that shines into the ten directions and brightly illuminates even Great Nonbeing. None among the host of celestial sages will dare not to show you respect and honor. The great demon kings of the Six Heavens at this time will elevate all practitioners who venerate the precepts to be registered in the Palace of Eastern Florescence. This office will then pass their names on to the Heavenly Palace of Great Brahma, which in turn will transfer them to the Golden Towers of Jade Capital, where they are inscribed into the ranks of the highest immortals.

The Heavenly King of Primordial Beginning said:

The *Perfect Scripture of Great Profundity*, if recited ten thousand times, makes a cloudy carriage descend to receive you. The scriptures of Numinous Treasure in Mystery Cavern are texts that survive the kalpas. Some people cultivate them and yet do not attain immortality or successfully concoct the numinous fluid of golden cinnabar. Why is this? It is because they do not venerate the precepts of self-observation in wisdom. These precepts are the most wondrous of all the wonders—all the nine hundred majestic deities, ultimate worthies, and immortals of golden florescence stand up and offer incense to them. They contain the perfect and arcane Dao which cannot be transmitted in words. You have to chant and practice them—and that is all.

[18b] Anyone studying the Dao who does not receive these precepts can ever attain immortality. Instead, they create karmic conditions and are enticed by sound and sights; start out diligently but soon lapse into laziness; enter mountain hermitages and encounter trials by the host of demons; give rise to strange thoughts and begin to doubt and misread the perfected scriptures; revert to following ordinary goals and lose their mind for the Dao; despise their teachers and friends or defame and shame their fellow students; develop signs of madness and let their temper and energy fall into wrong patterns; covet wealth, love, and sex, and go against the Three Treasures; are hindered by family involvement and develop resentment against all kinds of organizations; have bad dreams and confused imaginings—all this from not having the great precepts to sustain their mind and spirit. They thus allow the Three Deathbringers, poisonous and fickle, to cunningly deceive the five inner prefectures. Be sure to realize this affliction!

Also, this way you prevent the demon kings from erasing your name from the [ledgers of] the underworld springs of the dead. Instead, you will remain in the Three Worlds and never cross over to the ranks of the immortals.

The Heavenly King of Primordial Beginning said:

[19a] These precepts first appeared through the numinous immortals. Now all the immortals of the various heavens, earthly realms, and famous mountains venerate and practice them. Every new moon and full moon, on the days of the eight nodes and of original destiny as well as the constellations of the Primes—on all the purgation days of the various heavens—all students, teachers, and friends [of the Dao] enter the chamber to recite the precepts once in their entirety. They first pay obeisance to the ten directions, bowing once in each direction to the various heavens. As they present the precepts to the hearing of the gods, again they perform a bow for each.

If a disciple wishes to venerate the precepts, he or she must first give five pounds of gold as a pledge to the five emperors and ten *zhang* [ten feet] of cinnabar brocade as a gift to the ten directions. They must also swear an oath to be entered into the ledger that they will not disclose the precepts and statutes. The master in charge of the veneration of the precepts then sets up a three-day purgation for mindful meditation and instruction in the precepts.[52] On the eve of the event, participants first light ten lamps to present an offering of light to the ten directions. The great sages of the ten directions accordingly will come to manifest in their minds. If at the time there is violent wind and rain, thunder and lightning, transmission cannot take place. In that case, set up another purgation for the precepts and again prepare all with proper dignity. Then, as the time approaches, open your spirit and relax your intention.

After having venerated the precepts for nine years, your spirit candle will be naturally bright like the sun and the moon or the florescent cinnabar, and you will have a golden complexion rising from the inside, giving you the looks of a youngster with full and firm flesh. [19b] Your spirit will pervade the four far ends [of the universe], your virtue will be on par with that of the immortals, and you will be able to enter and leave the spaceless. Venerating these great statutes and precepts, you can bathe in the Pond of Flowing Calm, release your cloak on the Terrace of the Seven Treasures, wander to gaze beyond the Flowery Pool, or seclude yourself in the Fragrant Wood of Recovering Life, full of golden radiance, fresh and verdant. From kalpa to kalpa, forever, you will enjoy the perfection of the Dao.

Also, on the day of original destiny, at noon or midnight, face north and recite the "Highest Lord's Stanzas of Great Rank on Returning to the Mystery." This will connect you with the Highest Lord of the ten directions.

The Heavenly Emperor of Great Tenuity said:

These precepts are called "the precepts of self-observation in wisdom." They are also known as "the numinous writ of protecting immortality" or as "the numinous elixir for the salvation of life of highest, lofty Perfection Cavern." Unless a person has extensive karmic merit and virtue, successive blessings and a string of good karmic conditions, and is widely covered by good fortune, he can never see these precious arcana. Neither can he have a golden tablet and jade name in [the Palace of] Eastern Florescence, nor will he be able to encounter the right teacher.

One who venerates the precepts, on the other hand, will have a destiny leading directly to immortality. Having the scriptures and no precepts is like trying to cross the ocean without a boat or like trying to utter [speech] without a tongue. [20a] How can one, without them, find the karmic conditions to transcend all forms of body? Students may not even know how to search for the scriptures, or they may know how to search for the scriptures but have no idea how to obtain the precepts. This way they are missing the most essential root of enlightenment in perfection, stuck in a long dream with no chance of awakening. It is heart-wrenching indeed![53]

ll needs to be done in good measure. Those who wish to venerate the precepts can present their pledges and duly receive them. After that, in nine hundred years they may transmit the precepts orally to one other person—but not to more than one. If they try to pass them on to more than one person, this constitutes a slight on the precepts. The sin of slighting the precepts, moreover, causes one's ancestors of seven generations as well as one's father and mother to fall into darkness and hell, and oneself to tread the three bad rebirths, the five realms of suffering, and the eight difficult conditions—as kalpas end and begin again, one keeps transmigrating through the

---

[52] The text is cited on the subject of the three-day purgation in WSBY 47.8a.

[53] This paragraph, except the first sentence, is cited in *Essential Rules and Observances* 4.1a.

evil realms, daily more removed from immortality and time and again besieged by opponents and creditors. In all situations, then, watch carefully over what you do!

The Heavenly Emperor of Great Tenuity said:

If someone dares to listen to the precepts by stealth he will be accused by the great demons of the various heavens and will be subjected to all kinds of misfortunes, ten thousand without a doubt. [20b] Again, if disciples who venerate the precepts decide to go alone into the mountains, forests, or other dangerous places, they should sound the heavenly drum twelve times and in their minds visualize the gods of the precepts. These gods will protect them on a threefold level, and no sprite, demon, ghost, or goblin will dare to come close. Instead, good fortune and virtue will follow their bodies everywhere and the good deities of the various heavens will each come to support and protect them. The first thing to notice will also be that their opponents and creditors develop a merciful attitude.

The Heavenly Emperor of Great Tenuity said:

In the old days, when I first began to study, I only knew how to request the scriptures and had no idea how to obtain the precepts. For this reason, I continued to transmigrate through life and death.[54] Then the Highest Lord pitied my sincere mind for the Dao, and the lofty sages showed sympathy for me because of my lack of laziness. They appeared to me and told me: "You are studying with great dedication and diligence but you do not know how to venerate the great precepts of self-observation. How can you, from this base, ever attain immortality?" I thereupon prostrated myself for three thousand days at the foot of the Golden Towers. Then the Highest Lord appeared and transmitted the essential precepts to me. I duly venerated and cultivated them. Within nine years, a cloudy chariot arrived to receive me, and I have come to interact with the perfected of the Three Worlds and ten directions in mysterious emptiness.

[21a] For this reason, all students of the Dao must make the precepts and statutes a foremost priority. All ancestors and worthies among followers of the Dao have practiced and chanted them in accordance with the divine law, raising their voices up high, while the sages of old have kept them secret and recorded them in their entirety. Today, venerating them means the same thing—under no circumstances ever allow the texts to be released to common people.

Hymn to the Bright Lamps of the Highest Lord

Always chant the following text before the lamps are lit, not only when the precepts are being transmitted. Click your teeth together three times very subtly and without letting others hear any sound then, after the clicking is done, intone:

> The Highest Lord spreads flowery lamps all through the ten directions,
> Pervading them with essence and sincerity.
> The various heavens are equally lit up,
> The manifold earths are all shining bright.
>
> My body, too, has radiance which reaches the five organs,
> Bringing forth flowery glamour and burning brightness,
> Illuminating even Great Nonbeing in far-reaching vision

---

[54] These two sentences are also cited in the *Synopsis of Registers* (*Falu lueshuo* 法籙略説, DZ 1241, 1.3a).

And growing towards Jade Clarity in cinnabar essence.

Resting in the void of mystery yang in Great Nonbeing,
    I move towards containing the body
    While eliminating all darkness of the roots of suffering.
    Visions of wondrous and utmost perfection
    Float about, not seeming to be real.

Karmic connections show up like symbols of pure light,
    And I see that my body is just like that.
    Riding the changes, I entrust myself to flowing light,
    And with nightly radiance bring forth yang-type cinnabar. [21b]
    Going ever farther beyond, I illuminate the numinous chambers,
    See the various heavens equally shining in light.

All yin-darkness already gone,
    My spirit is bright and perceptive,
    And I play with wisdom and with insight.
    Wandering freely and following the cycles of the Dao,
    I move and rest in accordance with the patterns of Heaven.
    Raising my body up, I dance in empty pervasion,
    The nightly candles shining forth in flowing and density.

The Heavenly Emperor of Great Tenuity said:

If you foolishly light lamps without knowing this chant, the demon administrators of the Six Heavens will not let you go beyond human death and destiny, and the various heavens of the eight directions will not dispatch jade lads, jade maidens, flying celestials, or perfected to descend to you. The Three Worlds and the ten directions will not allow you to transfer your immortal name into the registers of the Southern Palace of Eastern Florescence and will not permit your ancestors of seven generations or your parents to enter the Dao of transforming life.[55]

The Heavenly Emperor of Great Tenuity said:

When someone working towards the Dao does not venerate the great precepts of self-observation, yet strives for ascension to the immortals by chanting the scriptures ten thousand times and living in the seclusion of mountains and forests, I am afraid he will still not have a hope.[56] Only by keeping the precepts intact on the inside and harmonizing radiance on the outside can one gradually get closer to the shore of the numinous goal. [22a] Without proper work toward the Dao and having difficulty in venerating the scriptures, all this becomes very hard. If you can keep the precepts intact, I will get the Highest Lord of the ten directions to help protect your climb to immortality. If you chant the precious scriptures and wear great talisman pendants while keeping your precepts intact, even if you do not attain immortality, you will realize the Dao of no-death in the world.

---

[55] This entire paragraph is also cited in WSBY 66.8a.
[56] This sentence is also found in WSBY 43.13b.

My precepts are regretfully hard to obtain even if pursued by people of the world. In a declining world, too many entrust their fame to what ultimately is merely floating and flourishing, and only few see the perfect mind of the Dao and its virtue. For this reason, the Three Treasures are deep in darkness and the sages are in hidden locations. How can the Dao be other than not spread? Once you have received the precepts, if you maintain them in their entirety, the great sages of the ten directions will spontaneously appear before you. Then even without study you will complete the Dao of immortality. These are not empty words! Not empty words! What else could one wish for?

I truly feel sympathy for the well-intentioned people of the world. May they find the good karmic opportunity to be taught! So, exert yourself! Delight in the practice! Soon you will reach the Dao of immortality—what other medicine could there be? Then you can wander freely in the highest Jade Capital, be at ease in the cities of spontaneity, [22b] have the joy and happiness of being at a stage before the creation even of the Highest Lord when the ten thousand kalpas had not yet begun. This is all I can say. It truly cannot be expressed through pen and paper.

The Heavenly Emperor of Great Tenuity said:

In the old days, I heard from the Highest Lord: Reciting the perfect scriptures of the Three Treasures without the great precepts—how can the Dao of immortality and multitude of wonders ever be achieved? For this reason, the [precepts] have been transmitted by word of mouth and never proclaimed in writing—resting solitary and withdrawn in the garden of the Three Treasures. Anyone who does not by fate have the marks and auspicious signs of the highest immortals will forever be prevented from seeing them. Also, unless you have accumulated blessings for seven [generations of] ancestors, are heir to a succession of manifold florescences, have karmic causes connected for generations, and have suitable merit over a whole kalpa— how would you even know to delight in the highest precepts of self-observation?

Only if you can venerate them do you belong to the lineage of the Highest Lord, the great preceptors, and the Three Treasures. As such all in the ten directions will respect you in the cloudy realm, and the host of immortals will guide you to the [Palace of] Eastern Florescence. There you can sit and summon the great demons of the heavens, and the demon kings will elevate your talismanic destiny from the Three Worlds, Six Heavens, and all departments of the underworld springs. [23a] The ruler of Mount Tai and the earth officials will never again hold any registers or ledgers of your death. Instead, your immortal name will be set up for good in the Green Palace, and you can become a lofty immortal of Jade Capital, a perfected of the Highest Lord.

The Perfected of Great Ultimate said:

The essentials of the Dao lie in practicing in accordance with the luminous rules and in accumulating goodness. Only on this basis can one first traverse the realm of the Great Dao. Who cannot do this will labor in the wind and grime in vain and fail to extend the inherent shortness of his life and destiny. The Dao is within me; it does not come from elsewhere. Mere kindness, mere love, mere forbearance, mere bashfulness—if you can practice these four virtues, you are getting closer to the Dao.[57] If then you can be diligent and trustworthy, can follow your natural beauty and be fully dedicated to all things, can expostulate with others and give up sex and wine, you are practicing the divine law of the six good qualities and turning into a companion of the perfected.[58]

Also, learn to receive wrong without complaint, yield to others at all times, be completely free from desires, allow the senseless without fighting it, [23b] hide in dark locations when away from the Dao, be free from all contrary mind, never turn your back on the scriptures and precepts, and ever diminish the oral rules—these are eight capabilities that make each and every goodness a good friend.[59]

The Perfected of Great Ultimate said:

The way in which the precepts activate the Dao is dignified and awe-inspiring, spiritual and wondrous. Unfortunately people should not take refuge in them and venerate them with conscious [ego-based] intention. For this reason, they should be kept secret and not written down. Thus never make the scriptures and writings of wisdom accessible to ignorant students. Being transmitted strictly by word of mouth, how could they ever leak out? Also, whenever you explain the precepts, be aware that the celestials of the ten directions are listening in respectfully and with folded hands, while the ghosts and spirits all pay obeisance to what is being heard. How can you undertake this lightly?

The Perfected of Great Ultimate said:

The way the people of old practiced the Dao was by being mindful of perfection in mysterious serenity and with tranquil spirit. They spontaneously attained total immobility [of mind] and sat firmly in oblivion. Thus their Dao of perfection was complete. Standing upright with hands folded over their chests, they were soon received by cloudy chariots. Or again, they would ride the wind and move into the void, harness dragons and race across emptiness, lift themselves up and dance on nonbeing, fly up and ascend to the Great Ultimate—in all cases embodying empty pervasion and being free from all obligations. [24a] Thus their traces cannot be discovered, and none in the world know me. Those who in fact know me are few; those who follow me are noble. This is just it. The complete match of [the cosmic] talisman and contract.

The Perfected of Great Ultimate said:

If a teacher or friend presumes to tell pretentious things, claiming them to be firm facts, then this is not the divine law of high antiquity, the system established by this lowly learner. If again by necessity a student imploringly requests the precious scriptures, in all cases take a close look at the person's intention. If he already has pervasive understanding, then set up the scriptures in

---

[57] The term used for "four virtues" is *sideng* 四等, literally "four levels." It is used in Buddhism to denote the four pure states of mind of the enlightened: kindness, compassion, joy, and equanimity. Only the first is identical with those listed here. See Soothill and Hodous 1936, 180.

[58] The six good qualities again uses a Buddhist term: *liudu* 六度, literally the "six ferries," the Chinese rendition of *pāramītas* or good qualities necessary for enlightenment. In Buddhism, they are: charity, morality, forbearance and bashfulness, efforts, concentration, and wisdom (Soothill and Hodous 1936, 134). The third appears in the above list of the "four virtues," while morality is expressed in the "abstention from sex and wine." The others do not seem to have a match.

[59] There does not seem to be a comparable Buddhist category of the "eight capabilities."

front of the Highest Lord and make a formal announcement and report before handing them over. Instruct him to obey the text and honor and venerate it. Doing so, you are in line with the mysterious rules and great divine law of the Highest Lord. Unless you have this talent of spreading the Dao, how could you call upon your ancestors of seven generations to witness before the ten directions that you will not go against them? But before you do any of this, first reflect and examine yourself very deeply as to whether you can really venerate [the precepts] or not. Because the three bad rebirths, the many hells, the ten realms of suffering, and the eight difficult conditions are not to be taken lightly.

Seeing this should make your heart freeze with terror in the face of all the wise and good ones. Be very careful and clear about the precepts, and good fortune will come of itself. If, on the other hand, you develop a mind that turns its back on them, then misfortune will arrive just as naturally. Suffering and pain will suffuse your body and your misfortune will grow with every hour. How much more so over an entire kalpa? [24b]

The Perfected of Great Ultimate said:

Even though kalpas may end and begin, these precepts are part of the unchangable Dao. People of old used to say: Receiving and bodily practicing the precepts, the Dao will be complete one day soon, whether one's traces are clearly apparent or not in the outside world. Their cultivation and activation are really unfathomable. In high antiquity they therefore cloaked their bodies and sat in oblivion, thus attaining the Dao. The Yellow Emperor cast nine tripods and was received by a dragon—he had pervasive insight into all ten directions and even beyond the Three Worlds. Wang Qiao and Master Redpine strode on purple haze and soared up high into the gardens of heaven. They were all of one kind. One cannot sufficiently explain or record this. Yet without speaking about it and not studying it properly, how would one ever complete one's Dao of immortality?

Text Nine

The Scripture of Prohibitions and Precepts

INTRODUCTION

The Scripture of Prohibitions and Precepts (*Jinjie jing* 禁戒經, DH 35) is a fragmentary manuscript from Dunhuang that can be placed in the context of early monastic manuals on the basis of its contentt and terminology. It is not cited in any works of the same or later periods, but provides a good overview of the different kinds of precepts and the concepts associated with them (see Ōfuchi 1978, 112). Section headings were added by the translator. Line numbers refer to the edition in Ōfuchi 1979a, 205-8.

TRANSLATION

Prohibitions

[The Heavenly Worthy said:][1]

[Not to] drink wine or eat the four kinds of blood-containing creatures or anything that is rotten in any way . . . . [Not to] think oneself right and cheat the members of the four ranks . . . Not to be proud . . .

Not to turn one's back on the teachers or oppose the Dao by establishing covenants or binding contracts. [5] [Not to] . . . transmit to the wrong people. Not to defile or cause shame to any holy person[2] . . .

[Not to] sit on the same mat as those who have not received the Dao. . . . sleep . . . Not to eat from the same dishes as those who have not received the Dao. Not to sojourn in the same house as those who have not received the Dao.

Not to give vestments and clothes, shoes and slippers, vessels and utensils, or other ritual implements to those who have not received the Dao.[3] Not to lend ritual vestments to those who have not received the Dao.

---

[1] The first part of the text is corrupt, with characters missing and lines only half visible. Missing sections are indicated with three dots or, if guessed at, supplied in brackets.

[2] This translates *fashen* 法身, literally the "body of the divine law," a concept used in relation to the Dao and problems of its embodiment (see *Pivotal Meaning of the Daoist Teaching*, DZ 1129, 2.3b-4b). In Buddhism, the term translates *dharmakāya* or "dharma body" and refers to the abstract body of the Buddha. In Daoist monastic literature, *fashen* is more concrete: it indicates the physical, sanctified body of the practitioner.

[10] Not to gossip about or insult the common people, the ignorant or mentally ill, or other people of this kind.

Not to curse or slander the sagely writings or denigrate their extraordinary study.

Not to fight with fellow students or create a sense of yours and mine among them.

Not to abandon perfection to pursue the false or fail to honor the divine law of the teachers.

Not to wander about with butchers and wine sellers, lechers and prostitutes, robbers and brigands, or other lawless sorts.

Not to interact with unclassified or anti-Daoist groups.

Not to squander or waste the wealth or property of the Three Treasures, their permanent staff,[4] the host of followers, or members of the four ranks, or anything given in sincere donation by the faithful.

[15] Not to levy fees from the common people to support the wealth or property of the permanent staff of the Three Treasures.

Not to fail to observe the scriptural precepts or encourage members of the four ranks to be lax and lazy and accumulate sinful karma.

Admonitions

[17] Always observe the scriptural precepts; recite, follow, cultivate, and practice them.

Always cleanse the self through purgations and be mindful of immortals and perfected.

Always be mindful of the Dao, the scriptures, and the teachers, maintaining sincerity without slackening.

Always burn incense and bow in prostrations, repent all sins and regret all transgressions.

Always cleanse your essence and mind, perform rites to the Dao, and offer prayers.

Always light lamps and create brightness, assisting Heaven in its bright radiance.

[20] Always at the new and full moon assemble with all fellow recluses to confess sins, repent transgressions, and recite the precepts.[5]

Always protect the holy body, vestments, clothes, and ritual implements, never allowing them to come in contact with the common people.

Always sweep the altar and oratory, and present offerings with a diligent mind.

---

[3] This is a precept often repeated. It appears most prominently in the *Rules and Precepts Regarding Ritual Vestments* of the eighth century (trl. "Supplement"). Its forty-six rules on the treatment of ritual vestments are also found in the *Precepts of Initial Perfection*, translated below.

[4] "Permanent staff" (*changzhu* 常住), also translated as "fixed assets," refers to the permanent residents of a monastery and its communal property. See Gernet 1995, 67; Twitchett 1956; 1957.

[5] This practice goes back to ancient Buddhist recitation of the *Pratimokṣa* at the new and full moon. See Prebish 1975.

Always be mindful of the three masters to soon attain the Dao of immortality and find salvation in the body.

Always establish merit and virtue on behalf of the country's ruler and the kings among men, so their sagely rule may flourish and be lofty without limits.

[25] Always create fields of blessedness for the people in all-under-Heaven, the men and women of the hundred families.

Always strive on behalf of those in the three bad rebirths and five realms of suffering, indeed of all living beings, that they may leave behind all suffering and afflictions and complete the Dao of immortality.

Always strive on behalf of the nine kinds of forebears and seven generations of ancestors, all fathers, mothers, males, and females, whether blood relatives or married in, that they may attain dissolution of their sins, exemption from their faults, and create all karma of good fortune.

Always use the all-highest, wondrous divine law to open salvation for the unenlightened.

Always use the mysterious karmic ways of utmost perfection to educate and guide all beings.

[30] Always use the great, divine law of the Three Caverns to widely set up rafts of salvation for the host of living beings.

Always lecture to open salvation for the ignorant and misguided, causing them to understand sin and good fortune.

Always use the various precepts and methods to transmit salvation to the celestial brotherhood.

Always copy the precious scriptures and keep them flowing through study and recitation, with the permanent staff present offerings to them to create fields of blessedness for kalpas everlasting.

Always teach and beg for [donations], thereby entering into karmic relations with all and allowing them to set up mysterious altars and numinous monasteries for all to take refuge.

[35] Always follow circumstances and develop a mind to create the highest possible holy body, be at peace wherever you are and perfectly accord with the transformations, establishing true sincerity everywhere.

Always produce banners and flowers, curtains and high seats, pennants and canopies, and all sorts of other ritual implements to painstakingly and with dignity present offerings to the Heavenly Worthies.[6]

Always maintain the property of the permanent staff, including their rice and millet, fabrics and silks to create fields of blessedness both for past and future.

Always admonish all fellow recluses to bring forth prayers for goodness and widely set up religious communities, to allow all living beings with the right karmic connection to earn good fruits in accordance with their lot.

---

[6] These are the three central deities of the Three Caverns. For a description, see *Rules and Precepts for Worshiping the Dao* 2.1a; Kohn 2004, sect. 4; Kohn 2003a, ch. 7.

[40] Always maintain and protect the Three Treasures, never allowing them to be harmed or destroyed.

Resolutions

[41] I would rather be violated in my body and have it become minute, subtle dust than ever violate the scriptural precepts of the Heavenly Worthies.

I would rather be harmed by wild tigers and poisonous snakes than ever harm the rules and prohibitions of the Heavenly Worthies.

I would rather be killed in this body and have my life cut short than ever not fulfill the covenant and my pledges to the Heavenly Worthies.

I would rather lose the sight of both eyes in my body than ever lose the dignified observances of the Heavenly Worthies.

[45] I would rather enter a great fiery pit than ever join the company of the impure and those outside the divine law.

I would rather sit and sleep on a bed of iron than ever sit and sleep on the bed of those who have not received the Dao.

I would rather be eaten by wild animals and consumed by fire than ever eat the food of those outside the divine law.

I would rather let a thousand pints of blood from my body than ever let words against the divine law out of my mouth.

I would rather lose a treasure worth a thousand gold pieces than ever lose this robe of the divine law.

I would rather fall into the defilement of the outhouse than ever be defiled by the various passions and desires.

[50] I would rather not eat for a thousand days than ever fail to observe the scriptural precepts for a single day.

I would rather lose my body and life than ever fail to preserve the foundation of the precepts.

I would rather be harmed bodily by accepting a blade [thrust] than ever accept any wealth or property of the permanent staff.

Metaphors

[52] For all those who follow these:

The precepts are the medicine of the divine law—they can eradicate life and death [*saṃsāra*] and all serious illness.

The precepts are the raft of the divine law—they can take us beyond life and death and the ocean of suffering.

The precepts are the sharp sword of the divine law—they can cut down all entanglements and attachments of life and death.

[55] The precepts are the bright mirror of the divine law—they can illuminate the truth of life and death.

The precepts are the fragrant water of the divine law—they can wash off the dust and grime of life and death.

The precepts are the sweet dew of the divine law—they can eradicate all false imaginings, all hunger and thirst.

The precepts are the wisdom lamp of the divine law—they can eradicate all darkness and delusion of life and death.

The precepts are the clouds of the divine law—they can cover all.

The precepts are the rain of the divine law—they can enrich all.

The precepts are like a vast ocean—they can contain all.

The precepts are like a big mountain—they can give life to all.

The precepts are like the sun in spring—they can give life to the myriad beings.

The precepts are like the fullness of summer—they can prolong all.

The precepts are like the sky in autumn—they can complete the myriad beings.

The precepts are like the moon in winter—they can harbor and preserve all beings.

Positive Effects

[61] Who scrupulously observes the precepts need not fear Heaven or man, need not fear demons and spirits. Instead in this life, the lads of the various heavens, the spirit kings of the diamond network, the five emperors of the Three Worlds, the spirit immortals, the soldiers and cavalry [of Heaven], the generals and strongmen—all the 1,200 [divine] personages will always come to attend and guard him. They will steer him clear of the host of misfortunes and disasters, official involvement and slander, capture and punishment, evil demon kings and nasty demons, water and fire, swords and weapons, tigers and wolves, scorpions and snakes, as well as all diseases and afflictions. None of them will ever dare to come to his door. Having passed through this [in this life], he will be born again in heaven as a spirit immortal and offer proper veneration to his father and mother and ancestors of seven generations. He will be reunited with his former companions, male and female, and together they will live in happiness and bliss, forever joyful and in spontaneity.

Failure to Observe

[67] However, who breaks the precepts and does not observe the divine law of the scriptures, who despite the admonitions by others to do good and despite of all the skillful instructions and metaphors, the many kinds of words and explanations [given by the teachers], still violates the

precepts and does not follow the divine law of the teachers, in this life will encounter the calamities of water and fire, swords and weapons, capture and prison, many thousands of strokes, evil winds and nasty demons. Shut off from perfection, he will suffer from madness, his eyebrows and beard will fall out, his body will overflow with rot and he will be covered with boils everywhere. His hands will be crippled and his feet deformed, tigers and wolves, scorpions and snakes will pester his family and take up residence in him, planting further weakness and adversity. He cannot gain life and he cannot find death![7]

[73] Eventually, a hundred pains course all through his body and he dies. Then, after death, he falls into the ninefold darkness and the eighteen hells, where he has to swallow fire and eat hot coals, is beaten with iron staffs and ground to dust on a stone mortar, submerged in hot water, and boiled in a bubbling cauldron. Iron plows will cut his tongue, his feet will tread the mountain of knives, his hands will grasp the tree of swords—thus he suffers on and on for a myriad kalpas.

When he finally attains rebirth, he comes back in the body of a domestic animal, a pauper or lowly person, a dumb, deaf, mute, or cripple, with warped hands and deformed feet and an overall ugly and repulsive appearance. He suffers from hunger and cold and from chronic diseases, a myriad pains stabbing his entire body. Then again, he may come back as a worm or fish, a cricket or ant, or in all sorts of body, each following its own lot in life. For kalpas eternal he will revolve around the cycle of transmigration, never able to get into a good karmic relation with the Dao.

All you men and women: Take good care to think of this!

Past Experiences

[79] The Heavenly Worthy said:

In the old days, there were 26,000 Daoists. They observed and venerated the scriptural precepts with all their hearts and without slackening. They obeyed the divine law in cultivation and practice, and in the course of twelve years, the administrators of Earth elevated them by memorializing their names to the various heavens. After one hundred years, they ascended to heaven in broad daylight. Today, they are still in the Brahma Heavens above, holding the rank of perfected.[8] As they further proceed in the highest divine law, they will transmigrate and enter utmost perfection and gradually go beyond even the Brahma Heaven to join the realm of the Three Clarities. As they refine their spirit and enter the wondrous [Dao], they will transform spontaneously and forever cut off all life and death. Calm and serene, they will attain eternal happiness in the primordial; refined and pure, they share in the flow of the Dao.

[85] Then there also were 72,000 women who went against the teachers and turned their backs on the Dao, instead pursuing an erroneous form of perfection. They did not venerate the scriptural precepts but instead destroyed their foundation, behaving contrarily and engaging in

---

[7] A detailed list of animal rebirths in relation to sins committed in human life is found in *Fengdao kejie* 1.2a-8b. See Kohn 2003b.

[8] The Brahma Heavens are located above the Three Worlds and below the Three Clarities. They are accessible only to enlightened and immortal beings.

slander and ruin, thus ever more falling into false teachings. In this life, they received a karma that brought them suffering of many kinds; after death, they fell into hell, undergoing tortures and pains unmentionable. Today, they are still in the ninefold darkness and still have not yet hit the bottom of their plight.

Thus I tell you: Heed it well! Be ever careful!

Understanding the Body

[89] The Heavenly Worthy said:

When someone comes to life in a human body, this is because of his or her accumulated good deeds and continued veneration of the scriptural precepts in a former life. Having attained birth among humans, she can then use this body to practice the various observations and visualizations, and bodily be liberated in the Dao of perfection.

Therefore, realize that the body is originally and eternally impure, smelly and full of defilement, composed of the four great elements, similar to the five species of beings, mere skin and muscles, flesh and bones. For a brief moment it is a composite entity; it is in apparent harmony for a short while. Then, soon, its constituting karma is exhausted and it disperses again, returning and reverting to dust and ashes.[9] In accordance with the accumulated karma, the person then receives his just rewards and continues to transmigrate through life and death, ever transforming, coming and going without pause.

Also, understand that the body is a fleeting thing, only borrowed for a time; it comes together and soon disperses.[10] For this reason, you must eradicate all evil and cut off all the roots of suffering. Look back on yourself and listen deep within, cleanse and purify your body and mind, undertake prolonged purgations and observe the precepts scrupulously. Recite and chant the numinous texts, pray and practice mindfulness every morning and evening, widely establish fields of blessedness, day and night never being lax about it.

[96] Visualize [the gods] within and meditate on perfection, vigorously perform rites to the utmost Dao. Guard the One and actualize the Three, refine your spirit and manifest your luminants.[11] Turn back to the origin and return to the source, so that your form and spirit may jointly fly [to heaven]. As you then wander easily about in Highest Clarity, you will be forever liberated from life and death to enjoy cosmic spontaneity.

Attachment to the Body

[98] If, on the other hand, you cannot develop this understanding and wisdom in regard to your body and instead bring forth ignorance and crazed imaginings, you will end up killing living beings and stealing the goods of others, engaging in debauchery and being all topsy-turvy. You

---

[9] This vision of the body is also reflected in Tang-dynasty mystical texts, such as the *Treatise On Sitting in Oblivion* (*Zuowang lun* 坐忘論, DZ 1036). See Kohn 1987.

[10] This notion is also reflected in the *Treatise on Sitting in Oblivion* as well as in the *Zhuangzi* (ch. 6).

[11] "Guarding the One" (*shouyi* 守一) refers to an exercise in concentration and visualization of the central deity in the body; "actualizing the Three" (*cunsan* 存三) indicates the practice of visualizing the Three Ones in the three cinnabar or elixir fields in head, chest, and abdomen. See Kohn 1989b.

will be greedy and full of anger, lying and cheating all around, slandering people and speaking double-tongued, cursing and yelling, scolding and shouting.

Giving license to your six senses, you will commit the ten evil deeds through all three karmic factors [body, speech, and mind], and thus will widely produce nothing but bad karmic connections. Never even believing in the karmic patterns of fate or in the cause and retribution of sin and good fortune, you will keep on revolving through life and death, yet maintaining all the time that this is merely natural. Attached to thinking of yourself as having a body, you give yourself over utterly to [the delights of] sounds and sights; riding on the flowing waves of worldliness, you pursue the mental categories of right and wrong. You continuously revolve through pleasures and desires, and never venerate the precepts of the scriptures, turn your back on the Dao, and doubt perfection. No cultivation in your past, you yet assume there will be good karma in the future.

[105] Then one day, your fate runs out, your body returns to dust and ashes, your spirit moves off, your spirit souls submerge, and you start suffering in the ninefold darkness. If after a myriad kalpas you get to be reborn again, it will not be in a human body. Following your karma and bound by its conditions, pains and afflictions pester you persistently. Then you start harboring resentment and complaints, whine in sorrow and shake with terror. Though I have great compassion, there is nothing even I can do. As sweet rain cannot bring a withered tree to blossom, so even the most compassionate father cannot heal a foolish child. It is most pitiful, indeed!

Constant Practice

[108] Oh, you good men and women! Once you have received life, regard your human body as most noble and begin the practice of cultivation: observe the purgations and venerate the precepts; perform prostrations and burn incense; offer rites to the Dao and chant and memorize [the scriptures]; give freely in donation; bring forth good prayers; sponsor the creation of statues and copy the scriptures; seek out a master and ask about the Dao; establish and erect mysterious altars; put others first and yourself last; rescue and save the impoverished and destitute; release living beings and sell them into life; repent your sins and pray for mercy; be forbearing and patient and make keen efforts; with courage and ferocity confront wrongness; find peace in your mind and develop a firm will; lecture and explain, teach and educate; open salvation for all in the celestial brotherhood.

As you maintain and protect the Three Treasure and widely establish bridges [to the Dao], the various heavens pronounce their blessings over you and support you in attaining the perfection of the Dao.

Final Blessing

[114] At this time the Highest Lord of the Dao and all the immortals, perfected, and sages, as well as the host of the celestial dragons, people, and demons, even those in the three bad rebirths and five realms of suffering, all the multitude of living beings equally received good fortune and benefits. They collectively praised goodness and withdrew.

Text Ten

Ten Items of Dignified Observances

INTRODUCTION

The *Ten Items of Dignified Observances* (*Shishi weiyi* 十事威儀, DZ 792) consists of seventeen pages and can be dated to the mid-seventh century. This date is suggested by the full title of the text, which also includes the term *xuanmen* 玄門, lit. "Gate to the Mystery." It is borrowed from late seventh-century Buddhism, where it plays a prominent role in the Huayan school and is found as the "Ten Gates to the Mystery" in Fazang's 法藏 (643-712) *Treatise on the Golden Lion* (*Jin shizi zhang* 金獅子章, T. 1880, 45.663b-67a; Chan 1963, 411).

Transmitted by the Highest Lord Lao to the Perfected of No-Thought (Wuxiang zhenren 無想真人), the *Ten Items* presents monastic behavioral guidelines in ten sections and 144 entries. In content it supplements the *Rules and Precepts for Worshiping the Dao* (see Kohn 2004), which it cites variously and to which it refers occasionally for details of incantations.

Both texts cover a similar ground, but the *Ten Items* focuses more on the concrete activities of Daoists rather than their material surroundings. For example, it has a detailed section on the performance of obeisances (sect. 2), describing exactly how far, with what body parts, and how many times to bow or knock the head in what situation, a feature taken entirely for granted in the *Rules and Precepts for Worshiping the Dao*.

TRANSLATION

[1a] At this time, after the Highest Lord Lao had addressed the Perfected of No-Thought[1] and a host of celestials on issues of "Rules and Precepts Regarding Ritual Vestments," he also said:

There are ten items of dignified observances that I have never explained to you. I will give their words to you today—they are most essential. Just like a person who wants to walk cannot take a step unless he has feet, so anyone wanting to progress in the wondrous Dao will not be able to enter unless he has the proper gate. These ten items of rules and precepts are the gate to the Dao. Those who enter through my gate all wish to be equal to the immortals and firmly separated from all outside commoners and ordinary people. Once they strongly uphold these ten items they truly deserve be called beyond the ordinary.

Now, according to the karmic retribution of life and death and the continuous revolution of sin and evil, desecrating and shaming holy persons and treating vestments with lightness and con-

---

[1] The name of this recipient of the scripture echoes Buddhist notions of in-depth meditation. It is typical of names of holy Daoist questioners, appearing especially in early-Tang scriptures. See Kohn and Kirkland 2000, 356-57.

tempt; joining the Dao with proper preparation and doing nothing to further good karmic conditions; interacting with others on the basis of lust and never developing a mind of shame; committing grave sins [punishable] in the nine realms of darkness and increasing them day and night; in all walking, standing, sitting, and lying down, as well as all entering and leaving losing the divine law—all these are forms of behavior no different from ordinary people and the mass of living beings. [1b]

The perfected, immortals, and great sages take no pleasure in seeing or hearing of them. The celestials, demon kings, demons, and spirits detest and abhor them. Also, they cause the kings, lords, and elders among humanity never to develop any respect, and the men and women of the ten directions to be contemptuous and unsympathetic. Without any merit or virtue, these forms of behavior increase the roots of evil; creating more sin in all directions, they cause suffering without end.

As I now see people acting in these ways, I ache with a chilled heart. For this reason, I repeatedly and diligently will tell you today to follow and obey, venerate and practice [my rules]. Holding up my fingers and palm, I clearly demonstrate to coming students that they must follow and embrace these ten items to attain access to the various heavens and learn to mirror and observe people and celestials in the ten directions. Then the celestials, demon kings, spirits, and demons all feel awe and respect for them, and all living beings develop good intentions [toward them]. As students never dare to violate or go against the rules they, moreover, constantly increase their fields of blessedness, bringing forth good karmic fruits in abundance, and creating merit and virtue without limit.[2]

Anyone who can practice in accordance with these rules is truly my disciple, worthy to receive transmission of the wondrous divine law. Such a one will quickly to closer to the Dao. On the other hand, anyone who does not practice like this will have the demon kings and demons for a close family joined by them day and night and never able to get away.

[The Perfected] No-Thought and the others listened to these wondrous instructions and knocked their heads in reverence, finding their minds startled into shame and compassion. Collectively they cried tears [of sadness] and bowed deeply, begging to hear the ten items of rules and precepts so that they would be able to venerate and practice them for countless kalpas. [2a]

The Highest Lord said:

(1) Handling the seat cloth; (2) Obeisances and formal greetings; (3) Coming and going; (4) Sitting and rising; (5) Handling the water pitcher; (6) Washing and rinsing; (7) Dishes and wiping cloths; (8) Ceremonial meals; (9) Requesting the divine law.

---

[2] "Good karmic fruits" are good fortune, prosperity, long life, extensive posterity, and the like. More particularly, in the higher levels of the Daoist teaching, this leads to the so-called "Dao fruits" (*daoguo* 道果) or five highest stages of immortality. As described in the seventh-century *Scripture of Haikong Zhizang* (*Haikong zhizang jing* 海空智藏經, DZ 9; ch. 1), these are: earth immortal, flying immortal, self-dependent, free from afflictions, and perfect nonaction (see Sunayama 1990). The three levels above them are borrowed from Buddhism: "self-dependent" = *isvara*, the state of complete freedom from resistance, the mind as free from delusion; "free from afflictions" = *asrava*, the end of all outflows, all afflictions and vexations; "nonaction" = *nirvāna*, ultimate liberation through cessation.

These ten items are key for entering the gate of my teaching. You must all follow and practice them, encouragingly teach them to the men and women, so they all can enter the ranks of the immortals.

No-Thought bowed deeply and knocked his head to the ground, then knelt upright to receive the divine words. [2b]

1. HANDLING THE SEAT CLOTH[3]

Kneeling before the altar, you are separated from ordinary people and removed from foulness. Preserving purity, you are self-possessed, solely concerned with the extraordinary nature of the Dao and the virtue, devoted to the lofty traces of the heavenly perfected.

1. Rising and sitting down, coming and going, the seat cloth must never be separated from your body. If, due to circumstances, you have to let it go for a moment, do not put it down abruptly or in a place of foulness or mixed nature. Instead, first wipe the place with a brush or use a clean object for placing the cloth.

2. Every time you wish to walk about, either hang the cloth from your shoulder or hold it in the left hand, with the hem facing out.

3. Every time you want to make an obeisance, first with your right hand pull out the edge of the cloth, so it hangs straight down. Then take three fingers of your left hand to unfold the two ends, and with both hands place it flat on the ground.

4. First, raise your left foot and place it firmly on the rim [of the cloth]. Second, stand up straight, raise your right foot, and step forward into a half kneel. Then arrange yourself in the proper posture.

5. [To get up] place your hands at chest level and raise the right foot backward to return to standing upright on the second rim [of the cloth]. Give three bows to end the activity. [3a]

6. After you have gotten up [from the cloth], with your right hand pick up its corner, gathering it with two fingers. Do not touch the ground or any impurities the cloth may have picked up.

7. Put on your shoes or slippers, then fold the cloth on the left side of your body without it coming close to your face.

8. After folding it, hang it from your left hand. This way it will cover your vestments and morning-mist cape. You can pull it forward as you rise to walk.

---

[3] The seat-cloth (*zuoju* 坐具) can be traced back to the mat used in ancient China by ministers when the formal presence of royalty (*Book of Rites* 11/1.18; Legge 1968, 2:6-7). In Daoism today it is "a piece of scarlet cloth about 1.5 meters long by 80 centimeters wide, with a black border approximately 10 centimeters wide," used for prayer and carried folded over one arm (Yoshioka 1979, 237-38). Called *zagu* in Japanese, it also still plays a role in all Zen obeisances. See Suzuki 1965, 12.

2. OBEISANCES AND FORMAL GREETINGS[4]

Obeisances and formal greetings show that: (1) you humble yourself; (2) you show respect in yourself; (3) you pay respects to others. It is hard to know how respectful the mind is, but the formally bent body can be clearly seen. For this reason, we must perform obeisances of the body in a diligent and attentive manner, so as to give expression to the worthiness and sincerity of the mind within. Thus humbling yourself, you express respect. This is what you are looking for.

There are, moreover, twelve situations when one performs obeisances: (1) to express shame; (2) to express repentance; (3) to request the divine law; (4) to remove pride and haughtiness; (5) to venerate virtue; (6) to condole or congratulate; (7) to expiate guilt; (8) to undergo discipline; (9) to repay kindness; (10) to present offerings; (11) to rejoice with people in the present life; (12) to pay respects to the future world. [3b]

1. All obeisances must be performed calmly and meticulously so that their underlying intent can be properly perceived.

2. Whenever holding the ritual tablet, be aware in mind, erect in body, and stand up straight.

3. Whenever prostrating with all five limbs touching the ground, be level back and front.

4. Whenever facing a statue of the [Heavenly] Worthies or the divine law of the scriptures, or when attending a rite of confession and repentance, perform an obeisance.

5. Whenever facing a venerable master or a master of great virtue, perform an obeisance.

6. Whenever facing a master of instruction, perform an obeisance.

7. Whenever facing a friend of goodness who is your superior, perform an obeisance.

8. Whenever facing a fellow student from anywhere in the four seas, perform an obeisance.

9. Having served the master and taking leave to return to quarters, perform an obeisance. Also, finding his instruction concluded and having important reason to take leave and return to the family the next day, first perform an obeisance. Only after that rise and ask for permission to leave.

10. Having taken leave to go into the outside world, be it after months or years, [upon return] always perform three obeisances. After that, kneel formally, knock the head to the ground, and repeatedly express your gratitude. [4a] After the obeisances are concluded, you can rise and stay to state the success and failure [of your mission]. This is the way of paying obeisance while serving one's master.

11. Whenever the master has to go away to a different province or separate district, be it near or far, for a short time, a month, or a year, always see him off with a formal obeisance. Kneel properly and express your feelings and regrets; bend the head to the ground and voice your sorrow and gratitude. Then get up and bow again. If the reason for the master's journey is an auspicious

---

[4] Similar instructions and explanations are also provided in contemporaneous Buddhist literature. For a study, see Reinders 1997. On Song practices, see Yifa 2002.

or inauspicious event [in his family or community], express your congratulations or condolences again with a proper bow.

12. After the proper expression of congratulations or condolences for the auspicious or inauspicious event is complete, again express your sympathy and that you will wait for him for a long time. After these words are concluded, bow once more. The same applies if you are the recipient of the congratulations or condolences.

13. Whenever receiving joyful words of teaching and instruction or reprimands and punishment from a senior, always perform an obeisance and express your apologies in a low voice, thus acknowledging that you have been taught the proper virtue.

14. Whenever receiving an obeisance from someone, stand with hands raised and palms together to express your regrets and apologies for assuming a high position and accepting veneration. [4b]

15. Whenever paying obeisance to a master, always wait until he is seated, then join him in simultaneous greeting. In all cases, he should be seated before receiving an obeisance. If the master is returning from a far-off outside place, escort him to the abbot's quarters and wait until he is comfortably seated. Only then perform an obeisance to him. Under no circumstances overwhelm him with your unexpected attentions at the gate or in the hallway.

16. Whenever in the presence of a sagely image, the senior master, or a master of great virtue in the sanctuary or sacred halls, never receive obeisances from others. If these others happen not to know this rule and unexpectedly pay their respects to you, explain the situation to them and prevent them from continuing. Also, if unexpectedly in the sanctuary or sacred halls you encounter an older recluse or one of higher virtue, explain the situation to him, saying: "I dare not perform an obeisance to you in the presence of these higher ones."

3. COMING AND GOING[5]

1. If you plan to travel or sojourn in a dangerous or suspicious area, always take a companion along and never travel all by yourself. This is so that you will remain clear and bright.

2. Coming and going to and from places, whether near or far, always take formal leave of your disciples and fellow monastics. If there are none, at least tell your servants where you are going and when you expect to be back.

3. If you go to a place where men and women are not segregated or to a purgation assembly that commemorates an auspicious or inauspicious event, [5a] even if staying only for a short time or freely coming and going, always stay in the same place as the multitude [of religious] and not all by yourself or with your family. Similarly, if the event takes place in a remote or secluded area, join up with companions or go along with the crowd.

---

[5] Unlike Buddhists, who never relinquished the ideal of the wandering ascetic, Daoists place a high value on *stabilitas loci* and, in continuation of the early communities of the Celestial Masters, place tight restrictions on outside travel. See Kohn 2003a.

4. Unless there is an urgent and serious affair or a necessary quest, you must not come and go repeatedly, lest you cause people to assume that you take your responsibilities lightly.

5. When upon coming and going, you meet an official or elder, withdraw to step out of the way. Never show yourself openly. Should there be no suitable place to withdraw or step out to, stand in the shadow of other people or of trees. Even from there, though, give the proper expression of paying your respects.

6. If upon coming or going you unexpectedly encounter a noble person riding in a horse-drawn carriage or a sedan-chair, you must immediately give way and lower your body into a posture of great awe.

7. Unless there is an urgent affair, do not walk about in rain or wind, mud or sleet, icy cold or scorching heat, swishing your gown about in great confusion. This is not what people like to see.

8. Coming and going in major cities or other places where people tend to congregate, always walk and stand with a composed expression and straight face, never raising your voice or laughing out loud. [5b] If addressed or questioned, answer politely with a bow. Unless there is an urgent affair, make it your goal not to speak at all.

9. If during your comings and goings you encounter some evil people, ignorant folk, or youngsters who use bad words and foul language, express their contempt for you, or make jokes about you, then act as if you had not heard them at all and never change your expression.

10. During all comings and goings, be they near or far, always carry your prayer cloth with you. As for the hand-cloth, water pitcher, and other utensils, you can obtain them wherever you stay, finding something suitable in the relevant present circumstances.

11. If it so happens that you have to spend a night in mixed company or in a donor's house, you should go and find some water to sprinkle over the bed or sleeping mat, then wipe it off with a clean cloth. This is called "calming the bedstead." You can then use it without being defiled.

12. If while coming or going from cities or towns, villages or hamlets, you see people doing indecent or illegitimate things, or again, if you hear unpleasant and jocular remarks, then lower your head and walk straight by, taking care not to pay them any heed.

13. Female Daoists, when coming and going, independent of whether [the road is] near or far, dangerous or plain, always must travel with a companion. This is to avoid arousing popular objections and suspicions. [6a]

14. When coming and going to a sacred place that contains scriptures or images, or again to the house of a superior person, never use the central gate but always pass through the small gate on one of the sides, turning your body sideways as you approach and withdraw.

4. SITTING AND RISING

1. In all rising and sitting, there is the distinction between noble and humble. Without above and below, there would be no difference between human beings and other species.

2. At all assemblies of the divine law, one male officiant should stand up front, bow three times, then kneel formally and, folding his palms over his chest, announce: "To commence the such-and-such rites, this humble master so-and-so asks all to be seated." Should the assembly be female, the same procedure applies with two lady Daoists asking all to be seated.

3. In the presence of a sacred image, the preceptor chants while bowing to the scriptures and statues, with the lads following suit. The good men just stay quietly in their places.

4. Whenever officiating at a rite facing the scriptures and sacred images, proceed with a sincere and sober expression, never behaving haughtily, disorderly, or speaking of non-ritual things.

5. Whenever officiating at a rite facing the scriptures and statues, never turn the back toward the divine law of the scriptures, the images of the Heavenly Worthies, the great ones, or the senior masters. [6b]

6. Whenever attending on a venerable master or elder, always stand upright, and never lean against a bed, wall, or other object.

7. Whenever attending on a master or elder, always be serious and stern, never asking questions or speaking out of turn.

8. Whenever attending on, or serving in the place of, a master or elder, always remain standing. If asked to sit down, wait until the order has been repeated three times, and only then touch the head to the ground, apologize [for the rudeness], and sit.

9. Whenever attending on a person in the residence of a master or elder, or again on someone even more venerable than they, only sit down after having received the appropriate order from the person immediately superior. Even then first express your apologies [for the rudeness] to the superior and only then sit down.

10. In the refectory and lecture hall, as well as during all rites of recitation and repentance, all sitting and rising occurs according to ritual rank. Never sit in a place beyond your station, but adhere to the order set up in the rules and precepts.

11. If in the lecture hall you come in late after the scriptural announcement has already been made, take the next available seat to sit down. Similarly, coming in after the masters, just take whatever spot is available and do not charge forward, creating clamor and disturbance. [7a]

12. Once seated, unless there is an urgent affair, do not get up again or undertake any coming and going that would disturb others.

13. Wherever and in whatever posture—walking, standing, sitting, or lying down—never mingle in the same place with people not of the same [monastic] kind.

14. If a master, elder, or venerable—or in fact any other person—is reading a letter or otherwise dealing with his own affairs, do not step before him or stealthily peek in on him, without him being aware of your presence.

5. HANDLING THE WATER PITCHER

1. Men must not use a water pitcher made from a pomegranate.

2. Women must not use a water pitcher made from a coconut.

3. Repeatedly change the water in the pitcher and polish and wash it so that it shines with cleanliness. Do not let it get dusty or dirty, foul or defiled.

4. Never keep water in the pitcher overnight.

5. In the summer months, change the water every day. If it has not been changed for one day, we call it "foul water."

6. In the winter months, change it once in two days. [7b]

7. If the pitcher is made from earthenware, change the water once in three days. But do not put it in a foul place; rather, observe all the relevant taboos.

8. In all places of urination and defecation, use a separate pitcher to wash yourself before and after. After you have washed yourself, use a brick to rub your hands, then clean it with ashes or black [plant] pods. Failure to comply means that you cannot attend an audience with the perfected, ascend to the sanctuary, or pay respects to the masters. Nor will you be able to receive the respects of others or join the great host of the faithful.

9. Every time you use the water pitcher, return it to its proper place. Never let it get dirty or fall down. This a great taboo.

10. In regard to the water pitcher, whenever there is a person who wants to examine it closely or a youngster who wants to lift it, make sure they do not touch it with dirty hands but have them wash and clean their hands first.

11. Protecting the water pitcher within and without is more important than other things. It is on the same level as the continued purity of the scriptures and sacred images.

6. WASHING AND RINSING

1. There are four kinds of washing and rinsing: (1) at dawn; (2) before reading a scripture; [8a] (3) after meals; (4) before bed.

2. Rinsing the mouth should always be done three times.

3. After meals use a willow branch and hot water, first to rinse out all foulness, second to take away bad breath [lit. "tooth wind."]. If no willow branch is available use purified ashes.

4. Whenever you use a new willow branch, chant the following incantation:[6]

> The great Yang [of the sun] harmonizes its energy
> To let spring arise and make the willow grow.

---

[6] This chant and the next are still in active use today. See Min 1990, 107-08. For more on Daoist discipline, see Kohn 2001b.

> Breaking it off, I take one branch,
> So I can clean my body and my mouth.
> Studying the Dao and cultivating perfection,
> May I go beyond the Three Worlds of existence!
> Swiftly, swiftly, in accordance with the statutes and ordinances!

5. Whenever you use ashes, chant the following:

> Washing with ashes to remove the dirt,
> Using the ashes as a primary means,
> May foulness go and perfection arise.
> Cleansing the heart and cleansing the mouth,
> Realizing the Dao and saving all people,
> Heaven is great and Earth everlasting!
> Swiftly, swiftly, in accordance with the statutes and ordinances!

6. All rinsing and washing should be done while turned to the side and with one's back to others. Never do it while facing someone.

7. When scooping water from the basin, never defile it by using your hands but always employ a wooden ladle to take water from the basin. Also do not defile the water by putting your chopsticks or personal ladle in the common basin. [8b]

8. If you have touched the water by mistake, you must make a formal confession and undergo repentance. There you should of your own volition perform the menial task of changing the water and setting [the basin] back up properly. This way you will not accumulate sin.

9. While rinsing the mouth and washing the face, do not contract your mouth to give forth sound. Nor must you make bubbles from either your nose or your mouth. Also, do not bang the water basin, startling everybody.

10. When using water, do not splash it all over the place. Do not paddle or trample around in it.

11. Do not spit or blow foul water from your mouth in front of others or onto the clean earth.

12. Whatever utensils you employ, and that applies not only to the water but to all objects and things, use them economically and with care. Do not use them wantonly or squander them in any way.

7. DISHES AND WIPING CLOTHS

1. Dishes and cloths are to be used during ceremonial [purgation] meals.

2. In ceremonial meals, the offering of food to sages and commoners is of utmost importance.

3. In garb be clean, in posture be straight and pure. Thus, first arrange a seating platform and only then sit.

4. Dishes and cloths have to be clean. Thus, first wash your hands and only then handle them. [9a]

5. First bring clean water, then set out your dishes to receive food. People of wisdom understand food as belonging to heaven; ordinary people take it to be part of destiny. Thus this rule is of utmost importance.

6. Although dishes and cloths are two, their use is one. Whenever at rest and not in use, they should be kept in the same place.

7. Although dishes and cloths are two, keep them clean as one. Only take them out at ceremonial meals, never use them elsewhere.

8. All ceremonial dishes must be stored in separate racks and must not be mixed up with ordinary vessels. That is why the old ones called them ceremonial dishes.

9. There are five parts to a set of ceremonial dishes, just as there are five phases in the application of the divine law and five tastes in the food we eat. Dishes can be made from copper or lacquer, depending on the spending power [of the institution].

10. Typically one has two wiping cloths, packed together. Each is about four inches in length, woven tightly, and with stitches removed. Always keep them white and spotless. [9b]

8. CEREMONIAL [PURGATION] MEALS[7]

1. As the time of the purgation approaches, first appoint one person to serve as the hall supervisor. He is called the purgation overseer. "Purgation" means "orderly arrangement," thus the overseer must know the rhythm and performance of the bells and chimes, and regulate the gain and loss [of all participants]. For this reason he is called "purgation overseer."

2. Before you ascend to the refectory, you must first wash and clean yourself, then don your vestments and headdress.

3. First wash your hands, then take your dishes and ascend to the hall. There put them down to your left, adding the wiping cloths.

4. Bow in supplication and sit down, all at the same time. Take off your slippers and place them underneath [the bench] but in such a way that they do not obstruct the servers.

5. First clear water is brought out, so that the dishes will not be treated with rudeness.

6. After everyone has received water, first take the cloth and lay it on the table with its central edge facing front. Spread it out to seven inches, then place the dishes on top. Use the second cloth to place on your knees, spreading it out with your hand.

7. Take out the ceremonial dishes, from the first to the fifth in their proper order and without creating confusion. [10a]

8. The hall supervisor stands erect at the chimes in front of the hall and sounds them once. All bow in veneration and offer good wishes to the sovereign emperor for an extended life and

---

[7] Another detailed description of the ceremonial meal is found in *Rules and Precepts for Worshiping the Dao*. See Kohn 2004, sect. 16. For comparable Buddhist rules, see Prip—Møller 1967.

great sageliness. As the present circumstances allow, in some cases prayers and offerings are also presented on behalf of the generous donors of the ten directions. Services like those on behalf of the various donors grant protection and give good karmic rewards.

Next, the officiating preceptor leads everyone in a series of incantations. The text of these prayers is found in the *Rules of Qizhen*.[8] [10a]

9. Chant the "Incantation for Presenting the Rice Gruel":

> Today this most fragrant rice gruel
> We offer above to the Three Worthies
> To benefit and increase our families and country
> And to ensure great abundance for our generous donor.
> May all numinous creatures contained in the six realms [of rebirth]
> Be equally and jointly filled and satisfied.

10. Chant the "Incantation for Presenting the Food":

> In all the fields of blessedness
> Donating food is by far the best.
> In the present it spreads pure happiness,
> After this life it gives rebirth in heaven
> And a future residence in the pure land
> Where all food and clothing arrive spontaneously.
> Therefore we present this offering today
> Spreading it equally to the various heavens.[9]

11. After the incantations have been sung, the food is brought out. Prior to this, the purgation overseer must have spoken with the food servers to make sure they announce the name of each dish, clearly calling out its qualities and amounts, thus making sure of equal distribution. [10b]

12. After the food has been all brought out, the purgation overseer sounds the chimes and announces that all purgation officers and participants should knock their heads once to pay respects. Only after this does everyone proceed to eat.

13. Generally you can receive three helpings of food to make sure you get enough. However, you must not take more than necessary in uncontrolled greed and then leave it. People seeing such bad behavior will never be able to develop respect or faith.

14. Whenever you hear the name of a dish being called out, take your bowl into your hands and bring it forward to receive the food.

15. If you do not want it, raise your finger and let it pass. If you wish to decline more food, move the bowl backward. If you wish to decline less, bring it slightly forward. Under no circumstances use words or make any noise.

---

[8] This refers to the prayer series found in section 16 ("The Noon Purgation") of the *Rules and Precepts for Worshiping the Dao* 6.4b-5b.

[9] This text, with minor variants, is also found in *Rules and Precepts for Worshiping the Dao*, sect. 16, 6.6a.

16. Always look around and remain attentive to the others up and down the hall. If you are behind, eat a little faster; if you are ahead, eat a little slower. Try to be in line with all other purgation participants.

17. During the entire period of the ceremonial meal, the purgation overseer must keep an eye on everything. When half the meal is over, he should begin another round [of inspection].

18. Do not give in to your basic nature [and eat with haste]. This will cause the slower eaters to dislike you. [11a]

19. During all eating, be meticulous to keep your mouth moving and your intention composed. Never make sucking or gulping noises, bang or clatter your spoon or chopsticks. This will cause you to bear sins necessitating mercy and compassion.

20. Once seated for a ceremonial meal—unless there is a military incident, an emergency, a fire or flood, an attack by robbers, or a sudden death—never abruptly speak up or make any noise in the refectory.

21. If during the purgation there is a matter that has to be taught or explained, use your hands and fingers to indicate the situation or, if absolutely necessary, speak in a very low voice.

22. If after the purgation there are fruit or other edibles left over, distribute them to those less fortunate, to beggars or the sick. Never throw them out in their entirety.

23. After you finish eating, first fold the lower cloth that is resting on your knees. Then stack up the ceremonial dishes, from fifth to first, and place them onto the cloth.

24. After the meal clear water is brought out to rinse the dishes. Once all have received water, the chimes sound and all chant an incantation of prayers for the donor. When this is over, chant them once again. Their text is found in the *Rules and Precepts of Qizhen*.[10] [11b]

25. If the assembly is not due to a special karmic connection [with a certain donor], there is no need to use this chant.

26. The next incantation runs:

> Now we have concluded the purgation.
> Still I fear
> That the accumulated merit is not complete
> And pledge to throw away more pure wealth
> And give massively to the Three Treasures.[11]
> May our generous donor be protected in good fortune
> And may his merit and virtue be full and complete.

27. The "Incantation for the Donation of Food" is next:

> The offering of the divine food to the Three Treasures is now complete.
> On behalf of the donor and his lads and servants,

---

[10] This refers to a chant of good wishes for the donor found also in section 16 of the *Rules and Precepts for Worshiping the Dao* 6.7a.

[11] To this point, the chant is also found as part of a larger prayer in *Rules and Precepts for Worshiping the Dao* 6.6b.

We now pray that
All the young people may jointly be steeped in equal merit
And remain without any impediment or obstacle.

28. The chimes are sounded, and all meal chants are complete. Next, with the meal over, all intone a prayer for the universal establishment of fields of blessedness, the liberation of all beings in the ten directions, and peace and prosperity throughout the Three Worlds.

29. If at any time during a purgation an unexpected violation of the precepts has occurred, at this time the purgation overseer makes an appropriate announcement and orders the culprit to pay obeisance.

30. Then he sounds the chimes again, and all chant the "Verse to Encourage Goodness":

As I and the multitude
Have now heard this divine law,
May our bodies and minds be pure and clear
Just as a clean glass vase.
Covered in joy and cheer,
We knock our heads in deep respect
To the All-Highest Three Worthies. [12a]

31. This must be sung three times with accompanying prostrations. If there is a different reason for the occasion, three prayers are sung, but not these chants also.

32. When the purgation affair is completely over, the overseer sounds the chimes and leads a chant he finds suitable. Then all knock their heads in deep respect, pick up their dishes and leave.

33. All rise and file out in their proper order, to immediately return to their quarters and buildings. Never congregate and chatter idly, disturbing the purity of all.

9. REQUESTING THE DIVINE LAW[12]

The divine law is often called a treasure. When people with respect receive it, this is truly wondrous. First, one gains benefit for oneself by transmitting the teaching of the divine law. Second, one also can assist others and jointly attain the wondrous karmic fruits.

Through the merit of transmitting the divine law we enter the ranks of the immortals. Therefore it is said: Requesting the divine law must occur with genuine seriousness and devout sincerity.

1. There are two ways of requesting the divine law from a preceptor. The first is to ask the preceptor to expound the law, lecture on the scriptures, transmit the rules, or hand down the precepts. The second is, in special circumstances, to ask for resolution of doubts. Either case necessitates the performance of obeisances. Once must always knock one's head with dedicated diligence, genuine seriousness, and devout sincerity. [12b]

---

[12] The procedures described in this section closely echo those used in reciting and lecturing on the scriptures as outlined in *Rules and Precepts for Worshiping the Dao*. See Kohn 2004, sects. 11-12.

2. Lecturing on the scriptures and expounding the divine law can occur in a big way or small, over a far distance or near. In all cases, explanations[13] must be prepared ahead of time. Their writing must be on good-quality paper and in perfect script. In due accordance with the divine law, all must be pure and clean, and there must be no writing that is smudgy or weak or words that invite contempt and laziness.

3. As for transmitting the explanations, if the event is of a smaller scale, begin by performing three obeisances. Once this is done, the master holds the explanations in his hand, while the recipients kneel formally and state their intention [for the Dao]. They then fold their hands over their chests while the master transmits the explanation, beginning with those up front. Once all have received the teaching, they perform three obeisances, excuse themselves, and withdraw.

4. In an event of a greater level, the master holds the explanations while all perform obeisances, either seven or nine. After that, the recipients kneel formally and state their request. After this, they give three more obeisances. This done, they kneel again and receive the explanations. Following this, they pay more obeisances and kneel again, then excuse themselves saying: "This insignificant person having widely received great mercy and compassion is now full of happiness unfathomable."

5. If the people up front have not yet received their explanations, they should just perform further obeisances without any fixed number, which will allow them to go beyond. If they are still not given their explanation at this time, they should withdraw in accordance with the situation and wait for a later time. [13a] At that time, they can knock their heads again three times and receive their explanations.

The *Scripture on Setting the Will on Wisdom* says:[14]

> Blood keeps flowing in numerous pecks,
> The mind, too, never stops.
> Without a spontaneously determined mind,
> One will only knock at the dark numinous enclosure
> And impede one's return to the masters' gates.
> With bowed head and contained virtue
> One can never receive transmission.

6. As regards the request in special circumstances to receive resolution of doubts, first pay obeisance three times, then kneel formally with hands folded over the chest. State your doubt and again give three obeisances. After resolution is given, rise with hands folded and excuse your-

---

[13] This translates *shu* 疏, a word of multiple meanings. In a scriptural context, it often means "subcommentary," the explanation of a sacred text in addition to standard or established commentaries. In a modern ritual context, it indicates the memorial, a formal document submitted to the gods inside the temple, whose text is also placed on a placard outside (see Lagerwey 1987, 61-63). Here the word seems to refer to interpretations of the scriptures or the rules written out formally by the master and handed over to one or more disciples in a ritual involving personal contact and the paying of obeisances. I have thus used the word "explanation(s)" to translate *shu*.

[14] This text is among the early Numinous Treasure corpus (LB 16) and found in DZ 325. The exact passage is not contained in today's version, but it fits well with the overall content, which focuses on the need for a determined mind to attain the Dao and contains an early version of the ten precepts later found prominently in the *Scripture of the Ten Precepts*.

self, saying: "This inferior disciple is stupid and dull. I bow before the grace of the preceptor who did not abandon me in my ordinariness and ignorance but himself explained the perfect principles, so now I feel joy and delight immeasurable." Pay obeisance three more times and withdraw.

7. When someone of obviously advanced years and grave virtue comes to receive explanation and requests a purgation, wishes to have an interpretation of the meaning of the scriptures or a specific topic, or desires a lecture on their principles, have him sit up straight and pay obeisance. Once the explanation is fully given, he is to excuse himself with the words: "This insignificant disciple is stupid and dull and had never heard such an interpretation before. Now bowing before the grace, I see my true destiny, which fills me with fear and awe immeasurable." Again, pay obeisance three times. The master should at this point reply with respect to the older person's virtue. [13b]

8. If masters and elders assemble to transmit the divine law, all those who receive their explanations and orders must wait properly, pay obeisance three times, then prostrate themselves on the ground for transmission. After that, they kneel formally, their hands interlaced above their heads. Remaining in this posture for a while, they release it and pay obeisance three more times, to end up again kneeling formally. Eventually they excuse themselves, saying: "Full of deadly sins, this insignificant disciple gives veneration to the dignified destiny, feeling terror and fear immeasurable." Or they may say: "I dare not." Again they are to give three obeisances and withdraw.

9. Whenever someone says "I dare not," it means one of two things – either "I receive and dare not speak" or "I speak and dare not receive."

10. SAFEKEEPING

There are seven kinds of safekeeping: (1) keeping the vestments safe; (2) keeping the divine law safe; (3) keeping the scriptures safe; (4) keeping the masters safe; (5) keeping oneself safe; (6) keeping the donors of the ten directions safe; (7) keeping all living beings safe. [14a]

1. All scriptures and sacred images have the same level [of safekeeping] without distinction. Just as the *Rules for Worshiping the Dao* says:[15] "Wherever scriptures and sacred images are housed, the place must be well protected and sparkling clean. They should be surrounded and properly separated by bamboo railings. If you leave them even for a short time, always take a clean cloth to cover then.

"At those times when practitioners study and read the scriptures, they must not unroll them more than three times in a row. Once they are done, they should use their free hand to roll the scripture back up. Even if the scroll has not been read completely, never leave it unrolled even for an instant. Should there be an urgent affair [to interrupt the reading], then start the scroll again later from the very beginning while uttering the proper expressions of repentance."

---

[15] This passage is not found in the *Rules and Precepts for Worshiping the Dao* as extant today. However, the content fits well with its section 6, "Copying the Scriptures."

2. Never let them be touched or handled by impure people or those of impure body or foul breath.

3. When holding the scriptures or sacred images, make sure you have clean hands and a pure intention. Do not place other things on the same racks, put them together with discarded objects, or allow people to handle them carelessly. If there is nobody else and you have to handle and place them carefully yourself, first wash your hands and wipe the scripture racks, equally on top and bottom. If you touch any other object in between, you have to wash your hands once more.

4. Do not keep scriptures and sacred images in your residence. Only those contained in wrappers of black lacquer or the like that are moreover placed in a special bookcase can expediently be stored in residences or bedrooms. [14b] Scriptures collected in wrappers of plain silk, even if placed in a bookcase, must not be so stored.

5. If you spend several days and nights continuously in a great hall or at a prolonged nocturnal assembly, you may get tired in performing services to the divine law and feel extremely fatigued and exhausted. In that case you may interrupt your activities for a short while to rest and recover. For that, you can lie down prostrate. But make sure that you do not move abruptly, spread your arms and legs, or make panting and snoring sounds with your nose and mouth. If you have someone doing these things near you, talk to him. Hearing these sounds and not addressing the person is as bad a sin as showing contempt for the divine law.

6. When you are sitting, rising, walking, or standing among the four crowds, do not let yourself be drawn into extended conversations or laughter with outsiders.

7. For diligent study, it is important to select the right master. If you find your master is rather shallow in virtue, be careful not to discard him or cut him off. There is still something you can learn from him. Ideally you want to be with an enlightened master—finding him is like obtaining a great treasure. If you have been so fortunate, exhaust all your strength to honor and learn from him, and you will easily achieve completion of the Dao. Never let yourself be separated from him.

8. If the master by mistake commits a transgression or an error, be careful not to speak ill of him or to discuss his faults. Rather, be withdrawing about it, then use skillful means to speak about it deferentially, bringing it up repeatedly if necessary, but always in accordance with the rule of worshiping the Dao. [15a] If another person speaks about your master's good or bad points, explain the facts to him. If you do not have the strength to do that, shake the questioner off, rise up, and leave. This is a manifestation of keeping the master safe.

9. All the master's possessions—his bedstead, table, bench, staff, vestments, vermilion ink, and all other things—you have to keep safe. Never allow them to be sullied or defiled.

10. If during a mass assembly someone unexpectedly violates the rules or the scriptures, and the crowd accuses him, see that he is punished appropriately. If you can do this with enthusiasm, joy, and shame, smilingly and happily, you can be called an able person who will extinguish innumerable sins. Such a person studying the Dao will quickly attain the all-highest fruits of good karma. We call this a great act of safekeeping.

11. To keep the donors of the ten directions safe—be they known personally or strangers, ranked high or low, men or women, tall or short, noble or humble, inside or outside, far or near—in all

cases venerate them with respect. Whether staying or resting, coming or going, calming or settling, sitting or rising, always urge them to give. Whether they are suffering or happy, hungry or satisfied, bad or good, law-abiding or contrary, present or absent, healthy or sick, [15b] whether they need your support and respect, comfort and instruction, reward and punishment, shame and reprimand—in all cases treat them equally in due accordance with your duties.

12. If you find any animated creature, whether crawling or running, drowning in water, burning in fire, or in any other life-threatening situation, with all the strength at your disposal rescue it, keep it safe, and see that it finds peace and security.

13. During your walking and staying, entering and leaving, if you stay overnight in any province or district and there encounter anyone—be they famous or influential, kin or stranger, man or woman—who makes fun [of you] and uses bad words, creating a disturbance among the host of living beings, do not do anything. This is called "keeping all beings safe." It brings great fruits of good karma.

14. Someone may repeatedly violate the rules and disturb the pure crowd, yet never submit despite strong reprimands, reject all good counsel, and gloss over his faults. In that case, announce to the crowd that he is to withdraw and leave the purgation, then discuss with him the dignified observances, precepts, and purgation rules.

15. To put on or take off your clothes of the Dao and ritual vestments, you should always have them carefully folded and arranged in an orderly manner. Placed in a wrapping kerchief or in any quiet and secure place, you first knock your head to them, and only then can you put them on or take them off.[16] [16a]

16. During an affair of requesting the divine law someone may again and again show himself haughty, rebellious, and fond of picking fights. In that case, make an announcement above and below on the good and bad fortune of certain behaviors. Do not let it happen again. Such a person is called a "guest of darkness" and should not be allowed to pester the crowd [of the faithful].

17. You may find yourself in a position to receive food or material goods. Take only little, always being modest and frugal. Do not allow the host of living beings to feel envy or doubt, or in any way diminished or humbled. They should not feel reduced in life or lessened in virtue. This way you can deeply attain the safekeeping of all.

The Highest Lord said:

I have now explained the ten items of dignified observances and their various statutes to you, all in all more than 140 entries. Using and reciting these ten items and their many rules, practicing them diligently—this is what we call keeping yourself safe from all violations. Teaching them to others, moreover, brings good karmic fruits too numerous to count. The host of living beings will look up to you with joy; the various celestials will be blushing with shame [in comparison]. A person like this in this life will receive ten kinds of good fortune, virtue, honor, and respect.

---

[16] A similar rule is also found in the *Rules and Precepts for Worshiping the Dao* (sect. 14, 5.8a).

As the *Scripture of Ascension to the Mystery* says: "Whoever follows the divine law and obeys the rules is called a 'perfected gentleman of great prosperity'." [16b] And afterwards he does not appear again in this [level of] existence but enters the ranks of the sages [above].

On the other hand, someone may mindlessly worship the Dao, take advantage of the followers of the divine law, stealthily seek his own profit and enrichment, and defile the ritual vestments of the Dao. He may bring shame to the followers of the Dao and the divine law, even plot with evil fellows. He may also hate others doing good, constantly violate the rules and precepts, and encourage others not to follow them either. Again, he may fail to honor the directives of the masters and think himself much superior when hearing the teachings. He may never bring forth any mercy or mindfulness, and may never give rise to any sense of shame or embarrassment.

People who behave like this are called sinful. Obstructive and evil, they are close to animals—they may have entered the human realm but have failed to obtain a human heart. In vain they engage in human relationships. Utterly polluted, they may listen to the divine law of the sages, yet their entire inclination is like that of animals kept in a dark pen. Even if all living beings were liberated, they would still not be awakened. With intentions of their low nature, they would only desire to return to their original bodies. It is indeed deeply painful! One feels deeply moved and saddened.

If, therefore, people in this life lose the ten kinds of merit and virtue, lose the ten kinds of honor and respect, and instead reap the ten kinds of contempt and loathing, separating themselves from the ten kinds of sageliness and wisdom, they will enter the five realms of suffering and eight difficult conditions, their whole being will be increasingly unfit for this [level of] life. As a result they will fall into the long night—the nine realms of darkness and the hells—where they will receive all kinds of suffering and pain. [17a] After this, they will continue to transmigrate through the three evil realms—without any chance for liberation.

The Perfected of No-Thought and the others listened to the Highest Lord revealing these essential words. They all had tears [of compassion] streaming down [their faces], yet felt deep cheer and joy and great enthusiasm. Thus they knocked their heads [to the Lord] and formally excused themselves to carry the teaching in good faith and practice it with proper veneration.

TEXT ELEVEN

Precepts of Initial Perfection

MASTER KUNYANG, WANG CHANGYUE

INTRODUCTION

The *Precepts of Initial Perfection* (*Chuzhen jie* 初真戒, JY 278, 292; ZW 404), is a long text that contains several sets of precepts and numerous behavioral rules. It is transmitted to ordinands of the first level of Complete Perfection, the Master of Wondrous Practice (*miaoxing shi* 妙行師) and represents the school's most fundamental guidelines and practical precepts.

Complete Perfection rules appear in various texts from the thirteenth century onward, however, systematic precepts and a clear ordination structure were only created in the seventeenth century under the leading abbot Wang Kunyang 王崑陽 (1622-1680), who is best known for the formalization of the Longmen 龍門 lineage (Kubo 1951, 37).Originally called Wang Ping 王平 (*zi* Changyue 常月), he was an avid Daoist traveler in his youth. In 1628, he met Zhao Fuyang 趙復陽, a sixth-generation Longmen patriarch, on Mount Wang-wu and received the Longmen precepts. For nine years, Wang continued to study with different masters until 1655, when he went to live in the Monastery of Numinous Darkness (Lingyou gong 靈幽宮) in the capital; one year later he became the abbot of the White Cloud Monastery (Esposito 2000, 629).

As abbot, Wang reorganized Daoist religious precepts in accordance with Neo-Confucian ethics as supported by the Qing court, outlining three sets of precepts as an indispensable means to enlightenment and an important element in the education of the Daoist clergy. He divided Daoist ordination into three ranks, beginning with the Master of Wondrous Practice and continuing though the Master of Wondrous Virtue to the Master of Wondrous Dao.

The initial precepts include the ancient five precepts of Lord Lao and the medieval set of ten "precepts of initial perfection" as contained in the *Ten Precepts of Initial Perfection* (*Chuzhen shijie wen* 初真十戒文, DZ 180), dated to around the year 700.[1] The latter rules include the classic five precepts plus rules against disloyal and unfilial behavior and other social misbehavior. Directed mainly at lay practitioners who had just made the decision to leave the family and pursue the Dao, they later became the first precepts for monastic novices.

---

[1] The text is mentioned in Zhang Wanfu's *Collected Precepts of the Three Caverns* (DZ 178). The rules are also listed in YJQQ 40.7a-8a. For a discussion, see Ren and Zhong 1991, 132-33; Kleeman 1991, 176-77; Yoshioka 1961a, 61.

The text also recovers medieval thinking in its list of the effects of certain numbers of good and bad deeds as an encouragement to behave toward better karma. Such lists are found, among others, in the *Essential Precepts of Master Redpine*, translated above, and in the *Statutes of Mystery Metropolis*, translated in the "Supplement." Beyond this, the text relies on earlier models in its set of forty-six rules regarding ritual vestments, which are originally contained in Zhang Wanfu's *Rules and Precepts Regarding Ritual Vestments* (trl. "Supplement"), and in its many guidelines for concrete behavior that are closely reminiscent of medieval monastic manuals.

The text deviates from the medieval model in its outline of specific Complete Perfection ranks and ritual practices. It also has a set of precepts for women aspiring to the Daoist path, acknowledging the importance of nuns in this tradition. The precepts are still used today (see Min 1990, 67-73). They were first brought to scholarly attention by Heinrich Hackmann, who found them at the Great Clarity Temple (Taiqing gong 太清宮) on Mount Lao (see Hackmann 1920). The page numbers below refer to his edition. The rules are still being used in Complete Perfection ordinations today.

TRANSLATION

[19a] Anyone who first joins the dharma gate of the highest orthodox lineage, independent of whether he is of Daoist or ordinary background, must honor and obey the highest gold rules and jade statutes and all the precepts texts of the Three Caverns. He must also present offerings to the statues of the worthies of the great Dao and send a formal memorial [19b] to the various heavens to make an official report to the kings and celestial lords and in prayer request to become part of the pure contrast. Next, he must take the precepts of the three refuges:

First: I take refuge with my body in the highest great Dao of Nonultimate.

Note: Through this they are forever liberated from the cycle of transmigration: thus it is called the Treasure of the Dao.

Second: I take refuge with my spirit in the venerable scriptures in thirty-six sections.

Note: Through this they get to hear the orthodox divine law: thus it is called the Treasure of the Scriptures.

Third: I take refuge with my life in the great preceptors of the mysterious center.

Note: Through this they will never fall into false views: thus it is called the Treasure of the Masters.

The Heavenly Worthy said: The precepts of the three refuges are the pivotal knob of Heaven and Earth and form the root foundation of spirit immortality. [20a] By developing and practicing them as you first enter the Dao, the primal state of your mind is set up. As you thereby act in accordance with the *qi* and encompass the numinous forces, you join perfection and enter the universal principle. As you further embrace the network and become part of the cosmic patterns, your body begins to be without bounds.

Anyone observing the three refuges will be blessed and enjoyed by the numinous deities of Heaven and Earth. His mind will be full of wisdom; his ears and eyes will be open and clear. The myriad beings will be respectful and awed; the six viscera will be harmonious and well functioning. The host of the perfected will come to stand guard and give protection; the multitude of living beings will be to him like father and mother. For long generations he will be free from decline, and his descendancts will be born in situations of prosperity.

Once the three refuges have been taken, next you must receive the five precepts revealed by Lord Lao so you may accumulate merit and return to the root. They are:

1. Do not kill any living being.
2. Do not take impure food or alcohol. [20b]
3. Do not say "yea" and think "nay."
4. Do not steal.
5. Do not engage in lasciviousness.

Whoever manages to observe these five precepts, making keen efforts without mishaps, will increase his reckoning and extend his years. The gods of Heaven will protect and assist him, and he will forever be liberated from the hardships of the five punishments; from generation to generation he will never forego human birth.

Once you have received the five precepts revealed by Lord Lao so you may accumulate merit and return to the root, every morning and evening burn incense and recite [21a] the highest perfect scriptures of the great emperors of the Three Primes, Three Ranks, and Three Bureaus. They protect the community, assist the people, extend life, and guard destiny.

You should also start memorizing the *Treatise on Impulse and Response.* As you chant and recite this text every day, examine and rectify your own body and mind, and see whether you have committed any violations. With every sentence of your recitation of scriptures and the *Treatise,* reflect and think to yourself: Can I properly receive this or not? Can I practice this or not? Like this, you are active and courageous in your keen efforts, and words and practice do not deviate from one another.

If you never violate the three refuges and are without error in your observance of the five precepts, then after following this discipline for one hundred days, all evil thoughts will dissolve completely, and your organs and vessels will all be pure. Once this state is reached, you will be permitted to receive [21a] the ten precepts of initial perfection revealed by the Heavenly Worthy, the Sovereign Emperor of Emptiness.

The Ten Precepts

1. Do not be disloyal or unfilial, without benevolence or good faith. Always exhaust your allegiance to your lord and family. Be sincere in your relation to the myriad beings.

2. Do not secretly steal things, harbor hidden plots, or harm others in order to profit yourself. Always practice hidden virtue and widely aid the host of living beings.

3. Do not kill or harm anything that lives in order to satisfy your own appetites. [22a] Always behave with compassion and grace to all, even insects and worms.

4. Do not be lascivious or lose perfection, defile or insult the numinous energy. Always guard perfection and integrity, and remain without shortcomings or violations.

5. Do not ruin others to create gains for yourself or leave your own flesh and blood. Always use the Dao to help others and make sure that the nine clan members all live in harmony.

6. Do not slander or defame the wise and good or exhibit your skill and elevate yourself. Always praise the beauty and goodness of others and never be contentious about your own merit and ability. [22b]

7. Do not drink wine beyond measure or eat meat in violation of the prohibitions. Always maintain a harmonious energy and peaceful nature, focusing on your duty in purity and emptiness.

8. Do not be greedy and acquisitive without ever being satisfied or accumulate wealth without giving some to others. Always practice moderation in all things and show grace and sympathy to the poor and destitute.

9. Do not have any relations or exchange with the unwise or live among the mixed and defiled. Always strive to control yourself; in your living assemble purity and emptiness.

10. Do not speak or laugh lightly or carelessly, increasing agitation and denigrating perfection. [23a] Always maintain seriousness and speak humble words, making the Dao and its virtue your main concern.

Having received the ten precepts of initial perfection is already a first fruit of your work towards being a perfected. If you then continue to make keen efforts with courage and enthusiasm, and observe and maintain the precepts in word and action without even the slightest transgression or violation, you will soon be permitted to receive the highest 300 Precepts of Medium Ultimate as revealed by Lord Lao.

However, if you recite the rules only with your mouth and go against them in your heart, or if you start out with diligence but soon become lazy and abandon them halfway, then we call this an intentional violation whilst in full knowledge. This sin is mortally serious and can never be expiated; it will cause you to fall into perdition forever and ever. Without proper feelings for the celestial precepts of Nüqing, [23b] even if the Highest Lord himself emerges again, there will be no way to save you. Students of the Dao and sons of immortality: consider this and be very, very careful!

General Outline of Practice and the Observation of Precepts

Whether monastic or lay, anyone who has joined the membership of the four ranks: after you have received the precepts and the divine law, set your will in determination and focus your spirit to give rise to great firmness and solidity. Just like Mount Kunlun, this must be so it can never be moved or shaken; just like a diamond crystal, it must be so it can never be ground or destroyed. Thoroughly concentrate on the one mind and never give rise to variegated thoughts. Every night practice with dedication, [24a] and the luminous spirits will come to merge with your body; every day abstain from sensual pleasures, and the demonic *qi* will have no way to enter your orifices.

Therefore, when you do even a single good deed, your mind will be settled and your spirit will be at peace.[2] 10 good deeds, and your essence and spirit will be healthy and vigorous. 20 good deeds, and you will no longer experience sickness or disease. 30 good deeds, and all your wishes will come true with ease. 40 good deeds, and your followers and family will blossom and flourish. 50 good deeds, and your sons and grandsons will grow numerous and prosperous. 60 good deeds, and you can change trouble into auspicious situations. 70 good deeds, and the luminous spirits come to support and protect you. 80 good deeds, and your earthly benefits and people will be in harmony. 90 good deeds, and you will excel among others. 100 good deeds, and the three *qi* will harmonize in your body. [24b]

When you do 200 good deeds, your virtue will spread all over the world. 300 good deeds, and you will be reborn as a person of great wealth. 400 good deeds, and you will be reborn as a person of high nobility. 500 good deeds, and you will be reborn as a person of extensive longevity. 600 good deeds, and you will be reborn as a person of good fortune. 700 good deeds, and you will be reborn as a person of great loyalty. 800 good deeds, and you will be reborn as a person of great filial piety. 900 good deeds, and you will be reborn as a person of excellent wisdom. 1,000 good deeds, and you will be reborn as a sagely king or spirit immortal.

On the other hand, if you give in to your emotions and follow your sensual desires and commit even one evil deed, your spirit soul and dreams will know no peace. 10 evil deeds, and all people will hate and reject you. 20 evil deeds, and your body will suffer from many ailments and diseases. [25a] 30 evil deeds, and your wishes will never be realized. 40 evil deeds, and you will experience much bad luck, decline, and damage. 50 evil deeds, and your family members will be separated and scattered. 60 evil deeds, and you will see nothing but wrongness, bad luck, and obstacles. 70 evil deeds, and the demons and spirits will come to invade you. 80 evil deeds, and water and fire will bring you disasters and harm. 90 evil deeds, and all future births will come with a short life. 100 evil deeds, and the celestial officers will come to capture and kill you.

Ultimately you should work hard to maintain an even and equanimous mind, practice the essential, secret, and wondrous methods, never go against a single precept or violate a single rule, never acquiesce to do any evil and still live but rather maintain goodness and die. If you can be a precepts follower like this, you will rightfully be called [25b] a disciple of pure faith of the great Dao. Then the ten thousand demon kings will support and guard you, and all the various heavens will give you guidance and protection.

In the end, the imperial kings of the Four Heavens will order the officers of the ten divisions to get into green carriages of flying clouds, float through the air to where you are, and descend to inspect and observe your wondrous practice. Even though your merits at the time may not yet be quite complete, the officers will be compelled to return and enter your seed name into the numinous charts and ledgers of immortality.

Still, there may yet be those who are not in awe of the heavenly entries and do not follow the precepts and statutes with diligence. They pretend to observe the rules and regulations, but in fact do not cultivate the boundaries of perfection. They are accordingly subject to the punishments of the office of Nüqing, which measures the weight of their sins and [26a] hands down

---

[2] A similar list is contained in the *Essential Precepts of Master Redpine* of the fourth century and recouped in various medieval sources. See Yoshioka 1967, 294-99.

appropriate deductions from their emoluments and life allotments. If there are too many [sins] so that they cannot be taken care of in this manner, the remainder will be visited upon the sinners' next life. From kalpa to kalpa it will continue this way, and they will never be able to find release and liberation.

Essential Rules for Practicing the Precepts

[27a] ITEM: A person who has received the Precepts of Celestial Immortality is called a Master of Wondrous Dao. A person who has received the Precepts of Medium Ultimate is called a Master of Wondrous Virtue. A person who has received the Precepts of Initial Perfection is called a Master of Wondrous Practice. Those who have received the precepts of the same level but at different times are called "same robes." Those who preside over them are called "earlier enlightened masters."

ITEM: At the time of the mid-winter festival, adepts are to observe the following practices. Followers of the Precepts of Celestial Immortality: hold on to the *Daode jing* steadily, and for one hundred days, every day at the hour of the rabbit [3-5 a.m.], practice devotions by bowing ten times to the ten directions. [27b] Both at noon and at midnight engage in quiet-sitting and inner observation. Do not concern yourselves with human affairs but strive to cleanse and purify your three karmic factors.

Followers of the Precepts of Medium Ultimate: Every day at the hour of the snake [9-11 a.m.], first pay respects at the feet of your discipline master, then rise to bow in audience rites and recite the "Celestial Repentance" and the "Great Repentance of Numinous Treasure." Continue this for one hundred days. After each recitation, focus in quiet-sitting.

Followers of the Precepts of Initial Perfection: Every day at the hour of the snake [9-11 a.m.], first pay respects at the feet of your discipline master, then rise, bow, and recite the "Repentance of the Divine Law for the Forgiveness of Sins." Continue this for one hundred days. After each recitation, focus in quiet-sitting.

These are the regulations to be observed at the beginning of the mid-winter festival. Anyone going against any part of them will be punished for his sins by the agents of Nüqing. Also, for those one hundred days a prohibition against walking about is in effect. Practitioners must not go into the outside world to perform offerings; they must not go into the outside world to recite scriptures. Once the hundred days are over, the taboo on these activities is lifted.

Also, in all interaction and contact with affairs and people, adepts must be forbearing and withdrawing, benevolent and pliant. They should not examine and discuss right and wrong. Rather, in all activities, whether rising or stopping, moving or resting, they should be circumspect and very careful. On every *wu* day [the fifth of the ten-day week], they should moreover join their fellow precept disciples or an earlier enlightened master to engage in the strong cultivation of virtue and participate in a lecture and discussion of a sacred scripture, such as the *Daode jing*, *Zhuangzi*, *Scripture of Master Wenshi*, *Book of Transformation*, and the *Yellow Court Scripture*, or other text of any of the major Daoist schools. [28a] If one studies one scroll with full dedication, the supervising officers will mark up a tenfold merit. If one even lectures on them with clarity, they will accord a hundredfold merit.

In all cases, those who have taken the precepts should place foremost emphasis on self-control and act in due accordance with the highest wondrous dignified observances and the highest wondrous observation and perception. Then the spirits of the precepts will spontaneously come to offer support and protection, and the members of the four ranks will of themselves be utterly respectful. Thus, always stick to solid forms and never chase the crooked shadow—the shadow will right itself of its own. Always be in harmony with solid sound and never pursue the matching echo—the echo will arrive naturally by itself.

ITEM: Regarding the rope bed, if at noon or midnight you find yourself on the bedstead, sit up cross-legged and practice quiet-sitting. [29a] Your hands should neither show outstretched fingers nor be rounded into a point; your legs should be neither extended nor tightly folded; your mouth should not utter any words; your eyes should not let your spirit shine forth; your head should not hang forward; and your body should not be hunched over. This practice, however, applies only to the monastic bedstead. You must never sit or sleep on a bed or a mat of an ordinary household.

When people come to pay their respects to you, there are three situations in which you do not rise: When you are sitting in meditation, reading a scripture, or taking a ceremonial meal. Just regard them steadily and receive their respects with an appropriate incantation. Wait until you have concluded your activity, then get off the platform and return the greeting.

Before going to sleep, always click your teeth and recite the following incantation: "May all my spirits come to rest now in the dark valley." Then cut off all thoughts and forget all words.

[29b] Never engage in laxity or recklessness or go outside the community of monks. If ever you have to go outside, travel and walk very carefully, stepping straight ahead without looking right or left. Do not extend your arms and legs in haste. Every time you go against this, the supervising officers will mark it up as one transgression.

ITEM: Each adept should have one cavern robe, pure robe, and faith robe, together with a headdress of the numinous chart of the five sacred mountains. They should also have a pure kerchief, a feathery skirt, and a pair of regulation straw sandals. Since local, earth, and other deities as well as green-robed divine lads watch over and protect these garments, never lend them out for others to use. Do not put them in an impure place, [30a] sell them, or mix them into a pile of ordinary clothing. If they get old and torn, burn them on the ninth of the ninth month while facing northwest. Then take the ashes and scatter them into an eastward flowing stream, allowing them to be taken off by the waves.

Follow these rules, and you will find your years extended, longevity increased, and your body utterly free from demonic obstructions. Go against them, and you will find your life beset by disasters and harm, and the supervising officers will mark you up for ten transgressions.

ITEM: The begging bowl should have the shape of the eight trigrams. Only the opening for the lid should be round. It should be kept in a special bowl bag and taken out only when it is time to eat. After concluding the incantation [at meals], collect your *qi* and visualize the spirit, then eat without opening your mouth widely or making any sucking noises. Use the spoon when appropriate. After food has been taken, wash the bowl and return it to its bag. Every time you go against this, it will count as one transgression.[3] [30b]

ITEM: The staff should be taken from a numinous mountain and made from a seven-notch bamboo facing the sun. Make it straight and smooth above and below. The sweet bamboo variety is most excellent. Once cut and smoothed, inscribe it with the seal of Primordial Beginning. Whether moving or resting, sitting or lying down, always keep it by your side. When you use the staff to point at things, hold it while reciting the Incantation of the Four Obscurities. [31a]

ITEM: The discipline board[4] should be made from peach wood and inscribed with talismans and seal script on all four sides. Use it to eliminate inauspiciousness and when more recent disciples commit a transgression. If the violation is very serious, however, you will have to destroy the offender's bowl and burn his robe. For the worst sins, you have to expel him entirely from the order. If he begs for leniency, use the discipline board to mete out punishment in the measure of the sin.

ITEM: As regards the pitcher for pure water, when you pour water into the pitcher, take care not to spill or lose any. Use a bag to cover it. On far-off travels always carry it on your person, so you can wash your hands with every convenience. [31b]

ITEM: The certificate pouch should be sewn into the seam of your precepts robe. Then fill the inside of your kerchief with the precepts and statutes.

ITEM: A fragrant frame should be used to hang the three robes. First construct the basic frame from white sandalwood, then hold it over the incense burner to give it fragrance.

ITEM: The tooth brush should be made of coconut palm. The comb, the clothes chest, the pillow, the seating mat, the coverlet, the bed platform, and all other necessities must be kept clean and pure. Never let ordinary people use them, sit on them, or sleep on them. [32a]

The above listed items are all taken and arranged on the basis of the Daoist canon. If students of later generations fail to venerate their traditional system, they risk getting egotistical and ruining their wisdom. Anyone who changes or modifies these items is a sinner within the order. Going against the statutes will be severely punished; there is no chance of pardon.

---

[3] Here ends the translation of this section by Hackmann (1920, 148-58). The following part he only summarizes briefly.

[4] This is a flat piece of wood used to hit students during meditation hours or for ritual misbehaviors. Called *jiechi* 戒尺 or in Japanese *kaishaku*, it is still actively used in Zen monasteries today.

Forty-Six Rules of Precepts Regarding Ritual Vestments[5]

1. [61a] Unless attired in ritual vestments, a Daoist must not ascend to the holy altar, enter the oratory, bow in prayer, make announcements or requests, confess transgressions, or seek kindness.

2. Unless attired in ritual vestments, a Daoist must not approach the scriptures and precepts, lecture or explain, recite or chant them.

3. Unless attired in ritual vestments, a Daoist must not perform rites of purgation and precepts, accept other people's obeisances, eat or drink holy food.

4. Unless attired in ritual vestments, a Daoist must not pay obeisance to the worthies, masters, and priests of extensive virtue nor accept the obeisances of disciples.

5. Unless attired in ritual vestments, a Daoist must not enter or leave any dwellings, [61b] travel among people, or be seen by ordinary folk.

6. Unless attired in ritual vestments, a Daoist must not offer spells, prohibitions, talismans, indictments, petitions, memorials, memoranda, or announcements.

7. Unless attired in ritual vestments, a Daoist must not go to see the ruler of the country, his or her parents, or other people of the world.

8. When sleeping, resting, or relaxing, Daoists must take off all ritual vestments.

9. When bathing, washing, or cleaning themselves, Daoists must take off all ritual vestments.

10. When using the outhouse, Daoists must take off all ritual vestments.

11. When in danger of getting spattered by mud and rain, Daoists must take off all ritual vestments.

12. When making offerings to the venerable masters and parents, Daoists should not take off their ritual vestments. [62a]

13. When preparing and cultivating services for the merit and virtue of all beings, Daoists should not take off their ritual vestments.

14. When preparing and setting out purgation offerings, flowers and fruit, Daoists should not take off their ritual vestments.

15. When preparing seeds and plants, Daoists should not take off their ritual vestments.

---

[5] These rules are taken verbatim from the medieval *Rules and Precepts Regarding Ritual Vestments* of the early eighth century. It is translated in the "Supplement." A rendition of the first few pages is also found in Kohn 1993, 335-43; for a brief discussion, see Kleeman 1991, 179. Comparative Buddhist rules are studied in Kieschnick 2003.

16. When free from imprisonment and disease, Daoists should not take off their ritual vestments.

17. Unclean hands or feet must never be allowed to offend the ritual vestments.

18. Dirty vessels or other objects must never be allowed to offend the ritual vestments.

19. Soiled beds or mats must never be allowed to offend the ritual vestments.

20. Dusty carriages or sedan chairs must never be allowed to offend the ritual vestments.

21. The naked or exposed body must never be allowed to offend the ritual vestments. [62b]

22. Birds and beasts, insects and fish must never be allowed to offend the ritual vestments.

23. Foul breath and spittle must never be allowed to offend the ritual vestments.

24. People who are not fellow students or disciples must never be allowed to offend the ritual vestments.

25. When Daoists first wish to leave the family, they should prepare a set of vestments.

26. When Daoists get ready to receive the scriptures and precepts, they should prepare a set of vestments.

27. When Daoists visit the master to request scriptures, precepts, and registers, they should put on ritual vestments.

28. When Daoists visit the master to request a blessing or spell to dissolve all danger and suffering, they should put on ritual vestments.

29. Daoists must not use five colors in creating ritual vestments. [63a]

30. Daoists must not use non-ritual materials in creating ritual vestments.

31. Daoists must not use damask or embroidery in creating ritual vestments.

32. Daoists must not use non-ritual procedures in creating ritual vestments.

33. Daoists must not lend their ritual vestments to others.

34. Daoists must not cast off their ritual vestments at their convenience.

35. Daoists must not rest on their beds wearing ritual vestments.

36. Daoists must not sit or lie down on their ritual vestments.

37. Daoists must not wash their ritual vestments by trampling them with their feet or pounding them. [63b]

38. If worn and torn, ritual vestments should be burned for pure transformation.

39. Daoists should not own more than three sets of ritual vestments; all in excess should be given to others.

40. Ritual vestments may be worn out, excessive, or not satisfactory; if not used, they should be given to others to wear.

41. Once the ritual vestments are complete, Daoists should offer incense and make an announcement to the Three Treasures. First offer the vestments up to the Three Treasures, then to the host of immortals, perfected, and sages. Only after that are they fit to be worn.

42. Ritual vestments that have been close to the scriptures or statues must never be worn among ordinary people or in an unclean location.

43. Ritual vestments must be carefully washed, purified with incense, [64a] and kept in a special clothes chest, lest they be soiled and defiled. They should always be kept in a clean room.

44. Daoists must not wear ritual vestments to the five kinds of ordinary families.

45. Daoists must not take off their vestments and travel incognito among ordinary people.

46. In all sitting, rising, laying down, and resting, Daoists should always follow the rules and precepts.

The Nine Precepts for Women

1. [65a] Be filial and respectful, soft and harmonious, careful in speech, and never jealous.

2. Be chaste and pure, controlled in body, and always separate from all foul activities.

3. Develop sympathy for all beings that have life, be compassionate and friendly, and never kill.

4. During rites and recitations, be diligent and circumspect, and give up eating meat and drinking wine.

5. In your garments be practical and simple, never favoring floweriness or ornaments.

6. Maintain an even and harmonious disposition, never giving rise to anger and afflictions.

7. Do not frequently go out to attend purgations and banquets.

8. Do not be cruel in your employment of servants and slaves.

9. Do not steal other people's things.

BIBLIOGRAPHY

Abe, Stanley. 1997. "Northern Wei Daoist Sculpture from Shaanxi Province." *Cahiers d'Extrême-Asie* 9:69-84.

Akizuki Kan'ei 秋月觀英. 1960. "Tonkō hakken Shinjin josetsu sangen igi kangyōkyō tanken to Dai bikuni sansen igi" 敦煌發見神人所說三元威儀觀行經斷簡と大比丘尼三千威儀. *Jimbun shakai* 人文社會 19:1-26.

_____. 1965. "Zairon sangen shisō no keisei" 再論三元思想の形成. *Hirosaki daigaku bunkyō ronsō* 弘前大學文經論叢 1:437-56.

_____. 1978. *Chūgoku kinsei dōkyō no keisei* 中國近世道教の形成. Tokyo: Sōbunsha.

Ames, Roger T. 1992. "Taoist Ethics." In *Encyclopedia of Ethics*, edited by Lawrence C. Becker and Charlotte B. Becker, 1226-31. New York: Garland.

Andersen, Poul. 1991. "Taoist Ritual Texts and Traditions with Special Reference to *Bugang*, the Cosmic Dance." Ph.D. diss., University of Copenhagen, Denmark.

Asad, Talal. 1997. "Remarks on the Anthropology of the Body." In *Religion and the Body,* edited by Sarah Coakley, 42-52. Cambridge: Cambridge University Press.

Bagchi, Prabodh C. 1927-38. *Le canon bouddique en Chine, les traducteurs et les traductions.* 2 vols. Paris: P. Guethner.

Baier, Kurt. 1958. *The Moral Point of View.* Ithaca: Cornell University Press.

Baldrian-Hussein, Farzeen. 1984. *Procédés secrets du joyau magique.* Paris: Les Deux Océans.

Barrett, T. H. 1997. "The *Feng-dao k'o* and Printing on Paper in Seventh-Century China." *Bulletin of the School of African and Oriental Studies* 60.3:538-40.

Baryosher-Chemouny, Muriel. 1996. *La quête de l'immortalité en Chine: Alchimie et payasage intérieure sous les Song.* Paris: Dervy Livres.

Beal, Samuel. 1871. *A Catena of Buddhist Scriptures from the Chinese.* London: Trubner & Co.

Becker, Lawrence C., and Charlotte B. Becker, eds. 1992. *Encyclopedia of Ethics.* New York: Garland.

Belgum, David. 1963. *Guilt: Where Psychology and Religion Meet.* Englewood Cliffs: Prentice Hall.

_____. 1967. "Patient or Penitent." In *Religion and Medicine*, edited by David Belgum, 207-15. Ames: Iowa State University Press.

Bell, Catherine. 1992. "Printing and Religion in China: Some Evidence from the *Taishang Ganying Pian*." *Journal of Chinese Religions* 20: 173-86.

Bemporad, Jack. 1987. "Suffering." In *Encyclopedia of Religion*, edited by Mircea Eliade, 14:99-104. New York: Macmillan.

Benn, Charles D. 1991. *The Cavern Mystery Transmission: A Taoist Ordinarion Rite of A. D. 711.* Honolulu: University of Hawai'i Press.

_____. 2000. "Daoist Ordination and *Zhai* Rituals." In *Daoism Handbook*, edited by Livia Kohn, 309-38. Leiden: E. Brill.

Bergson, Henri. 1933. *The Two Sources of Morality and Religion.* London: Macmillan.

Bokenkamp, Stephen R. 1983. "Sources of the Ling-pao Scriptures." In *Tantric and Taoist Studies*, edited by Michel Strickmann, 2:434-86. Brussels: Institut Belge des Hautes Etudes Chinoises.

_____. 1986. "The Peach Flower Font and the Grotto Passsage." *Journal of the American Oriental Society* 106:65-79.

_____. 1989. "Death and Ascent in Ling-pao Taoism." *Taoist Resources* 1.2:1-20.

_____. 1990. "Stages of Transcendence: The *Bhūmi* Concept in Taoist Scripture." In *Chinese Buddhist Apocrypha*, edited by Robert E. Buswell, Jr., 119-46. Honolulu: University of Hawai'i Press.

_____. 1993. "Traces of Early Celestial Master Physiological Practice in the *Xiang'er* Commentary." *Taoist Resources* 4.2:37-52.

_____. 1997a. *Early Daoist Scriptures*. With a contribution by Peter Nickerson. Berkeley: University of California Press.

_____. 1997b. "The Yao Boduo Stele as Evidence for the 'Dao-Buddhism' of the Early Lingbao Scriptures." *Cahiers d'Extrême-Asie* 9:55-68.

Boltz, Judith M. 1987. *A Survey of Taoist Literature: Tenth to Seventeenth Centuries*. Berkeley: University of California, Center for Chinese Studies.

_____. 1996. "Singing to the Spirits of the Dead: A Daoist Ritual of Salvation." In *Harmony and Counterpoint: Ritual Music in Chinese Context*, edited by Bell Yong, Evelyn Rawski, and Rubie S. Watson, 177-225. Stanford: Stanford University Press.

Boltz, William G. 1982. "The Religious and Philosophical Significance of the *Hsiang-erh Lao-tzu* in the Light of the Ma-wang-tui Silk Manuscripts." *Bulletin of the School for Oriental and African Studies* 45:95-117.

Bourdieu, Pierre. 1977. *Outline of a Theory of Practice*. Cambridge: Cambridge University Press.

_____. 1990. *The Logic of Practice*. Stanford: Stanford University Press.

Brokaw, Cynthia. 1990. *The Ledgers of Merit and Demerit: Social Change and Moral Order in Late Imperial China*. Princeton: Princeton University Press.

Bumbacher, Stephan Peter. 2000a. *The Fragments of the Daoxue zhuan*. Frankfurt: Peter Lang.

_____. 2000b. "On Pre-Tang Monastic Establishments at Mao Shan, According to *Daoxue zhuan*." *Journal of Chinese Religions* 28:145-60.

_____. 2001. "Zu den Körpergottheiten im chinesischen Taoismus." In *Noch eine Chance für die Religionsphänomenologie?*, edited by D. Peoli-Olgiati, A. Michaels, and F. Stolz, 151-72. Frankfurt: Peter Lang.

Buswell, Robert E., Jr., ed. 1990. *Chinese Buddhist Apocrypha*. Honolulu: University of Hawaii Press.

_____. 2000. "Ordination into the Chögye Order." In *The Life of Buddhism*, edited by Frank E. Reynolds and Jason A. Carbine, 74-83. Berkeley: University of California Press.

Campany, Robert F. 2002. *To Live As Long As Heaven and Earth: A Translation and Study of Ge Hong's Traditions of Divine Transcendents*. Berkeley: University of California Press.

Chan, Wing-tsit. 1963. *A Source Book in Chinese Philosophy*. Princeton: Princeton University Press.

Chang, Kwang-chih. 1977. *Food in Chinese Culture*. New Haven: Yale University Press.

_____. 1980. *Shang Civilization*. New Haven: Yale University Press.

Chappell, David W. forthcoming. "The Precious Scroll of the Liang Emperor: Buddhist and Daoist Repentance to Save the Dead." In *Going Forth: Visions of Buddhist Vinaya*, edited by William Bodiford. Honolulu: University of Hawai'i Press.

Chard, Robert L. 1988. "Master of the Family: History and Development of the Chinese Cult of the Stove." Ph.D. Dissertation, University of California, Berkeley.

_____. 1990. "Folktales on the God of the Stove." *Hanxue yanjiu* 漢學研究 8:149-82.

_____. 1995. "Rituals and Scriptures of the Stove Cult." In *Ritual and Scripture in Chinese Popular Religion*, edited by David Johnson, 3-54. Berkeley: Chinese Popular Culture Project.

Chavannes, Edouard. 1910. *Le T'ai Chan: Essai de monographie d'un culte chinois*. Paris: Annales du Musée Guimet.

Chen Guofu 陳國符. 1975. *Daozang yuanliu kao* 道藏源流考. Taipei: Guting.

Chen-Hua. 1992. *In Search of the Dharma: Memoirs of a Modern Chinese Buddhist Pilgrim*. Edited by Chün-fang Yü. Translated by Denis C. Mair. Albany: State University of New York Press.

Ch'en, Kenneth. 1963. "A Propos the *Feng-fa-yao* of Hsi Ch'ao." *T'oung Pao* 50:79-92.

_____. 1964. *Buddhism in China*. Princeton: Princeton University Press.

_____. 1973. *The Chinese Transformation of Buddhism*. Princeton: Princeton University Press.

Cleary, Thomas. 1984. *The Flower Ornament Scripture*. Boston: Shambhala.

_____. 1987. *Understanding Reality: A Taoist Alchemical Classic by Chang Po-tuan*. Honolulu: University of Hawaii Press.

_____. 1992. *The Secret of the Golden Flower: The Classic Chinese Book of Life*. San Francisco: Harper.

Coakley, Sarah, ed. 1997. *Religion and the Body*. Cambridge: Cambridge University Press.

Cole, Alan. 1998. *Mothers and Sons in Chinese Buddhism*. Stanford: Stanford University Press.

Collcutt, Martin. 1983. "The Early Ch'an Monastic Rule: *Ch'ing-kuei* and the Shaping of Ch'an Community Life." In *Early Ch'an in China and Tibet*, edited by Lewis R. Lancaster and Whalen Lai, 165-84. Berkeley: University of California Press.

Cook, Francis. 1977. *Hua-yan Buddhism: The Jewel Net of Indra*. University Park: Pennsylvania State University Press.

Davis, Edward L. 2001. *Society and the Supernatural in Sung China*. Honolulu: University of Hawai'i Press.

DeGroot, J. J. M. 1969 [1893]. *Le côde du Mahāyāna en Chine: Son influence sur la vie monacale et sur le monde laïque*. Amsterdam: Verhandelingen der Koninklijke Akademie van Wetenschappen.

Demiéville, Paul. 1929. *Hōbōgirin*, vols. I, II. "A-Bussokuseki." Tokyo: Maison Franco-Japonaise.

Despeux, Catherine. 1990. *Immortelles de la Chine ancienne: Taoïsme et alchimie feminine*. Paris: Pardés.

_____. 2000a. "Women in Daoism." In *Daoism Handbook*, edited by Livia Kohn, 384-412. Leiden: E. Brill.

_____. 2000b. "Talismans and Sacred Diagrams." In *Daoism Handbook*, edited by Livia Kohn, 498-540. Leiden: E. Brill.

Despeux, Catherine, and Livia Kohn. 2003. *Women in Daoism*. Cambridge, Mass.: Three Pines Press.

Drexler, Monika. 1994. *Daoistische Schriftmagie: Interpretationen zu den fu im Daozang*. Stuttgart: Franz Steiner, Münchener Ostasiatische Studien, 68.

Dutt, Nalinaksha. 1960. *Early Monastic Buddhism*. Calcutta: Calcutta Oriental Books.

Dutt, Sukumar. 1924. *Early Buddhist Monachism*. London: Kegan Paul.

Eberhard, Wolfram. 1933. Beiträge zur kosmologischen Spekulation der Han-Zeit. Berlin.

_____. 1967. *Guilt and Sin in Traditional China*. Berkeley: University of California Press.

Eichhorn, Werner. 1957. "T'ai-p'ing und T'ai-p'ing Religion." *Mitteilungen des Instituts für Orientforschung* 5:113-40.

Emmrich, Thomas. 1992. *Tabu und Meidung im antiken China: Aspekte des Verpönten*. Bad Honnef: Bock + Herchen.

Eskildsen, Stephen. 1998. *Asceticism in Early Taoist Religion*. Albany: State University of New York Press.

Esposito, Monica. 2000. "Daoism in the Qing (1644-1911)." In *Daoism Handbook*, edited by Livia Kohn, 623-58. Leiden: E. Brill.

_____. 2001. "Longmen Taoism in Qing China: Doctrinal Ideal and Local Reality." *Journal of Chinese Religions* 29:191-232.

Evans-Wentz, W. Y. 1983 [1958]. *Tibetan Yoga and Secret Doctrines*. New York: Oxford University Press.

Foulk, T. Griffith. 1987. "The 'Ch'an School' and Its Place in the Buddhist Monastic Tradition." Ph.D. Dissertation, University of Michigan, Ann Arbor.

_____. 1991. "The Sinification of Buddhist Monasticism." Paper presented at the 44th Annual South Asia Seminar, Philadelphia.

_____. 1993. "Myth, Ritual, and Monastic Practice in Sung Ch'an Buddhism." In *Religion and Society in T'ang and Sung China*, edited by Patricia B. Ebrey and Peter N. Gregory, 147-208. Honolulu: University of Hawai'i Press.

Foulk, T. Griffith, and Robert H. Sharf. 1994. "On the Ritual Use of Ch'an Portraiture in Medieval China." *Cahiers d'Extrême-Asie* 7:149-220.

Gernet, Jacques. 1995. *Buddhism in Chinese Society: An Economic History from the Fifth to the Tenth Centuries*. Translated by Franciscus Verellen. New York: Columbia University Press.

Gert, Bernard. 1970. *The Moral Rules*. New York: Harper & Row.

Girardot, Norman. 1983. *Myth and Meaning in Early Taoism*. Berkeley: University of California Press.

_____. 1985. "Behaving Cosmogonically in Early Taoism." In *Cosmogony and Ethical Order: New Studies in Comparative Ethics*, edited by Robin W. Lovin and Frank E. Reynolds, 67-97. Chicago: University of Chicago Press.

Goffman, Erving. 1961. *Asylums: Essays on the Social Situations of Mental Patients and Other Inmates*. Garden City, NY: Anchor Books.

Gombridge, Richard F. 1971. *Precept and Practice: Traditional Buddhism in the Rural Highlands of Ceylon*. Oxford: Clarendon.

Gomez, Luis. 1993. "The Avatamsaka Sutra." In *Buddhist Spirituality: Indian, Southeast Asian, Tibetan, and Early Chinese*, edited by Takeuchi Yoshinori, 160-70. New York: Crossroad.

Goossaert, Vincent. 1998. "Ph.D. Dissertation Abstract: The Creation of Modern Taoism—The Quanzhen Order." *Journal of Sung and Yuan Studies* 28:303-9.

_____. 2000. "Counting the Monks: The 1736-1739 Census of the Chinese Clergy." *Late Imperial China* 21:40-85.

_____. 2003. "The Quanzhen Clergy, 1700-1950." In *Religion and Chinese Society: The Transformation of a Field*, edited by John Lagerwey, 10-35. Hong Kong: Chinese University of Hong Kong Press.

Graham, A. C. 1983. "Taoist Spontaneity and the Dichotomy of 'Is' and 'Ought'." In *Experimental Essays on Chuang-tzu*, edited by Victor H. Mair, 3-23. Honolulu: University of Hawai'i Press.

Green, Ronald M. 1978. *Religious Reason*. New York: Oxford University Press.

_____. 1987. "Morality and Religion." In *Encyclopedia of Religion*, edited by Mircea Eliade, 10:92-106. New York: Macmillan.

Groner, Paul. 1984. *Saichō: The Establishment of the Japanese Tendai School*. Berkeley: Berkeley Buddhist Studies Series 7.

_____. 1990a. *A History of Indian Buddhism*. Honolulu: University of Hawai'i Press.

_____. 1990b. "The *Fan-wang ching* and Monastic Discipline in Japanese Tendai: A Study of Annen's *Futsu jubosatsukai kōshaku*." In *Chinese Buddhist Apocrypha*, edited by Robert E. Buswell, Jr., 251-90. Honolulu: University of Hawai'i Press.

Güntsch, Gertrud. 1988. *Das Shen-hsien-chuan und das Erscheinungsbild eines Hsien*. Frankfurt: Peter Lang.

Hackmann, Heinrich. 1920. "Die Mönchsregeln des Klostertaoismus." *Ostasiatische Zeitschrift* 8:141-70.

_____. 1931. *Die dreihundert Mönchsgebote des chinesischen Taoismus*. Amsterdam: Koninklijke Akademie van Wetenshapen.

Hahn, Thomas H. 1989. "New Developments Concerning Buddhist and Taoist Monasteries." In *The Turning of the Tide: Religion in China Today*, edited by Julian F. Pas, 79-101. Hong Kong: Oxford University Press.

Hare, R. M. 1965. *Freedom and Reason*. New York: Oxford University Press.

Harper, Donald. 1985. "A Chinese Demonography of the Third Century B.C." *Harvard Journal of Asiatic Studies* 45:459-98.

Hendrischke, Barbara. 1991. "The Concept of Inherited Evil in the *Taiping Jing*." *East Asian History* 2:1-30.

_____. 2000. "Early Daoist Movements." In *Daoism Handbook*, edited by Livia Kohn, 134-64. Leiden: E. Brill.

Hendrischke, Barbara , and Benjamin Penny. 1996. "*The 180 Precepts Spoken by Lord Lao*: A Translation and Textual Study." *Taoist Resources* 6.2:17-29.

Hervouet, Yves, ed. 1978. *A Sung Bibliography, Bibliographie des Sung*. Hong Kong: Chinese University Press.

Heyd, David. 1982. *Supererogation: Its Status in Ethical Theory*. Cambridge: Cambridge University Press.

Hillery, George A. 1992. *The Monastery: A Study in Love, Freedom, and Community*. Westport: Praeger.

Hiltebeitel, Alf, and Barbara D. Miller. 1998. *Hair: Its Power and Meaning in Asian Cultures*. Albany: State University of New York Press.

Hirakawa Akira 平川彰. 1960. *Ritsuzō no kenkyū* 律藏の研究. Tokyo: Sankibō busshorin.

Höllmann, Thomas O., and Michael Friedrich, eds. 1999. *Botschaften and die Götter: Religiöse Handschriften der Yao*. Munich: Bayerische Staatsbibliothek.

Holt, John C. 1981. *Discipline: The Canonical Buddhism of the Vinayapitaka*. New Delhi: Motilal Banarsidass.

Hopkins, Jeffrey, ed. 1982. *Tantric Practice in Nying-ma*. Outlined by Khetsun Sangpo Rinbochay. Ithaca: Snow Lion Publications.

Horner, I. B. 1936. *The Early Buddhist Theory of Man Perfected*. London: Williams and Norgate.

Hou, Ching-lang. 1975. *Monnaies d'offrande et la notion de trésorérie dans la religion chinoise*. Paris: Mémoires de l'Institut des Hautes Etudes Chinoises.

Huang, Jane, and Michael Wurmbrand. 1987. *The Primordial Breath: Ancient Chinese Ways of Prolonging Life Through Breath*. Torrance: Original Books.

Hurvitz, Leon. 1956. *Wei Shou on Buddhism and Taoism*. Kyoto: Jimbun kagaku kenkyūjo.

_____. 1962. *Chih-i (538-597): An Introduction to the Life and Ideas of a Chinese Buddhist Monk*. Brussels: Institut Belge des Hautes Etudes Chinoises.

Hymes, Robert. 2002. *Way and Byway: Taoism, Local Religion, and Models of Divinity in Sung and Modern China*. Berkeley: University of California Press.

Idziak, Janine Marie. 1980. *Divine Command Morality*. Lewiston: Edwin Mellen Press.

Jaini, Padmanabh S. 1979. *The Jaina Path of Purification*. Berkeley: University of California Press.

Jan, Yün-hua. 1986. "Cultural Borrowing and Religious Identity: A Case Study of the Taoist Religious Codes." *Hanxue yanjiu* 漢學研究 4.1: 281-93.

Juergensmeyer, Mark. 1990. "The Monastic Syndrome in the Comparative Study of Culture." In *Monastic Life in the Christian and Hindu Traditions*, edited by Austin B. Creel and Vasudha Narayanan, 541-61. Lewiston, NY: Edwin Mellen Press.

Kaltenmark, Maxime. 1953. *Le Lie-sien tchouan*. Peking: Université de Paris Publications.

_____. 1979. "The Ideology of the *T'ai-p'ing-ching*." In *Facets of Taoism*, edited by Holmes Welch and Anna Seidel, 19-52. New Haven: Yale University Press.

Karlgren, Bernhard. 1946. "Legends and Cults in Ancient China." *Bulletin of the Museum of Far Eastern Antiquities* 18:199-365.

Kamitsuka Yoshiko 神塚淑子. 1988. "Taiheikyō no shōfu to taihei no riron ni tsuite" 太平 經の承負と太平の理論について. *Nagoya daigaku kyōyobu kiyō* 名古屋大學教養部紀要 32:41-75.

_____. 1998. "Lao-tzu in Six Dynasties Sculpture." In *Lao-tzu and the Tao-te-ching*, edited by Livia Kohn and Michael LaFargue, 63-85. Albany: State University of New York Press.

_____. 1999. *Rikuchō dōkyō shisō no kenkyū* 六朝道教思想の研究. Tokyo: Sōbunsha.

Kandel, Barbara. 1979. *Taiping jing: The Origin and Transmission of the 'Scripture on General Welfare' — The History of an Unofficial Text*. Hamburg: Gesellschaft für Natur- und Völkerkunde Ostasiens.

Kant, Immanuel. 1948. *Fundamental Principles of the Metaphysics of Morals*. Edited by J. Paton. London: Hutchinson.

_____. 1959. *Foundations of the Metaphysics of Morals*. New York: Bobbs-Merrill.

_____. 1960. *Religion within the Limits of Reason Alone*, edited by Theodore M. Greene and Hoyt H. Hudson. New York: Harper & Row.

Kanter, Rosabeth Moss. 1972. *Commitment and Community: Communes and Utopias in Sociological Perspective*. Cambridge, Mass.: Harvard University Press.

Kaptchuk, Ted J. 1983. *The Web that Has No Weaver: Understanding Chinese Medicine*. New York: Congdon & Weed.

Kawamura, Leslie S., ed. 1981. *The Bodhisattva Doctrine in Buddhism*. Calgary: Canadian Corporation for Studies in Religion.

Keightley, David N. 1978a. *Sources of Shang History: The Oracle Bone Inscriptions of Bronze Age China*. Berkeley: University of California Press.

_____. 1978b. "The Religious Commitment: Shang Theology and the Genesis of Chinese Political Culture." *History of Religions* 17:211-225.

Kennett, Jiyu. 1976. *Zen Is Eternal Life*. Emeryville: Dharma Publishing.

Keown, Damien. 1992. *The Nature of Buddhist Ethics*. New York: St. Martin's Press.

Kieschnick, John. 1997. *The Eminent Monk: Buddhist Ideals in Medieval Chinese Hagiography.* Honolulu: University of Hawai'i Press.

_____. 2003. *The Impact of Buddhism on Chinese Material Culture.* Princeton: Princeton University Press.

Kirkland, Russell. 2001. "Responsible Nonaction in a Natural World: Perspectives from the *Neiye, Zhuangzi,* and *Daode jing.*" In *Daoism and Ecology: Ways Within a Cosmic Landscape,* edited by Norman Girardot, James Miller, and Liu Xiaogan, 283-304. Cambridge, Mass.: Harvard University Press, Center for the Study of World Religions.

Kjellberg, Paul, and Philip J. Ivanhoe, eds. 1996. *Essays on Skepticism, Relativism, and Ethics in the Zhuangzi.* Albany: State University of New York Press.

Kleeman, Terry. 1991. "Taoist Ethics." In *A Bibliographic Guide to the Comparative Study of Ethics,* edited by John Carman and Mark Juergensmeyer, 162-94. Cambridge: Cambridge University Press.

_____. 1998. *Great Perfection: Religion and Ethnicity in a Chinese Millenarian Kingdom.* Honolulu: University of Hawai'i Press.

_____. 2002. "Ethnic Identity and Daoist Identity in Traditional China." In *Daoist Identity: History, Lineage, and Ritual,* edited by Livia Kohn and Harold D. Roth, 23-38. Honolulu: University of Hawai'i Press.

Knapp, Keith. 2004. "Reverent Caring: The Parent-Son Relationship in Early Medieval Tales of Filial Offspring." In *Filial Piety in Chinese Thought and History,* edited by Alan K.L. Chan and Sor-hoon Tan, 44-70. London: RoutledgeCurzon.

Knaul, Livia. 1985. "The Winged Life: Kuo Hsiang's Mystical Philosophy." *Journal of Chinese Studies* 2.1:17-41.

Kobayashi Masayoshi 小林正美. 1990. *Rikuchō dōkyōshi kenkyū* 六朝道教史研究. Tokyo: Sōbun-sha.

_____. 1992. "The Celestial Masters Under the Eastern Jin and Liu-Song Dynasties." *Taoist Resources* 3.2:17-45.

Kohn, Livia. 1987. *Seven Steps to the Tao: Sima Chengzhen's Zuowanglun.* St.Augustin/Net-tetal: Monumenta Serica Monograph XX.

_____. 1989a. "The Mother of the Tao." *Taoist Resources* 1.2: 37-113.

_____. 1989b. "Guarding the One: Concentrative Meditation in Taoism." In *Taoist Meditation and Longevity Techniques,* edited by Livia Kohn, 123-56. Ann Arbor: University of Michigan, Center for Chinese Studies Publications.

_____. 1991a. *Taoist Mystical Philosophy: The Scripture of Western Ascension.* Albany: State University of New York Press.

_____. 1991b. "Taoist Visions of the Body." *Journal of Chinese Philosophy* 18:227-52.

_____. 1993. *The Taoist Experience: An Anthology.* Albany: State University of New York Press.

_____. 1994. "The Five Precepts of the Venerable Lord." *Monumenta Serica* 42:171-215.

Kohn, Livia. 1995a. "Zur Symbolik des Bösen im alten China." In *Der Abbruch des Turmbaus. Studien zum Geist in China und im Abendland,* edited by Ingrid Krüssmann, Hans-Georg Möller, and Wolfgang Kubin, 113-33. St. Augustin: Monumenta Serica Monograph 34.

_____. 1995b. "Kōshin: A Taoist Cult in Japan. Part II: Historical Development." *Japanese Religions* 20.1:34-55.

_____. 1995c. *Laughing at the Tao: Debates among Buddhists and Taoists in Medieval China.* Princeton: Princeton University Press.

_____. 1997a. "The Date and Compilation of the *Fengdao kejie*: The First Handbook of Monastic Daoism." *East Asian History* 13:91-118.

_____. 1997b. "Yin Xi: The Master at the Beginning of the Scripture." *Journal of Chinese Religions* 25:83-139.

_____. 1998a. *God of the Dao: Lord Lao in History and Myth*. Ann Arbor: University of Michgan, Center for Chinese Studies.

_____. 1998b. "Steal Holy Food and Come Back as a Viper: Conceptions of Karma and Rebirth in Medieval Daoism." *Early Medieval China* 4:1-48.

_____. 1998c. "Counting Good Deeds and Days of Life: The Quantification of Fate in Medieval China." *Asiatische Studien/Etudes Asiatiques* 52:833-70.

_____. 2000a. "The Northern Celestial Masters." In *Daoism Handbook*, edited by Livia Kohn, 283-308. Leiden: E. Brill.

_____. 2000b. "Chinese Religion." In *The Human Condition: A Theory and Case-Study of the Comparison of Religious Ideas*, edited by Robert C. Neville, 21-47. Albany: State University of New York Press.

_____. 2001a. *Daoism and Chinese Culture*. Cambridge, Mass.: Three Pines Press.

_____. 2001b. "Daoist Monastic Discipline: Hygiene, Meals, and Etiquette." *T'oung Pao* 87:153-93.

_____. 2002a. "The Symbolism of Evil in Traditional China." In *Living with the Dao: Conceptual Issues in Daoist Practice*, edited by Livia Kohn, 1-16. Cambridge: Three Pines Press, E-Dao Series (electronic publication).

_____. 2002b. "The Sage in the World, the Perfected Without Feelings: Mysticism and Moral Reponsibility in Chinese Religion." In *Crossing Boundaries: Essays on the Ethical Status of Mysticism*, edited by G. William Barnard and Jeffrey J. Kripal, 288-306. New York: Seven Bridges Press.

_____. 2003a. *Monastic Life in Medieval Daoism*. Honolulu: University of Hawai'i Press.

_____. 2003b. "Monastic Rules in Quanzhen Daoism: As Collected by Heinrich Hackmann." *Monumenta Serica* 51:1-32.

_____. 2003c. "Medieval Daoist Ordination: Origins, Structure, and Practices." *Acta Orientalia* 56:379-98.

_____. 2004. *The Daoist Monastic Manual: A Translation of the Fengdao kejie*. New York: Oxford University Press.

Kohn, Livia, and Russell Kirkland. 2000. "Daoism in the Tang (618-907)." In *Daoism Handbook*, edited by Livia Kohn, 339-83. Leiden: E. Brill.

Komjathy, Louis. 2002. *Title Index to Daoist Collections*. Cambridge, Mass.: Three Pines Press.

Kroll, Paul W. 1996. "Body Gods and Inner Vision: *The Scripture of the Yellow Court*. In *Religions of China in Practice*, edited by Donald S. Lopez Jr., 149-55. Princeton: Princeton University Press.

Kubo Noritada 窪德忠. 1951. "Dōkyō no shingi ni tsuite" 道教の清規について. *Tōhōshūkyō* 東方宗教 1:28-44.

Kuo, Li-ying. 1994. *Confession et contrition dans le bouddhisme chinois du Ve au Xe siècle*. Paris: Publications de l'Ecole Française d'Extrême-Orient.

Kusuyama Haruki 楠山春樹. 1982. "Dōkyō ni okeru jukai" 道教における十戒. *Waseda daigaku daigakuin bungaku kenkyūka kiyō* 早田大學文學研究科紀要 28:55-72.

_____. 1983. "Dōkyō to jukyō" 道教と儒教. In *Dōkyō* 道教, edited by Fukui Kōjun 福井康順 et al., 2:49-94. Tokyo: Iwanami.

_____. 1984. "Seishin deshi kō" 清信弟子考. In *Makio Ryōkai hakase sōshu kinen ronshū: Chūgoku no shūkyō shisō to kagaku* 牧尾良海博士頌壽記念論集：中國の宗教思想と科學. Tokyo: Kokusho kankōkai. Reprinted in Kusuyama 1992, 114-35.

_____. 1992. *Dōka shisō to dōkyō* 道家思想と道教. Tokyo: Hirakawa.

Lagerwey, John. 1981. *Wu-shang pi-yao: Somme taoïste du VIe siècle*. Paris: Publications de l'Ecole Française d'Extrême-Orient.

_____. 1987. *Taoist Ritual in Chinese Society and History*. New York: Macmillan.

Lai Chi-tim 黎志添. 2002a. "The *Demon Statutes of Nüqing* and the Problem of the Bureaucratization of the Netherworld in Early Heavenly Master Daoism." *T'oung Pao* 88:251-81.

_____. 2002b. "Tiandishui sanguan xinyang yu zaoqi tianshi dao zhibing jiezui yishi" 天地水三官信仰與早期天師道治病解罪儀式. *Taiwan zongjiao yanjiu* 台灣宗教研究 2.1:1-30.

_____. 2003. "Daoism in China Today, 1980-2002." *The China Quarterly* 174:413-27.

Lai, Whalen. 1984. "Symbolism of Evil in China: The K'ung-chia Myth Analyzed." *History of Religions* 23:316-43.

_____. 1987. "The Earliest Folk Buddhist Religion in China: *T'i-wei Po-li Ching* and Its Historical Significance." In *Buddhist and Taoist Practice in Medieval Chinese Society*, edited by David W. Chappell, 11-35. Honolulu: University of Hawai'i Press.

Lamotte, Etienne. 1987. *History of Indian Buddhism*. Louvain: Institut Orientaliste.

Le Blanc, Charles. 1987. "From Ontology to Cosmogony: Notes on *Chuang-tzu* and *Huai-nan-tzu*." In *Chinese Ideas About Nature and Society: Studies in Honor of Derk Bodde*, edited by Charles Le Blanc and Susan Blader, 117-29. Hong Kong: Hong Kong University Press.

Le Blanc, Charles. 1992. "Resonance: Une interpretation chinoise de la réalité." In *Mythe et philosophie a l'aube de la Chine impérial: Etudes sur le Huainan zi*, edited by Charles Le Blanc and Remi Mathieu, 91-111. Montreal: Les Presses de l'Université de Montreal.

Legge, James. 1968 [1885]. *The Li Ki—Book of Rites*. 2 vols. Delhi: Motilal Bernasidass.

_____. 1969 [1893]. *The Shoo King—Book of Historical Documents*. 2 vols. Taipei: Jinxue.

_____. Lemoine, Jacques. 1982. *Yao Ceremonial Paintings*. Bangkok: White Lotus Co.

Lévi, Jean. 1983. "L'abstinence des céréals chez les taoïstes." *Etudes Chinoises* 1:3-47.

Levy, Howard S. 1956. "Yellow Turban Rebellion at the End of the Han." *Journal of the American Oriental Society* 76:214-27.

Lewis, Mark E. 1990. *Sanctioned Violence in Early China*. Albany: State University of New York Press.

Li Yangzheng 李養正. 1993. *Dangdai Zhongguo daojiao* 當代中國道教. Beijing: Zhongguo shehui kexue chubanshe.

Little, Stephen, and Shawn Eichman. 2000. *Taoism and the Arts of China*. Berkeley: University of California Press.

Liu Tsun-yan 劉存仁. 1986. "Sandong fengdao kejie yifan juan diwu: P. 2337 zhong Jin Ming Qizhen yice zhi tuice" 三洞奉道科戒儀範卷第五：P. 2337 中金明七真遺冊之推測. *Hanxue yanjiu* 漢學研究 4.2:509-31.

Liu Zhongyu 劉仲釪. 1990. *Zhongguo daojiao wenhua xiushi* 中國道教文化修史. Shanghai: Xielin.

Liu, Yang. 2001. "Origins of Daoist Iconography." *Ars Orientalis* 31:31-64.

_____. 2003. "Sakyamuni and Laojun Seated Side by Side: Catching a Glimpse of the Northern Dynasties Buddhist/Taoist Relationship from a Popular Iconography." In *Ancient Taoist Art from Shanxi Province*, edited by Lin Yiying, 54-63. Hong Kong: Unversity of Hong Kong, University Museum and Art Gallery.

Liu, Yanzhi. 1988. *The Essential Book of Traditional Chinese Medicine*. 2 Vols. New York: Columbia University Press.

Loon, Piet van der. 1979. "A Taoist Collection of the Fourteenth Century." In *Studia Sino-Mongolica: Festschrift for Herbert Franke*, edited by Wolfgang Bauer, 401-5. Wiesbaden: Franz Steiner: Münchener Ostasiatische Studien.

_____. 1984. *Taoist Books in the Libraries of the Sung Period*. London: Oxford Oriental Institute.

Loori, John Daido. 1998. *Invoking Reality: Moral and Ethical Teachings of Zen*. Mt. Temper: Dharma Communications.

Lu Kuan-yü. 1970. *Taoist Yoga: Alchemy and Immortality*. London: Rider.

Mabbott, J. D. 1969. *An Introduction to Ethics*. Garden City: Anchor Books.

Maeda Shigeki 前田繁樹. 1985. "Rōkun ippyaku hachiju kaijo no seiritsu ni tsuite" 老君一百八十戒序の成立について. *Tōyō no shisō to shūkyō* 東方の思想と宗教 2:81-94.

Mahony, William K. 1987. "Karman: Hindu and Jain Concepts." In *Encyclopedia of Religion*, edited by Mircea Eliade, 8:261-66. New York: Macmillan.

Major, John S. 1993. *Heaven and Earth in Early Han Thought: Chapters Three, Four, and Five of the Huainanzi*. Albany: State University of New York Press.

Makita Tairyō 牧田諦亮. 1968/1971. "Tonkōhon Daiikyō no kenkyū" 敦煌本提魏經の研究. *Bukkyō daigaku daigakuin kenkyū kiyō* 佛教大學大學院研究紀要 1:137-85 and 2:165-97.

Malek, Roman. 1985. *Das Chai-chieh-lu*. Frankfurt: Peter Lang.

Mansvelt-Beck, .J. 1980. "The Date of the *Taiping jing*." *T'oung Pao* 66: 149-82.

Maruyama, Hiroshi. 2002. "Documents Used in Rituals of Merit in Taiwanese Daoism." In *Daoist Identity: History, Lineage, and Ritual*, edited by Livia Kohn and Harold D. Roth, 256-73. Honolulu: University of Hawai'i Press.

Maspero, Henri. 1981. *Taoism and Chinese Religion*. Translated by Frank Kierman. Amherst: University of Massachusetts Press.

Mather, Richard B. 1979. "K'ou Ch'ien-chih and the Taoist Theocracy at the Northern Wei Court, 425-451." In *Facets of Taoism*, edited by Holmes Welch and Anna Seidel, 103-22. New Haven: Yale University Press.

Matsunaga, A., and D. Matsunaga 1976. *Foundation of Japanese Buddhism*. 2 vols. Los Angeles: Books International.

Mauss, Marcel. 1979. *Sociology and Psychology: Essays*. London: Routledge & Kegan Paul.

Michaud, Paul. 1958. "The Yellow Turbans." *Monumenta Serica* 17: 47-127.

Min Zhiting 閔智亭. 1990. *Daojiao yifan* 道教儀範. Beijing: Zhongguo daojiao xueyuan.

Misra, G. S. P. 1969. *The Age of Vinaya*. New Delhi: Mushiram Manoharlal.

Mizuno, Kogen. "Karman, Buddhist Concepts." In *Encyclopedia of Religion*, edited by Mircea Eliade, 8:266-68. New York: Macmillan.

Mochizuki Shinkō 望月信享. 1936. *Bukkyō daijiten* 佛教大辭典. 7 vols. Tokyo: Sekai seiten kankō kyūkai.

Mollier, Christine. 1997. "La méthode de l'empereur du nord du mont Fengdu: une tradition exorciste du taoïsme médiévale." *T'oung Pao* 83:329-85.

_____. 2000. "Les cuisines de Laozi et du Buddha." *Cahiers d'Extrême-Asie* 11:45-90.

Mori Yuria 森由利亞. 1994. "Zenshinkyō ryūmonha keizu kō" 全真教龍門派系譜考. In *Dōkyō bunka e no tembō* 道教文化への展望, edited by Dōkyō bunka kenkyūkai 道教文化研究會, 180-211. Tokyo: Hirakawa.

Mugitani Kunio 麥谷邦夫. 1985a. *Rōshi sōjichu sakuin* 老子想爾注索引. Kyoto: Hōyū shoten.

_____. 1985b. "Rōshi sōjichu ni tsuite" 老子想爾注について. *Tōhō gakuhō* 東方學報 57:75-109.

_____. 1987. "Yōsei enmei roku kunchu" 養性延命綠訓注. *Report of the Study Group on Traditional Chinese Longevity Techniques*, no. 3. Tokyo: Mombushō.

Munroe, Kristen Renwick. 1996. *The Heart of Altruism: Perceptions of a Common Humanity*. Princeton: Princeton University Press.

Nagel, Thomas. 1970. *The Possibility of Altruism*. Oxford: Clarendon Press.

_____. 1979. *Mortal Questions*. Cambridge: Cambridge University Press.

Nakajima Ryūzō 中島隆藏. 1984. "Taijō gyōhō innenkyō ni okeru ōhōron" 太上業報因緣經 における應報論. In *Makio Ryōkai hakase sōshu kinen ronshū Chūgoku no shūkyō shisō to kagaku* 牧尾良海博士頌壽記念論集：中國の宗教思想と科學, 335-54. Tokyo: Kokusho kankōkai.

Nakamura, Hajime 中村元. 1964. "A Critical Study of Mahayana and Estoeric Buddhism Chiefly Based on Japanese Studies." *Acta Asiatica* 6:57-88; 7:36-94.

_____. 1975. *Bukkyōgo daijiten* 佛教語大辭典. Tokyo: Tokyo shoshiki.

Needham, Joseph, et al. 1983. *Science and Civilisation in China*, vol. V.5: "Spagyrical Discovery and Invention—Physiological Alchemy." Cambridge: Cambridge University Press.

Ni, Maoshing. 1995. *The Yellow Emperor's Classic of Medicine*. Boston: Shambhala.

Nickerson, Peter. 1996. "*Abridged Codes of Master Lu for the Daoist Community*." In *Religions of China in Practice*, edited by Donald S. Lopez Jr., 347-59. Princeton: Princeton University Press.

_____. 2000. "The Southern Celestial Masters." In *Daoism Handbook*, edited by Livia Kohn, 256-82. Leiden: E. Brill.

Nylan, Michael. 1992. *The Shifting Center: The Original 'Great Plan' and Later Readings*. St. Augustin/Nettetal: Monumenta Serica Monograph.

O.D.A. 1998. *The Blue Book: A Text Concerning Orthodox Daoist Conduct*. Santa Cruz: Orthodox Daoism of America.

Obeyesekere, Gananath. 1968. "Theodice, Sin and Salvation in a Sociology of Buddhism." In *Dialectic in Practical Religion*, edited by Edmund Leach, 7-40. Cambridge: Cambridge University Press.

Ōfuchi Ninji 大淵忍爾. 1964. *Dōkyōshi no kenkyū* 道教史の研究. Okayama: Chūgoku insatsu.

_____. 1974. "On *Ku Ling-pao ching*." *Acta Asiatica* 27:33-56.

_____. 1978. *Tonkō dōkei: Mokuroku hen* 敦煌道經--目錄篇. Tokyo: Kokubu shoten.

_____. 1979a. *Tonkō dōkei: Zurokuhen* 敦煌道經一圖錄篇. Tokyo: Kokubu shoten.

_____. 1979b. "The Formation of the Taoist Canon." In *Facets of Taoism*, edited by Holmes Welch and Anna Seidel, 253-68. New Haven: Yale University Press.

_____. 1991. *Shoki no dōkyō* 初期の道教. Tokyo: Sōbunsha.

_____, ed. 1983. *Chūgokujin no shūkyō girei* 中國人の宗教儀禮. Tokyo: Fukubu.

_____. 1997. *Dōkyō to sono kyōten* 道教とその經典. Tokyo: Sōbunsha.

Ōfuchi Ninji 大淵忍爾 and Ishii Masako 石井昌子. 1988. *Dōkyō tenseki mokuroku, sakuin* 道教典籍目錄。索引. Tokyo: Kokusho kankōkai.

Ōgata Tōru 大形徹. 1995. "Hihatsu kō: Kamikatachi to reikon no kanren ni tsuite" 被髮考：髮型と靈魂の關連について. *Tōhō shūkyō* 東方宗教 86:1-23.

Ohnuki-Tierney, Emiko. 1984. *Illness and Culture in Contemporary Japan: An Anthropological View*. Cambridge: Cambridge University Press.

Ōno Hōdō 大野法道. 1954. *Daijō kaikyō no kenkyū* 大乗戒經の研究. Tokyo: Risōsha.

Orzech, Charles D. 2002. "*Fang Yankou* and *Pudu*: Translation, Metaphor, and Religious Identity." In *Daoist Identity: History, Lineage, and Ritual*, edited by Livia Kohn and Harold D. Roth, 213-34. Honolulu: University of Hawai'i Press.

Outka, Gene, and John P. Reeder. 1973. *Religion and Morality*. New York: Doubleday.

Overmyer, Daniel L. 1990. "Attitudes Toward Popular Religion in Ritual Texts of the Chinese State: *The Collected Statutes of the Great Ming*." *Cahiers d'Extreme-Asie* 5:191-221.

Ōzaki Masaharu 尾埼正治. 1979. "Kō Kenshi no shinsen shisō" 寇謙之の神仙思想. *Tōhō shūkyō* 東方宗教 54:52-69.

_____. 1986. "The Taoist Priesthood: From Tsai-chia to Ch'u-chia." In *Religion and Family in East Asia*, edited by George DeVos and T. Sofue, 97-109. Berkeley: University of California Press.

Pachow, W. 1955. *A Comparative Study of the Pratimokṣa*. Santinitekan: Sino-Indian Cultural Society.

Pas, Julian F. 1986. "Six Daily Periods of Worship: Symbolic Meaning in Buddhist Liturgy and Eschatology." *Monumenta Serica* 37:49-82.

Peerenboom, R. P. 1991. *Law and Morality in Ancient China: The Silk Manuscripts of Huang-Lao*. Albany: State University of New York Press.

Penny, Benjamin. 1990. "A System of Fate Calculation in *Taiping Jing*." *Papers on Far Eastern History* 41:1-8.

_____. 1996. "Buddhism and Daoism in *The 180 Precepts Spoken by Lord Lao*." *Taoist Resources* 6.2:1-16.

Petersen, Jens O. 1989/1990. "The Early Traditions Relating to the Han-dynasty Transmission of the *Taiping jing*." *Acta Orientalia* 50:133-71 and 51:165-216.

Poo, Mu-chou. 1997. *In Search of Personal Welfare: A View of Ancient Chinese Religion*. Albany: State University of New York Press.

Porkert, Manfred. 1974. *The Theoretical Foundations of Chinese Medicine*. Cambridge, Mass.: MIT Press.

Prebish, Charles S. 1974. "The Pratimoksha Rule: Fact versus Fantasy." *Journal of the American Oriental Society* 94:168-76.

_____. 1975. *Buddhist Monastic Discipline: The Sanskrit Pratimoksha Sutras of the Mahasamghikas and Mulasarvastivadins*. University Park: Pennsylvania State University Press.

Prip-Møller, J. 1967. *Chinese Buddhist Monasteries*. Hongkong: Hongkong University Press.

Pruden, Leo. 1967. "Some Notes on the *Fan-wang-ching* [*Brahmajāla-sūtra*]." *Indogaku bukkyōgaku kenkyū* インド學佛教學研究 15.2:70-80,

Qing Xitai 卿希泰. 1996. *Zhongguo daojiao shi* 中國道教史, vol. 1. Chengdu: Sichuan renmin chubanshe.

_____. 2000. *History of Chinese Daoism*. Translated by David C. Yu. Vol. 1. Lanham: University Press of America.

Rao Zongyi 饒宗頤. 1992. *Laozi xianger zhu jiaojian* 老子想爾注校箋. Shanghai: Wenyi.

Reinders, Eric. 1997. "Ritual Topography: Embodiment and Vertical Space in Buddhist Monastic Practice." *History of Religions* 36.3:244-54.

Reiter, Florian C. 1985. "Ch'ung-yang Sets Forth His Teachings in Fifteen Discourses." *Monumenta Serica* 36:33-54.

Ren Jiyu 任繼愈. 1990. *Zhongguo daojiao shi* 中國道教史. Shanghai: Renmin.

_____, and Zhong Zhaopeng 鐘肇鵬, eds. 1991. *Daozang tiyao* 道藏提要. Beijing: Zhongguo shehui kexue chubanshe.

Rhys-Davids, T. W., and T. Oldenberg. 1965 [1882]. *Vinaya Texts*. 2 vols. In *Sacred Books of the East*, vols. 13 and 17. Edited by Max Müller. New Delhi: Motilal Barnasidass.

Richards, David. 1971. *A Theory of Reasons for Action*. Oxford: Clarendon Press.

Richter, Antje. 2001. *Das Bild des Schlafes in der altchinesischen Literatur*. Hamburg: Hamburger Sinologische Schriften.

Ricoeur, Paul. 1967. *The Symbolism of Evil*. Boston: Beacon Press.

Robinet, Isabelle. 1983. "Kouo Siang ou le monde comme absolu." *T'oung Pao* 69:87-112.

_____. 1984. *La révélation du Shangqing dans l'histoire du taoïsme*. 2 Vols. Paris: Publications de l'Ecole Française d'Extrême-Orient.

_____. 1989a. "Original Contributions of *Neidan* to Taoism and Chinese Thought." In *Taoist Meditation and Longevity Techniques*, edited by Livia Kohn, 295-38. Ann Arbor: University of Michigan, Center for Chinese Studies Publications.

_____. 1989b. "Visualization and Ecstatic Flight in Shangqing Taoism." In *Taoist Meditation and Longevity Techniques*, edited by Livia Kohn, 157-90. Ann Arbor: University of Michigan, Center for Chinese Studies Publications.

_____. 1993. *Taoist Meditation*. Translated by Norman Girardot and Julian Pas. Albany: State University of New York Press.

_____. 1995. *Introduction a l'alchimie interieure taoïste: De l'unité et de la multiplicité*. Paris: Editions Cerf.

_____. 1997. *Taoism: Growth of A Religion*. Translated by Phyllis Brooks. Stanford: Stanford University Press.

_____. 2000. "Shangqing—Highest Clarity." In *Daoism Handbook*, edited by Livia Kohn, 196-224. Leiden: E. Brill.

Roth, Harold D. 1999. *Original Tao: Inward Training and the Foundations of Taoist Mysticism*. New York: Columbia University Press.

Saddhatissa, H. 1970. *Buddhist Ethics*. London: George Allan & Unwin.

Sailey, Jay. 1978. *The Master Who Embraces Simplicity: A Study of the Philosophy of Ko Hung (A.D. 283-343)*. San Francisco: Chinese Materials Center.

Sargent, Galen E. 1957. "T'an-yao and His Time." *Monumenta Serica* 16:363-96.

Sasaki, George H. 1956. "The Concept of Kamma in Buddhist Philosophy." *Oriens Extremus* 3:185-204.

Saso, Michael. 1974. *Zhuang-Lin xu daozang* 莊林續道藏. Taipei: Chengwen.

_____. 1997. "The Taoist Body and Cosmic Prayer." In *Religion and the Body*, edited by Sarah Coakley, 231-47. Cambridge: Cambridge University Press.

Schafer, Edward H. 1978. "The Capeline Cantos: Verses on the Divine Loves of Taoist Priestesses." *Asiatische Studien/ Etudes Asiatiques* 32:5-65.

Schipper, Kristofer M. 1967. "Gogaku shingyōzu no shinkō" 五嶽真形圖の信仰. *Dōkyō kenkyū* 道教研究 2:114-62.

_____. 1975. *Concordance du Tao Tsang: Titres des ouvrages*. Paris: Publications de l'Ecole Française d'Extrême-Orient.

_____. 1978. "The Taoist Body." *History of Religions* 17:355-87.

_____. 1980. *Concordance du Yun ki ki kian*. 2 vols. Paris: Publications de l'Ecole Française d'Extrême-Orient.

_____. 1984. "Le monachisme taoïste." In *Incontro di religioni in Asia tra il terzo e il decimo secolo d. C.*, edited by L. Lanciotti, 199-215. Firenze: Leo S. Olschki.

_____. 1985. "Taoist Ordination Ranks in the Tunhuang Manuscripts." In *Religion und Philosophie in Ostasien: Festschrift für Hans Steininger*, edited by. G. Naundorf, K.H. Pohl, and H. H. Schmidt, 127-48. Würzburg: Königshausen and Neumann.

_____. 1994a. *The Taoist Body*. Translated by Karen C. Duval. Berkeley: University of California Press.

_____. 1994b. "Purity and Strangers: Shifting Boundaries in Medieval Taoism." *T'oung Pao* 80:61-81.

_____. 2001. "Daoist Ecology: The Inner Transformation. A Study of the Precepts of the Early Daoist Ecclesia." In *Daoism and Ecology: Ways Within a Cosmic Landscape*, edited by Norman Girardot, James Miller, and Liu Xiaogan, 79-94. Cambridge, Mass.: Harvard University Press, Center for the Study of World Religions.

Schmidt, Hans-Hermann. 1985. "Die hundertachtzig Vorschriften von Lao-chün." In *Religion und Philosophie in Ostasien: Festschrift für Hans Steininger*, edited by. G. Naundorf, K.H. Pohl, and H. H. Schmidt, 151-59. Würzburg: Königshausen and Neumann.

Seidel, Anna. 1969. "The Image of the Perfect Ruler in Early Taoist Messianism." *History of Religions* 9:216-47.

_____. 1984. "Taoist Messianism." *Numen* 31:161-74.

Shahar, Meir, and Robert P. Weller, eds. 1996. *Unruly Gods: Divinity and Society in China*. Honolulu: University of Hawai'i Press.

Siivals, Aarne. 1962. "The Meaning of an Illness." *Journal of Religion and Health* 1.2:153-64

Silber, Ilana Friedrich. 1995. *Virtuosi, Charisma, and Social Order: A Comparative Sociological Study of Monasticism in Theravada Buddhism and Medieval Catholicism*. Cambridge: Cambridge University Press.

Silber, John R. 1960. "The Ethical Significance of Kant's Religion." In *Religion Within the Limits of Reason Alone*, by Immanuel Kant, edited by Theodore M. Greene and Hoyt H. Hudson, lxxix-cxxxiv. New York: Harper & Row.

Simmons, Harold E. 1956. *The Psychosomatic Aspects of Cancer*. Washington, D.C.: Pea- body Press.

Sivin, Nathan. 1969. "On the *Pao-p'u-tzu nei-p'ien* and the Life of Ko Hung." *Isis* 40:388-91.

Skar, Lowell, and Fabrizio Pregadio. 2000. "Inner Alchemy (*Neidan*)." In *Daoism Handbook*, edited by Livia Kohn, 464-97. Leiden: E. Brill.

Soothill, William E., and Lewis Hodous. 1937. *A Dictionary of Chinese Buddhist Terms*. London: Kegan Paul.

Soymié, Michel. 1956. "Le Lo-Feou chan: Etude de géographie religieuse." *Bulletin de l'Ecole Française d'Extrême-Orient* 48: 1-139.

_____. 1977. "Les dix jours du jeune taoiste." In *Yoshioka Yoshitoyo hakase kanri kinen Dōkyō kenkyū ronshū* 吉岡義豐博士還歷記念道教研究論集, 1-21. Tokyo: Kokusho kan- kōkai.

Staal, Julius. 1984. *Stars of Jade: Calendar Lore, Mythology, Legends and Star Stories of Ancient China*. Decatur, GA: Writ Press.

Stein, Rolf A. 1963. "Remarques sur les mouvements du taoïsme politico-religieux au IIe siècle ap. J.-C." *T'oung Pao* 50:1-78.

_____. 1971. "Les fêtes de cuisine du taoïsme religieux." *Annuaire du Collège de France* 71:431-40.

Strickmann, Michel. 1978a. "The Mao-shan Revelations: Taoism and the Aristocracy." *T'oung Pao* 63:1-63.

Strickmann, Michel. 1978b. "A Taoist Confirmation of Liang Wu-ti's Suppression of Taoism." *Journal of the American Oriental Society* 98:467-74.

_____. 1981. *Le taoïsme du Mao chan: Chronique d'une révélation*. Paris: Collège du France, Institut des Hautes Etudes Chinoises.

_____. 1982. "The Tao among the Yao." In *Rekishi ni okeru minshū to bunka* 歴史における民族と文化, edited by Sakai Tadao kinen kai 酒井忠夫記念會, 23-30. Tokyo: Kokusho kankōkai.

_____. 1985. "Therapeutische Rituale und das Problem des Bösen im frühen Taoismus." In *Religion und Philosophie in Ostasien: Festschrift für Hans Steininger*, edited by. G. Naundorf, K.H. Pohl, and H. H. Schmidt, 185-200. Würzburg: Königshausen and Neumann.

Stuart, G. A. 1976. *Chinese Material Medica*. Taipei: Southern Materials Center.

Sunayama Minoru 沙山稔. 1990. *Zui To dōkyō shisōshi kenkyū* 隋唐道教思想史研究. Tokyo: Hirakawa.

Suzuki, Daisetz T. 1965. *The Training of the Zen Buddhist Monk*. New York: University Books.

_____. 1968. *Outlines of Mahayana Buddhism*. New York: Schocken Books.

Suzuki, Daisetz T., and Paul Carus. 1973 [1906]. *Treatise on Response and Retribution*. LaSalle: Open Court Publishing.

Switkin, Walter. 1987. *Immortality: A Taoist Text of Macrobiotics*. San Francisco: H. S. Dakin Company.

Tang Yongtong 唐用彤 and Tang Yijie 唐顗節. 1961. "Kou Qianzhi de zhuzuo yu sixiang" 寇謙之的著作與思想. *Lishi yanjiu* 歴史研究 5:64-77.

Tao Bingfu 陶秉福, ed. 1989. *Nüdan jicui* 女丹集萃. Beijing: Beijing shifan daxue.

Taylor, Paul. 1972. *Problems of Moral Philosphy*. Encino: Dickenson.

Teasdale, Wayne. 2002. *A Monk in the World*. Novato, Calif.: New World Library.

Tokuno, Kyoko. 1991. "Chinese Buddhist Ethics." In *A Bibliographic Guide to the Comparative Study of Ethics*, edited by John Carman and Mark Juergensmeyer, 125-61. Cambridge: Cambridge University Press.

Tonkō kōza 敦煌講座, ed. 1983. *Tonkō to Chūgoku dōkyō* 敦煌と中國道教. Tokyo: Daitō.

Trauzettel, Rolf. 2002. "Grundsätzliches zur altkonfuzianischen Morallehre." In *Und folge nun dem, was mein Herz begehrt: Festschrift für Ulrich Unger zum 70. Geburtstag*, edited by Reinhard Emmrich and Hans Stumpfeldt, 137-53. Hamburg: Hamburger Sinologische Gesellschaft.

Tsuchihashi Shūkō 土橋秀高. 1956. "Kairitsu shisō no tenkai" 戒律思想の展開. *Ryūkoku daigaku ronshū* 龍谷大學論集 352:88-107.

_____. 1957. "Juzenkai no keifu" 十善戒の系譜. *Ryūkoku daigaku ronshū* 龍谷大學論集 355:45-65.

_____. 1964. "Sho hassai kaigi no hensen" 受八齋戒儀の變遷. In *Iwai hakase koseki kinen tenseki ronshū* 岩井博士古稀記念典籍論集, 379-400. Tokyo: Dai'an.

_____. 1980. *Kairitsu no kenkyū* 戒律の研究. Tokyo: Nagata bunchōdō.

Tsuchiya, Masaaki. 2002. "Confession of Sins and Awareness of Self in the *Taiping Jing*." In *Daoist Identity: History, Lineage, and Ritual*, edited by Livia Kohn and Harold D. Roth, 39-57. Honolulu: University of Hawai'i Press.

Tsui, Bartholomew P. M. 1991. *Taoist Tradition and Change: The Story of the Complete Perfection Sect in Hong Kong*. Hong Kong: Christian Study Centre on Chinese Religion and Culture.

Tsukamoto, Senryū, and Leon Hurvitz. 1985. *A History of Early Chinese Buddhism*. 2 vols. Tokyo: Kōdansha.

Turner, Bryan. 1997. "The Body in Western Society." In *Religion and the Body*, edited by Sarah Coakley, 15-41. Cambridge: Cambridge University Press.

Turner, Victor W. 1969. *The Ritual Process: Structure and Anti-Structure*. Chicago: Aldine.

Tuzuki Masako 都築晶子. 2000. "Tōdai chūki no dōkan: kūken, keisai, kairitsu" 唐代中期の道觀− 空間經濟戒律. In *Tōdai no shūkyō* 唐代の宗教, edited by Yoshikawa Tadao 吉川忠夫, 269-96. Kyoto: Hōyō shoten.

_____. 2002. "Dōkan ni okeru kairitsu no seiritsu" 道觀における戒律の成立. In *Chūgoku chūsei shakai to shūkyō* 中國中世社會と宗教, edited by Mugitani Kunio 麥谷邦夫, 59-82. Kyoto: Dōkisha.

Twitchett, Dennis W. 1956. "Monastic Estates in T'ang China." *Asia Major*, New Series, 5:123-46.

_____. 1957. "The Monasteries and China's Economy in Mediaeval China." *Bulletin of the School of Oriental and African Studies* 19:526-49.

Vankeerberghen, Griet. 2001. *The Huainanzi and Liu An's Claim to Moral Authority*. Albany: State University of New York Press.

Varma, Vishwanath P. 1963. "The Origin and Sociology of the Early Buddhist Philosophy of Moral Determinism." *Philosophy East and West* 13:25-48.

Veith, Ilza. 1972. *The Yellow Emperor's Classic of Internal Medicine*. Berkeley: University of California Press.

Wagner, Roy. 1987. "Taboo." In *Encyclopedia of Religion*, edited by Mircea Eliade, 14:233-36. New York: Macmillan.

Wang Ming 王明. 1979. *Taiping jing hejiao* 太平經合校. Beijing: Zhonghua.

Wang, Yi-t'ung. 1984. *A Record of Buddhist Monasteries in Lo-yang*. Princeton: Princeton University Press.

Ware, James R. 1933. "The *Wei-shu* and the *Sui-shu* on Taoism." *Journal of the American Oriental Society* 53:215-50.

_____. 1966. *Alchemy, Medicine and Religion in the China of AD 320*. Cambridge, Mass.: MIT Press.

Watson, Burton. 1968. *The Complete Works of Chuang-tzu*. New York: Columbia University Press.

Welch, Holmes. 1967. *The Practice of Chinese Buddhism, 1900-1950*. Cambridge, Mass: Harvard University Press.

Wijayaratna, Mohan. 1990. *Buddhist Monastic Life*. Cambridge: Cambridge University Press.

Williams, Bernard. 1980. *Three Rival Versions of Moral Inquiry*. University of Notre Dame Press.

Yamada Takashi 山田俊. 1992. *Kohon Shōgenkyō* 古本昇玄經. Sendai: Tōhōku daigaku.

Yamada Toshiaki 山田利明. 1989. "Longevity Techniques and the Compilation of the *Lingbao wufuxu*." In *Taoist Meditation and Longevity Techniques*, edited by Livia Kohn, 97-122. Ann Arbor: University of Michigan, Center for Chinese Studies Publications.

_____. 1999. *Rikuchō dōkyō girei no kenkyū* 六朝道教儀禮の研究. Tokyo: Tōhō shoten.

_____. 2000. "The Lingbao School." In *Daoism Handbook*, edited by Livia Kohn, 225-55. Leiden: E. Brill.

Yan Shanchao 嚴善忩. 2001. "Shoki dōkyō to kōshi konki hōchūjutsu" 初期道教と黄赤混氣 房中術. *Tōhō shūkyō* 東方宗教 97:1-19.

Yang Liansheng 楊聯陞. 1956. "Laojun yinsong jiejing jiaoshi" 老君音誦誡經校釋. *Zhong-yang yanjiu yuan lishi yuyen yanjiusuo jikan* 中央研究院歷史語言研究所集刊 28:17-54.

Yao, Tao-chung. 1980. "Ch'üan-chen: A New Taoist Sect in North China During the 12th and 13th Centuries." Ph.D. Dissertation, University of Arizona, Phoenix.

_____. 2000. "Quanzhen—Complete Perfection." In *Daoism Handbook*, edited by Livia Kohn, 567-93. Leiden: E. Brill.

Yifa. 2002. *The Origins of Buddhist Monastic Codes in China*. Honolulu: University of Hawai'i Press.

Yokoi, Yūhō. 1986. *The Shōbō genzō*. Tokyo: Sankibō.

Yoshikawa Tadao 吉川忠夫. 1987. "Seishitsu kō" 靜室考. *Tōhō gakuhō* 東方學報 59:125-62.

_____, ed. 1992. *Chūgoku ko dōkyōshi kenkyū* 中國古道教史研究. Kyoto: Dōhōsha.

_____, ed. 1998. *Rikuchō dōkyō no kenkyū* 六朝道教の研究. Kyoto: Shunjusha.

Yoshioka Yoshitoyo 吉岡義豐. 1955. *Dōkyō kyōten shiron* 道教經典史論. Tokyo: Dōkyō kankō-kai.

_____. 1959. "Kōka kaku shisō no ichi genryū" 功過格思想の一源流. *Tōhō shūkyō* 東方宗教 15:25-36.

_____. 1960. "Shisōji chūkaikyō to kōka shisō" 赤松子中誡經と功過思想. *Fukui hakase sōshu kinen Tōyō shisō ronshū* 福井博士頌壽記念洋方思想論集, 722-37. Tokyo: Waseda daigaku.

_____. 1961a. "Bukkyō jukai shisō no Chūgoku teki shuyō" 佛教十戒思想の中國的受容. *Shūkyō kenkyū* 宗教研究 35.1:51-72.

_____. 1961b. "Tonkō hon jukaikyō ni tsuite" 敦煌本十戒經について. In *Tsukamoto hakase sōshu kinen Bukkyō shigaku rombunshū* 塚本博士頌壽記念佛教史學論文集, 925-38. Kyoto: Hōzō-kan.

_____. 1967. "Zaikairoku to chigonsō" 齋戒錄と至言總. *Taishō daigaku kenkyūjo kiyō* 大正大學研究所紀要 52:283-302.

_____. 1970a. *Dōkyō to bukkyō* 道教と佛教, vol. 2. Tokyo: Kokusho kankōkai.

_____. 1970b. *Eisei e no negai: Dōkyō* 永生への願い：道教. Kyoto: Tankōsha.

_____. 1976. *Dōkyō to bukkyō* 道教と佛教, vol. 3. Tokyo: Kokusho kankōkai.

_____. 1979. "Taoist Monastic Life." In *Facets of Taoism*, edited by Holmes Welch and Anna Seidel, 220-52. New Haven: Yale University Press.

Yūsa Noboru 遊左昇. 1989. "Tōdai ni mirareru kyukutenson shinkō ni tsuite" 唐代に見られる救苦天尊信仰について. *Tōhōshūkyō* 東方宗教 73:19-40.

Zhu Yueli 朱越利. 1992. *Daojiao yaoji gailun* 道教要籍概論. Beijing: Yenshan chubanshe.

Zürcher, Eric. 1959. *The Buddhist Conquest of China*. 2 vols. Leiden: E Brill.

_____. "Buddhist Influence on Early Taoism." *T'oung Pao* 66:84-174.

INDEX

283